THE REPUBLICAN PARTY AND WENDELL WILLKIE

THE REPUBLICAN PARTY
AND WENDELL WILLKIE

BY DONALD BRUCE JOHNSON · UNIVERSITY OF ILLINOIS PRESS, URBANA, 1960

TO CLARENCE A. BERDAHL
teacher, scholar, colleague, friend

PREFACE

The assumption underlying this book is that political parties in a democracy play essential roles in the accommodation of diverse interests and in the conversion of individual and group opinion into public policy. It follows from this assumption that given the party structure as it exists in the United States, together with the present values and character of America, a healthy Republican party is an important and representative instrument through which these roles could be fulfilled. In this volume, I have endeavored to examine the performance of the GOP primarily as reflected in the words and actions of Wendell Willkie and his contemporaries during a crucial and formative period in American history. I have also tried to observe in this performance the way in which party leadership may be obtained and lost, and the way in which the operations of the Republican party revealed its strengths and frailties, its limitations and potential, and its developments, stresses, and strains from 1936 to 1944.

Political parties are, in many ways, similar to giant uncompleted tapestries in which threads of persons, groups, actions, ideas, and aspirations run left and right, north and south, high and low, and in which many threads are intertwined and overlapping. Such party tapestries are usually flexible but occasionally rigorous of line. And as the picture grows, changes of color and pattern often alter the complexion of the whole tableau.

The activities of Willkie, a truly unique figure in American political history, provide the thread woven throughout this volume illustrating the changing patterns of the Republican party just before and during World War II. This dynamic and argumentative outsider, who never held public office, stimulated the bridging of a gap between two eras of Republicanism, only to pass from the scene before his task was completed — before the many threads of intraparty strife had been untangled. But during this period, his ideas, his exhortations, his opposition, and the inexorable pressure of world events had forced the Republicans to accept much of his philosophy while they rejected his leadership. This volume is, therefore, less a study of leadership than a study of the basic raw materials of politics, the interactions of a man and other men within a party. It is more a study of impact than a survey of achievement. And it is more an analysis of the activities of Willkie that left a mark on current history than a complete biography. The major portion of this work covers only five years, but threads of influence from those years continue to be significant. They can be seen in the current party struggle over liberalism and conservatism as party leaders strive to represent what they consider to be the majority view within the rank and file of their constituencies. They can also be observed by reviewing the suggested, but incompletely accepted, reforms and new orientations that Willkie laid out for his party. In the final analysis, however, these threads of party life still leave the Republican tapestry — as all examinations of contemporary politics must be left — unfinished to this present day.

For assistance in this work, I am indebted to many persons. To all those who have advanced opinions, facts, and arguments, I express my gratitude. Professor Clarence Berdahl of the University of Illinois not only made available a wealth of his own collected materials, he supervised the original draft of this study and provided patient and enlightening criticism and encouragement. For reading portions of the manuscript, I want to thank Lem Jones, Professor DeVere Pentony of San Francisco State College, Professor Harry Morris of Southern University, Mrs. Romayne Ponleithner, Dr. Donald Jackson, and Professor D. Philip Locklin of the University of Illinois, and my colleagues at the State University of Iowa, Lane Davis, Kirk Porter, and Vernon Van Dyke. All made valuable suggestions. I should like to acknowledge a special debt to those administrative officials here at Iowa who, through the research professorship program, provided a semester free from teaching duties that enabled me to travel for interviews and to search for new information.

I am also grateful to many persons, in and out of public life, who gave time and energy to this undertaking. Former Secretary of Commerce Sinclair Weeks was particularly helpful. So were the late Robert A. Taft and Harold L. Ickes. Of those still in Congress, Senators Styles Bridges, George Aiken, and Homer Capehart, together with Representatives Fred Schwengel, Joseph Martin, and Charles Halleck, all deserve a special word of thanks. I also want to express my gratitude to, and acknowledge the assistance of: Harold E. Stassen, Samuel F. Pryor, Harrison E. Spangler, Floyd E. Mc-Caffree, Joseph Barnes, Dr. Harry Elmer Barnes, Oren Root, Frank D. McKay, Roscoe Drummond, John Orr Young, Albert Leman, James P. Selvage, and Philip Willkie, in addition to those individuals who supplied information but who requested that no attribution be made. Their data and opinions added greatly to the authenticity of the manuscript. Any errors of interpretation are, of course, mine. I want to thank Mrs. Marilyn Christensen of the Political Science Department at Iowa for cheerfully typing the manuscript. And finally, to my wife for her understanding and generous help, I express my deep appreciation.

Iowa City, Iowa   Donald Bruce Johnson
                                     Department of Political Science
                                     State University of Iowa
                                     June 1, 1959

CONTENTS

And they, whether they will hear,
or whether they will forbear
(for they are a rebellious house),
yet shall know that there hath
been a prophet among them.

EZEKIEL 2:5

1 PROLOGUE TO 1940

Just before the Republican convention of 1940, while searching for an explanation of his meteoric rise to national political prominence, Wendell Willkie declared: "I would like to think it means I'm a hell of a fellow . . . but I think it means . . . I represent a trend, or am ahead of a trend."[1]

Whether Willkie or any of his contemporaries fully realized the meaning of his words is doubtful, but with the benefit of twenty years of hindsight, it is now clear that Wendell Willkie was the herald of several trends in both national and international affairs. Moreover, the fact that he was in a position to make such a statement at all is fascinating and significant. For Willkie was the most unique phenomenon of American politics in the twentieth century. In 1938 he was a Democrat almost unknown outside of his own circle of associates. By 1940 he was the Republican candidate for President of the United States. As a tycoon of the discredited and feared utilities industry, he nevertheless became the only corporation chief ever to be nominated for the presidency of the entire nation. He was an amateur politician who without ever holding public office captured a major American party only to conclude his life estranged from both parties. As a nineteenth-century liberal, Willkie was chosen the standard-bearer of the GOP. As a twentieth-century liberal, he eventually walked too far ahead of his party to lead it. His political career was a pattern of political incongruity

---

[1] *Time,* June 24, 1940, p. 18.

that has no parallel in American history. Strangely enough, it probably never would have developed if his principal political opponent, Franklin Roosevelt, had never become President and had never undertaken the dramatic program he called a "new deal."

Today, opinions of the New Deal, even in retrospect, range from judgments that it was a failure, if the material well-being of the people was the principal objective,[2] to the conclusions that it maintained "a democratic system of government and society in a world swept by confused alarms of struggle and flight,"[3] or that it brought a "new condition for man."[4]

In this present era of a four hundred billion dollar national productivity and a national employment of seventy million persons, it is difficult to remember that only a quarter of a century ago the New Deal came into existence when banks were failing throughout the country, when businessmen were testifying before congressional committees that nothing could be done other than cut the national budget,[5] while nonprofessional beggars jockeyed for street corners in large cities. With seventeen million people out of work, sickness, unemployment, and poverty in old age were accepted as the normal course of human existence. Clearly, in 1933 this was an emergency situation necessitating emergency measures when Roosevelt asked for "broad executive power to wage a war against the emergency as great as the power that would be given me if we were in fact invaded by a foreign foe."[6]

During the following four years, the United States underwent what was virtually a psychological and economic revolution as the result of the New Deal's experiments in the use of broad executive power in agriculture, social legislation, finance, and government. In order to preserve the capitalistic system, laissez faire was partially abandoned and social control in national, state, and local politics was highly developed. While the businessmen lost their preponderance of power, the farmers, the laborers, the intellectuals, and the

---

[2] Arthur Larson, *A Republican Looks at His Party* (New York, 1956), p. 185.

[3] Samuel Eliot Morison and Henry Steele Commager, *The Growth of the American Republic* (New York, 1942), p. 641.

[4] James M. Burns, *Roosevelt: The Lion and the Fox* (New York, 1956), p. 268.

[5] Arthur Schlesinger, Jr., *The Crisis of the Old Order* (Boston, 1957), p. 5.

[6] Robert E. Sherwood, *Roosevelt and Hopkins* (New York, 1950), I, 49.

artists obtained greater access to governmental decision-making.

Politically, the significance and success of the New Deal were inextricably bound to the multifarious groups that received benefits from the many programs.

For the farmers, the Agricultural Adjustment Act made the first effective endeavor to re-establish some sort of parity between what they received for their crops and what they paid for their industrial necessities. Commodity prices were raised, credit was eased, loans for mortgages were made available at low interest rates, and marginal land was taken out of cultivation. When Roosevelt came into office, the index of prices received by farmers for their products (based at 100 for the average of the years 1909-14) stood at 65; by 1936, it was back to 114. Millions of dollars were poured into crop reduction, and the program, aided by the drought, successfully eliminated surpluses. The efforts of the Rural Electrification Administration promoted the increased use of electricity, reduced the rates for larger consumption, and doubled the number of electrified farms. The Commodity Credit Corporation, organized under the Reconstruction Finance Corporation, made direct loans that enabled hundreds of thousands of farmers to refinance their debts, thereby preventing the foreclosures that were panicking rural residents. Finally, another New Deal program included relief measures for the nearly three million tenant and sharecropping families. In 1934 the Division of Rural Rehabilitation of the Federal Emergency Relief Administration was practically the sole support of more than a quarter of a million persons.

For the large numbers of people concerned about the nation's fiscal collapse, Roosevelt acted with alacrity if not always to their satisfaction. The banking industry was stabilized; the country was taken off the gold standard; and the dollar was devalued in order to aid debtors. The Glass-Steagall Banking Act established the Federal Deposit Insurance Corporation to protect small bank deposits, and reformed some practices previously permitted in the banking industry. To stimulate the purchase of new homes and the refinancing of old ones, the Home Owners' Loan Corporation was created. Within the first year, nearly one billion dollars were loaned to more than 300,000 people, and literally thousands of homes were saved from foreclosure. The Reconstruction Finance Corporation, a carryover from the Hoover administration, was authorized to lend large additional amounts of money to business and industry. More-

over, a long overdue reform of investment and securities practices was achieved within the first fifteen months of the New Deal.
A Securities and Exchange Commission was created to license stock
exchanges, register securities, require the publication of information
concerning all stocks available for sale, and to prevent many of the
malpractices which allegedly had brought on the stock market crash
of 1929.

When Franklin Roosevelt became President in March of 1933,
the total number of nonagricultural employees was estimated at
27,775,000. By 1937, nearly thirty-six million persons were employed. Nevertheless, during this period hundreds of thousands of
other citizens were subsidized by the government. The cost of the
agricultural adjustment program, unemployment relief, and the
public works program rose from $823,000,000 to more than $4,156,-
000,000 four years later, and assistance was provided to more than
twelve million people. The Civilian Conservation Corps gave
temporary work to nearly two million young men. The Civil Works
Administration, which was followed by the Federal Emergency
Relief Administration, and eventually, the Work Projects Administration, disbursed billions of dollars to enable the jobless to preserve their morale until they could obtain employment in private
industry. Governmental buildings, slum clearance, parks, artistic
and literary projects, resource preservation, highway improvements,
and many other related undertakings added to the national product
while individuals were kept from starvation. Concomitant with
this result, local economies were stimulated by the federal money
placed in circulation, though in the process, to be sure, a strong
element of centralization thoroughly challenged the traditional
concept of state-federal relations.

A plan for the elderly and underprivileged groups brought about
one of the most extensive and permanent changes in the concept
of governmental welfare to come out of this period. As the result
of pressure from large groups of reformers, social workers, cham-
pions of aid plans, and the more progressive state administrators,
the national government set up a system of social security which
also provided assistance for the unemployed, the blind, crippled
children, dependent mothers, underprivileged children, and other
groups needing direct aid. In one swoop, the New Deal cemented
a political doctrine under which American politicians of both major
parties for generations to come would recognize the obligation of

the government to provide security for an ever-increasing segment of the population that was no longer employable.

Among those who *were* employed, the New Deal offered more opportunities for labor reform than any administration in history. To further the advances of organized labor made under Woodrow Wilson and to combat the many inequities that still existed throughout much of the nation's industrial plant, section 7(a) of the National Industrial Recovery Act was lifted from the Norris-LaGuardia Act of 1928 in an effort to guarantee workers the right to organize and bargain collectively without interference by employers. The law established a National Labor Board which mediated thousands of grievances and strikes. Later, this board was replaced by a more permanent National Labor Relations Board which had broad powers over union representation and industrial disputes. When the NRA was declared unconstitutional in 1935, the labor provision of the statute was placed in a new National Labor Relations Act shepherded, with little presidential assistance, through the Congress by Senator Wagner of New York. This law provided the foundation for industrial relations during a period of transition in the labor movement and, in one of the most far-reaching decisions ever handed down by the Supreme Court, it was eventually upheld. As a result, union membership underwent a phenomenal growth. The craft-oriented American Federation of Labor increased its membership to more than four million members, and, more important politically, the Committee of Industrial Organization was established among the semi-skilled and unskilled industrial workers. In the short period of two years, the CIO, under the energetic and fluent John L. Lewis of the United Mine Workers, recruited an additional four million new members who had not been organized previously.

During this entire period, partly in an effort to obtain a status that had been denied it in the 1920's and partly in an effort to share the fruits of recovery, organized labor fought managerial reluctance to accept the new role of unions in a series of bitter strikes. Confident that the government would not be committed against them in the conflicts, the workers in the steel, automobile, and textile industries fought about hours, wages, and recognition. Violence flared and articulate public opinion seemed to be so aroused that for a time the new rights of labor seemed jeopardized for the future. Opponents of Roosevelt charged him with fomenting class warfare,

and in a sense, this was true. But out of the militance of the labor-
ing classes came a new and devoted political force, more unified
than ever before, to which the New Deal meant job security, governmental access, shorter hours, and better pay.

Strangely enough, the National Recovery Administration that
originally brought to labor new strength and encouragement was
designed mainly as a psychological shot in the arm for business. In
order to stimulate production and organize business more coopera-
tively, the National Industrial Recovery Act provided that industrial leaders, complying with certain stipulations in the law which
established minimum wages and maximum hours and outlawed
child labor, drew up codes for their industries for approval by
governmental administrators and, eventually, the President. For a
time, the plan looked as though it might succeed. Millions of
unemployed went back to work under more than seven hundred
different codes, and there was a general upswing in the economy.
But soon it became evident that confusion and noncompliance
with the codes were making the law unworkable. Big business
dominated smaller firms, monopolies developed, labor relations disintegrated; charges of unconstitutionality were brought against the
law, and neither liberals nor conservatives were satisfied with the
way in which the experiment was actually working out. In May of
1935, the Supreme Court declared the statute unconstitutional as
an excessive delegation of congressional power to the President.
Many of the activities which the NRA had outlawed were promptly
resumed by business, and liberals everywhere called for a more
vigorous prosecution of antitrust laws, for new wages and hours
legislation, and for new reform legislation to benefit working
groups. Battle lines, in the courts, throughout the economy, and on
the political front, became more sharply drawn.

Nowhere in the American economic order was the battle between
the government and private control more assiduously fought than
in the field of public utilities in the name of conservation and new
sources of power. To be sure, public power projects had been
initiated under Theodore Roosevelt, Woodrow Wilson, and Herbert
Hoover, but the scope and philosophy which enveloped this field
during the early period of the New Deal dwarfed all previous efforts.
The political implications of the most publicized of these projects —
the Tennessee Valley Authority — will be treated elsewhere in this
study. Suffice it to say here that the Roosevelt administration made

the most extensive effort in history to halt soil erosion, the destruction of natural resources, and flood damage in the United States. At the same time it instituted a program that bordered more closely on socialism than its other experiments, and concocted a change in policy that is still the subject of debate twenty-five years later. The CCC, flood control bills, the PWA, the Agricultural Resettlement Administration, and the erection of the Boulder, Grand Coulee, Bonneville, and Fort Peck Dams, together with many others, were all part of the grand scheme. An entire experiment in governmental planning was involved, and heated opposition from private utilities resulted in dramatic battles both in and out of the courts. The government eventually won them all, and in August of 1935, Congress passed the Wheeler-Rayburn Public Utility Bill, which authorized the government to regulate the production, transmission, security issues, and sale of electricity and gas. The statute also forced the dissolution (in the famous "death-sentence" clause) of all holding companies not in the public interest. Opposition to this bill, which "challenged the American business community as it had not been challenged by earlier New Deal measures," was led by the president of Commonwealth and Southern Corporation, Wendell L. Willkie, who was pushed into national prominence by the violence of the struggle.[7] Finally, however, on September 6 of 1935, President Roosevelt wrote to publisher Roy Howard that he "saw 'substantial completion' of the experimental phases of the Administration's program as far as business was concerned, and promised a breathing spell."[8] Actually, the New Deal lasted at least three more years, but opposition forces were marshalling so rapidly that the breathing spell had to be taken to allow for an electoral evaluation of the program in 1936.

This brief review of the Roosevelt program indicates the tremendous scope of activities and changes wrought between 1932 and 1936. There was no doubt of the New Deal's popularity with a majority of the voters. In 1934, for the first and only time in the history of our government, the "in" party actually increased its

---

[7] Joseph Barnes, *Willkie* (New York, 1952), p. 93. The death-sentence clause was written by Benjamin Cohen and Thomas Corcoran of the Roosevelt administration. Though the clause was originally placed in the bill only for bargaining purposes, the eventual controversy became so vituperative that a fight had to be made for it in the Congress.

[8] *Ibid.*, p. 94.

congressional delegation.[9] Nevertheless, it must be realized that such sweeping reforms and adjustments were not made without offending large segments of the population. Any attempt at a readjustment of the status quo — any endeavor to effect a more equitable distribution of the available wealth — produces an opposition. Groups regulated rebelled as their freedom of enterprise was curtailed. The President was charged with "dictatorship," his program with unconstitutionality. Class antagonisms were certainly fostered, the merit system was weakened by a large influx of new political workers, and, contrary to the campaign pledges of President Roosevelt in 1932, the budget was imbalanced with an impunity never known during time of peace. Much of the money was obviously wasted. Confused experiments were occasionally unsuccessful. The cost of administration was often excessive, and the physical products of some of the programs were "jerry-built." Republicans cried that partisanship influenced the spending of money, relief, and the hiring of workers for the governmental projects.

On the whole, however, the New Deal undoubtedly reduced despair across the nation. Aged people, the unemployed, labor, persons interested in civic improvement, better schools, investment, slum clearance, and the preservation of farms, homes, and culture were all grateful for the achievements made under the Roosevelt administration. And it was with this backlog of gratitude that the Democrats entered the election campaign of 1936.

THE ELECTION OF 1936

The strength of the Republican party was an unknown quantity, however, and this was not a campaign which Roosevelt faced without apprehension. Opposition was intense, and the barbs thrown at the President were particularly irritating, for they accused him of destroying the very institutions that he in his own mind was dedicated to preserve. Among his most persistent critics were some former Democrats such as John J. Raskob, who had been Democratic National Chairman in 1928, Alfred E. Smith, the 1928 party nominee, and John W. Davis, who had been the party leader in 1924. These men, together with several other prominent right-wing

---

[9] In 1932, the Democrats had 59 members in the Senate and 314 members in the House. The voters in 1934 elected 322 Democrats to the House and nine new Senators. Nearly all of the House seats were gained by a sweeping victory in Pennsylvania, called by James Farley, "the sweetest . . . in the country. . . ." *Time*, November 21, 1932, p. 11, and November 19, 1934, p. 12.

Northern Democrats, were part of the American Liberty League, which had been chartered in August of 1934 as an organization to protect property rights, initiative, enterprise, and economic freedom. Many leading industrialists from the automotive, chemical, oil, mail-order, and other large industries formed the backbone of this organization which poured huge amounts of money and propaganda into the campaign — though with little effect.

Moreover, by this time, more than seventy-five per cent of the nation's newspapers were against the President as a leader who had not kept his 1932 platform and campaign promises, as a reckless spender, as a radical leading the nation to socialism, and as a politician utilizing the nation's misery to build a political bureaucracy. Similar criticisms were widely broadcast over the radio, as conservative forces became more concerned over a perpetuation of New Deal policies. Though the money spent by the GOP in 1936 did not compare with the large expenditures in the name of relief and rehabilitation emanating from Washington, the Republicans were not without extensive avenues of expression.

Unfortunately, however, the party selected a competent but rather colorless standard-bearer who could not effectively utilize these available channels. At their June convention, the Republicans nominated Kansan Alfred M. Landon, the one Republican governor who had twice defeated the Democrats in the midst of Democratic landslides.[10] Landon, seemingly, had all of the characteristics necessary to oppose Roosevelt — except possibly that important and illusive quality, glamour. He was a businessman from a farm state. He had supported Theodore Roosevelt and was identified with the liberal wing of the GOP. Though he had made few speeches heard outside of Kansas, he had been given a careful build-up as both a conservative in economics and a liberal humanitarian. As proven a vote-getter as any Republican on the scene at the time, he was a solid, substantial, budget-balancing, average representative of the midwestern middle class. By convention time, he had outdistanced any of the other contenders — Borah, Knox, and former President Hoover — and he was nominated by acclamation on the first ballot.

Landon ran on a platform under which the Republicans assumed

[10] Malcom Moos, in his *The Republicans* (New York, 1956), p. 396, wrote that Landon undoubtedly was victorious in 1932 and 1934 because of a third-party candidate, John R. Brinkley, who drew votes from the Democrats.

"the obligations and duties imposed upon Government by modern conditions," but which also stated that "We affirm our unalterable conviction that . . . the fate of the nation will depend, not so much on the wisdom and power of government, as on the character and virtue, self-reliance, industry and thrift of the people and on their willingness to meet the responsibilities essential to the preservation of a free society." The document charged that the powers of Congress and the rights reserved to the states had been usurped by the President, that the political liberties and individual opportunities of Americans were being threatened by the government itself for the first time, and that the New Deal had been guilty of frightful waste and extravagance using public funds for partisan political purposes. Measures of the Roosevelt administration, it asserted, had "bred fear and hesitation in commerce and industry, thus discouraging new enterprises, preventing employment and prolonging the depression."

The GOP promised to continue social security, unemployment insurance, the protection of labor, aid to agriculture, and federal public works, but maintained that these programs would be administered more economically and without partisanship. A balanced budget, decentralized regulation of agricultural agencies, and "the return of responsibility for relief administration to non-political local agencies familiar with community problems" were all pledged by the Republican leaders. Deference was, of course, paid to many other interest groups, but essentially, the platform set forth the issues and established the tone for the 1936 campaign. The statements clearly meant that the President and his policies were the principal considerations to be placed before the voters for endorsement or repudiation.

Landon began his campaign in August, but Roosevelt waited until late in September to make his first appeal. The President campaigned primarily on his record of recovery, constantly contrasting the situation in 1936 with that of 1932. He defended relief spending in terms of conserving human resources and argued that the cost was balanced by the rising national income. Rarely mentioning the Republican candidate by name in the course of his entire campaign, he preferred to castigate "the selfish forces who have ruined commerce," or the "unscrupulous enemies alien to the American spirit," or his "organized money" foes. Finally, he always promised to carry on the spirit of the New Deal.

Governor Landon, on the other hand, followed his platform rather closely. He devoted much of his time to "the American Way" — a way of life to which he promised to return — a way of life which he contended the New Deal had rejected in favor of regimentation, radicalism, interference with business, infringement of liberties, and extravagant spending.

Both parties favored a balanced budget, but neither party offered a plan to achieve the aim. Neither party was for a reduction in expenditures for the unemployed, the farmer, the veteran, or national defense, items to which two-thirds of the budget was devoted. Both candidates wanted to continue relief, though Landon stood for more local administration while Roosevelt suggested a division of authority between the localities and the national government. On agriculture, both men were for soil conservation, subsidies, retirement of submarginal land, and liberal credit to farmers. Landon declared that he would recommend repeal of the Reciprocal Trade treaties, but that he favored reciprocity for noncompeting products; Roosevelt favored more trade, and "a revival of foreign imports" as a realistic necessity.[11]

Landon suffered from the handicap under which Republican presidential candidates have had to labor since 1932. He was for economy, sound money, protectionism, less governmental interference with the business community, more freedom of enterprise — in agriculture as well as in commerce — and all of the other principles advocated by those whose voices are most powerful in the party, while at the same time he realized that the voters supporting these ideas were in the minority. He therefore had to temporize and equivocate his stand in an effort to obtain additional votes from the middle and lower classes. In 1936, when the nation's economy was just barely emerging from chaos and eleven million workers were still unemployed, this position was disastrous. Moreover, Landon as an inspirational force could not compete in personality with the President. His voice sounded flat, almost monotonous, and his negative approach did not kindle the fire necessary to obtain converts to his Republicanism. Added to this dilemma was a pitiful depression of spirit and lack of organization within the party ranks. When John D. M. Hamilton took over the chairmanship of the

---

[11] Foreign policy was not an important issue in 1936. Though fascism was secure in Germany and Italy, "the sound of Europe, the threat of war — grows fainter and further with each mile beyond the seaboard. . . ." Anne O'Hare McCormick in the *New York Times,* November 1, 1936, sec. 8, p. 1.

national committee, he discovered that his headquarters did not even have a list of the county chairmen, and that in many counties there was no longer a Republican chairman.[12] In view of this situation, Hamilton found it necessary to spend huge amounts of money for broadcasting facilities and local organization. By election eve, prospects looked bright, and the *Literary Digest* even predicted a Republican victory.[13] The consensus of two hundred forecasters polled by the *New York Times,* however, was that the President would win with 406 electoral votes. They conceded twelve certain votes and a probable ninety-one more to Landon.

On November 3, 1936, more than forty-four million voters went to the polls. The astounding results upset all predictions except those of Democratic Chairman James Farley, who had correctly forecast the final electoral count. Roosevelt defeated Landon by more than ten million votes, the biggest presidential plurality in history. He won 523 of the 531 electoral votes, the largest ratio since 1820, and carried with him into the Congress the largest Senate majority since 1869 and the largest House majority since 1855.[14] The Republican congressional delegation dropped from twenty-three to seventeen in the Senate and from one hundred four to eighty-nine in the House of Representatives. There was no Democratic swing to the "Jefferson Democrats" who had bolted the party, and the Republican progressives like Senators Borah and Hiram Johnson, who had refused to support the President this time, had no discernible effect on the results. Of the thirty-three governorships at stake, the Republicans won only three, while they lost four of the ten they had previously held.[15]

Immediately after the election and constantly during the following six months, Republican leaders, commentators, and analysts searched for the meaning of the election together with a future course for the Republican party. The Republican National Committee had spent a record amount of nearly nine million dollars

---

[12] Moos, *op. cit.,* p. 401.

[13] The *Digest,* which had had an excellent record of predictions until this time, mailed more than ten million ballots to persons listed in telephone directories and in automobile registration files. The magazine thus ignored the millions of citizens who could not afford such luxuries and also forgot that upper-class voters respond to questionnaires more readily than individuals in lower economic groups.

[14] *Newsweek,* November 7, 1936, p. 7.

[15] *Ibid.,* p. 13.

on the campaign,[16] had gone \$900,000 into debt[17] and yet, as one source put it, "more experienced observers agreed only that the Old Guard brand of Republicanism was dead."[18] Many Republicans thought that the 1936 election was a victory for liberalism over conservatism and advocated a leftward swing for the GOP. Governor Harold G. Hoffman of New Jersey said, "the Republican Party is hampered by leaders who are still living among cobwebs and mothballs,"[19] and New York Republican leader Kenneth Simpson, Governor George Aiken of Vermont, and Emporia editor William Allen White all agreed with another commentator who remarked: "It can never be victorious while it is Victorian."[20] John D. M. Hamilton, the national chairman, declared: "I think that the Republicans will have to recognize . . . that they have lost the pulse of the people, the confidence of the great masses of Americans — that the party has been a closed corporation. It means that our leadership has lost touch with others who lead other great groups."[21]

Fortune magazine, however, in a most comprehensive analysis, pointed out that the issue was not that of liberalism against conservatism, but simply whether or not the people liked Franklin D. Roosevelt as President, and that the election meant that they did. The editors examined the Roosevelt record and found that his economic beliefs rested more solidly on the preservation of capitalism than on socialism, that the NRA, the continuation of the RFC and the Banking Act of 1935 could not be reconciled with a Federal Relief Administrator, a public-works program, and the TVA under any one politico-philosophical term such as liberalism. They concluded that the liberalism argument came almost solely from the fact that a Roosevelt victory was a victory over the big business forces that opposed him, and that the voters' response was materialistic, not humanitarian. "The lesson the Republican party should learn," the magazine asserted, "is the lesson that prosperity is still the best election argument."[22] The policies that had brought a resurgence of prosperity on which the President had campaigned

---

[16] *New York Times,* January 6, 1937, p. 3, and March 5, p. 17.
[17] *Ibid.,* March 10, 1937, p. 21.
[18] *Newsweek,* November 14, 1936, p. 14.
[19] *New York Times,* February 7, 1937, p. 18.
[20] *Ibid.,* January 31, 1937, sec. 2, p. 9.
[21] *Ibid.,* January 17, 1937, p. 9.
[22] *Fortune,* February, 1937, pp. 67 ff.

had been formulated almost entirely within the executive branch, and the people had endorsed both the program and the man.

Thoughtful Republicans wondered what road the party should take. Several avenues were open. The party leaders could go back to the old pre-New Deal philosophy and become a truly conservative organization devoted to individualism, states' rights, a restoration of the gold standard, a balanced budget, and an elimination of governmental controls. The obvious difficulty with this turn to the right was that practically no one, in 1937, would have supported it.[23] A second alternative, which several progressive leaders suggested, was the expulsion of the Old Guard and the offering of a liberalism reminiscent of the Progressive party of 1912 — or, more drastically, a more liberal program than that offered by President Roosevelt. This course was patently nonsense. It would have required a contradiction of much of the party dogma, a repudiation of the principal supporters of the party, and a renunciation of the party's historical philosophy. The leaders of the GOP, outside of a small section on the eastern seaboard, were simply incapable of thinking in terms more liberal than the New Deal.

A third alternative was the rather widespread, but silent, conviction that the Republican party should *go quietly out of existence.* Though few leaders of the GOP would openly discuss this possibility, evidence indicates that it was frequently considered during the early months of 1937. Nicholas Murray Butler, in an interview, declared: "There isn't any Republican party any more, and there hasn't been a Republican party for some time."[24] He predicted a complete realignment of political forces in the United States within the following ten years. Delbert Clark, writing in the *New York Times Magazine,* commented that "no one of any responsibility will publicly discuss his thoughts," but that such self-constituted leaders as Senator Borah, Representative Snell, Ogden Mills, Representatives Wadsworth and Hamilton Fish would talk volubly in private. "From private discussion with some," he wrote, "one startling fact emerges. That is a willingness, inconceivable four years ago, to consider the possibility of discarding the party, as the Republican party, altogether and of issuing a new manifesto under a new name with the salutary purpose of eliminating fundamental antagonisms and starting afresh on a solid, if small, basis."[25]

---

[23] *American Mercury,* June, 1938, p. 133.
[24] *New York Times,* April 2, 1937, p. 25.
[25] *Ibid.,* June 20, 1937, sec. 7, p. 22.

The editors of *Fortune,* who four years later were to be among the principal spokesmen for the Republican party, in February of 1937 gave the party leaders similar advice: "What then can the Republicans do? Whether they like it or not they can reflect upon the phrase by which the Democrats now know this era. They can make the Era of Good Feeling unanimous by doing what the Federalists did a hundred years ago. They can disappear. . . ."[26] John Hamilton, when asked about changing the name of the party, seriously stated that any new party would have to be based on the present Republican party,[27] and as late as September of 1937, Senator Vandenberg, who was believed by many observers to be the real leader of the party in Congress, said that he thought party labels were comparatively unimportant.[28]

The theory behind the dissolution of the Republican party in favor of a new conservative party arose from the belief that a new group could rally to its banner many Democrats who would not vote under the Republican label but who were sufficiently out of step with the Roosevelt philosophy to enlist in a new organization that more fully represented their true beliefs. It was no secret that the President was strengthening a personal nucleus of New Dealers within the Democratic party, and that he was privately critical of Democrats who were hesitant to go along with many of his policies. It was thought that such Senators as Bailey of North Carolina, Burke of Nebraska, Byrd and Glass of Virginia, Clark of Missouri, Copeland of New York, Gerry of Rhode Island, King of Utah, Tydings of Maryland, and many right-wing Democratic congressmen might welcome a way out of their difficulties with the Administration. As *Fortune* put it:

. . . if the Republicans liquidate, the Democratic party will split. And if the Democratic party splits the split will run along economic rather than economic-geographic lines, and then there will be no more Solid South. And if there is no Solid South, the major part of the splitting party will be attracted toward the stronger pole. And with Republicans released from their old allegiance the stronger pole will be the conservative pole. Which would mean that the liberal pole would be a truly liberal pole. And U.S. politics might then quicken with a conservatism that would really conserve, a liberalism that would really liberalize, an opposition that would really oppose. From such a state of affairs there

---

[26] *Fortune,* February, 1937, p. 188.
[27] *New York Times,* May 2, 1937, p. 1.
[28] *Ibid.,* September 23, 1937, p. 26.

might spring something this country has not yet known in this century: a set of intelligent political principles. . . .[29]

As students of American political history well know, however, any endeavor to form a new major party is fraught with such overwhelming difficulties that unless a dynamic and soul-burning issue exists about which people can coalesce, the movement never really comes off. The technical necessities of getting on ballots, the spiritual persuasion essential to move large groups to new allegiances, and the nearly impossible task of organization preclude any new party based merely on the weakness of one of the old coalitions. Political parties have their strengths in the local precincts, and a decision from the top to change a label needs more than a renunciation of a temporarily discredited name. In 1937 the Republican party was still a symbol of loyalty and respect for seventeen million people, and there was no real evidence that the many disaffected Democrats would switch to a new organization that had clouded principles and no apparent leadership. As Arthur Krock put it: "There is a breadth in the Democratic party of fealty . . . which exceeds that in any other political group. Not only in the South, where it is almost a matter of social consciousness to vote Democratic, but in New England and the Northwest, where Democrats labored sturdily in the minority for decades, it would require prayerful renunciation to enlist under a new banner. With the party symbol and chief leader ranged under the old flag, Democrats in a broad space of the nation's surface would find it most difficult to leave the fold."[30] Thus, in spite of thoughtful consideration of a new conservative party by some Republican leaders and organs in the spring of 1937, the GOP followed a fourth alternative line of action. This was a policy called "loyal opposition" by some individuals and "just muddling along" by others. The theory behind it was merely to lie low while endeavoring to rebuild at the local political level. The term "loyal opposition" was inappropriate for the Republicans in the Seventy-fifth Congress because of the size of the delegation, and because, as one source put it: "A useful opposition can function only in a country in which the vital decisions are made in the legislature."[31] In 1937 Roosevelt was making the decisions, formulating the policy, and establishing a trend

[29] *Fortune,* February, 1937, p. 190.
[30] *New York Times,* October 24, 1937, sec. 8, p. 2.
[31] *Fortune,* February, 1937, p. 70.

toward presidential leadership in legislation, while the interests normally represented by the Republican party turned more and more to direct negotiation with Democratic federal administrators and, when rebuffed, to the courts.

The retreat of Republicans to the courts had been enormously successful. New Deal statutes and administrative decisions had been delayed, modified, or invalidated by court decisions, and the President seemed impotent to do anything about this debilitation of his program. His next dramatic and characteristic endeavor to remedy the situation, however, produced the most memorable political event of 1937, and eventually altered, for a generation, the judiciary's interpretation of the Constitution.

Flushed with an almost personal victory and carrying a record number of Democratic congressmen into office with him, the President, early in February, announced his plan to enlarge the Supreme Court. The proposal had been well thought out, and was one of several different possibilities he had considered to enable him to place some additional liberals on the court which had rejected so much of his New Deal. The heart of the plan was merely a proposal to add one new judge, up to a maximum of six, for every justice of the Supreme Court who failed to retire within six months after becoming seventy years of age. Considering (1) the mandate the President had received at the polls; (2) the fact that in his first four years he had not had an opportunity to name a single judge to the high court; (3) that never before in the court's history had it been called upon to pass on so much extremely controversial legislation in so short a period; (4) that never before had the court nullified so many acts indirectly sponsored by a president; and (5) that the court was virtually frozen into a 5-4 split favoring the conservatives against Administration measures, the bill was relatively moderate.

What Roosevelt had failed to take into consideration, however, was the deep-seated respect for the Court as an institution and the widespread opposition to any outright alteration in the traditional concept of the Court as a guardian of the Constitution, a concept that existed among people of all economic and social strata. Immediately the press, the organized bar, the business community, members of both parties, and even some leaders of labor joined thousands of ordinary citizens in denouncing the plan as another attempt by the President to assume dictatorial power and to end constitutional government.[32]

The tremendous majorities and cohesive group coalitions that had produced the President's victory in November evaporated as the implications of the proposal were broadcast throughout the country. For more than six months, the Court struggle dominated the political news. Finally, the President accepted a compromise — the main portion of his bill was defeated in the Senate Judiciary Committee — when circumstances indicated that a liberal majority had been established, and Justice Van Devanter resigned to give Roosevelt a controlling first appointment. Throughout the entire fracas, the President's tactics, rather than the critical role of judicial review in a representative government, had been constantly at issue, and the American public had not supported the President's maneuvers.

The opposition to the President in this struggle was led by Democratic senators, and in the final committee session in which the proposal was defeated, six Democrats and four Republicans constituted the majority that killed the bill. The Republican delegation in the Senate, however, on orders from minority leader Charles McNary, maintained almost a complete silence on the Court measure. Fearful that any open attack would result in an impression that the fight involved only a Democratic-Republican split and despite tremendous pressure from constituents, the small band of GOP senators reserved comment during the debate, and even curtailed the statements of other Republican leaders outside of Congress. This strategy met with mixed reactions. To be sure, the maneuver illustrated to the nation the division within the Democratic party and provided a vacuum which newsmen avidly filled by emphasizing the opposition to Roosevelt by Chief Justice Charles Evans Hughes. But it also vividly emphasized that on one of the liveliest constitutional issues ever debated in Congress, the Republican party was silent. The voters undoubtedly knew, from the few statements that were made by Chairman Hamilton, that the GOP was unanimously against the measure, but the long debate produced no hint of what, in these dramatic times, the Republican party was *for*.

The Court fight was in a sense symbolic of the Republican atti-

---

[32] For an excellent summary of the Court fight, see Burns, *op. cit.*, pp. 291-315. For a more comprehensive discussion, see Joseph Alsop and Turner Catledge, *The 168 Days* (Garden City, N.Y., 1938).

tude during the first months of 1937. The leaders of the party, Senators Vandenberg and McNary, Representatives Bacon, Fish, Snell, and others, realized that it was futile to base a campaign wholly on negativism, but they were too weak to organize anything more constructive. Moreover, the members of this high command were at odds as to the best strategy.[33] The party stood for economy, sound finance, and an end to extravagance. Hamilton repeatedly asked for "a positive program of cooperation between capital and labor," for he felt that the Republicans had to cultivate the groups that had supported the Democratic party in November. Vandenberg and three other Republican senators did draft a "cash and carry" bill for American neutrality, and the Michigan senator also sponsored a "pay-as-you-go" amendment to the Social Security Act, which, among other items, would have expanded the number of people reached by the statute.[34] He also called for a rejection of the Reciprocal Trade Agreements renewal as "an unconstitutional delegation of legislative power to the executive," for a policing of the maladministration of relief appropriations,[35] and for the protection of the employer as well as the employee in labor relations. As the first hints of the 1938 recession were appearing in the spring of 1937, cries of "all-powerful" or "omnipotent" government that restricted opportunities for employment and destroyed competitive enterprise were again widely heard. Gradually party leaders became more optimistic and began to reassert that the Republican party was alive, vibrant, and potent.

Actually, it was Franklin Roosevelt who was determining Republican policy and he forced it to be essentially negativistic. When the President failed to act on the mushrooming sit-down strikes, the Republicans charged that he had "sold out to the C.I.O," and a revision of the Wagner Act became a part of their program. The GOP opposed the Black-Connery wages and hours bill as a new move for a "centralized authoritarian state with . . . government-blessed monopolies."[36] Roosevelt's relief appropriation bill for 1938 passed the Senate in spite of Republican attempts to cut out one-

---

[33] See the *New York Times,* May 23, 1937, sec. 4, p. 10.

[34] *Ibid.,* February 24, 1937, p. 2. This move represented almost the first Republican effort of its kind since 1932.

[35] Senator Vandenberg and Representative Robert L. Bacon of New York introduced a bill which would have provided direct federal relief in place of work relief. The plan, administered by the states, allegedly would have saved forty cents on every dollar of relief funds. *Ibid.,* May 24, 1937, p. 6.

[36] *Ibid.,* June 6, 1937, p. 4.

sixth of the money, but the administrative reorganization bill, following closely in the President's timetable the Supreme Court enlargement proposal, was so bitterly denounced by Republican and Democratic congressmen alike that it didn't come up for a vote.

Thus, the Republican position of opposition was always present, but observers were doubtful that Republicans, as such, were making an impression on the nation's voters. Chairman Hamilton undertook a modest radio campaign featuring prominent party leaders, but too frequently the speakers substituted generalities for specific plans. In an effort to formulate something more explicit, former President Hoover suggested a mid-term party convention for 1938 "to take stock of the party's position" and work out some sort of program.[37]

THE REPUBLICAN PROGRAM COMMITTEE

What Hoover originally had in mind was a meeting of a few prominent Republicans, both laymen and those who had been candidates for state or national office, who would meet and formulate a set of principles in advance of a larger mid-term convention patterned after the quadrennial national convention. The principles were to establish the base for a document eventually to be placed before the nation as an off-year platform of the Republican party about which Republicans, independents, and disgruntled Democrats could rally. Will Hays had appointed a similar committee to draft a declaration of principles in 1919 with great success.

The suggestions produced an immediate division of ranks among the Republicans. Hoover was accused of making a bid for power though he later denied that he wanted any public office. He said the mid-term convention would be merely an "intellectual session of the party." Governor Landon and many congressional leaders, however, felt that such a convention would show that the Republi-

---

[37] In the September 26, 1937, issue of the *New York Times*, Charles R. Michael wrote that the grass-roots convention was really Hamilton's suggestion, and that it had been favorably discussed by the executive committee of the Republican National Committee. On August 9, however, Hamilton had told a reporter that he had heard of it, but wanted to reserve comment. *Ibid.*, Aug. 10, p. 5. The convention was publicly proposed, however, in an article by Hoover which appeared in the September, 1937, issue of the *Atlantic Monthly*. In another article entitled "The Republican Program Committee," by Ronald Bridges, reference is made to the fact that a convention had been discussed in both the March and September meetings of the executive committee, but that action was postponed until the full committee met in November. *Public Opinion Quarterly*, 3 (April, 1939), 300.

can party had no constructive program and that it would develop breaches which would be difficult to heal. Senator McNary declared that "nothing can be gained from such meetings," and former Senator James E. Watson seemed to epitomize the position of state leaders when he asserted that "next year is not the proper time to rouse intra-party controversies."[38] Newspaper accounts of the differences between Hoover and Landon on the controversy ranged from a "gentle duel" to "deep seated hostility" over the issue. Representative Hamilton Fish said that he hoped both Hoover and Landon would "from now on sit on the sidelines and let someone else carry the ball."[39] The *New York Times* reported that the Republican party "is in a remarkably confused and disjointed state."[40] Harrison Spangler, national committeeman from Iowa who five years later became the Republican National Chairman, sent out 11,000 questionnaires to Republican Clubs and prominent party workers to determine their stand on the convention. He received 6,000 replies, indicating that of the Republican rank and file, ninety-four per cent were in favor of the mid-term convention.[41]

At the November 5 meeting of the national committee, however, opponents of the convention, led by Landon, Colonel Frank Knox, Senator Borah, and Representative Joseph Martin, who was then chairman of the Republican Congressional Campaign Committee, defeated the Hoover forces directed by Hamilton and supported by the party's Old Guard. The idea of a convention was given up in the interests of party harmony. The compromise agreed upon was a program committee of 100 persons chosen by the executive committee of the Republican National Committee, whose duty it would be to make a comprehensive study of the issues and the positions of the major parties on them and to report its findings to the national committee. The job was formidable indeed. More than 3,000 names were quickly suggested as participants in the conference, and several party leaders compiled lists of their own.

At a December meeting at the Coronado Hotel in St. Louis, the executive committee members who were authorized to select the "most representative" Republicans soon discovered that they would not be able to confine the list to 100 persons. They raised the number to 150, and then to 200 in an effort to bring in representa-

---

[38] *New York Times*, October 20, 1937, p. 6.
[39] *Ibid.*, October 17, 1937, sec. 4, p. 8.
[40] *Ibid.*, October 24, 1937, sec. 4, p. 7.
[41] *Ibid.*, September 26, 1937, sec. 4, p. 10.

tives of more groups. The final list included farmers, manufacturers, labor and commerce representatives, professional men, editors, social workers, and representatives from minority, religious, and miscellaneous groups,[42] but many party loyalists, including some public officials (even national committeemen) had to be excluded from the ultimate selection of laymen. Dr. Glenn Frank, who had been ousted as president of the University of Wisconsin by Governor Philip La Follette, was chosen as chairman of the committee in spite of the fact that he occasionally had been mentioned as a possible presidential dark horse. Acceptable to all groups and identified with none, Frank, at the age of fifty, had been a one-time editor of *Century Magazine,* a university president, and at the time of his selection was editor of a popular farming "free-sheet" called *Rural Progress.* Raymond Clapper, writing for the Scripps-Howard newspapers, hailed the selection of Frank as "unexpectedly progressive," a choice that turns "the clock forward a couple of decades, which is pretty good when you bear in mind that the party began marking time thirty years ago." The *New York Herald Tribune,* however, felt that "as a leader fitted to lift the Republican party above its personal rivalries, its feuds, and its confusion of outlook, his choice is a grave disappointment."[43] Similar opinions were voiced by other papers and party leaders, but Frank was acceptable to both Landon and Hoover, and all discussion of him soon disappeared. Frank himself helped quash opposition when he stated on several occasions that it was not the business of his group to write a 1938 or 1940 platform or to promote the candidacy of anyone for any office.[44]

The program committee went to work immediately, setting up a Chicago headquarters and nine regional committees each instructed

---

[42] *Time,* December 27, 1937, p. 12, called it "an eclectic list" with a solid underpinning of businessmen, manufacturers, publishers, and local Republican leaders. Publisher Frank Gannett declined to be a member.

[43] The *Literary Digest,* January 1, 1938, p. 9.

[44] Commenting on the meeting, the pro-Administration *Nation* said that the Republicans faced a dilemma in that members of the party did not agree on what strategy would best capitalize on the ready-made issues presented to them by the Democratic party. "The dilemma of the Republicans is that on one hand they are being driven increasingly toward a fascist position by the powerful interests of the economic groups they represent, yet are held back from it by the whole character of their ideology, which is traditionally liberal in the laissez faire sense. On the other hand, they are straining increasingly to broaden the base of their popular appeal and are being held back by the roots of their economic interest." *The Nation,* December 25, 1937, p. 705.

to sound out rank-and-file party members on questions of interest as political issues. The Chicago office was to act as a clearing house for comments and as a center for research on thirty-five topics of vital interest. At the first full meeting of the program committee in March, 1938, Frank outlined the duties of the committee saying "this commission: (1) must make an utterly honest and objective audit of the New Deal . . . (2) must rethink, restate, and reinterpret to the nation the political and economic philosophy with which the Republican Party faces the new circumstances of this new age — and (3) must . . . create a comprehensive report of policy respecting the long array of stubborn problems confronting us as a people. . . ." Mrs. Chester C. Bolton of Ohio and Robert P. Bass of New Hampshire were chosen as vice-chairmen. The members present were united in their determination to provide a solid piece of Republican philosophy, but as they got down to work, multifarious problems soon became apparent, and much of the solidarity of the group gave way to differences of opinion.

From March to August, 1938, the committee conducted interviews, held hearings, and attempted to draft the fundamentals of the party doctrine. The magnitude of the job became overwhelming, personal bickering flared among the members, and political considerations kept interfering with proposed statements of policy. Early in June of 1938, Dr. Thomas H. Reed was selected to be director of studies for the committee. He arranged some round tables at which all of the principal pressure groups, including labor, had an opportunity to express their opinions to the Republican policy-makers, and he also established work plans on agriculture, social security, old-age insurance, unemployment, and kindred subjects in order to analyze alternative courses of action by the party.

In August the program committee met at Northwestern University's Thorne Hall in Chicago to assess, in closed sessions and at public forums, the progress of the group and the status of the parties. After some debate, a lengthy report was issued which warned that the country was threatened with a twofold disaster, "a breakdown of its economic system and the disintegration of responsible and effective government." The report added that "effective recognition of [our] obligation to youth and age is essential through individual action, voluntary social action, and government action . . ." and that "the key to the whole program the committee is engaged in drafting is to determine such stimulations, regulations, and freedoms for labor, agriculture, business, industry, and finance as will make the mature years of Americans a period of high and sustained productivity.[45]

Several observers stated that the sessions accomplished little tangible good and that national interest in the meeting was lacking but that the gatherings were the kind of Republican promotion that kept the ball rolling.[46] The *Saturday Evening Post,* however, thought that the statement put forth was too liberal, and that "the Republican Party . . . lost an opportunity to make a clear challenge and raise a fighting standard."[47] The venerable publication then called for a "rebirth of the conservative principle"! Charles Michelson, the Democratic publicity director, declared that the meeting showed that "the minority party hasn't the slightest idea of where it is going or how it shall get to any destination. . . . Nowhere in the report is there any suggestion as to how the alleged breakdown of the economic system is to be averted or the disintegration of government is to be checked."[48]

At the August meeting it was decided that the program committee's report would not be brought out before the 1938 elections. Many of the congressmen who had opposed the creation of the group in the first instance did not want to be committed to any program in which they had no hand, and the committee itself dropped its original objective of preparing a comprehensive long-range policy in favor of an elaborate study of the needs and desires of the American people. As a result, interest in the project waned during 1939, and it was not until a 33,000-word report was issued in February, 1940, that the country again heard from the Frank committee.

THE EMERGING CANDIDATES

Meanwhile, other political activities dominated the scene. In spite of the President's repeated statements that he intended to balance the budget, the financial ledger continued imbalanced with increasing pressure to raise taxes or to cut relief. A split in labor became constantly wider as jurisdictional strikes and differences among leaders multiplied during the expansion period of the CIO.

---

[45] Bridges, *op. cit.,* p. 302.

[46] *Newsweek,* August 15, 1938, p. 11. The pro-New Deal magazines concurred.

[47] *Saturday Evening Post,* December 10, 1938, p. 22.

[48] *New York Times,* August 7, 1938, p. 4.

Labor leaders began to criticize Roosevelt because of his ingratitude for their assistance in 1936. The stock market declined rapidly and a new depression was in the making. Unemployment was again on the rise, and the Administration seemed to be genuinely confused about what steps to take. To top the beleaguered domestic situation, a war crisis in Europe was threatening the stability of our foreign affairs.[49] Unfortunately for the Republicans, the party could not fully capitalize on these ready-made Rooseveltian issues. It was still looking for both a leader and a positive program.

Herbert Hoover made statements from time to time that kept him in both the party and the public eye, and reports were widespread that Hamilton had slipped from Landon to the protection of Hoover and the Old Guard. On the other hand, the resignation of the conservative Charles D. Hilles of New York from the Republican National Committee was considered as a liberal omen, for he was succeeded by Kenneth F. Simpson, Republican chairman of New York County, who was a fusionist willing to cooperate with anyone from any party to strengthen the GOP. But as Arthur Krock wrote: "The Republican Party fails to provide clear opposition leadership. . . . No Republican has yet appeared who can effect the junction [between American conservatives and liberals opposed to the New Deal]."[50] New York district attorney Thomas E. Dewey was mentioned by party leaders as "a Moses for the 1940 campaign," but he still had to become governor, and his fame was limited outside of eastern GOP circles. Henry Cabot Lodge, Jr., of Massachusetts, Styles Bridges of New Hampshire, and Glenn Frank of Wisconsin also were frequently mentioned, in addition to the top candidate, Senator Vandenberg, as possible eventual nominees.

For a fleeting several months in 1937 and 1938, Governor George D. Aiken of Vermont catapulted himself into the small circle of nationally influential Republicans, but his constant criticism of the party as "a party of old men"[51] whose leaders were "more concerned

---

[49] In 1937, the implications of the foreign situation had not yet become a crucial issue within the Republican party, and no one became excited when John Hamilton, over NBC on August 28, declared: "The Republican party had no panacea in 1920 for the solution of the problem of peace, but by reason of its victory in that election, it saved the nation from active entanglement, foreign quarrels and alarms under the nobly-conceived but still impracticable and dangerous commitments of the League of Nations." *Vital Speeches,* September 15, 1937, p. 709.

[50] *New York Times,* September 23, 1937, p. 26.

[51] The *Literary Digest,* December 18, 1937, p. 7. On April 30, 1938,

with controlling party machinery than with American welfare," and his efforts to purge the "baneful influence" of committeemen from the South were too much for those who were trying to promote party harmony. Nevertheless, he was widely publicized as "a man of the Coolidge type" who had the courage to demand the expulsion of reactionaries from the GOP.[52]

Charles McNary, as the official leader of the Republican delegation in the Senate, said little, but broke into print frequently enough to be considered as a possible 1940 candidate. He stood for sound public credit, a tariff adequate to encourage production for home markets, and a strong national government that would not absorb the powers of the states. He was, of all Republicans, closer to the farm problem than any others, and he believed that his old equalization fee or export debentures plan that had been vetoed by Coolidge was still superior to the AAA. He wanted more economy and decentralization in the handling of relief, simpler forms of taxation, and a conduct of international relations that would maintain American rights with a minimum of risk of embroilment in foreign wars.[53] Usually unmentioned in McNary's qualifications, however, were the facts that he was a consistent supporter of the New Deal's program of public power development and that he had voted for the social security program, the Wagner Act, and the full work relief bill proposed by the Administration.

The acknowledged leader of congressional Republican policy and front-runner for the 1940 nomination in 1938 was Arthur Vandenberg of Michigan. While columnists complained that the Republicans had no program, Vandenberg frequently asserted five,- seven,- or ten-point programs — some planks of which eventually became law in the 1940's. It is a curiosity of the era that Vandenberg did not emerge more dominantly in Republican councils before he revised his position on foreign policy. He fought for a remodeled Wagner Act "to encourage mutual responsibility and to punish

Chairman Hamilton told the Eastern Intercollegiate Republican Clubs conference meeting at Princeton, New Jersey: "The Republican party is no longer made up of the Old Guard. It is, in effect, of at least near-youth." *New York Times,* May 1, 1938, sec. 2, p. 3.

[52] In a Lincoln Day address in 1938, Aiken declared: "If Lincoln were alive, he would be ashamed of the leadership of the Republican party. . . ." He warned that, unless the methods of leadership changed, there would be a permanent third party of "ordinary folks, workers and farmers." *Ibid.,* February 13, 1938, p. 1.

[53] *Christian Science Monitor Magazine,* April 27, 1938, p. 1.

mutual irresponsibility," a repeal of the surplus-profits and the capital-gains taxes, a single appropriations bill, and a "firm policy of insulating neutrality." He took the position that the United States could not be the world's protector or the world's policeman, and that the limitation of arms was the sole defense against the final calamity of bankruptcy or conflict.[54] He wanted protective tariffs, a prohibition of sit-down strikes but no part of the wages and hours bill, and an investigation of the advisability of exempting industrial firms from certain taxes in return for the installation of "profit sharing" systems.[55] But in 1938, when Arthur Vandenberg was advancing issues he was not always advancing party solidarity. He was the Republican of whom it was most frequently said that he would not hesitate to junk the old party if necessary to obtain a new right-wing coalition with any Democrats who would vote against Roosevelt but not for the Republican label.[56] Delbert Clark wrote: "[Vandenberg] appears to be entirely honest in his talk of coalition. He is not a progressive, as progressives are rated these days, but he is a realist, and he knows that a party label is a pitiful thing if it can't inspire victory at the polls."[57]

Vandenberg, however, was not the head of the party out of Congress, and consequently his influence was only one of many forces pulling in different directions. Landon and Hoover were also involved in the struggle for control of the national committee and party affairs, and though Hoover and Hamilton apparently supported Vandenberg's position on a coalition, Landon and Colonel Knox did not, and thus the Landon faction of the party was favorably disposed toward the resignation of Hamilton in favor of ex-Governor Kohler of Wisconsin as national chairman.[58] Actually Landon had been cool toward Vandenberg ever since the Michigan senator had declined to be his running mate in 1936, and both of the 1936 Republican standard-bearers had refused to be members of the Hoover-Hamilton–inspired Republican program committee. Nevertheless, Vandenberg in 1938 quietly built himself up as the most available nominee, and until the elections in November, he continued to be the most talked-of prospect for the party's 1940 nomination.

---

[54] *New York Times,* November 23, 1937, p. 6, and *Vital Speeches,* April 1, 1938, p. 354.

[55] *New York Times,* March 13, 1938, p. 2.

[56] *Ibid.,* July 31, 1938, sec. 4, p. 3.

[57] *Ibid.*

[58] *Ibid.,* June 28, 1938, p. 2.

Political parties, however, consist of more than just their top echelons, and discordant factions among the leaders are not always reflected among the rank and file at the lower levels of party organization. Public events, socioeconomic reverberations, and reactions to the opposition party all tended in 1938 to influence the unity of the party workers. As the year entered the "dog days," Republican activity over the nation began to quicken. At the national level, Franklyn Waltman, Jr., was hired as the new publicity chief, and a Gallup poll indicated that sixty-nine per cent of the Republicans polled were optimistic and wanted dissident Democrats to join their ranks. Moreover, ninety per cent opposed any change in the name of the party.[59] The GOP was, after all, still the only existing vehicle for those opposed to the New Deal; it had an existing organization, an experienced mechanism, and a hard core of voters about which independents could coalesce.[60] In the 1936 election, fifteen seats had been lost by less than two per cent, forty-one by less than five per cent, and fifty-eight by less than ten per cent. If these marginal districts could be recaptured it would mean substantial gains in Congress and an opportunity for more vigorous opposition. Furthermore, while the Democrats continued their internecine warfare, the popularity of the Roosevelt administration had dropped substantially. The newspapers were full of talk of a purge by the President of congressional Democrats, and if this move were made by the Administration, Republican leaders reasoned, the loss of approximately seven million votes would be risked by Roosevelt. Finally, another AIPO poll indicated that in spite of the President's personal popularity, the dominant pull of public opinion was definitely toward greater conservatism.[61]

As the nation viewed the political scene in anticipation of the 1938 election, one eye was cocked on the disturbing turmoil in Europe where, in a few brief months, Hitler had invaded and captured Austria, the debacle at Munich had alternately raised hopes and produced despair, and Franco's maneuvers were successfully strengthening the Fascist forces all over the Continent — all while America buried its head in indecisive isolationism.

At home, Roosevelt seemingly had lost his control over the Con-

---

[59] *Newsweek,* February 21, 1938, p. 15.

[60] See Chester Rowell, "Resources of the Republican Party," *Yale Review,* 27 (ns) (March, 1938), 443.

[61] *New York Times,* August 29, 1938, p. 11.

gress. In an effort to placate congressional leaders, he had neglected many liberal supporters who, after supporting him, now had to stand for re-election in their home districts without visible evidence of reciprocal admiration.[62] The gigantic new political forces of organized labor and organized agriculture beseeched the President to do something about the really serious recession that had set in, but the New Deal program had been curtailed by the conservative Democrats, and even bottled up in the House Rules Committee headed by anti-Administration John O'Connor. Social welfare legislation for relief, labor, agriculture, and other groups had either been defeated or had come through the Congress so watered down that it failed to meet mass expectations.[63] Accordingly, the President, over the opposition of his political advisers, decided to take his case to the voters, thereby forcing a showdown with his congressional opponents within the party.[64] In a fireside chat late in June, he vigorously called for the election of candidates who supported his liberal principles, and shortly thereafter he left for a trip that took him and his mission throughout the entire country. He endorsed some candidates, merely appeared with others, and ignored still others. For a handful of conservative southern senators, including Walter George of Georgia, "Cotton Ed" Smith of South Carolina, and Millard Tydings of Maryland, he reserved public, personal, and Administration opposition. He also let it be known that he disliked Guy Gillette of Iowa, and he sent Corcoran into New York to personally run the grass-roots campaign against O'Connor. He endorsed Wagner and Lehman in New York, and vigorously supported Alben Barkley against A. B. "Happy" Chandler in Kentucky.

The President was pleased by the reception he received on his travels; the masses of the voters whom he encountered were still under his charming spell. He was not at all pleased, however, by the trend that the campaign took in its closing phases. The old dependable issues of security, reform, and optimism were shunted aside. Prosperity was not a weapon, for there was no prosperity;

[62] For an excellent summary of the Democratic side of this dilemma, see Burns, *op. cit.*, pp. 346-50.

[63] In 1937, the wages and hours bill had been defeated. In 1938, a weaker version of it was passed only after the Rules Committee was forced by a discharge petition to surrender it. The administrative reorganization bill passed the Senate in February, but was defeated 204-196 in the House.

[64] Burns, *op. cit.*, p. 359.

nine million people were still unemployed. Instead, in the primaries as well as the general election, Administration critics harped on the sit-down strikes, the appointment of a former Klan member (Justice Black, who later made an excellent record in civil rights) to the Supreme Court, the President's intervention in state elections, the domination of the country by a near-dictator, and "a destruction of the Constitution." As one observer later wrote, during these weeks "Roosevelt's political fortunes reached the lowest point of his presidency."[65]

In the primary elections, Roosevelt received his first blows. All of the southern conservatives were victorious, and several New Deal Democrats were defeated. O'Connor was narrowly upset in New York, but others against whom the President had waged no campaign, but who also had opposed his program, won decisively in the West. The more conclusive evidence of a shift in the country came in the general elections. The Republicans nearly doubled their delegation in the House of Representatives — from 89 to 170; they picked up eight new seats in the Senate while losing none; they gained fourteen new governorships, and in New York, they came so close to defeating Governor Lehman that his opponent, District Attorney Thomas E. Dewey, became a national prospect for the presidential nomination. The Farmer-Labor and Progressive dynasties in Minnesota and Wisconsin were swept away, and the entire Midwest moved back to the Republican column — though, to be sure, these were normally Republican states for generations before the New Deal. Nationally, the Republicans polled 53.1 per cent of the votes cast in twenty-eight of the thirty-three states that elected governors. If these majorities could be translated into electoral votes in 1940, a few optimistic national committee members reasoned, the party would capture the presidency with 365 votes.

According to George Gallup, the American middle-class vote determined the outcome of the 1938 election. The conservative shift was primarily the product of four factors: the sit-down strikes, the President's proposal to enlarge the Supreme Court, the business recession, and, finally, the attempt to purge conservative congressmen.[66] Arthur Krock added that "the average taxpayers . . . shifted their allegiance from the President and the post-1936 New Deal," to "emphatically abolish" one-party government under the domina-

[65] *Ibid.*, p. 363.
[66] *New York Times,* November 13, 1938, sec. 4, p. 8.

tion of the President—"a domination often exercised through young doctrinaires. . . ."[67] Other observers claimed that the election was also a revolt by the farmers against the New Deal agricultural programs and the tactics of the CIO, a repudiation of the partisan manner in which relief had been administered, and, strangely enough, a rejection of the Old Guard of the Republican party. Turner Catledge wrote: "It can hardly be stressed too much that most of the Republicans who won last Tuesday had long since accepted the social and humane objectives of the First New Deal. . . . Many of them subscribed in general to the basic reform intentions of the Second New Deal. . . . The complaint which they detected on the part of the voters was against some of the methods employed by this Administration to follow out its objectives."[68]

The election provided the Republican party with a fresh group of leaders. Raymond Baldwin in Connecticut was only forty-five years of age, and the new Governor of Minnesota, Harold Stassen, was still in his early thirties. In addition, Julius Heil of Wisconsin, John Bricker of Ohio, Leverett Saltonstall of Massachusetts, and Governors-elect James of Pennsylvania and Fitzgerald of Michigan were, for a time, looked upon as bringing a more progressive brand of Republicanism to the state offices. The victory of Robert Taft over Senator Bulkley in Ohio was immediately evaluated in presidential terms, and indeed Taft rapidly indicated that he would be a vigorous junior senator. Presidential Democrats were alarmed; though the party still held a large majority in Congress, a conservative Democrat-Republican coalition was obviously in the making, and it was accurately predicted that the new legislature would be in no mood for programs of social innovation.

At year's end, Republican National Chairman John D. M. Hamilton observed that the Republicans had won 150,000 jobs, including 400 county seats, in November. He made plans to visit the states in which the party had triumphed in order to organize these thousands and many more as active workers for a party victory in 1940.

In New York, however, liberal National Committeeman Kenneth Simpson came under criticism because certain Dewey supporters felt that New York City had not cast a large enough vote for the District Attorney. Anti-Simpson Republicans sent letters to all members of the national committee stating that Simpson had formed

[67] *Ibid.*, p. 3.
[68] *Ibid.*

alliances with radical parties, and that this had cost Dewey the election.[69] Simpson, in rebuttal, declared: "The people have left the President, but they will return to the Republican Party only if they are sure that it is not under the domination of Mr. Hoover, the Liberty League and some of the reactionary influences of the past. If we turn that way, we might as well fold up!"[70] When the Dewey-Simpson feud was carried to Washington, however, Simpson was defeated for a position on the party executive committee by Old Guardsman and former Senator Daniel O. Hastings of Delaware, "than whom no man in Congress [had] a more reactionary record."[71]

The result of this minor election was in complete contrast to the speeches made at the luncheon after the executive committee's business meeting, at which Senators Vandenberg, Wiley (Wisconsin), and Gladys O. Pyle (South Dakota) made promises of adherence to liberal doctrines in the next Congress, and it served to point up the power of the conservatives within the national committee.[72] Simpson felt bitter about his defeat,[73] and though reconciliations were made with the Dewey forces the following year, they were never quite complete. In 1940, after Simpson had become more solidly entrenched as a party leader, the scars were still evident, and Simpson was one of the leaders of the exodus from the Dewey camp.

THE SEVENTY-SIXTH CONGRESS

The Seventy-sixth Congress that convened in January of 1939 was determined to temper the New Deal and to maintain America's neutrality in world affairs. Publicly, and therefore politically, it was touted as an "Economy Congress," in which the balance of power was held by the Southern Democrats, many of whom were anti-

---

[69] *Ibid.*, November 22, 1938, p. 2, and November 29, p. 1.

[70] *Time,* December 12, 1938, p. 16.

[71] *Ibid.* Arthur Krock wrote: "There is not a New Deal critic among the Senate or the House Democrats, and there never has been one since 1933, whose voting record would not rate as liberal in contrast to Mr. Hastings'. Even to his Republican colleagues he was established as the firmest representative of the right wing of their party, a heritage from the Harding-Coolidge era. Most of Herbert Hoover's speeches . . . take ground to the left of Mr. Hastings." *New York Times,* November 30, 1938, p. 22.

[72] *New York Times,* November 30, 1938, p. 1.

[73] *Time* magazine stated that Hastings was given his seat to encourage contributions from the party's "fat cats." The money was badly needed. "National Treasurer C. B. Goodspeed . . . reported a deficit of $724,910, but this, despite a $636,452 outlay for this year's election, was $50,000 less red ink than on January 1, 1938." December 12, 1938, p. 16.

Administration. Before it adjourned, it did pass an improved social security bill in which old-age benefits were liberalized, unemployment insurance rates were limited, and new groups were added. It also authorized the President to reorganize part of his administrative staff, renewed his power to revalue the dollar, and increased the subsidy for farmers (which the President opposed). Finally, it gave the army and navy all the money they wanted, and more. Without an increase in taxes, the Congress appropriated more than thirteen billions of dollars — the largest peacetime appropriation in the nation's history. Reporters noted that among conservative groups there was a growing feeling against the use of deficit financing for relief or recovery but also a strong feeling for spending money to improve national defense in spite of the fact that this had to be done with borrowed funds.[74] The Wagner Act and the Fair Labor Standards Act were frequently attacked, but they were left unamended and the TVA was investigated, but not injured. Essentially, these were the positive achievements of the session.

On the negative side, the House, by a 193-167 vote refused even to consider the President's Spend-Lend bill by which he hoped to lift the country from its economic plight. The Administration's $800,000,000 housing bill went down by a 193-166 vote, and WPA was cut by fifty million dollars. The term "Republocrat" was coined and took on meaning as an identification of those who guillotined the Administration measures. The greatest personal defeat for the President, however, came on the Neutrality Act. Here the congressmen reflected the effects of more than two decades of isolationist thought. The disillusionment that followed the first World War, bolstered by the propaganda of the twenties and thirties against munitions makers and foreign capital, was so thoroughly ingrained in both the legislators and their constituents that they were blinded to the events in Germany and Italy. More important, the public pressure created forced the President himself into a state of indecision that temporarily prevented any vigorous leadership. This "feeling" of isolationism, that seemed to be so evident, plus the loss of the Court fight and the recession of 1938, made Roosevelt reluctant to advance, publicly and forcibly, the true facts of the international crisis and his thoughts on the already existing threat to American democracy. Moreover, his concern for his domestic pro-

[74] *New Republic,* November 1, 1939, p. 368.

gram placed him at a political and philosophical disadvantage in bringing his change in foreign policy before the Congress.

When the President opened the Congress, he stated that it was becoming increasingly clear that though war had been averted, world peace had not been assured. He therefore asked the legislators to repeal the portions of the Neutrality Act that would prevent him from aiding invaded or attacked nations as well as the invaders. Clearly, this meant aid for the democracies which would need American resources if Germany continued to expand. The measure was hotly debated both in and out of Congress. The President called senators to the White House to argue, plead, or discuss the bill. When the measure came up for a vote, however, his supporters were unable to marshal the votes to amend the act, and "Explosion after smoky explosion blew away Franklin Roosevelt's last vestige of control over both houses of Congress."[75]

Meanwhile, Hitler absorbed Czechoslovakia in March, formed a mutual military alliance with Mussolini in May, and rebuked every attempt by the President to obtain a commitment to peace; Japan continued to expand her empire; and Italy invaded Albania.

Strange bedfellows made up the forces that defeated the Administration's preparedness efforts in the Senate. Hiram Johnson, William Borah, and Arthur Vandenberg found themselves surrounded by Progressive Robert La Follette, Democrats David Walsh of Massachusetts, Carter Glass and Harry Byrd of Virginia, Bennett Champ Clark of Missouri, and some of the ardent New Deal, but isolationist, first-term senators. These men believed that they had sources of information superior to those of the President, that there simply would be no war in Europe, and that the "war propaganda" in the United States was being distributed by a relatively small group of Anglophiles. Their position was symbolized by Senator Taft, who was already being suggested for the White House, in a speech before the American Forum of the Air in which he declared:

No one has ever suggested before that a single nation should range over the world . . . protecting democracy. . . . Such a policy is not only vain, but almost inevitably leads to war. . . . Now it is suggested that the whole world is different. It is said that distances are so short we cannot possibly avoid being involved in a general war. I don't believe it. . . . It seems essential that Congress shall strengthen the Neutrality Bill rather than repeal it . . . that the President shall not have discretion to take sides in foreign wars, or to impose sanctions against those nations

---

[75] *Time,* July 31, 1939, p. 8.

which he might find to be aggressor nations. . . . [Congress] should not permit the Executive to go too far towards war, without consulting Congress. . . ."[76]

Taft's final sentence also summarized the first session of the Seventy-sixth Congress — that the Executive should not go very far in any direction without consulting the legislative branch. The "Republo-crats" had defied Roosevelt twelve times and knuckled under on only four occasions. They had shown the conservative wing of Congress to be stronger than the followers of the President, and they had greatly encouraged the members of the Republican party. In August, they adjourned the session, but not before New Dealer Claude Pepper scourged them for "putting personal grudge and party feeling above the welfare of the American people" just because they hated the President.[77]

Even in a period of crisis, the year before an election year is a time for trial balloons, polls, publicity build-ups, and speculation about the possible nominees — and 1939 was no exception. Imme-diately after the November elections, Washington political observers placed Robert A. Taft in the running for the nomination, and it was reported that "around G.O.P. headquarters . . . he was 'the real whitehaired boy.' "[78] A month later, however, at a luncheon given by Chairman Hamilton, Taft asserted that Senator Vanden-berg "is still in the lead" as the party's choice. It was about this time, however, that the first comments that Vandenberg's record was too long and that he had had to go on record on too many con-troversial issues began to appear widely in both magazines and news-papers. The man who had led conservatives in the Senate during the drought period for the Republican party was slowly having his availability withdrawn in favor of newer, less controversial aspirants.[79]

Most of the polls, however, indicated that in spite of his loss in the gubernatorial election in New York, Thomas E. Dewey was the most popular Republican, with thirty-three per cent of the rank-and-file Republicans favoring him for the nomination. Dr. George Gallup reported that his surveys indicated that the members of the

[76] *Vital Speeches,* February 1, 1939, p. 254.

[77] *Time,* August 14, 1939, p. 12.

[78] *New York Times,* November 10, 1938, p. 15, and *Newsweek,* January 23, 1939, p. 7.

[79] *Ibid.,* December 18, 1938, p. 4.

GOP wanted new faces and a more liberal program. Another example of such a new leader was Bruce Barton, the advertising executive, who was considered by one author as one of "two people [who] stand out distinctly as the people's choice" for the nomination in 1940.[80] In January, 1939, Barton wrote:

> The good old conditions are gone. . . . The time has come to review the mass of New Deal Legislation, preserve the good, and modify or repeal the rest. Both parties are agreed on adequate relief, collective bargaining, the regulation of exchanges, social security, and low-price housing; these, in principle, have ceased to be matters of political controversy. . . .[81]

Indicating the extent to which at least some Republicans had revised their thoughts in 1939, he continued:

> We Republicans admit that the distribution of the national income was faulty at that time [1928]; there was too much money at the top and not enough down below. We favor a fairer distribution, but we favor first and foremost a policy that will create something to distribute. . . . The Republican party is the party of business (little "b," not big "B"), and makes no apologies for that fact. It understands and knows how to promote cooperation. It knows, too, how sensitive and easily destroyed is that elusive but all-important element called confidence. . . . The Republican party recognizes that there are still business maladies to be cured. But we would proceed cautiously, quietly, with one thing at a time.[82]

Governor Bricker, who had become the first Republican Governor of Ohio in a decade, also came in for his share of speculation, and Joseph N. Pew of Philadelphia wanted to launch a nationwide right-wing Bricker-for-President campaign early in 1940. Bricker, however, refused to sanction the move[83] for it was pretty obvious that at this early stage most Ohio leaders seemed to favor Taft. F. F. Taggart, the national committeeman from Ohio, stated that Bricker "had better go slow," and Mrs. Katherine Kennedy Brown, the national committeewoman, served a dinner the motif of which was "Taft, White House, 1940." Other Ohio party workers who had helped elect Bricker, including Ed Schorr, chairman of the state committee, declared that they did not prefer him to Taft. It was agreed among newspapermen that if Bricker had an inclination to

---

[80] Ted Patrick, "Electing a Republican President," *Scribner's Magazine* (November, 1938), p. 20. The other candidate was Dewey, who, the publication stated, "could not have a better build-up."

[81] *Collier's,* January 21, 1939, p. 12.

[82] *Ibid.,* p. 36.

[83] *Newsweek,* December 11, 1939, p. 15.

run, he would have to declare his intentions early in order to pre-empt the Ohio delegation.[84]

Some sentiment in the party favored the nomination of New York Mayor Fiorello LaGuardia as the Republican nominee. A *Fortune* poll, taken in February among voters in both parties, indicated that he was tied with Vandenberg and only .7 per cent behind Dewey in preference for the GOP nomination. LaGuardia's strength, how-ever, was almost wholly within the lower economic classes, while Dewey held a strong position among those polled in the lower middle class and was within one per cent of Vandenberg's popu-larity with the upper middle class.[85] As the year wore on, La-Guardia's popularity among Republicans declined, and by July only two per cent of the Republicans polled by the Gallup organization stated that they preferred the New York mayor for the nomination.[86]

Senator Lodge, Senator Borah, and former President Herbert Hoover were usually mentioned in surveys of Republican prefer-ence, but no large groups were ever strongly in support of their candidacies.[87] Governor James of Pennsylvania was talked about but seemed to lack popular appeal. On February 23, Arthur Krock mentioned utility magnate Wendell Willkie as a possible candidate, but called development of any affirmation a "highly improbable event." Raymond Moley, writing in *Newsweek* in March, stated that a few "timid feelers" about Willkie had been circulating, and added: "Brilliant, resourceful, experienced, well-schooled in public affairs, he might conceivably go far. . . . But I cannot imagine a convention composed of politicians venturing to nominate a busi-nessman in 1940, regardless of his ability."[88] Moley then defined the characteristics necessary for anyone nominated by the Republi-cans in 1940: "He must be able to capitalize on the growing drift toward conservatism in this country. And yet, somehow he must make it clear that he knows 1932 marked the end of an era in American history."

In 1939 many men were forming myth patterns that fitted this description; others were making records that showed that they did not; the Republican situation was still in a state of flux and would

---

[84] *Ibid.*, February 13, 1939, p. 17.

[85] *Fortune*, February, 1939, p. 69.

[86] *New York Times*, July 8, 1939, p. 2.

[87] Hoover was reported in December of 1939 to have 102 "friendly dele-gates" lined up for himself. *Newsweek*, December 11, 1939, p. 15.

[88] *Ibid.*, March 27, 1939, p. 52.

remain so for nearly a year. At the party headquarters John Hamilton worked out a program of dinners and rallies at which party leaders were to face their party workers. He called it a "preview of the 1940 convention" to enunciate the party principles and to build some party unity. Hamilton himself, at one of these meetings, stressed that the Republicans had to "keep close to the people" — an ingredient in which, he said, the party was lacking. He declared that the party had to win the confidence of labor and become closer to the people "across the tracks." Other programs were held and they obtained publicity, but it was too early to sustain interest in a political world topsy-turvy with international and domestic upheaval.

In Congress, Vandenberg, Taft, and McNary fought for isolation, economy, and "solvent government." Vandenberg's philosophy was epitomized by a June 5 speech in which he rejected the "war psychology" of the times, and asserted: "Protected by a great ocean on either side, the United States need fear no other nation if we mind our own business, concentrate our attention on domestic problems of our own and 'decline to surrender' to the propaganda that we cannot escape participation in other people's wars. . . . Our challenge is not abroad, it is at home!"[89] It was a reflection of the times that Vandenberg's statements that his principal activity was "to keep America out of other people's wars" produced a six per cent increase in his popularity among Republicans (and a corresponding seven per cent decline in the popularity of Dewey, who had no Senate sounding board) between January and July of 1939. *Time* asserted: "Vandenberg's stand looked like first-class Grade A politics. For he stood to win much, to lose little. He had in his grasp the kind of issue politicians dream about: national, emotional, impeccably honorable. With that stick he could drum a roll that would be felt by every mother's heart in the U.S. 'I will never vote to send your sons to war.' "[90] The Michigan senator also fought the President's attempt to continue the operation of the two billion dollar stabilization fund, Hull's tariff program, and advocated "pay-as-you-go" taxes for national defense expenditures.

Taft, who reached an agreement with Governor Bricker that he would be Ohio's favorite son in 1940, stressed private enterprise and a balanced budget during the congressional term. In his maiden speech in the Senate he criticized TVA spending. On many occa-

[89] *New York Times,* June 6, 1939, p. 20.
[90] *Time,* October 2, 1939, p. 13.

sions, he castigated governmental competition with business and said the "S.E.C. still takes the attitude that businessmen are crooks." He advocated direct relief, old-age pensions, unemployment insurance, and some form of housing subsidy, but usually in smaller amounts than the Administration asked. He opposed foreign loans and intervention in European affairs.[91] On August 3 he announced that he would be in the 1940 Republican presidential race. He called the farm situation the "greatest and most difficult" problem before the Republicans: "The present policy is most unsatisfactory, it hasn't produced results and I feel we have got to abandon restriction of production, though I say we don't have to go back to the old way."[92]

But a much more difficult problem for both parties was brewing. On August 24, Germany signed a nonaggression pact with Russia and a week later invaded Poland. The war was on, and Germany declared an economic blockade against Britain to be enforced by submarines. The President called a special session of Congress to make a second attempt to repeal the arms embargo. This time, in spite of the threats of the isolationists that repeal would eventually mean war, the majority sentiment seemed to have changed. Clearly the majority did not want to see Britain lose the war for lack of supplies. After a forty-four-day session, Congress revised the Neutrality Act to ban belligerent submarines from United States ports, to define combat areas, and to lift the embargo on the sale of arms (but only on a "cash and carry" basis) to warring nations. In the Senate, the vote was 63 to 30; the Republicans stood firm, but the Southern bloc of senators returned to support the President. Almost immediately, stocks rose, hard products industries, particularly steel and aircraft, began to hire additional workers, and the country made ready to become an arsenal of democracy.

Among the Republicans at the close of 1939, there was talk of the emergence of the conservative wing from oblivion to a place of challenging dominance within the party. The Pew organization of Pennsylvania was reportedly working quietly behind the scene for

[91] In March, after he had finished a speech at the National Republican Club, Taft said of Hitler's seizure of Czechoslovakia: "I think it was a little overdone in some of the language used, but I certainly approved of the government registering disapproval of such high-handed grabbing as Hitler has put on in the past few days." *New York Times,* March 19, 1939, p. 33.

[92] *Ibid.,* August 4, 1939, p. 1.

Governor James or Senator Taft or Governor Bricker. Senator Bridges was sounding out party leaders to determine if there was any support for his candidacy while Landon, usually associated with Kenneth Simpson as a liberal, was presumably supporting Dewey. The New York district attorney still led all of the popularity polls, though his appeal had declined when the outbreak of war drew attention to his inexperience in foreign affairs. Magazine editors who ventured predictions usually picked Taft or Vandenberg as the nominee with Dewey on the ticket as the vice-presidential candidate. Late in December a poll of 481 of the 1,728 editors of daily newspapers in the United States showed eighty-six per cent of them against a third term for the President and a majority convinced that Security Administrator Paul V. McNutt of Indiana and Senator Vandenberg would be the respective party nominees.[93] There was continuing talk among a very small number of journalists, such as former NRA Administrator Hugh S. Johnson and Arthur Krock, that Wendell Willkie would still make a very strong candidate, but even at this time, only six months before the nomination, Krock said that such a nomination would take a miracle, and "miracles don't happen any more."[94] What was obvious was that no Republican had a personal following comparable to the President's, that the race was wide open for favorite sons or dark horses, and that since the President had not as yet declared whether or not he would run, the American people were more confused than indifferent.

1940

During the early months of 1940, both the President and the conservatives in the two major parties were for "economy." The Administration's foreign policy was generally accepted and expenditures for preparedness were authorized, but the big cuts came in relief spending for the poor. Funds for the PWA, the WPA, the CCC, and NYA were shockingly reduced at a time when only ten to twelve per cent of the workers who were subsequently hired could be absorbed immediately by industry. The war boom did not take up the slack because the expenditures for armaments were less than the amounts of relief cuts. Moreover, the war industries needed specialists located in certain areas, not the mass of unskilled dislocated by the budget slashes. The "inventory boom" of the autumn

[93] *Newsweek,* December 25, 1939, p. 12.
[94] *New York Times,* November 29, 1939, p. 22.

of 1939, based on expected war profits, declined, and the Federal Reserve Board index dropped fifteen points between December and March.[95] England and France, instead of buying more products, substituted war materials for foods and other items previously purchased, so that the rise in total exports to these nations was slight.

The Congress also investigated the NLRB and deliberately found it in a state of confusion. It cut two million dollars off the White House staff appropriation, and temporarily cut, but later restored, a portion of the agricultural aid. This was still the Congress dominated by the "Republocrats" who had one eye on their constituents and the other on the forthcoming presidential nominations. The House committees were dominated by anti-New Deal southerners loyal to Vice-President John Garner, and though the Senate was more friendly to the President, many of its members were either presidential aspirants or supporters of potential candidates anxious to make records of their own. The President, reserving his energies and his powers of persuasion for the foreign situation, was ineffective and unimaginative in his management of Congress on his domestic program. His leadership again declined in spite of daily visits to the White House of local party leaders urging him to run for re-election.

Republican National Chairman John D. M. Hamilton also claimed that he wanted the President to run for a third term, for many political analysts early in 1940 thought that this issue alone would end the New Deal. At a meeting of the national committee in February, Hamilton stated that the Democratic party was so demoralized and embittered by internecine feuds that it could not present a common front against a Republican party which had half a dozen or more men who could defeat Roosevelt.[96] The GOP was also finally out of debt, and the committee decided to hold the 1940 national convention in Philadelphia — which outbid Chicago by offering the committee $200,000 and a free convention hall.

At this meeting of the committee, the Glenn Frank program committee finally submitted its long-awaited report. The document was a 33,000-word statement which accepted the essentials of the social program of the New Deal and directed its offensive at the spending, borrowing, taxing, and business regulating policies of the Roosevelt

---

[95] *New Republic*, February 19, 1940, p. 235.
[96] *New York Times*, February 17, 1940, p. 1.

administration.[97] Couched in cautious, qualifying phrases on many issues, the report declared that the New Deal's restrictive legislation had failed to encourage private enterprise, that the budget could be and should be reduced by twenty per cent, that all tax exemptions of future issues of government securities should be eliminated, that income surtaxes should be reduced, and that the capital stock tax and the excess profits taxes should be repealed. In addition, the document argued that the emergency monetary powers of the President should be withdrawn, that the Wagner Act should be kept but amended, that the Reciprocal Trade Agreements Act should be revised, that the Wages and Hours Act should be abolished in industries with collective bargaining but preserved elsewhere, that relief expenditures should be maintained but reduced, that national defense should be strengthened, that business should be protected rather than restricted, and that unemployment insurance and old-age pensions should be placed on a pay-as-you-go basis. The report also contained a nine-point farm program which endorsed subsidies and soil conservation, and added that the nation should depend primarily on private enterprise for housing. The document recognized the need for regulation of the stock market, governmental "yardsticks" in some areas, and the impossibility of returning to the gold standard at the time. Finally, presaging a proposal advocated by a Republican president a decade later, the Frank committee proposed that a national health program should be carried out through the cooperation of the government, the medical profession, and voluntary groups.

Even from impartial observers, the report met with mixed reactions. It was conceded that the report was a liberal document with some good advice for Republican platform-makers, but observers noted that it did not specify just *how* all of the programs were to be implemented. The *New York Times* thought it was equivocal in spots and that it contained many conditional phrases. ". . . the caution of the present report," the editors stated, "once generalities are left behind, tends to draw attention to the strong differences of opinion which actually exist within the party."[98] Landon, however, liked the Frank program. He called it "good, sound, and construc-

---

[97] *Ibid.*, February 19, 1940, p. 2. See "The Republican Opposition," by Thomas H. Reed and Doris D. Reed, *Survey Graphic*, 29 (May, 1940), 286 ff.

[98] *New York Times*, February 20, 1940, p. 20.

tive." Hamilton endorsed the document, as did other leaders who had supported the project from the beginning. The pro-New Deal *Nation* declared that the Frank report came out for the New Deal with *ifs* and *buts,* and showed the extent to which the Republican party had been forced to accept the leadership of Roosevelt. "Mr. Hoover still belongs to the Republican Party, but [read in the light of the 'rugged individualism' campaign of 1932] the Republican Party no longer seems to belong to Mr. Hoover."[99] *Newsweek,* on the other hand, declared that the Frank program committee had "produced an impressive document, persuasive in many respects, clear and definite far beyond most party statements. . . . If the Frank report represents Republican opinion, then the Republican party has whizzed forward through eons of philosophic time since 1932. . . ."[100]

There were three factors, however, which prevented the Frank report from having the impact that it might have had at another time. First, the report, in 1940, did *not* represent Republican opinion throughout the party. This was particularly true in Congress where GOP congressmen were uniting to sabotage some of the New Deal projects which the report implicitly endorsed. Secondly, though it was obvious that the forthcoming political campaign would be waged much less over broad principles than over the governmental management of reform programs instituted by the Roosevelt administration, the Republican party had not yet found a man to espouse the issues. To push the program without a candidate and possibly eventually select a man out of sympathy with the study would be a hazardous undertaking, so publicity on the report was quietly shelved for several months. Finally, and most important, the Frank report had no word relative to the totally new set of conditions which existed in foreign affairs by the time a candidate was finally selected. On April 9 the Germans invaded Norway; by the end of May the Netherlands and Belgium had been conquered; and by the time the Republican National Convention met, France had fallen. The war seemed much closer than it had four months earlier. The conventional platitudes concerning reciprocal trade treaties and a balanced budget seemed less important. William Allen White wrote that among those who were framing the Republican platform, the world-wide events had had such an impact that the cries of the

---

[99] *The Nation,* March 9, 1940, p. 325.
[100] *Newsweek,* March 4, 1940, p. 56.

Republican isolationists had just about been stopped.[101] This proved to be untrue; eighteen more months were to pass before Pearl Harbor finally stopped the cries of the Republican isolationists. But early in 1940 the foundation for a decline of isolationism within the party ranks was established by the most volatile ascension to party leadership in the history of American political parties.

---

[101] *New York Times,* June 9, 1940, p. 2.

2 MAN IN A HURRY— PARTY IN CONFUSION

The rise of Wendell L. Willkie to leadership of the Republican party and nomination by the 1940 GOP convention was almost incredible in terms of the criteria by which Americans usually select their presidential candidates. Until two years before he received the Republican nomination, he was a registered and voting Democrat![1] He was not only a business tycoon in an area in which businessmen had not previously been allowed, he was a prominent member of the utility industry, one of the most distrusted fields of American enterprise. He had never held public office, and only two men, both generals (Ulysses S. Grant and Zachary Taylor), had ever become President without having previously run for public office; and Willkie had no outstanding military career behind him. Moreover, until the year in which he was nominated, he was almost completely unknown outside of his own business circles. In a Gallup poll taken among Republican voters seven weeks before the conven-

---

[1] As late as 1935, Wendell Willkie was elected to the Tammany county committee in the Thirty-seventh Election District of the Fifteenth Assembly District in New York City. James A. Farley, who was the Democratic National Chairman until 1940, was elected to a similar post at the same time. Also elected as committee members were Mrs. Elizabeth Farley, Mrs. Edith Willkie, and Frank C. Walker, then treasurer of the Democratic National Committee, and later Postmaster General. Willkie was a member of the committee for one year. *New York Times,* July 26, 1940, p. 11. At the *New York Herald Tribune* Forum on October 26, 1938, he told Farley that he had voted for Governor Lehman and the rest of the Democratic ticket. Joseph Barnes, *op. cit.,* p. 155.

tion, Willkie was the favorite of only three per cent of those who expressed an opinion; two weeks before his nomination, he was favored by only seventeen per cent of the Republicans polled.[2] Finally, his known views on foreign policy were out of focus with a host of congressional Republicans, and he had openly endorsed many of President Roosevelt's reforms.

On the other hand, Willkie emerged in 1940 as the most articulate critic of the New Deal's economic philosophy. He was a big, colorful, expansive champion of the business community, of government regulation without government competition, and of a more productive industrial plant. In spite of his associations in the utility field, he was an acknowledged liberal in civil rights. He had a carefree, attractive personality capable of filling the vacuum that existed among the leaders of the GOP. And, most important, he was exceedingly appealing to the editors, publishers, and publicists who write the news. As a result, he became the focus of the most rapid and astute public relations campaign in political annals. The way in which these characteristics of Wendell Willkie were blended with the events of 1940 and the activities of his supporters to obtain the Republican presidential nomination makes an interesting chapter in American party history.

THE MAN WILLKIE, 1940

Wendell Willkie was a curious mixture — a man of complex personality and vigorous action. He was called "the most exciting young man to run for the presidency since William Jennings Bryan," and the excitement pervaded many fields.[3] He was a dramatic debater as well as an expert witness before congressional committees; a big businessman and a small farmer; a familiar figure on Wall Street and a renowned son of Elwood, Indiana; a one-time révolté and a driving corporation president. He read voraciously, traveled widely, argued vociferously without regard for personal feelings, and was at home among capitalists, socialists, and New York's intellectual elite. He owned nearly two thousand books and on several occasions declined the presidencies of colleges and universities.[4]

Willkie was a man of tremendous energy. Although he had a

---

[2] *New York Times,* June 12, 1940, p. 23.

[3] Irving Stone, *They Also Ran* (New York, 1944), p. 340.

[4] Janet Flanner, "Rushville's Renowned Son-in-Law," *New Yorker,* 6 (October 12, 1940), 28.

comfortable childhood and adolescence, he worked hard all his life
— and he believed that labor resulting in high production was in
itself a good. Though he was an articulate businessman, he never
abandoned his Indiana twang, and pronounced "power" as "pahr"
and "interests" as "intersts." He and his wife were members of the
Presbyterian church, and in New York he belonged to the Century,
University, Recess, Lawyers, and Blind Brook clubs. He was rela-
tively wealthy, and his close friends included Perry Hall of the
Morgan Stanley firm, Thomas Lamont of J. P. Morgan, Sloan
Colt, George Howard of the United Corporation, Roy Howard,
Gardner and John Cowles, Sam Pryor, vice-president of Pan-
American Airways, Sinclair Weeks, and Russell Davenport.[5]

Willkie's humor was a joshing repartee rather than a subtle, wry,
agreeable comment, and his remarks often gave the not completely
erroneous impression that he was extremely self-assured. Many who
wrote about Willkie felt that underneath his external confidence
there was a real humility, but Roscoe Drummond, who knew
Willkie well, wrote:

He was his own closest adviser. He was independent, occasionally
stubborn. He was something of a revivalist even in private conversation.
His mind was stimulated in his contact with people, and his thought
processes seemed more inspirational than logical. Not that he was
illogical; he just didn't tick things off under Roman numerals I, II, III.
The impression of one of his writing friends is that he used to snipe at a
subject from all sides; then, finally grabbing hold, he would roll it up
in a ball and throw it at you.
Willkie was no more humble than he was simple. There was no self-
doubt in his make-up. He was neither modest nor immodest; it just
never occurred to him that he could be anything other than successful.[6]

Wendell Willkie's views on business, whether they were the
product of his environment or merely the result of the position
which he had acquired, accounted for his rise to national fame. He
believed in a vigorous private economy not merely as a money-
making device but as a force capable of maintaining a high stand-

---

[5] Willkie's top salary at Commonwealth and Southern was $75,000 a
year. He refused raises and once rejected an offer of a quarter of a
million dollars a year from another corporation. When he died, his assets
totaled approximately $500,000. He gave generously to private charities
and put nearly fifty young people through college. The five farms he owned
near Rushville, Indiana, were the only real estate he ever possessed. *Ibid.*,
p. 34.

[6] Roscoe Drummond, "A Study in Courage," in *The Aspirin Age,* Isabel
Leighton (ed.), (New York, 1949), p. 449.

ard of living for an entire people. He elevated himself by sheer drive and ability and he was intolerant of those who tried to deny him the fruits of his efforts. He called himself a liberal and he thought of the word as one who refused to have his freedom curtailed. In his speeches defending utilities he often said, "In the pre-war years, we fought against the domination of the people by Big Business. We now face the domination of the people by Big Government. The liberal who fought against one kind of domination thirty-five years ago should find himself fighting against this new kind of domination today."[7] A liberal was also one who set himself up to "increase freedom"[8] or to "make men free."[9] Therefore, he could not countenance the tactics of Franklin Roosevelt which he thought to be restrictive and damaging to private enterprise.[10] He nevertheless agreed that many of the specific reforms of the New Deal were necessary, thus creating a mental conflict which debilitated his value as an alternative to the President before the public. In the thirties, if liberal meant one advocating government protection, Willkie would have accepted the inference, but to Willkie the government was gaining control and ownership, not regulatory and protective power. He said:

I'm the last person in the world to say that social control is not necessary in industrial organizations in order to protect us from greed and injustice. But look over the world today and tell me if governments are less greedy or more just than individuals. I know that there is a superstition that governments are exempt from moral frailties and that industry will be cured of all its ills once the bureaucrats take hold of it. I'm willing to leave it to the students of history to decide whether the evils of excessive profit-taking are not more easily cured than the evils of excessive power-taking on the part of the government.[11]

Willkie's willingness to have the citizens of America decide the questions he was presenting to them found its source in his basic

[7] Stone, *op. cit.*, p. 341.

[8] "Brace Up, America!" *Atlantic Monthly*, 163 (June, 1939), 749-56.

[9] "With Malice Toward None," *Saturday Evening Post*, 212 (December 30, 1939), 23 ff.

[10] *The Nation*, October 5, 1940, p. 295, reflecting its attitude toward utility presidents, characterized Willkie's liberalism as "freedom for the victims of poverty, fear, and adversity to 'fight their own battle' and the cessation of government interference with free economic enterprise."

[11] *New York Times*, February 20, 1938, sec. 8, p. 21. Willkie's most thorough public discussion of his liberalism can be found in his address at Indiana University delivered on May 4, 1938, reprinted in Wendell Willkie, *This Is Wendell Willkie* (New York, 1940), pp. 156-70.

affection for masses of individuals and the exhilaration he felt in trying to persuade them. He enjoyed being with people, and to those who were not diametrically opposed to him, he had a warm and friendly personality. He frequently described himself as the "best gadget salesman in the country," and as president of Commonwealth and Southern he was essentially a public relations man and he knew it. He said: "Good, bad, or indifferent, Commonwealth and Southern's public relations consist solely of my statements."[12] In reality, however, he also knew his business very well; he worked diligently at the task of comprehending the vast superstructure of operating and holding companies that he supervised and he tirelessly devoted his energies to their promotion.

Politically, Willkie was a mugwump, and during most of his brief political career he was engaged in a struggle with the leaders of both parties. In his final analysis of the world situation, however, there were no two sides, and he refused to compromise his principles. As a politician, Wendell Willkie never learned a primary rule of politics — unswerving loyalty to one's party. This fact made Willkie, the Democrat, the stalwart opponent of the means but not the social ends of the New Deal. It also made Willkie, the titular head of the Republican party, a factional champion rather than a true party leader. Wendell Willkie was a "small 'd' democrat" during his entire life, and he felt that party philosophies were variable quantities which could be altered, to a greater or lesser degree, by the leaders who made the effort. Willkie, moreover, was not one to shy away from such an effort. Early in his career, opposing the confiscation of Commonwealth and Southern was his job and he considered it a trust. Later, a progressive Ohio publisher who knew Willkie well said: "Given the chance, . . . Wendell Willkie will dedicate himself to serving all the people, not only the privileged few. Deep down he is an idealist and a born crusader."[13] Wendell Willkie's dedication to what he considered to be his task from 1933 to 1940 brought him into party leadership; his devotion to his conception of world peace disintegrated that same leadership. In the process, his party was split to the degree that the eventual synthesis of the parts, a decade later, produced a "middle-road" to the left of the conservative highway it had traveled in previous administrations.

[12] Flanner, *op. cit.,* p. 34.
[13] Dorothy Dunbar Bromley, "The Education of Wendell Willkie," *Harper's,* 181 (October, 1940), 483.

THE WILLKIE LEGEND

Lewis Wendell Willkie was born on February 18, 1892, in the town of Elwood, Indiana. He was the son of Herman Willkie, a brilliant, humanitarian lawyer, and Henrietta (Trisch) Willkie, a former schoolteacher who became the first woman to be licensed by the Indiana bar. He was the fourth of six children who grew up in a home of stimulating debate and vigorous learning.[14] Politically, the family was Democratic, and this indoctrination carried over into Willkie's university and business career. At Indiana University, young Willkie was frequently called a Socialist, but he was actually a leader of the campus Jackson club — an organization that staged a mock Democratic convention in 1912.[15]

Willkie completed five years of academic work in less than four years. He was graduated with the class of 1913 with a year and a half accomplished toward his law degree. After receiving his bachelor's degree, he accepted a position teaching history in the high school of Coffeyville, Kansas, in order to earn money with which to finish law school. After a year in Coffeyville and a summer working with his brother as a chemist with the Fajardo Sugar Company in Puerto Rico, he returned to Indiana for his final year of study. The summer in Puerto Rico was significant in Willkie's life. He never forgot the squalor and brutality he saw there and years later he told Gardner Cowles that scenes he remembered of *peon* life on the sugar plantations were more responsible than anything else for his not thinking like a typical American millionaire.[16]

Willkie's record in law school was excellent; he won every first prize awarded by the faculty for scholastic achievement. As a result, he was chosen class orator and created a mild sensation when he criticized the Indiana law school and the Indiana constitution before an audience which included a majority of the Supreme Court

---

[14] For information concerning Willkie's early years, see Stanley Walker, "A Biographical Introduction," in Willkie, *op. cit.,* p. 16; Alden Hatch, *Young Willkie* (New York, 1944); Herman O. Makey, *Wendell Willkie of Elwood* (Elwood, Ind., 1940); Mary Earhart Dillon, *Wendell Willkie, 1892-1944* (New York, 1952), pp. 15-28; and Joseph Barnes, *op. cit.,* pp. 3-29.

[15] Willkie was a member of a Friday night discussion group which was tabbed "The Socialist Club" by the university yearbook. In later years, Willkie remarked: "Any man who is not something of a socialist before he is forty has no heart; any man who is still a socialist after he is forty has no head." Drummond, *op. cit.,* p. 446.

[16] Barnes, *op. cit.,* p. 28.

justices of the state. The address, entitled "The New Freedom," was an outspoken condemnation of economic domination of the nation by private interests, coupled with eulogies for President Wilson's reforms and pleas that Indiana follow them. Members of the law faculty were furious, and for three days Willkie's fate in regard to his diploma was in doubt. He was, however, finally called to the administration office and informally given his diploma and his prizes.

After graduation, Willkie returned to Elwood, where he practiced law for several months. With the outbreak of the first World War, he enlisted as a private, became an officer-candidate, and after several different assignments, became a counsel for enlisted men involved in courts-martial. In January, 1918, he obtained a leave and was married. In September, he went overseas. The armistice was signed a month later, and so Willkie was not involved in combat. He returned, a captain, in February, 1919.

After Willkie was discharged from the army in April, he joined the legal department of the Firestone Tire and Rubber Company in Akron, Ohio. With Firestone, his activities were largely confined to supervising the legal problems of the employees, and he resigned in 1921[17] to accept a position with Mather and Nesbitt, utility lawyers whose clients included the Ohio Edison Company, a "utility . . . in politics both state and municipal, up to its ears."[18] Within a year, the hard-driving Willkie was made a junior partner in the business.

The years in Akron were a formative period in Willkie's life. He began to emerge as a public figure, a civic worker, a frequent public speaker, and a competent trial lawyer. Apparently he represented clients on all sides of legal problems. Though most of his work in the courtroom was for the utility, he evidently also fought for individual clients, some of whom were from lower income groups. But he was neither a crusader for unions and the poor as his father had been, nor a labor baiter or utility speculator as was later

---

[17] When Harvey Firestone heard of Willkie's decision to leave the company, he offered to increase his salary to $10,000 a year. Willkie had made his choice, however, so turned down the raise. "Young man," said Firestone in parting with him, "I like you, but I don't think you will ever amount to a great deal." "Why not?" asked Willkie. "Because," said the rubber magnate, "I understand you are a Democrat. No Democrat can ever amount to much." Stanley Walker, in Willkie, *op. cit.,* p. 20.

[18] *Fortune,* May, 1937, p. 202.

charged.[19] He was simply a very ambitious and talented young lawyer who accepted the business values as he found them, and who used those values to make money and further his career. He found an economic freedom that was thrilling to develop, and many of his attitudes toward progress, industrial expansion, and the national government that he publicized a decade later stemmed from this period when economic freedom was unquestioned and the business of the country was business.

Politically, however, he repeatedly spoke for civil liberties and against the Ku Klux Klan. He advocated abolition of the labor injunction and a restraint on monopolies. He supported the overhauling of the Ohio state governmental administration under Governor Cox, and he consistently urged membership in the League of Nations — making scores of speeches against war and for international cooperation. Though he refused opportunities to run for public office, he was active in the Democratic party. He was a delegate in 1924 to the lengthy convention which took 103 ballots to nominate John W. Davis. Willkie's support was given to Al Smith, primarily because William Gibbs McAdoo was supported by the Klan and Klan sympathizers. He worked for a plank in the platform clearly endorsing the League, but this "fight for international cooperation we lost," he declared, "and lost largely because the New York delegation, under the leadership of Franklin D. Roosevelt and others, voted two to one against it."[20]

During this period, Willkie attracted the attention of B. C. Cobb, a utility tycoon who had an interest in the Northern Ohio Power and Light Company. In 1926, Cobb wrote to an officer in Akron, "Do not let this young man get away from us. . . . He is a comer and we should keep an eye on him."[21] Thus in 1929, when Cobb's plans to form a gigantic utility holding company were completed, he asked Willkie to join, at $36,000 a year, the New York firm of Weadock and Weadock, the legal representatives of the newly formed Commonwealth and Southern Corporation. Though he was reluctant to leave Akron, Willkie accepted the new position in New York which, he felt, held greater opportunities for him.

The activities of Wendell Willkie as counsel for, and later as

---

[19] See C. Nelson Sparks, *One Man — Wendell Willkie* (New York, 1943), pp. 34-35, and Bromley, *op. cit.,* pp. 482-83.

[20] Joseph Barnes, *op. cit.,* p. 37.

[21] *Fortune,* May, 1937, p. 202.

president of, Commonwealth and Southern have been extensively publicized.[22] It was charged during the 1940 campaign, some eleven years after Willkie joined the Weadock firm, that the utilities purchased by companies represented by Willkie "wrote up" the ledger value of its investments in the utilities it had merged, and that the Republican candidate had contributed to the financial collapse of the period.[23] This was denied by Willkie, but in the minds of the voters, it remained a moot point during the campaign. Willkie frequently asserted that he was proud that he had had nothing to do with the "speculative orgies of the 1920's" and that he agreed with later "strictures about unloading on the public of common stocks beyond their true value." The Democrats, however, attached little validity to the statements and the issue figured prominently in Democratic propaganda against the 1940 candidate.[24]

From 1929 to 1933, B. C. Cobb became increasingly ill and depended heavily upon Willkie. Upon Cobb's retirement early in 1933, he selected Wendell Willkie to be the new president of Commonwealth and Southern. It was believed at the time that, other factors aside, the selection of Willkie, one of the few Democrats among the utility magnates, was a shrewd choice, considering the Democratic administration which was to assume power in Washington. Almost immediately, Willkie replaced the investment bankers on the board with five operating heads from the subsidiaries, and by 1937 only one banker remained among the directors. In the face of the desperate financial dilemma of the utility industry, in which private expenditures for appliances were practically nil and the corresponding sales of light and power were being cut to a minimum, Willkie began his own revolution in utility public relations and appliance salesmanship. He hired hundreds of new salesmen when salesmen were being discharged elsewhere; he liberalized the already easy credit terms; and he cut rates when

---

[22] See Makey, *op. cit.,* pp. 156 ff., Dillon, *op. cit.,* pp. 41-121, Joseph Barnes, *op. cit.,* pp. 43-125, *Fortune,* May, 1937, pp. 202 ff., and Stone, *op. cit.,* pp. 346-50.

[23] *Congressional Record,* vol. 86, p. 19640 (76th Cong., 3rd Sess., Oct. 17, 1940).

[24] Actually, Commonwealth and Southern Corporation was incorporated on May 23, 1929. Its offer to exchange its stock for that of the companies which were party to the merger was made on June 12, 1929. Willkie did not join the Weadock firm until October 1, 1929. Until that time, he remained in Akron. Willkie lost a large portion of his own savings in the 1929 crash.

others in the industry claimed it was impossible. He devised a complicated bonus plan called the "objective rate," under which the consumer was granted additional free electricity if he would use electricity liberally. Willkie himself traveled extensively in an endeavor to create enthusiasm among small appliance dealers and local power officials.[25] He tried mightily to improve the public relations of his organization, talking with housewives, farmers, merchants, and newspapermen, attempting to prove that a higher standard of living could be achieved by the additional use of electricity without additional cost. Willkie's efforts were rewarded. In six years, the sale of electricity by Commonwealth and Southern subsidiaries was more than doubled; appliance sales were quadrupled, while the company reduced its rates until they were 27 per cent below that of the entire industry's average for the United States.[26] Willkie, by this time, had become chairman of the board of the Consumers Power Company and the Ohio Edison Company and director of the Central Illinois Light Company and the Southern Gas and Electric Company. Moreover, he had impressed many businessmen with his energy, his candor, and his salesmanship.

The economic rejuvenation of Commonwealth and Southern was only one of Willkie's two parallel problems, and it was not the principal achievement which eventually catapulted him to national fame. The second facet of his difficulties involved the government of the United States, which was threatening the business of which he was now a representative. Early in 1933, when Willkie became president of the utility, Franklin Roosevelt recommended the creation of the Tennessee Valley Authority: ". . . a corporation clothed with the power of government but possessed of the flexibility and initiative of a private enterprise. It should be charged with the

---

[25] After sleeping in Pullman berths on his eleven-state tours, Willkie frequently looked disheveled in his personal appearance. When asked about it, he replied, "It's an asset to my business to look like an Indiana farmer." Stone, *op. cit.,* p. 347.

[26] For precise figures concerning income and rates of Willkie's companies, see the *Congressional Record,* vol. 86, p. 19640 (76th Cong., 3rd Sess., Oct. 2, 1940). Opponents of Willkie correctly charged, however, that it was the TVA that forced Willkie's rates down. The *New Republic,* September 2, 1940, p. 324, stated: "One solid fact to remember is that Mr. Willkie reduced the rates of Commonwealth and Southern subsidiaries that are in direct competition with TVA sooner and farther than the others. A second fact is that his companies in the South are making money at the new low rates, which suggests that there must have been something funny about the earlier ones."

broadest duty of planning for the proper use, conservation, and development of the natural resources of the Tennessee River drainage basin and its adjoining territory for the general social and economic welfare of the Nation. This authority should also be clothed with the necessary power to carry these plans into effect."

TVA was an experiment in public ownership and operation which was to vitally affect the life of Wendell Willkie. As one writer expressed it, "If Willkie hadn't got into a fight with Mr. Roosevelt's T.V.A., it is doubtful if Mr. Roosevelt or the American public would ever have heard of him, and it is sure that he would never have run for President."[27] The battle raged in and out of the courts, the operating utility areas, and all the media of communication from October, 1933, until the transfer of the properties of Commonwealth and Southern's Tennessee Electric Power Company to TVA on August 15, 1939.

The court cases testing the validity of the Tennessee Valley Authority were all won by the government. The *Ashwander* case substantiated the right of the government to purchase certain properties of the Mississippi Power Company, a portion of the facilities of the Alabama Power Company, and some property belonging to the Tennessee Electric Power Company, all subsidiaries of Commonwealth and Southern.[28] In *Alabama Power Company* v. *Ickes,* the Court upheld the constitutionality of the PWA grants made to municipalities already served by Commonwealth and Southern so that they might erect local power distribution facilities,[29] and in 1939 the court announced its decision in the case of *Tennessee*

[27] Flanner, *op. cit.*, p. 28.

[28] 297 U.S. 288. The suit was brought against the power company by a group of stockholders to enjoin it from completing the contract. It was reported by Commonwealth and Southern that the suit was being financed by the stockholders, who were contributing twenty-five cents each. Stone, *op. cit.*, p. 348. However, an investigation brought out the fact that the Edison Electrical Institute, of which Wendell Willkie was a director, was providing fifty thousand dollars to support the suit. Whether or not Willkie, who had agreed in a conference with President Roosevelt to carry out the contract, was present at the meeting at which the fifty thousand dollars was appropriated became part of the smear campaign during 1940. Willkie denied that he was present when the matter was discussed. Nelson Sparks (*op. cit.*, pp. 24-27) claimed that Willkie was present "and encouraged the trustees to appropriate $50,000 to fight the case through the courts although Mr. Willkie himself had signed the sales contract." Sparks also accused Willkie of trying to expunge from the record of the meeting any reference to the fact that he was present.

[29] 302 U.S. 464.

Electric Power et al. v. *T.V.A.,* holding that the private utilities had no standing in court to question the constitutionality of the TVA and that the power program was not invalid.[30]

The court cases closed, for the most part, the procurement of power systems by the TVA. The prolonged and bitter struggle between the government and private power companies in the area became history, and though Willkie lost the battle in the courts, he emerged as one of the foremost critics of the New Deal, a champion of private enterprise, and a member of the Republican party.

While the litigation was in progress, however, Willkie fought the government by taking his case to the people in frequent articles and speeches, and also by attempting to stymie every effort of the New Deal in the areas in which the TVA was operating. His addresses were usually presented to prominent business groups — investment bankers, economic clubs, the Harvard Business School Club, or similar organizations. The theme, for five years, remained essentially the same, though it developed from a condemnation of the government's utility policy to an eventual ringing criticism of the entire administration of the New Deal. He claimed that given the same privileges, tax exemptions, and other differentials that government corporations received, private enterprise could perform any service more efficiently.

During one address in 1935, Willkie made an ill-fated remark which was hurled at him many times during the 1940 campaign: ". . . I want to say to you that no duty has ever come to me in my life, even that in the service of my country, which has so appealed to my sense of social obligation, patriotism and love of mankind as this, my obligation to say and do what I can for the preservation of public utilities privately owned. . . ."[31] In 1940 it was difficult for some voters to believe that anyone who placed private utilities higher in his structure of values than service to his country would make a satisfactory chief executive. Nevertheless, in 1935, the words exemplified the epitome of leadership in the public utility field, and Willkie was its outstanding spokesman. He defended holding companies before congressional committees, stressing the great advantages and unfounded myths that surrounded these structures. On other occasions, he charged that the Roosevelt

---

[30] 306 U.S. 118.
[31] Wendell Willkie, *Government and the Public Utilities* (pamphlet copy) in the University of Illinois library.

administration stimulated a "New Fear" among businessmen and investors that prevented industrial expansion — that government ownership of the utilities was the goal of a political leadership already entrenched in power. But by 1937, in view of the great odds against him, Willkie's views became more conciliatory, and his proposals for the utility field more conducive to government-corporation cooperation.

On January 6, 1938, Willkie spoke to his first nationwide audience in a debate over the Town Meeting of the Air with Robert H. Jackson, then Assistant Attorney General of the United States. He called for an end to the bitterness between business and government and claimed that there was no general disagreement between the government and business on the principles of social legislation. He declared: "There is nothing against the interests of the ill-housed, ill-fed or ill-clad in the demand of business for a cessation of government competition," and he summoned the government to discontinue its attack on business so that investors would provide the funds with which the nation could regain industrial prosperity. The address was a ringing defense of capitalism, and correspondents agreed that Willkie so thoroughly outclassed Jackson that the latter's presidential aspirations melted in the course of one night's debate.[32]

Willkie's opinions began to command a wider audience and he became a sought-after writer and speaker. He frequently wrote for the magazine sections of leading New York newspapers, defending the profit system "as one of the principal spurs to human progress" while analyzing the weakness of government in economic enterprise. Big business, according to Willkie, had identical interests with each little business, and their destinies were conditioned by the same economic circumstances such as taxation, government aid or hostility, and investment confidence by the public. He believed that their prosperities were interdependent.

Nevertheless, Willkie claimed to be something other than a cut-and-dried conservative. He incessantly declared that he was a liberal by nature and upbringing and that he realized that big business had been the cause of many social evils. His principal

---

[32] See comments by General Hugh Johnson and Raymond Moley in *This Is Wendell Willkie, op. cit.,* p. 31; by Congressman Bruce Barton in *Official Report of the Proceedings of the Twenty-Second Republican National Convention* (Washington, D.C., 1940), p. 212; and by Freda Kirchwey, in "Pre-Mortem on Willkie," *The Nation,* 151 (October 12, 1940), 318.

opposition to government regulations was that they were indefinite and administered at the whim of a few individuals in the government. He disliked what he called the "punitive attitude" of the independent commissioners and their implication that operators of large enterprise were more sinister than persons who followed other lines of endeavor. He demanded unity and cooperation between business and government but apparently failed to see the parallel implicit in his demand, that decisions among corporation heads were also made at the whim of a few individuals, and that left unrestricted, they too were often punitive toward competitors. Two years later, when Willkie's charges of government strangulation of business had broadened from the utilities to the nation's economic welfare, "unity" became one of his most frequently used words. He claimed that he could obtain it merely by being elected — by restoring the faith in America which had made the United States the most productive nation on earth. Wendell Willkie wanted everyone to "pull together," but Willkie, in his own relations with his fellow men, was living evidence that a meeting of minds within a complex economic and political system was an elusive goal almost impossible of attainment.

While Willkie argued his case against government power in the courts and before the people of the nation, a third facet of the dispute took place in the specific areas served by the TVA and Commonwealth and Southern. Willkie's company conducted a gigantic propaganda campaign against the Authority which produced full-page advertisements in southern newspapers and thousands of letters to the White House and Congress. His subordinates intimidated farmers in an attempt to keep them from joining rural electrification cooperatives. The company erected power lines where they had refused to install them on previous dates — often in areas where they duplicated cooperative facilities and sometimes in such a way as to practically block the erection of lines by the TVA. Commonwealth and Southern, moreover, withdrew all advertising from the pro-public power *Chattanooga News* and gave it to the *Chattanooga Free Press,* a forty-grocery store semi-weekly trade sheet which eventually became a daily paper in competition with the *News.*[33] The incident led Senator George Norris to charge, during the 1940 campaign, that the power company "was the one

---

[33] See the *New Republic,* September 2, 1940, pp. 321-23, and the *Congressional Record,* vol. 86, p. 18956 and p. 19639 (76th Cong., 3rd Sess., Oct. 2, 1940).

great instrumentality in killing the *Chattanooga News,* one of the oldest papers in the South." Willkie did not deny the reports of bitter contests over the construction of rural lines, but he flatly asserted that the Tennessee Electric Power Company of Commonwealth and Southern had nothing to do with the founding of the *Free Press* and that the *News* would have gone bankrupt anyway.[34]

When the smoke of the verbal and legal battles had cleared, both Willkie and David Lilienthal of the TVA were anxious for a settlement of the struggle. Willkie had long been advocating that the government, if it were going to remain in the power business, should purchase the existing facilities rather than erect new systems alongside those already present in the Tennessee Valley. Finally, in 1939, the government offered to buy the Tennessee Electric Power Company for $55,000,000, a price Willkie considered too low. The Commonwealth and Southern president then proposed arbitration by the Federal Securities and Exchange Commission, but the government refused. Willkie had offered to sell the properties for $100,000,000, so a compromise figure was agreed upon — $78,600,-000. This amount enabled Commonwealth and Southern to pay off outstanding bonds and preferred stock at par value and realize about $6,000,000 for the holders of common stock.[35] On the floor of the Senate, George Norris claimed that the price was more than the property was worth, but that the TVA wanted to lean backward so that no private investment would be injured.[36] Subsequently Willkie summed up his view of the episode of the TVA in answer to his critics:

They forget when they criticize me on the power issue that I was a trustee for a number of stockholders. What did they expect me to do? Give the company away? If I were a public official, then I would have the Government's interests as my interest and I would work on behalf of the Government's interests. The only test that could be logically and fairly applied was whether or not I was an effective representative of the people whom I was hired to represent.

Look what I did for them! I got $25,000,000 more than the government offered me for the Commonwealth and Southern properties in the T.V.A. area. I was a special pleader, yes. I was getting $75,000 a year to be a special pleader. With regard to the dispute over the constitu-

---

[34] The entire episode is shrouded in conflicting data. For the charges and coun, countercharges, see the *Congressional Record,* p. 19246 (Sept. 27, 1940), and p. 19965 (Oct. 7, 1940), pp. 19645-19647 (Oct. 2, 1940).

[35] Drummond, *op. cit.,* p. 448.

[36] *Congressional Record,* vol. 86, p. 19247 (76th Cong., 3rd Sess., Sept. 27, 1940).

tionality of the T.V.A., why I was a party to that dispute. It was my duty. I helped to develop the issue. That was my social function.[37]

Willkie was on sound intellectual ground during most of his struggle with the TVA. He cited his record and financial statements with fluency, and many of his criticisms of the government policy were justified. There were, however, two facets of the government-in-business debate that Willkie never recognized. The first was that in spite of any duplications or alterations of the businesses involved, great economic and social benefits were produced throughout the entire Tennessee Valley. The standard of living in the area was substantially raised, and this was the crux of many of the New Deal's basic reforms. Secondly, Willkie, because of the nature of his position and the philosophy under which he matured, never accepted the fact that a public utility is, by its very nature, a business into which the government may enter. It is a natural monopoly, the investment in which, by private capitalists, presents a potential threat both to capital as such and to the welfare of the consuming public.

Nevertheless, the immediate results of Willkie's polemics consisted of a satisfactory price obtained for his properties and the governmental operation of the power facilities in the Tennessee Valley. Also, out of the venture came an articulate *former* Democratic businessman to whom anti-New Dealers everywhere — whose fight he had been fighting and with whom he had been increasingly closely associated — could look for economic leadership.

Willkie's activities against the New Deal were watched and applauded in the business world. *Fortune* magazine, in May, 1937, published a lengthy review of his work at Commonwealth and Southern together with another separate article on his personality and ability. It called him "the Mississippi Yankee, the clever bumpkin, the homespun, rail-splitting, cracker-barrel simplifier of national issues . . . [who] feels a dedication to the cause of private ownership; he knows all the arguments; they are persuasive on his tongue not because they are new but because he frames them intelligently and hence makes them sound new."[38] Other feature articles about Willkie appeared in *Time, Newsweek, Life,* the *Literary Digest, Printer's Ink, Financial Age, Savings Bank Journal, Nation's Business, Dynamic America, Scribner's Commentator, Contemporary*

---

[37] *Propaganda Analysis,* October 15, 1940, p. 1.
[38] *Fortune,* May, 1937, pp. 83 ff.

Affairs, and *Barron's.* For the *Atlantic Monthly* of June, 1939, he wrote a stirring article called "Brace Up, America!" which was a commendation of economic freedom practiced with humanitarianism,[39] and he followed with several others in the *Saturday Evening Post* and the *Reader's Digest.*

By the end of 1939, through such articles, speeches, interviews, and appearances on radio programs, Willkie finally obtained a national audience. He was no longer only the voice of the businessman against the New Deal, he was rapidly becoming one of the outstanding critics of the President as an administrator — a critic of Franklin Roosevelt's right to be the President at all. Willkie occasionally had been mentioned as a presidential possibility, but such statements were quickly qualified as irrational. An editorial in the *New York Times* explained: ". . . party conventions must approach desperation before they will consider nominating a man who, like Mr. Willkie, was registered with the other party. . . ." The paper nevertheless suggested that since the thought of a Republican nomination was no worse than daydreaming, Willkie should consider himself a dark horse.[40] Dark horse Willkie's progress became phenomenal. He was politically "unavailable," but he was an outstanding member of the President's opposition; how was he to become the leader of it?

DARK HORSE IN THE LIMELIGHT

In reality, Willkie had had isolated support for the presidential nomination from certain quarters for more than a year before the Philadelphia convention. Perhaps the first suggestions that he would be a desirable Republican nominee were made early in 1937 by Edward E. Whiting, a New England columnist,[41] and by the *New York Sun* in a special profile on Willkie published on November 2, 1937.[42] Whiting's column went almost unnoticed and the *Sun's* profile was merely one of many which appeared in cosmopolitan newspapers on prominent political and business personalities.

Evidence exists that in informal gatherings of New York business and financial leaders, Willkie's availability and attributes were often discussed. Among those impressed by the utility executive's talents were Raymond Moley, Alfred E. Smith, Thomas Lamont, Alfred

[39] *Atlantic Monthly,* 163 (June, 1939), 749-56.
[40] *New York Times,* February 1, 1940, p. 22.
[41] Makey, *op. cit.,* p. 181.
[42] Joseph Barnes, *op. cit.,* p. 152.

P. Sloan, and Raoul Desvernine, New York lawyer and industrialist. Moreover, as the result of one such meeting, Ernest T. Weir, president of the National Steel Corporation, began an individual campaign to raise funds for a Willkie boom.[43]

Arthur Krock referred to Willkie's outstanding qualifications for candidacy in his column as early as February, 1939, and his comments received wide endorsement from his readers. Letters seconding the proposal soon reached Willkie, and he began to reply to inquiries by saying that although the suggestions could not be taken seriously, he would, of course, like to be President.[44] In November, 1939, General Hugh S. Johnson, at a luncheon in New York City, suggested Willkie as a prospective nominee.[45] He followed this by a statement in his syndicated column to the effect that if Willkie were nominated, he would make a powerful candidate and if elected, a great President. Willkie soon began to receive hundreds of letters and telegrams offering congratulations together with requests for speaking and writing engagements.

Hundreds of messages are insufficient, however, to obtain a nomination by a major political party. Outside of the groups familiar with the government-versus-business controversy, Willkie was, in spite of his writing and speaking, still relatively unknown to the millions of people who were to be the voters during the following November; the bulk of the American public did not have a mental image of him at the beginning of 1940. Even among his acquaintances there were some who thought he would be wasting his time striving for the nomination, and among his utility cohorts there were many who wanted him to remain in the background

---

[43] *New Republic,* July 8, 1940, p. 48, and Dillon, *op. cit.,* pp. 123-26.

[44] In Wooster, Ohio, on January 30, 1940, Willkie made the characteristic reply: "But I'm not running for President. Of course, it isn't going to happen, but if the nomination were given to me without any strings, I would have to accept it. No man in middle life and in good health could do otherwise. But I couldn't go out and seek delegates and make two-sided statements. I value my independence. That's what I've been fighting for all these years." *New York Times,* January 31, 1940, p. 5.

[45] C. Nelson Sparks, in an anti-Willkie tract, *One Man — Wendell Willkie* (pp. 8-9), wrote: "Johnson, in his lifetime, never had the credit for this job of super-selling but everyone remembers how Willkie suddenly burst on the national picture; . . . how Johnson himself catapulted Willkie in the political arena in an article in the *Saturday Evening Post.* . . . The basic framework of the whole buildup — a necessary factor in American politics on occasion — was Johnson's. A good buildup, inevitably appears to be the result of a spontaneous public interest, *and this was a good buildup.*"

lest the industry's record of the twenties and early thirties again be dragged into the headlines.

Nevertheless, Willkie did not request that his name be withdrawn from the list of presidential possibilities. Indeed, during the first months of 1940 he spoke several times each week — against business curbs, government abuses, and the New Deal — "a maker of depressions" — at the same time endorsing reciprocal trade agreements, Roosevelt's foreign policy, and the Allied cause. If Willkie's views were inconsistent with those of the Old Guard Republicans, this fact did not deter him from expressing them. Said the *New York Times:* "Mr. Willkie . . . endorses . . . points of view, support of which is supposed to be fatal to anyone hoping for the Republican nomination."[46] In the April issue of *Fortune,* Willkie wrote a ringing declaration called "We, the People, A Foundation for a Political Platform for Recovery." In reality, it was merely another short, cogent, castigation of the New Deal couched in general phrases, which illustrated Willkie's faith in private enterprise, but the response to the article among those in business circles was immediate and extensive. It was widely circulated and discussed, and along the eastern seaboard, bankers, industrialists, and financiers began to think about what they could do — what specific steps they could take — to foster the Willkie movement.[47]

It remained for a twenty-nine-year-old lawyer to take the first step that made Willkie a truly nationwide personality actively supported by thousands of people. Oren Root, Jr., was greatly impressed by Willkie's speeches at Princeton University. Subsequently, when he read "We, the People" he concluded that Willkie "ought to be President and that a lot of others thought so, too." Young Root spent forty dollars on the printing and mailing of petitions to determine what sentiment existed among his associates for Willkie's candidacy.[48] The circulars raised such a tremendous response that Root temporarily abandoned his legal practice and opened the first "Willkie for President" headquarters in his home. Hundreds of

---

[46] *New York Times,* April 27, 1940, p. 14.

[47] *Ibid.,* April 6, 1940, p. 22.

[48] The Pandick Press, which printed the first Willkie petitions, eventually published more than 277,000 before the national convention. Twenty other shops in almost as many cities went into the Willkie-for-President petition business. *New York Herald Tribune,* June 30, 1940, p. 3. At the time that Root sent the original petition, he did not know Willkie, and in his life saw him "only fifteen or twenty times." Interview with Oren Root.

people who signed the original petitions began to send out facsimiles with their own money. Contributions began coming into Root at the rate of two hundred dollars a day. Root rented an empty store and the Willkie crusade got underway. Thousands of Willkie "kits" were distributed. Root placed personal advertisements in the want-ad columns of newspapers throughout the country requesting that local Willkie clubs be established; residents quickly volunteered their services, time, and money for the cause. More than three million signatures eventually were obtained on the petitions.

Meanwhile, the entire Willkie boom had grown to such proportions that Russell "Mitch" Davenport, managing editor of *Fortune*, took leave from his position to devote his entire time to managing Willkie's personal campaign. In addition, Harold E. Talbott, the investment banker of Wall Street who later became Assistant Secretary of the Air Force under Eisenhower, Charlton MacVeagh, an eastern industrialist, and Frank Altschul, a former chairman of the finance committee of the GOP, were important forces in giving impetus to the Willkie campaign. It was Altschul who interested Kenneth Simpson and Styles Bridges in the Willkie potentiality, and it was MacVeagh who sold John D. M. Hamilton on the desirability of having the utility executive as a presidential candidate.[49] Working with these men was a large group of professional public relations experts who made the first great, though uncoordinated, effort by this segment of the population to engineer mass consensus behind a presidential nominee. These men, whose contemporaries and successors today have become essential fixtures in any well-developed political campaign, were as enthusiastic about supporting an articulate businessman for the nomination as were any of the financial leaders of Wall Street. They gave generously of their talents with the result that the Willkie preconvention build-up, called a "masterpiece of disorganization" by mass circulation magazines, was actually the most skillful piece of publicity that had ever been exhibited in a political campaign.

The nucleus of the organization was made up of Stanley Walker, newspaper editor; Steve Hannagan and Ned Stevenson, public relations counsels; Fred Smith,[50] of Selvage and Smith, who had

---

[49] Dillon, *op. cit.*, pp. 126 and 131.

[50] After the nomination, Smith is reported to have said: "Neither Willkie's personality, nor the weight of his ideals, could conceivably have produced even a fraction of the phenomenon that we lived through. It should never be forgotten that the 'Willkie boom' was one of the best engineered jobs in history." Joseph Barnes, *op. cit.*, p. 165.

been the director of Bruce Barton's campaign for Congress; Harry M. Schackleford, advertising manager of Johns-Manville; Chester LaRoche and Ted Patrick of Young and Rubicam; Thomas Ryan of Pedlar and Ryan; Stanley Resor of J. Walter Thompson; Raymond Leslie Buell of *Fortune;* Robert L. Johnson of *Promenade;* Stephen Walter, publicity director for the Committee of Utility Executives, and John Orr Young, the distinguished advertising consultant. Working both individually and in concert but with practically no direction from a political headquarters, these opinion leaders stimulated chain letters, petitions, telegrams, and the distribution of propaganda. For example, Stevenson sent out publicity at no cost to Willkie for more than two months before the convention. Schackleford organized the Indiana Box Supper to raise funds and help conceptualize the myth of Willkie's rural background; LaRoche and Patrick wrote and paid for advertising directed to the delegates of the convention, and Ryan put notices for Willkie's candidacy into newspaper columns to solicit donations from readers.[51] John Orr Young contributed about $10,000 worth of his *time* publicizing Willkie, in addition to financing some of the early ads before the advertising campaign became self-supporting. Later, Young was subpoenaed to testify before a federal grand jury and a special Senate committee investigating violations of the Hatch Act regarding campaign expenditures. In his activities, however, he had been well within the law and he was dismissed without penalty or censure.[52]

These, then, were the principals who quickened the pulse of the American people and helped create the spontaneous uprising for Willkie.[53] In their publicity, they stressed Willkie's tumultuous youth, his dynamic rise to business prominence and the fact that he had cut power rates fifty per cent in the areas his companies served; they noted that he once called Wall Street speculators "a bunch of jugglers" and that Samuel Insull had expressed determination to destroy him. In short, these men placed before the public not a utilities-identified tycoon or the Akron corporation counsel, but instead a fascinating picture of a homespun, hard-working Indiana small-town boy; a carelessly dressed, friendly, Horatio Alger type,

---

[51] *Tide,* July 15, 1940, pp. 9-10.

[52] Personal letter to the author.

[53] *Propaganda Analysis,* October 15, 1940, p. 2. Also, see Peter Odegard, *Prologue to November, 1940* (New York, 1940), p. 49.

opposed in a mighty crusade to the Country Squire in the White House.

In the spring of 1940 Willkie also spoke to a group of publishers in New York, including John Cowles of the *Minneapolis Star,* and his brother Gardner Cowles, Jr., of the *Des Moines Register.* These men were favorably impressed by Willkie and desired to support him, but they did not know (in Willkie's words) "how much discount to give me as a resident of New York City, a public utility man, and a former Democrat."[54] Nevertheless, they arranged for a midwestern test speech in St. Paul on May 11, where Willkie addressed a large crowd of Republican leaders. After a prepared statement attacking the growing governmental deficit, praising the aims of the Hatch Act, and urging all aid short of war to the free nations of Europe, Willkie gave an extemporaneous peroration that was received with such exceptional enthusiasm that the Cowles brothers decided to give him their complete backing for the nomination.[55] It was after this speech that Willkie, for the first time, openly admitted that he had decided to run for the Republican nomination. "It was the way the speech went off," said Willkie, "that decided me in my own mind."[56] This was just forty-four days before the convention. Two weeks earlier, however, Willkie had become such a threat to the declared candidates, Dewey, Taft, Vandenberg, and Frank Gannett, that he had to deny a charge that he was engaged in "stopping the campaign of other candidates." Willkie declared, "I am not engaged in any campaign to start or stop any candidate. . . . I have not participated and I do not expect to participate in any preconvention activities for or against any aspirant for the Republican nomination."[57] Willkie's decision was heralded throughout the business world. Here was a man who, though individualistic and dynamic, believed, like Calvin Coolidge, in the efficiency and ability of business to run the business of government.

Thus, from its inception the Willkie preconvention movement was spearheaded by two groups which ordinarily played neither an active nor an open role in presidential primary campaigns: the

---

[54] Flanner, *op. cit.,* p. 39.

[55] *PM* credited this speech with much of the very favorable press Willkie received during the campaign, though as the GOP candidate, he probably would have had it in any event. *PM,* June 28, 1940, p. 7.

[56] Flanner, *op. cit.,* p. 39.

[57] *New York Times,* April 23, 1940, p. 12.

Willkie-for-President Clubs, organized by Oren Root among non-party amateurs who displayed more enthusiasm than local party organizations generated in support of either political party in 1940, and the businessmen, financiers, and publishers, led by the mass distributors of the Willkie saga, *Fortune* and the *Saturday Evening Post*. These groups utilized the consistently successful formula for selling candidates by presenting Willkie as the political newcomer who did not want to be President but who felt that it was his public duty and destiny.

From St. Paul, Willkie went to Des Moines, where he conferred with farm and labor groups, then to Indiana before returning to New York. Back in Manhattan, he told reporters that he felt he had some "secondary strength" in Massachusetts and New York, and expressed the belief that he probably had made inroads in the delegations in Connecticut, Rhode Island, New Jersey, Iowa, Indiana, Minnesota, and Missouri.[58]

In the middle of May, Willkie opened his eastern campaign in New Jersey. In what he called his first address to an "out and out political gathering," he blasted the Administration for the waste of defense funds. Two days later, he addressed the previously mentioned Hoosier Box Supper and dance which was attended by four thousand friends in New York. He warned of Nazi trade aims which, he said, threatened world commerce. In a Kansas City speech three days later, he declared that the New Deal was not capable of properly spending the money needed for defense because a strong military position was impossible without strong industry. He then attacked the Roosevelt administration for refusing to remove restrictions on industry even during an emergency, and disparaged the idea of a "coalition cabinet" which was rumored at that time. In Akron, Willkie again affirmed his belief that Britain and France were America's first line of defense, which the United States had to strengthen by all means short of war. The following day, he opened a Willkie-for-President headquarters in Chicago, and in Denver, on May 31, he said to reporters: "I would be delighted to be the nominee for President and I would be doubly

[58] *Ibid.*, May 19, 1940, p. 2. According to Dillon, Sinclair Weeks, national committeeman from Massachusetts at that time, agreed to support Willkie in the spring of 1940. For making this commitment without consulting Joe Martin, Weeks was reportedly "taken over the coals." *Op. cit.*, p. 132. This account does not square with the impression I obtained from Weeks personally.

delighted if President Roosevelt were my opponent. I'd love to go to the people against that fellow."[59]

During this period, Willkie supporters worked feverishly on his publicity campaign. Oren Root predicted that if the convention went beyond the second ballot, Willkie would get the nomination. A week earlier, Root's Willkie Clubs had stimulated, in three days, a write-in campaign in the New Jersey preferential election. Dewey was the only avowed entrant, and he had received 340,744 votes, but Willkie had obtained 24,240 "write-ins," a sign Willkie enthusiasts interpreted as a display of surprising strength.

In the western part of the country, Willkie talked with delegates from twenty-five states and came to the conclusion that "no person controls any substantial number of delegates." He added that the "overwhelming sentiment" throughout the nation for the granting of all possible aid short of war to the Allies precluded any possibility that an isolationist plank could be included in the Republican platform to be adopted at the national convention — an observation and prediction that proved to be incorrect.

During this week, a fortnight before the convention opened, forty-three Willkie clubs were formed, making a total of nearly five hundred in existence by June 12. In addition, requests for Willkie buttons totaled 50,000 a day, over 350,000 having been distributed by this time along with more than 150,000 copies of what his headquarters called "Willkie's principles." A Gallup poll showed Willkie in second place with seventeen per cent of the Republicans in favor of him (Dewey still had fifty-two per cent) a percentage jump of seven per cent in one week. A Democrats-for-Willkie organization was established by Lewis Douglas, president of the Mutual Life Insurance Company and former Director of the Budget under Roosevelt, John W. Hanes, former Under Secretary of the Treasury, and Alan Valentine, president of the University of Rochester. Plans were made to stress the fact that Willkie was a Democrat whom the party had left, and that other dissident Democrats could legally support him as a means of defeating Roosevelt.

When Willkie returned to the East for the conclusion of his pre-convention campaign, he was full of confidence. He told a group

---

[59] *New York Times,* June 1, 1940, p. 7. Wrote Robert E. Sherwood of this remark, "A shrewder politician would not have said that. The people interpreted Willkie literally as saying, 'The hell with the third term tradition. Let's make this a *real* fight.' " Robert E. Sherwood, *op. cit.,* I, 215.

of Washington reporters that Representative Charles A. Halleck of Indiana would place his name in nomination, and that Representative Bruce Barton of New York would be among those who would second the nomination.[60] He then added: "My supporters say that I will be nominated on the sixth or seventh ballot and I think I should be." Willkie was uncertain as to the exact number of delegates he had obtained, but thought that he would have at least seventy votes on the first ballot. In Boston he declared his opposition to war, and stated that if he became the President he would resist entry into any armed conflict. He said that it was up to the people to decide whether or not the United States should enter a war, but he asserted that he believed that the Allies should be sent all supplies possible — food if not armaments. Willkie spent the next three days in the New England states, during which time he was assured of a "substantial bloc" of delegates, including those from Rhode Island, where he received the support of Governor William H. Vanderbilt, who promised him six of the eight Rhode Island votes; those from Connecticut, where he expected to get sixteen votes on the second ballot; and from Massachusetts, where he claimed that twenty-two of the thirty-four delegates would fall to him after the token vote for Representative Joseph Martin on the first ballot.

This period of the preconvention activities represented the hiatus in Willkie's life. Though he had been driven by the inexorable pressure of political events and his opposition to the New Deal into a defense of certain conservative forces with which he was not always in agreement, he was still not completely obligated to the Republican party and all of the principles for which it had historically stood. In Boston he told Sinclair Weeks that his plans for organization in Washington included only MacVeagh, Davenport, and Gardner "Mike" Cowles. Willkie was still, at this point, writing most of his own speeches and making others extemporaneously

---

[60] According to Dillon, *op. cit.,* p. 135, the question of who was to nominate Willkie had bothered his supporters for some time. "Hamilton urged that the nominating speech be made by a politician from Indiana, and suggested Charles A. Halleck as the logical man. . . . Ambitious but cautious, Halleck was dubious whether his nomination of Willkie would advance his own career in the Republican Party. Finally, Hamilton and Altschul persuaded him to take the risk. Willkie hastened to make a public announcement of this decision before Halleck quite realized that he had committed himself." Halleck termed this account of his indecision "a lot of nonsense!"

without caution or concessions to expediency. He often challenged the voters to vote against him if they did not like his ideas or statements, and he had not yet assembled about him the heterogeneous group leaders that later made compromise seem so desirable.

THE OTHER CONTENDERS

Meanwhile, other Republican presidential aspirants searched for delegates and encouragement. By January of 1940, the favorite of 1938, Arthur Vandenberg, was still a contender but his popularity had decreased. "I do not consider myself a candidate in the usual sense of that word," he wrote to Kansas State Republican Chairman Walter Fess, "I have indicated my willingness to serve in this terrific responsibility, but I have also indicated that I have absolutely no personal aspirations in this direction and I shall not personally participate in any pre-convention campaign for delegates."[61] Nevertheless, Senator Nye came out for Vandenberg, and as support continued to pile up, Vandenberg entered primaries and met with group leaders in an effort to obtain some firm commitments. After a February conference with farm, labor, and party leaders in St. Paul, the Michigan senator declared that he thought he could count on 199 delegates from the Northwest area, though his friends believed that he would have to carry the Wisconsin and Nebraska primaries before he could count the western states in his fold.

In Wisconsin, Vandenberg supporters openly encouraged Progressive voters to vote for their candidate in the Republican primary. Progressives were told that there was no point in voting in the Democratic primary, which Roosevelt was certain to win, and that by voting for Vandenberg, a liberal in the White House would be assured no matter which party won the November election. In Nebraska, Vandenberg was endorsed by Senators McNary of Oregon and Capper of Kansas, who sent messages calling the Michigan candidate a "champion of agriculture." The efforts were unsuccessful, however, for the Vandenberg slate lost to the Dewey delegates in both states. Vandenberg received only 72,108 votes to Dewey's 99,905. Nonetheless, by convention time Vandenberg still had the Michigan delegation and scattered support in other areas, and he asserted that he would be nominated if his pledged delegates could hold the line for five or six ballots. It was clear, however, that he

---

[61] *New York Times,* January 10, 1940, p. 1.

was counting on a deadlock to turn the convention to him in view of his lack of a large number of initially pledged delegates.

The overwhelming choice for the Republican nomination when the convention opened, according to all of the polls, was the New York district attorney, Thomas E. Dewey. In spite of the fact that he was only thirty-eight years of age in 1940, he led all other aspirants in popular support — though James A. Hagerty thought that this lead could be attributed to a lack of popular interest in the other candidates.[62] Dewey traveled widely during the early months of 1940, making more than forty-five speeches to Republican rallies in the Midwest and Pacific Northwest. In addition, he had most of the New York delegation behind him, he swept the primaries in both Wisconsin and Nebraska, and in Illinois, where he ran unopposed, he acquired an impressive 977,000 votes.[63] His supporters sent a letter to each of the two thousand delegates and alternates stating that the Gallup, *Fortune,* and *Pathfinder* polls gave him fifty-nine per cent of the "vote-getting strength," and asked five questions, the answers to which indicated that Dewey would have the greatest chance of defeating the Democratic candidate. On the other hand, an unauthorized, but Dewey-pledged, delegation in Massachusetts was defeated by an unpledged delegation headed by Governor Saltonstall, and in New York, both Frank Gannett and Kenneth Simpson represented defections from solid support in Dewey's home state.

Observers noted inconsistencies in Dewey's speeches. In Wisconsin, where he spoke to German groups, he seemed to veer toward isolationism. Subsequently, in other parts of the country, he spoke more favorably of aid to the Allies. He also advocated both a balanced budget and a "two ocean navy." On the whole, however, Dewey's speeches were similar to many of Willkie's. He criticized the shackling of industry and initiative, the shifting New Deal policies, and punitive taxes which paralyzed business. And in an effort to parallel the propaganda for Willkie, Dewey's supporters stressed

---

[62] *Ibid.,* January 31, 1940, p. 12.

[63] The *New York Times* reported that a "Stop Dewey" investigation of primary expenditures in Wisconsin and Nebraska indicated that approximately $75,000 was spent by Dewey backers in each state, while Vandenberg supporters spent about $13,000 on each of the primaries. Remembering that in 1920 General Leonard Wood and Governor Frank O. Lowden had been put out of the running by last minute disclosures of heavy spending in primary campaigns, Dewey sympathizers charged that the investigation was a "smear" attempt on their candidate. April 22, 1940, p. 1.

that their candidate had much of his strength among banking and corporate interests. Strangely enough, however, though Dewey had popularity and pledged strength as the convention approached, a general sentiment existed among reporters and political analysts that the vice-presidential nomination, if he would accept it, would be the best that Dewey could win in 1940. Even among his close advisers it was agreed that the young prosecuter would have to be victorious within the first three ballots or give up his aspirations. William Allen White thought that Dewey reached the crest of his popularity too early and that his equivocation on foreign policy diminished his chances of success.

Behind the scenes in the preconvention campaign of 1940 remained the unknown, well-organized strength of Senator Robert A. Taft of Ohio. Taft was the professional who preferred to negotiate for his delegates within the states. He had solid support among many conservative members of the national committee, and reportedly was the favorite of delegates from the South. He refused to enter primaries, he said, because he could not spare the campaigning time from his Senate duties. Later, he did decide to enter the Maryland primary but he promptly withdrew when Dewey decided to oppose him in the Old Line State.

On the vital issue of foreign policy, Taft was frankly negative. He gave the impression that it made little difference to him who won the war,[64] and he preferred to concentrate his ammunition on the New Deal's policies for agriculture and business. Even at this early date in his senatorial career, Taft was acknowledged to be most representative of his party's philosophy, and his loyalty to Republican principles was above question. As a result, he was personally confident that after the first ballot the delegates would turn to his banner. He predicted that running entirely "on his own," he would have 275 first-ballot votes on which to build.

In addition to these prominent personalities from whose ranks most newsmen thought the candidate would come, there were many "favorite sons" who had remote hopes of being nominated in case the convention became a stalemate, but who realized that for the most part their influence would be used for bargaining purposes.[65] Included in this group were Styles Bridges, who had won the New

[64] *Ibid.*, June 9, 1940, p. 2.

[65] For a full discussion of "favorite sons," see Clarence A. Berdahl, "Presidential Selection and Democratic Government," *Journal of Politics,* 11 (February, 1949), 35-40.

Hampshire primary; Hanford MacNider of Iowa, a former national commander of the American Legion and minister to Canada; Joe Martin of Massachusetts; Senator Charles McNary of Oregon; and Governor Arthur James of Pennsylvania. In California, a group of citizens started a "Draft Hoover" drive, but the former President, though certainly both anxious and available, refused to sanction the action. Several dark horses were also in the field. Suggested for nomination if the delegates could not agree on one of the more prominent candidates were Supreme Court Justices Harlan F. Stone and Owen J. Roberts. Neither of these men would agree to seek the nomination, but it was understood that they would recognize a draft movement. New York publisher Frank Gannett traveled across the country trying to obtain delegate commitments and spent large amounts of money for radio broadcasts, but he was unable to inspire any great enthusiasm for his conservative cause.

These, then, were the candidates as the 1940 Republican convention assembled under the sinister shadow of war in Europe. In the elections of 1938, foreign policy had not been a major consideration, but by June, 1940, the most fundamental considerations of the party were to name a candidate and frame a platform, both of which would be acceptable to the various factions within the organization. The *New York Times* noted that the war fury had upset the entire background against which the Republican convention would be staged, and observed that, section by section throughout the country, the citizens were for all-out aid to the Allies.[66] That many members of the Republican party did not feel so strongly about aiding the democracies of Europe was to be brought out during the convention proceedings; that Wendell Willkie was the one Republican candidate who was in complete accord with the *Times'* survey had been well established by his declarations on many occasions. Though it was conceded that neither Dewey nor Taft would insist upon an isolationist platform, both men had vacillated in their foreign policy statements, and delegates were uncertain about their positions in view of the Fascist threat in Europe. Thus, as the Republicans entered the 1940 convention, a deep schism developed over the international issue — the issue which William Allen White accurately predicted would "unquestionably dominate the Republican convention and probably . . . name the Republican candidate."[67]

[66] *New York Times,* June 16, 1940, sec. 4, pp. 6-7.
[67] *Ibid.,* June 9, 1940, p. 2.

3 WE WANT WILLKIE

The Republican National Convention of 1940 was scheduled to begin on June 24, 1940, in Philadelphia. The traditional fanfare, bands, parades, and bunting dominated the scene in the convention area as the candidates set up their campaign headquarters. Senator Taft and his general staff occupied 102 rooms in the Benjamin Franklin Hotel; Senator Vandenberg had forty-eight rooms, most of which were at the Adelphia Hotel; Frank Gannett took over the Harvard Club and forty-eight rooms in the same hotel with Taft; Dewey had seventy-eight rooms in the Hotel Walton; and the national committee had the entire fifth floor of the Bellevue-Stratford. Wendell Willkie had a two-room suite at the Benjamin Franklin.

This shrewdly conceived lack of ostentation on Willkie's part indicated no lack of facilities; adequate and spacious Willkie headquarters were set up by Oren Root in the Land Title Building and in a store in the block between the Benjamin Franklin and the Bellevue-Stratford Hotels. Moreover, two rooms proved to be sufficient in which to meet most of the delegates to the convention — which Willkie did. And finally, every effort was made to eliminate any thought from the minds of the delegates and spectators that Willkie had access to large sums of money to help obtain the nomination. Willkie's advisers did everything possible to suppress independent activities by his friends which might have altered the carefully cultivated impression among the delegates that he was "just plain folks, just like you." During the convention period, newspapers were asked to reject several full-page advertisements for the utility president for fear the delegates would wonder where all the money was coming from. Thomas W. Lamont reportedly was asked not to appear at the Willkie headquarters, and efforts were made to quash a telegram campaign similar to those that the utilities had used on Congress during the fight over the holding company bill in 1935.[1]

Newspapers began to print daily headlines such as "Willkie Now Chief Fear of Other Candidates," "Willkie Now Is Man to Beat," or "Stop Willkie Plans in Making." James E. Watson, former majority leader of the Senate and a Dewey supporter, suggested that the New York prosecutor and Senator Taft cooperate to bring about the defeat of Willkie; he estimated that the two leading first-ballot candidates had more than a majority, 650 ballots, between them. This proposition was promptly rejected by both men, however; Dewey asserted that he would refuse second place on the ballot, while Taft felt that his success after the first ballot would increase steadily until the nomination was his.[2] Many observers believed that Alf Landon held the key to the Republican nomination, and the pro-New Deal paper, *PM*, actually credited Landon with the Willkie victory, but this was denied in other quarters.[3]

The commentators were unanimous on one point in their agreement that the professional politicians were to have less influence in the 1940 GOP convention than at any political gathering in recent United States history — that this would be an unbossed assembly in which the rank-and-file Republicans would have more voice in the selection of a leader than they had had in many years.

During the week prior to the convention, a number of events took place which were aimed at re-establishing the power of the professionals and at stopping the Willkie boom. The arguments against Willkie were based upon the same charges that many columnists had predicted would make Willkie unavailable from the beginning of his preconvention campaign. He was accused of being a former Democrat, the head of a public utility, pro-

---

[1] *Propaganda Analysis*, October 14, 1940, p. 3.

[2] *New York Herald Tribune*, June 22, 1940, p. 1.

[3] *PM*, June 28, 1940, p. 7. A very close associate of Willkie who was present at nearly all of the private meetings wrote me: "In my judgment, Landon did not play an important part in the final result."

interventionist, and a supporter of reciprocal trade agreements adverse to the interests of the voters in the Rocky Mountain areas and the far West. In addition, many Republicans believed that the very fact that he was probably being supported by the Wall Street financial interests would make him a weak candidate to place in opposition to any Democratic nominee. David S. Ingalls, campaign manager for Senator Taft, made a widely distributed declaration in which he asserted that the "next president should be a Republican . . . deeply experienced in the science of government. He should know by experience how to cooperate with the legislative branch. . . . He should be the most available standard bearer in the Republican party. . . ."[4]

On the floor of the House of Representatives, Usher L. Burdick, Republican of North Dakota, made a more direct attack that was circulated among the delegates:

Is the great Republican Party of Abraham Lincoln to be sacrificed on the utility altar by nominating Wendell Willkie for the highest office in our country? . . . I believe I am serving the best interests of the Republican Party by protesting in advance and exposing the machinations and attempts of J. P. Morgan and the other New York utility bankers in forcing Wendell Willkie on the Republican Party. Money, I know, talks.

There is nothing to the Willkie boom for President except the artificial public opinion being created by newspapers, magazines, and the radio. The reason back of all this is money. Money is being spent by someone and lots of it. This is a good time to find out whether the American people are to be let alone in the selection of a Republican candidate for the Presidency, or whether the "special interests" of this country are powerful enough to dictate to the American people. If that power cannot be broken, then this Republic is lost.[5]

Three days later, Ezra Whitla, national committeeman from Idaho, a supporter of Dewey, called a meeting of the delegates from thirteen western states and the Territory of Alaska, at which resolutions were adopted opposing American intervention in any European or Asiatic wars and denouncing reciprocal tariff legislation.[6] Senator John Thomas of Idaho was selected to submit the views to the convention committee on resolutions. The following day, about

<hr>

[4] *New York Times,* June 20, 1940, p. 20.

[5] *Congressional Record,* vol. 86, p. 12960 (76th Cong., 3rd Sess., June 19, 1940).

[6] *New York Times,* June 24, 1940, p. 10. The states represented were Idaho, Utah, Montana, Wyoming, Nevada, Arizona, New Mexico, Colorado, Oregon, Washington, North Dakota, South Dakota, and Oklahoma.

forty members of the House and five senators from western and other states, representing more than two-thirds of the states which had Republican representatives in Congress in 1940, attended a meeting to oppose the nomination of Willkie. Eight members of the group[7] signed a lengthy appeal requesting that the delegates to the convention "nominate a candidate for President whose personal views will present an opportunity for a clear-cut vote on foreign and domestic issues in harmony with the Republican record in Congress." Representative Stephen Bolles of Wisconsin said that if Willkie became the Republican nominee, Wisconsin would be lost by the GOP by 50,000 to 100,000 votes. Senator Thomas declared that the nomination of the utility man would be fatal to Republican candidates in the Rocky Mountain and other western states and added that he would not support him and would not be a candidate for re-election in case Willkie were nominated.[8] He declared that the public utility interests had "done enough" to the Republican party "without wishing their man Willkie on us as a Presidential candidate with his endorsement of Roosevelt's intervention policies and reciprocal tariff."

On the same day, though not at the meeting, Senator McNary, who ironically was to become Willkie's running mate, said that the western states, which he assumed the Republican nominee for President would have to carry in order to win the election, would not support Willkie. He predicted that the Willkie boom would decline as quickly as it had risen when the balloting began, and that the Republican party would win the election in November with the proper candidate.

While these "stop Willkie" movements were in progress, Willkie supporters were quietly trying to line up additional support. For example, on Thursday morning, June 20, Sam Pryor, a Republican committeeman from Connecticut who had decided that Willkie could be nominated, talked with Sinclair Weeks, and the two men decided to fly to Washington to talk with Joe Martin. After having dinner with the House leader that evening, they told him that in view of the fact that he might have presidential aspirations of his

---

[7] The eight who signed the petition were Harold Knutson, Minnesota; Cliff Clevenger, Ohio; Karl Mundt, South Dakota; George W. Gille, Indiana; Stephen Bolles, Wisconsin; Earl Lewis, Ohio; Frank Keefe, Wisconsin; and Roy O. Woodruff of Michigan.

[8] Senator Thomas did not consummate his threat. He died while still in office on November 10, 1945. *Ibid.*, November 11, 1945, p. 42.

own, they had decided to lay the cards on the table quite frankly. They declared that in spite of their long friendships with him, they felt that the political and world situations demanded a man of Willkie's type and that they thought his cause was making very rapid headway. Martin, however, undisturbed and inclined to discount the whole movement, indicated that he thought a Willkie nomination could not possibly happen.

The Commonwealth and Southern president, meanwhile, continued to meet delegates in his two hotel rooms. By June 25 he claimed to have seen more than six hundred of the one thousand delegates attending the convention. With regard to the meeting of the western congressmen, Willkie expressed "particular gratitude" to Representative Knutson for his organization movement, which he thought had rebounded for his benefit. "Only today," he said, "a half dozen western congressmen came in to tell me that the Knutson statement did not represent their views; some thought it presumptuous of seven [sic] congressmen to speak for others. It is too much like the New Deal."[9] Willkie then cited figures to show that a majority of the county chairmen and precinct chairmen in Knutson's district were in favor of his candidacy.

Willkie's drive was exceedingly successful. With the rise of open opposition on the part of the Republican congressmen, however, it was obvious to the candidate's advisers that his organizational plans, which Willkie had told reporters were "in my hat," had to be succeeded by a coordination of the numerous delegates who had expressed interest in voting for him after two or three ballots.[10]

---

[9] *Ibid.*, June 26, 1940, p. 18.

[10] A column written by Arthur Krock after Willkie's death illustrated just how unprepared Willkie personally appeared to be at this date. About midnight on June 22, 1940, Krock and Turner Catledge met Mr. and Mrs. Willkie, who were on their way to a quiet room in the Chancellor Hall, a small apartment hotel in Philadelphia. Willkie invited the newspapermen to come up to his room to discuss the convention. When Krock asked how everything was going, Willkie replied that things were going very well. But in response to a question concerning whether or not he had a floor leader, Willkie did not seem to know what the correspondent meant, and asked if one was needed. Somewhat astonished, Krock and Catledge explained the duties of the floor leader, the necessity for one, and the additional need for a strategy committee. Krock emphasized the desirability of having well-known politicians who were acquainted with state leaders to roam the floor and inform the respective delegations which other states were about to throw their support to the Hoosier candidate. In this way, when the time came for Willkie to make his bid, the pace of it could be regulated. "Mr. Willkie seemed surprised that so much organization was

Therefore, John D. M. Hamilton, who had to be publicly neutral toward all candidates, privately organized a group to support Willkie on the convention floor. Acting through Representative Halleck, he recruited a strategy committee composed of Governor Harold Stassen, Senator Bridges, Samuel Pryor, James Allen of the Kansas delegation, Mayor Rolland B. Marvin of Syracuse, Kenneth Simpson, Governor Baldwin of Connecticut, Sinclair Weeks, Representatives Bruce Barton of New York and Frank Horton of Wyoming, Charlton MacVeagh, Russell Davenport, Mike Cowles, Walter Hallanan, Edgar M. Queeny of Missouri, and James Douglas of Illinois to guide the balloting for the Commonwealth and Southern chief. On the Sunday night preceding the opening of the convention, the group met secretly in Hamilton's hotel suite at the Bellevue-Stratford.

As a result of the strategy board's meeting, and after a caucus with the Connecticut delegation, Governor Baldwin announced that he would withdraw from the Republican race to second the nomination of Willkie.[11] This meant that sixteen votes would go to Willkie on the first ballot from Connecticut — the only state from which he had such a commitment. It also meant that Willkie's total would probably trail only Dewey and Taft on the first ballot. Willkie announced that in addition to the Connecticut votes, he had assurances of votes from at least some delegates in every state of the Union except three.[12] He had spent most of the day meeting new

required; . . . he gave the impression the plan was wholly new to him. . . ." In his memorandum written on the following day, Krock added: "There was more discussion, so naive on his part . . . that as his visitors departed they expressed the opinion that so unprepared an attempt against the powerful professionals might not be able to produce even Mr. Willkie's strength among the delegates. But they concluded that perhaps this apparent lack of organization . . . was deliberate and would be most effective in the end, since it showed that little money had been used and that the one-man nominating bid was as real as it had been represented." *New York Times*, October 10, 1944, p. 22. Willkie, who had attended previous conventions, was being facetious during this interview. He knew of the organization already being developed for him, but he thought the reporters would enjoy thinking he had followed their advice. After Krock and Catledge left, he remarked, in effect, "Someday they will write about how naïve I was, but I didn't want to spoil their illusions."

[11] Dillon, *op. cit.*, p. 137, wrote that Baldwin agreed to release his delegates at a church dinner in Greenwich shortly before the convention. The decision to give Willkie the votes on the first ballot was the strategy of Sam Pryor, who prevailed upon Baldwin to make the sacrifice. *Ibid.*, p. 147.

[12] The states were Mississippi, South Carolina, and Louisiana. Willkie was evidently mistaken on this assurance or else those who promised to

arrivals and holding conferences with supporters. These meetings were handled by Willkie's amateur supporters, who ushered one group into one of the hotel rooms while Willkie was speaking to a gathering in the other. This process continued for three days from nine o'clock each morning until two the following morning up to the night of June 27.

While Willkie and the other candidates were contacting delegates in hotel rooms, and while the members of the various convention committees were preparing their reports, the crowds in the streets were rabidly advocating their favorite candidates. No groups were more avid than those supporting Wendell Willkie. In response to letters from Oren Root sent on June 15, Willkie Club members by the thousands flocked to Philadelphia to help create enthusiasm among the delegates and increase the appearance of overwhelming Willkie support. Though Arthur Krock related that the "approximate truth" about Willkie's expenditures was that the candidate, personally, had spent only "from three to four thousand dollars" on the campaign and that the volunteer committees had spent "about $23,000 more," Willkie pamphlets and other literature littered the streets, Willkie buttons were worn by thousands of people, and the two Willkie headquarters were working at top speed supplying additional propaganda. Much of the money which financed this wave of enthusiasm was actually collected and disbursed by local groups and organizations, and Oren Root said that he had no record of the "countless amounts" spent by Willkie amateurs during this preconvention period.[13] The entire movement truly became "an uprising of the people" such as the nation had never before seen. If

___

support him did not fulfill their pledges. It was the strategy of the organizational committee that Willkie should not have more than sixty or seventy votes on the first ballot — a steady increase in subsequent ballots would then look impressive. However, since no one knew exactly how many ballots would be needed to nominate a candidate, the fact that by the fourth ballot twelve states had not as yet cast a single ballot for Willkie indicated that some of the delegates who promised support either changed their minds or decided to support Willkie only if their own candidates were definitely out of the race. Even on the fifth ballot, Kentucky, Louisiana, Idaho, Michigan, Mississippi, Ohio, Washington, Wisconsin, and Wyoming failed to support him.

[13] Louise Overacker wrote that the Associated Willkie Clubs of America, as one organization, spent $1,355,604 during the entire campaign. "Campaign Finance in the Presidential Election of 1940," *American Political Science Review*, 35 (August, 1941), 709.

anyone was directing it, it was not apparent then, and it has been neither proved nor admitted since 1940.

The Twenty-Second National Republican Convention was called to order shortly before noon on June 24, 1940, by National Chairman John Hamilton. After the traditional welcoming speeches, the temporary roll of delegates was referred to the committee on credentials, and Governor Stassen was elected temporary chairman. Though Stassen's election on the floor was unanimous, he had been selected by the committee on arrangements only after a dispute between the liberals and conservatives in the group. It was argued by some members of the committee that Glenn Frank, because of his extensive effort in formulating the preliminary platform, should be the keynoter, but he was unacceptable to certain ultraconservative members.[14]

The second session was an "Americanism-Patriotism" period devoted to speeches which merely served to stall for time while the committees worked on their reports. At the third session, Stassen gave his address. Though some reporters considered it "long and uninspired," it served the traditional function of setting the tone of the convention, and the Minnesota governor received a standing ovation when he finished. It is interesting to note that his principal points of stress, National Preparedness, Fifth Column Defense, and Governmental Effectiveness and Integrity, were still viable a dozen years later when the Republicans again selected a political amateur to conduct a "crusade." At 11:26 P.M., the convention recessed until the following morning.

Meanwhile, Willkie continued to pick up support. By the time of the keynote address, Baldwin and Company, Wall Street betting commissioners, placed Willkie in front of the field at even money. As a consequence of the Willkie Club volunteer movement and the hundreds of phone calls made by prominent businessmen to friends back home, thousands of messages demanding Willkie's nomination were pouring in to the delegates. To climax the efforts, the *New York Herald Tribune,* under the heading, "Wendell Willkie for President," printed a three-column appeal to the delegates on its front page which called him "Heaven's gift to the nation in its time of crisis," and added: ". . . such timing of the man and the hour

---

[14] Odegard, *op. cit.,* p. 50.

does not come often in history.[15] . . . We ask the convention to nominate Wendell Willkie for the Presidency."[16]

The first session of the convention's second day featured committee reports and a ringing speech by Permanent Chairman Joe Martin in which he declared that constitutional government was in danger of being extinguished. The evening session heard a speech by Herbert Hoover. He avowed that the Republicans were for peace and preparedness (though Republicans in Congress had opposed nearly every effort to arm or fortify the country's defenses) but that they were opposed to war except for defense. He called for a restoration of "American Living," and accused the New Deal of weakening the structure of liberty. The address was warmly received, and the ovation given to Hoover made it impossible for Martin to re-establish order for fifteen minutes. Undoubtedly there were delegates who would have liked to see Hoover emerge as the candidate, but the movement for Willkie was building up with such magnitude that by the time the balloting began, the former President was not seriously considered by the delegates. On the third ballot, Hoover received thirty-two votes, his highest total of the 1940 convention.

Outside the convention hall, another event was taking place that was to have a future impact on the Republican party. Harold Stassen, freed of the necessity for neutrality which bound him while he was temporary chairman, telephoned both Dewey and Willkie to ask for a clarification of their views. Later, he called in reporters and announced: "After weighing all the factors and in view of the critical situation facing this country, . . . I have decided to cast my vote on the first ballot for Willkie because I believe him best fitted for leadership in utilizing our mass-production system and preparing to make this country safe for any eventuality."[17] At least

---

[15] The paper used almost identical words recommending the nomination of Dwight D. Eisenhower in 1952.

[16] *New York Herald Tribune*, June 27, 1940, p. 1. Both C. Nelson Sparks and Harry Elmer Barnes have charged that Ogden Reid, publisher of the *Herald Tribune* at that time, was one of two men (the other was allegedly Thomas Lamont, New York financier) who dictated Willkie's nomination. That Willkie and the *Herald Tribune* were philosophically affiliated is evidenced by the following extract from a letter to the author by Philip Willkie. "During most of his years in New York, he was closely associated with the *New York Herald Tribune* and their news and editorial columns gave him full and complete treatment during not only his political career but also his business career and reflected his thinking."

[17] *New York Times*, June 27, 1940, p. 4.

one observer stated that there had been a tacit understanding all along that Stassen would support Willkie, because he had been chosen as the keynoter by Hamilton, who was known to be for Willkie.[18] In any event, Willkie asked Stassen to be his floor leader, and the young Minnesota governor worked tirelessly during the convention coordinating the utility magnate's campaign. He chose twelve floor leaders, including Halleck, Sinclair Weeks, Walter Hallanan, Governors Baldwin, Carr, and Vanderbilt, and a few of his own delegates from Minnesota, to obtain someone to keep in constant touch with every state delegation and to encourage the delegates to get on the Willkie bandwagon. It was a highly successful strategy, and coupled with the floor activities of Sam Pryor, Harold Talbott, and the scores of Willkie supporters circulating in and out of the hall, the entire operation worked very smoothly. It served to make Stassen a newly recognized force within the Republican party; on the other hand, it also meant that he incurred the political opposition of Tom Dewey, who was himself a force within the party who eventually proved to be capable of frustrating the thirty-three-year-old Minnesotan's future political aspirations.

But all of this was still four and eight years away. On that hot June night of 1940, Stassen was riding the tidal wave of support for another rising political personality who was receiving astounding support from throughout the nation. Nearly a million messages reached the delegates between Saturday and Tuesday nights demanding the Hoosier's nomination.[19] Kenneth F. Simpson told reporters that he had received more than one hundred thousand telegrams, letters, and postal cards during the twelve days preceding the balloting. "The sentiment in New York is overwhelmingly for Wendell Willkie," he said. "I have never seen anything like it."

Philadelphia also had never seen anything like it, for the enthusiasm of the Willkie Club members surpassed anything even the oldest observers could remember. It reminded historians of the Tammany Hall march of six hundred organization workers to the Democratic convention in Chicago in July of 1884. As tension continued to mount, delegates talked, argued, and wondered what decisions were being made elsewhere. Negotiators and representatives of the candidates hurried around, trying to arrange conferences or to trade votes in case of certain eventualities. Dewey estimated

[18] Dillon, *op. cit.*, p. 148.
[19] *New York Herald Tribune,* June 26, 1940, p. 1.

that his vote on the first ballot would run somewhere between 375 and 410 ballots, with the likelihood of its being above 400. "At least," he added, "I will have a minimum of one-hundred more votes than anyone else, according to my own discussions of the last twenty-four hours."[20]   Taft would not comment, but his supporters claimed the twenty-six-vote Texas delegation after the delegates had received both Willkie and the Senator in succession. Styles Bridges visited thirty-five different delegations, but no one knew at the time whether he was an emissary for the other candidates or whether he was actively campaigning for himself. Vandenberg refused to make a claim, but predicted that there would be no candidate named in a "smoke-filled room" at this convention. As a veteran politician, the Michigan senator could see that party discipline had broken down, that members of the national committee were already thinking more in terms of a colorful personality than party service, and that the events of the few days prior to the convention were having more effects on the delegates than the previous four years. The field was wide open — to the Old Guard and newcomers alike.

The convention adjourned after the Hoover speech and reassembled at two o'clock on the afternoon of June 25 to receive the report of the committee on resolutions, which was trying to frame the platform. Because the committee could not reach agreement, however, Martin had to recess the convention. The principal political and philosophical difficulty involved was the foreign relations plank. In the preliminary hearings, majority sentiment on the committee seemed to favor those individuals who advocated unlimited aid to Britain "short of War." As a result, Alf Landon, a pro-Ally member of the group working on the preliminary draft of the platform, was made chairman of the subcommittee on national defense and foreign policy.

Landon's work progressed relatively smoothly until President Roosevelt, with his shrewd sense of timing the dramatic, announced the appointment of 1936 vice-presidential candidate Frank Knox to the position of Secretary of the Navy and interventionist Republican Henry L. Stimson to the post of Secretary of War.[21]   Republican leaders in Philadelphia were appalled; both men were bitterly

---

[20] *New York Times,* June 25, 1940, p. 1.

[21] Stimson was seventy-three at the time. He had been Secretary of State under Hoover. Roosevelt had originally wanted Landon and Knox, but Landon agreed to accept only if the President would renounce a possible third term. Burns, *op. cit.,* p. 424.

denounced. Late in September of 1939, when President Roosevelt had suggested that there be an "adjournment of partisanship" during the European crisis, John Hamilton had rejected the idea, saying, "Nothing would be more disastrous to this nation than an adjournment of politics which would permit a black-out of domestic problems. . . . There is no reason to surrender our American birthright of frank and open discussion to any leadership. . . ."[22] Now Hamilton was even more infuriated. He literally read Stimson and Knox out of the party, and in his statement he actually sounded the keynote for a revised platform and even a revised campaign. He announced to the press: "Having entered the Cabinet, these men are no longer qualified to speak as Republicans for the Republican organization. . . . Since Colonel Knox and Colonel Stimson have long desired to intervene in the affairs of Europe and the *Democratic party has become the war party,* we may accept that issue at its face value."[23]

By accusing the Democrats of being the war party, Hamilton not only endeavored to label the Republicans the peace party, he also made Landon's position infinitely more tenuous. For eight days Landon's subcommittee had labored in one day-long session after another to write a keep-out-of-war-plank that would not offend those determined to aid the Allies. At one point in the discussion, the subcommittee proposed to leave the foreign relations plank up to the candidate who might be nominated, but this proposal was rejected by the isolationist faction. Now, all of the work had been futile. On June 25, C. Wayland Brooks of Illinois and Senator Henry Cabot Lodge, Jr., of Massachusetts entered the committee meetings to protest any Landon report endorsing aid to the Allies. Brooks read to the resolutions committee a strong noninterventionist platform that had been adopted a few weeks previously by the Republican delegation from Illinois; this platform made no mention of aid to anyone. He told the committee that the Illinois Republicans did not propose to be left out on a limb, to say nothing of the prevailing sentiment in the Middle West.[24] Supported by Senator Thomas of Idaho and Herbert K. Hyde of Oklahoma, the anti-war, anti-New Deal, anti-European involvement chairman of the com-

---

[22] Odegard, *op. cit.,* pp. 42-43.
[23] Italics mine. *New York Herald Tribune,* June 21, 1940, p. 1; see page 6 of this issue for comments by prominent Republicans.
[24] *New York Times,* June 26, 1940, p. 16.

mittee, Brooks forced a redraft of the contemplated statement of foreign policy making it more noninterventionist and including a sharp denunciation of the Roosevelt administration of international relations. The terms of the final statement, which Hyde claimed had unanimous approval, were not agreed upon until shortly before midnight of June 26. The national defense plank of the watered down version stated, after a condemnation of the New Deal: "The Republican party stands for Americanism, preparedness and peace. We accordingly fasten upon the New Deal full responsibility for our unpreparedness and for the consequent danger of involvement in war . . . we shall support all necessary and proper defense measures proposed by the Administration in its belated effort to make up for lost time; . . . We favor the extension to all peoples fighting for liberty, or whose liberty is threatened, of such aid as shall not be in violation of international law or inconsistent with the requirements of our own national defense."

This last statement was included at the insistence of Landon, aided by former Senator Walter Edge of New Jersey, but even it did not escape the isolationist axe. Landon originally had used the word "Allies," but this was dropped because Great Britain was considered at the time to be the only nation still at war with Germany, and we were not her ally. "Peoples fighting for liberty" was the substitute. The *New York Times* denounced the Republican claim of "preparedness" in view of the party's record in the Senate against increased appropriations for strategic materials, new planes, and ships, and H. L. Mencken cracked: "[The plank] is so written that it will fit both the triumph of democracy and the collapse of democracy, and approve both sending arms to England or sending only flowers."[25]

Actually, the approved plank was what the representatives of the forces sparring for power within the resolutions committee could agree upon; the compromises necessary to obtain approval were symbolic of the diverse attitudes within the party. Eastern seaboard presidential Republicans who were about to select the next GOP candidate were unable to dictate the national defense plank, and the congressional Republicans, though too divided to name the candidate, nevertheless exerted a veto power commensurate with the anti-involvement sentiment that split Republicans throughout the nation.

---

[25] *Time,* July 1, 1940, p. 17.

Committee members considered all other planks as "basket" proposals, vague general statements designed to offend no factions
within the party. Generally, these sections followed the Frank
report closely. When the convention reassembled at 4:45 P.M.,
Hyde presented the Republican platform of 1940. Brooks moved
its adoption and said: ". . . the voice of this Convention to the
people of America should be, above all, that we stand for *America
first,* and for *preparedness* to defend this country against any and
every form of attack. . . ."[26] Henry Cabot Lodge, Jr., seconded the
motion by presenting a summary of the resolutions committee report
which Peter Odegard termed "a masterpiece of equivocation, evasion, ambiguity and generalization."[27] In reality, the Republicans
produced a platform which suited nearly all of the candidates in
that virtually every positive statement on any issue of significance
to interest groups was qualified by a relative generality. And this
was as it should have been. This was the function of the platform —
to act as a catalytic agent for the many divergent opinions within
the party in a crucial and confusing year while reflecting the strongest pressures through qualified positive statements.

The delegates, after hearing a violent anti-interventionist blast in
which Hamilton Fish denounced President Roosevelt for leading the
country on the road to war, adopted the platform without debate.
For as *Time* put it, ". . . the expedient weasel words faded out of
mind as fast as ink dried on the newsprint. Something bigger was
afoot than mean, dishonest words. The trend that Willkie was in
front of spread like flood water."[28]

At 4:30 in the afternoon on June 27, before crowded galleries
which the Democrats and some Republicans charged were "packed"
with Willkie supporters, Chairman Martin called the state "Alabama" and the nominations began. Alabama yielded to New York
and John Lord O'Brian of New York placed the name of Thomas
E. Dewey before the convention. He told of the candidate's
success in checking racketeering in New York City and destroying
alliances between crime and politics by his prosecutions. He
characterized Dewey as a man of trustworthiness and proven ability
both as an executive and as a vote-getter, as demonstrated by
the fact that in 1938, when the young district attorney was a candi-

---

[26] *Proceedings,* pp. 152-53.
[27] Odegard, *op. cit.,* p. 52.
[28] *Time,* July 8, 1940, p. 12.

date for governor, he polled more votes in New York than had ever been cast for a Republican presidential nominee. When the speech was over, the New York delegation paraded down the aisles. Other state delegations with their standards quickly joined in the procession — Illinois, Oklahoma, Kentucky, Florida, Idaho, Wisconsin, South Carolina, Montana, and Tennessee. Martin was unable to restore order for twenty-five minutes, but, in intensity, the demonstration fell short of those which were to be given to Willkie and Taft. The managers of Dewey's campaign actually had been caught "flat-footed" in arranging the demonstration; they had not expected him to be placed in nomination so early and, as a result, many of his supporters had not reached the hall. Thus, to many of the Dewey supporters, the display was a disappointment. After seconding speeches, the secretary of the convention called the name of the next state, Arizona.

Arizona again yielded to New York so that Representative James W. Wadsworth could place the name of Frank E. Gannett, Rochester newspaper publisher, before the convention. Wadsworth presented Gannett as a successful businessman, a man of outstanding ability and enterprise, a thrifty candidate who understood both the system of government and foreign relations. Unfortunately for Gannett, his demonstration was handicapped by the lack of any great number of supporters among the delegates while his friends in the galleries were forbidden to participate. He received a two-minute round of applause after which it must have been obvious to him that the $500,000 he had poured into the effort to obtain the candidacy had been spent in vain.[29]

Arkansas yielded to Ohio, and Senator Taft was nominated by Grove Patterson, editor of the *Toledo Blade*. Patterson said that the Senator's equipment for leadership of the nation at this time of crisis consisted of experience, training, education, and ability. He quipped, "If our candidate is not the best backslapper, he has the best backbone," and called Taft "as common as an old shoe." He cited Taft as courageous, imaginative, distinguished, and above all, a great vote-getter. Taft receive a more impressive reception than Dewey. His supporters were better organized and there were more placards, banners, and standards to impress the spectators.

The next eight states on the roll passed, and the clerk finally came to Indiana. This was the moment for which the galleries had been

---

[29] *New York Times*, June 27, 1940, p. 1, and *Time*, July 8, 1940, p. 12.

waiting. ". . . from the moment the nominations were opened the jammed and frenzied galleries set up a chant of 'We Want Willkie!' . . . When the chairman demanded that they watch their manners since they were guests, one (spectator) . . . shouted: 'Guests, hell! We're the People!' "[30] In a hard-hitting, well-read speech written by Russell Davenport, Congressman Charles Halleck of Indiana reviewed the achievements, the life, and the attributes of Wendell Willkie. He claimed that Willkie understood, from experience, the problems of business, labor, and agriculture; that Willkie had become, in nine weeks, the hope of people in every walk of life and in every corner of the land. He cited Willkie's position as a utility head as an illustration of his success. He admitted that Willkie had only recently become a member of the GOP, but asked, "Is the Republican Party a closed corporation? Do you have to be born in it?" Cries of "No" came from the galleries. Halleck's conclusion was a signal for pandemonium to reign: "There is a man big enough to be President of the United States: Wendell Lewis Willkie."

The words produced the convention's most tumultuous demonstration. Though Willkie's parade had fewer placards and fewer standards representing state delegations than those for Dewey or Taft, the roar from the galleries made it the loudest, the most determined, and the most impressive to the millions of listeners outside the hall. Led by Mayor Rolland Marvin of Syracuse, and relatively unplanned, it actually was more spontaneous than the other demonstrations; it resembled a cheering session rather than a conventional demonstration by those who would ultimately make the decision on the nominee.[31] Mingled with the applause for Willkie were the first "boos" from the floor of the convention. They were particularly evident when Halleck asserted that his candidate would stand with his party, "win, lose or draw," and when he described the Willkie boom as growing "without campaign funds." Many delegates resented the uprising of a well-heeled newcomer and they resented the shouting galleries that were supporting him. Delegates are professionals, chosen in most states only after extended party service. They will support a potential winner, but they are essentially party loyalists, and during this period of nomination in the 1940 convention, they were devoted to the party. It was obvious

---

[30] Stone, *op. cit.*, p. 354.

[31] Halleck, according to Dillon (*op. cit.*, p. 160), had made no provisions for a demonstration following his nominating speech.

that more than frantic galleries were needed to place them on the Indiana bandwagon.

After the uproar had subsided, Willkie's nomination was seconded by Representative Bruce Barton of New York, who shouted: "I do not mind those boos. You will be in the parade next January when he is inaugurated President." Miss Ann Stuart of Minnesota presented her endorsement and Governor Raymond E. Baldwin of Connecticut concluded the seconds with what Sinclair Weeks called "really one of the best speeches I have ever listened to." There was more applause, after which the convention was recessed until the following morning, and the delegates went back to their hotels.

Awaiting the delegates out on the streets, however, were the Willkie volunteers, a persuading, shouting, exhorting mass. Many distributed newspapers — some from the delegates' home towns — all demanding the nomination of Wendell Willkie. The delegates were sick of the badgering, the demands, and the arguments, and yet the streets were filled with crusading Willkie enthusiasts urging them to switch to the utility magnate. Even the most sophisticated and hard-bitten old political observers — Frank Kent, Westbrook Pegler, Walter Lippmann, Dorothy Thompson, and Mark Sullivan — insisted that only Willkie had the glamour and freshness to run against the President, and more important, that only Willkie understood the implications of the fall of France and the Fascist threats.

When the delegates returned to their hotels, they found additional evidence of vigorous support by Willkie volunteers. The Willkie Mailing Committee, formed three months earlier by Oren Root at the suggestion of Harold Talbott, presented them with bundled petitions and chain letters containing thousands of names of people from their districts who wanted Wendell Willkie nominated for the presidency. John Chamberlain wrote: ". . . the 'amateurism' of Willkie's approach had a professional skillfulness behind it; and the Willkie strategy proved the Dewey-Taft-Joe Pew 'professionals' to be the . . . real amateurs."[32] Willkie's supporters had, of course, organized many of the latent and actual interest groups that would support a businessman. Lawyers received messages from their firms and their clients; businessmen heard from their creditors and their customers; delegates in other fields from their constituents of all classes; they were literally deluged with telegrams and letters.

---

[32] *Yale Review*, 30(ns) (September, 1940), 48.

A few opponents of Willkie charged that the messages were "canned" and that there had been a systematic control over them from one central source, but this was never proved. Many Willkie followers belonged to both the Associated Willkie Clubs and the Willkie Mailing Committee. That members of these organizations all over America contributed to, inspired, and solicited for, the avalanche of messages there can be no doubt. But the convention deluge was something more in 1940. Many individuals actually were spontaneously inspired to wire delegates, and the combined movement and its publicity produced a phenomenon that gained constant momentum until the balloting began. Oren Root stated: "There was absolutely no one directing it. There couldn't have been, it was too colossal!" and Sam Pryor substantiated Root by declaring, "The telegram barrage was spontaneous. There is no possible way this great spark of enthusiasm can be manufactured."[33] The spadework had been done by Willkie for months; he was a businessman who desired and received the support of business; he was an attractive, vigorous candidate in a year when a vacuum of leadership existed within the Republican party; he had had no previous political experience — a qualification that appeals to many Americans; he had hundreds of friends among the people of the financial world; and the Willkie Clubs had brought thousands of persons who ordinarily were apolitical into an association through which they were eager to influence their delegates. These were the characteristics of the candidate and the era that produced the spontaneity for Wendell Willkie.

The "spontaneous" uprising for the Hoosier received an assist from the galleries, and this prompted a number of the anti-Willkie Republicans to attempt to determine the manner in which the galleries had been filled with spectators so overwhelmingly in favor of

[33] C. Nelson Sparks (*op. cit.*, pp. 16-17) charged that "thousands of telegrams were unauthorized and unsent by the persons whose names were signed to them," but on July 11, 1940, Senator Guy Gillette, chairman of the Senate Campaign Expenditures Committee, stated to the press that the members of his committee had agreed unanimously that information given to it to justify an investigation of reports that a high pressure telegram drive was employed in the preconvention campaign of Wendell Willkie was insufficient to warrant committee action "at this time." *New York Times,* July 12, 1940, p. 16. A similar statement was made in the final committee report. See *Report of the United States Senate Special Committee to Investigate Presidential, Vice-Presidential, and Senatorial Campaign Expenditures, 1940,* Senate Report No. 47, p. 31. (77th Cong., 1st Sess., Feb. 15, 1941).

Willkie. Colonel R. B. Creager, national committeeman from Texas, a member of the committee on arrangements and a Taft floor leader, together with former Senator David A. Reed of Pennsylvania charged that the galleries were packed with Willkie supporters who led his demonstration. The two men, and Owlett W. Mason, national committeeman from the Keystone State, demanded that Samuel S. Lewis, assistant sergeant at arms, make an investigation. The investigation revealed that the committee on arrangements, of which Samuel F. Pryor was chairman, had issued thousands of tickets admitting the bearers to Entrance 23 of the convention hall.

When this was reported to Creager, he lashed out at Pryor, saying, "You issued them without authority from the committee for the candidacy of your man Willkie. You have perpetrated an outrage on the Republican Party and dealt unfairly with the other candidates. You will hear more of this. No other candidate knew of the issuance of these tickets." Mason and Creager declared their intention to ask John Hamilton to put new doormen in the galleries the following night, fearing that a similar uprising might take place during the balloting. Creager wanted only those persons possessing the previously and carefully allotted official tickets to gain admission.

Pryor, however, maintained that the galleries were not "stacked." He issued standing room tickets to anyone and everyone who wanted them; they were practically unlimited in number. He said:

Those tickets went to the average people on the street who, I knew, were ardent supporters of Wendell Willkie. Every regular ticket was numbered and allotted. Taft had as many standing room tickets as anyone; the only restriction on those tickets was that of the fire marshal who closed the doors when the hall was legally full. A political party belongs to the people; it is not a country club — not a private organization. The people had every right to be there. On the following night I again ordered those at the doors to keep them open for anyone who wanted to stand and watch the proceedings until the fire marshal halted their entry.[34]

The assembling of the convention on the morning of the fourth day was anticlimatic; additional candidates were yet to be nominated, but most observers felt that one of the three nominated on the previous day was certain to be the GOP standard-bearer.

Verne Marshall, who was neither a delegate nor an alternate to

---

[34] Interview with Mr. Pryor.

the convention, received unanimous consent to nominate Hanford MacNider for the state of Iowa. He praised MacNider as the only battle commander who was a candidate for the nomination, a holder of the Distinguished Service Cross, a former National Commander of the American Legion who hated war, and a former United States Minister to Canada.

Senator Arthur Vandenberg was placed in nomination by Congressman Roy O. Woodruff of Michigan, Chairman of the Republican caucus of the House of Representatives, who asked that "in view of the solemnity of this occasion, in view of the tragic conditions facing the country and the world . . . there be no demonstration . . . following my remarks." There was none.

Woodruff praised Vandenberg as a man of social vision who wrote the amendment to the Banking Act of 1933 under which the FDIC was inaugurated; as a faithful "protectionist" on tariff legislation; as a "hard and popular campaigner"; and as a man who had never failed his party or his nation. He declared that Vandenberg's record was "substantially his Party's platform"; that the Michigan senator had spent a lifetime defending George Washington's Farewell Address; and that he had "long since ceased to be an 'isolationist' in the sense that we can be immune to great events in this fore-shortened world, but who long since became an unchangeable 'insulationist' in a sense that we must think, speak, dream, hope and plan for 'AMERICA FIRST AND AMERICA LAST' in dealing with the forces . . . in other lands."

At this stage of the proceedings, Vandenberg thought that the final showdown on the nomination would be between Willkie and himself. As a result, he rejected a Dewey offer of the vice-presidential nomination, made through Senator Bridges by saying: "Tell Dewey that I think the vice presidency is very important and that if I were not a Senator I would take it, but I think — as I did in 1936 — that my place on the Senate floor is more important than on the Senate rostrum. Also tell him that if he will take the vice-presidency with me . . . I shall be a pre-pledged one-termer [and] he will be in direct line for the White House in 1944. Also tell him that if this is too much for him to swallow all at once, I'll make him a sporting proposition. I'll meet him at eleven o'clock and flip a coin to see which end of the ticket we each take."[35]

[35] Arthur H. Vandenberg, Jr., *The Private Papers of Senator Vandenberg* (Boston, 1952), pp. 6-7.

Vandenberg heard no more from Dewey, though he and the New York district attorney probably could have won the nomination as a combined slate. As it was, defections from both men were taking place while the nominations were in progress, and the move to Willkie continued. Later, Vandenberg wrote in his diary: "The Willkie blitzkrieg hit me just as it hit everybody else."

Back on the convention floor, Congressman Foster Stearns of New Hampshire nominated Senator Styles Bridges for President as a man of "spunk," "hard work," and an advocate of "intelligent liberalism." This speech was followed by the nomination of Senator Charles L. McNary of Oregon by William A. Ekwall, a former member of Congress and a delegate for the state of Oregon, who declared:

> Charles L. McNary is typically a self-made man. In 1918 Senator McNary was elected to his first full term in the Senate and has since been re-elected three times by ever-increasing and overwhelming majorities. . . . During the past seven years Senator McNary has been of the Republican minority and has been recognized as shrewd, resourceful and a splendid strategist. . . . His judgment is universally respected because it is always mature and always progressive. . . . Senator McNary has been a friend of labor . . . Senator McNary's record on farm legislation is too well known throughout the country to need any detailed discussion at this time. . . . Senator McNary has a tremendous vote appeal to those in all walks of life. . . . Senator McNary is perhaps the most beloved Senator of the present day.[36]

Senator James J. Davis of Pennsylvania, in nominating Governor Arthur H. James for the Presidency, asked that all demonstrations and parades in his behalf be postponed until after James had been nominated by the convention itself. Davis lauded James as a man with practical experience in government, and added, "Government is not industry." He called James a fearless, tireless, magnetic, vigorous, and inspiring campaigner; a man of the people; and a man of courage and will, pluck and skill, an administrator who understands government and freedom.

The final name to be placed before the convention was that of Governor Harlan J. Bushfield of South Dakota. He was described by former United States Senator Gladys Pyle of South Dakota as a successful lawyer, businessman, and administrator.

The roll thus completed, the convention recessed for an hour and a half before the balloting on the nominees.

---

[36] *Proceedings*, pp. 255-62.

HOW WILLKIE WON

The convention reassembled promptly at 4:30. At 4:35, the balloting opened: Alabama gave 7 votes to Dewey and 6 to Taft; Arizona's 6 went to Frank Gannett; it was not until Arkansas was called that Willkie received his first 2 votes. California gave 7 votes to Willkie, but cast 1 vote more than it was entitled to — a roll call was demanded. Colorado's Ralph Carr was able to muster only 3 votes for Willkie on the first ballot, but Connecticut contributed its slate of 16. Georgia's vote was protested; over gallery shouts of "No," an additional roll call was held. Illinois' vote was 52 for Dewey, 2 for Taft, and 4 for Willkie; Indiana's delegation gave 9 of its 28 to the former Hoosier; Minnesota contributed only 6 Stassen-controlled votes of 22; New Jersey, 12 of 32, all of which had been pledged to Dewey. The balloting went on, Willkie obtaining 8 out of New York's 92, and small numbers of votes from nine of the remaining twenty-three delegations. With each Willkie vote the galleries roared, and while the first ballot was being tabulated, the spectators chanted, "We want Willkie." The hall was so filled with confusion that several delegates protested that they could not hear what was going on. George H. Moses of New Hampshire complained that there were many people in the aisles "buttonholing delegates who have no right to be on the floor of the Convention." Chairman Martin called upon the sergeants at arms to clear the aisles, and ordered the clerk to read the results of the first ballot. The clerk stated:

The result of the first ballot is as follows: 1,000 votes were cast. Bridges, 28; Bushfield, 9; Dewey, 360; Gannett, 33; James, 74; McNary, 13; MacNider, 34; Taft, 189; Vandenberg, 76; Willkie, 105; Hoover, 17; Martin, 44; and Capper, 18.

Willkie had received votes from twenty-five states. "The Dewey men squirmed; 360 was not 400, much less 450. The Taft men sat tight; too early to pour in their extra strength."[37]

On the second ballot, California gave Willkie 2 additional votes; Colorado and Delaware added 2 more with the galleries' riotous sanction. The first break came when Maine shifted 9 of her 13 votes from Bridges to Willkie. Four votes were given from Maryland; 7 new ballots from Massachusetts; 7 more from Missouri; 5 from New Jersey. Willkie received 5 additional votes from New York, 4 from North Carolina, and 3 from West Virginia. It was

[37] *Newsweek*, July 8, 1940, p. 12.

obvious that Dewey was slipping, but while Willkie was on the rise, so was Taft.

The secretary read the results of the second poll:

1,000 votes were cast. Bridges, 9; Capper, 18; Dewey, 338; Gannett, 30; Hoover, 21; James, 66; La Guardia, 1; Martin, 26; McNary, 10; MacNider, 34; Taft, 203; Vandenberg, 73; and Willkie, 171.

After 6:45, the managers of the candidates agreed to recess until 8:30. Harold Stassen, who had set up a complete Willkie floor organization with someone responsible for the delegation of every state (coordinated from Stassen's seat) and who also had a direct wire telephone to Willkie installed underneath his chair, hurried to a conference with Alf Landon in a freight elevator behind the stage of the convention hall. "This was the only place we could avoid interruptions," Stassen wrote, "and with a policeman at the entrance to the elevator, we talked through the situation, and Mr. Landon decided to swing his votes to Mr. Willkie."[38]

During the recess, deals of all kinds were considered, and some were already too late. Phone calls, secret meetings, hurried conversations were all concerned with the same question: Could Willkie be stopped? Stassen called Willkie and said: "You are gambling with the biggest thing you've ever gambled with . . . we could use Pennsylvania's seventy-two votes at this point. Shall I have a talk with Joe Pew?" Willkie hesitated and then replied, "No." He wanted no commitment to Joe Pew.[39]

As the second ballot was being taken, Willkie, with a small group

---

[38] Letter to the author from Harold E. Stassen. Sinclair Weeks, in his personal notes on the convention, recorded an interesting sidelight on the situation in New York: "Simpson and Marvin were most anxious to poll the delegation on the third ballot, because they thought it would produce two results: first, that it would give the folks back home an opportunity to learn how their delegates were voting; and second, that it would create quite favorable propaganda to have men like Bert Snell and others to stand up and declare themselves for Wendell Willkie. Stassen and some others were inclined to disagree on the ground that to poll 92 delegates would take a lot of time and create unfavorable reaction and that it might be interpreted as injecting the Simpson-Dewey feud into the Convention proceedings. The matter was argued back and forth, and after changing the decision several times, it was finally decided not to do it on the third ballot. However, New York voting on the third ballot — 17 for Willkie, Walter Mack, President of Pepsi-Cola Company and a delegate told Simpson that he proposed to call for a poll regardless, that he had been cheated out of a vote for Willkie on two ballots and that he was going to have an opportunity to see what was going on. The poll, therefore, was taken and resulted in 27 votes for Willkie instead of the 17 previously announced."

[39] Bromley, *op. cit.*, p. 485.

of reporters, listened to the radio in his hotel room. He conducted a running commentary on the balloting. As his vote mounted, he cut into a steak, and followed this with a bowlful of raspberries. When Tennessee gave him five votes, he smiled and said: "That's where that utility fight of mine occurred."[40]

Taft forces were confident. The professionals had planned well for Dewey's decline and they were sure that they could pick up the votes finally released by such candidates as Hoover, James, Mac-Nider, and Martin from safe Republican areas of the country. A few observers were so certain that the Republican party, in its hour of resurgence, would select its most representative figure that they had stories of his nomination on the streets before the third ballot had been taken. But these observations were premature. The crowds in the street were still violently pro-Willkie; messages from home continued to pour in to the delegates; and the Stassen floor organization for Willkie was working superbly. In addition, the galleries kept up their agonizing, compelling chant, "We want Willkie!"

The third session of the convention's fourth day was convened at 8:30 in the evening. After the invocation, Chairman Martin immediately ordered the secretary to call the roll for the third ballot. Some large breaks developed. New York changed 14 votes to Willkie; Delaware went entirely into the Willkie column; Joe Martin released 21 Massachusetts votes, 20 of which went to the Hoosier; even the Pennsylvania delegation raised its 5 votes for Willkie on the second ballot to 15 on the third. Dewey lost 23 votes but was still leading with 315; Taft gained 9; Willkie's total, increased by 88 votes, was now second in rank with 259.[41]

On the fourth ballot, the Dewey vote dropped to 250.[42] Governor Dwight Green, the chairman of the Illinois delegation, temporarily passed, then a few minutes later announced that the delegation had

---

[40] *Newsweek,* July 8, 1940, p. 16.

[41] If Dewey had promptly released his delegation to Taft, the victory would have gone to Taft. But Dewey delayed and did not send word to Taft of his support until after the third ballot. By this time the bandwagon movement for Willkie was already started. Dillon, *op. cit.,* p. 161. It was also after the third ballot that Governor Baldwin tried unsuccessfully to get Joseph N. Pew, Jr., of Pennsylvania, to switch to Willkie. When Baldwin reported Pew's refusal, Willkie reportedly said, "Pew be damned!" *Ibid.,* p. 163.

[42] Other candidates had the following totals on the third ballot: Bridges, 1; Gannett, 11; Hoover, 32; James, 59; MacNider, 28; McNary, 10; Vandenberg, 72. *Proceedings,* p. 290.

changed 22 votes to Taft and 3 to Willkie. Willkie, however, continued to acquire additional ballots in nearly every state in which he had previously made an inroad. On this ballot, he gained 47 votes to Taft's 43; Willkie was ahead with 306 but Taft was beginning his climb with 254.[43]

Martin moved immediately to the fifth ballot. This was the time for action. Dewey was obviously out of the race; MacNider was about to release 26 crucial votes — nearly all from the Midwest; and the Arthur James-Joe Pew combination still had 51 undecided votes from Pennsylvania.

Taft received 10 of Arkansas' 12 votes and the bulk of MacNider's relinquished delegates. He needed the James votes and most of those who left Dewey in order to catch Willkie. Willkie picked up 34 votes before the secretary reached the name of Kansas. Then, Alf Landon gave Willkie the state's entire delegation.[44] New York switched 40 votes to Willkie while New Jersey and North Carolina each moved more votes to the Willkie column. Dewey's support collapsed as his total dwindled to 57. Pennsylvania's James vote was crucial; if it had gone to Taft, he would have been only one vote behind Willkie with almost certain additional support from Wisconsin, California, Illinois, and Oregon on the sixth ballot. Pew, however, chose to hold out; 51 votes were again cast for the Pennsylvania governor. As evidence of the intensity of the race, it should be noted that both Taft and Willkie increased their totals on the fifth ballot by exactly the same number of votes, 123. Willkie obtained 429 votes, 72 short of the nomination, while Taft received 377.[45]

Earlier in the evening, the Taft forces had decided to stay and fight it out that night rather than vote for an adjournment. Now, however, the time was 12:20 on Friday morning. Governor Bricker,

---

[43] Votes for the remaining candidates on the fourth ballot were: Bridges, 1; Gannett, 4; Hoover, 31; James, 56; McNary, 8; MacNider, 26; Vandenberg, 61; absent, 3. *Proceedings,* p. 301.

[44] The following morning *PM* credited Landon with being the "hero" behind Willkie's victory. The paper said Landon had decided that a Taft ticket would be controlled by Hoover and possibly bossed by Joe Pew. Willkie, with all his political and personal handicaps visible in him, was, therefore, Landon's man. *PM,* June 28, 1940, pp. 6-7.

[45] Totals for the other candidates: Gannett, 1; Hoover, 20; James, 59; McNary, 9; MacNider, 4; Vandenberg, 42; absent, 2. *Proceedings,* p. 306. "Willkie had previously asked one thing of Joe Martin: 'If the tide is running my way, you will not recess.' Martin promised and kept his word." Source withheld by request.

floor manager for Senator Taft, tried to move for a recess — and an opportunity to stem the Willkie tide the following day; he was too late. Joe Martin had called for a sixth ballot.

During the balloting by the first few states on the sixth ballot, Willkie gained few new votes. Maine, which had been strong for Willkie since the second ballot, passed.[46] Back in the hotel room, Willkie, losing some of his composure and confidence, admitted, "Well, he [Taft] might get it. At least I scared them." The clerk reached the name of Michigan — a state which, up to this ballot, had given its vote to Arthur Vandenberg. As the state was called, Howard Lawrence of Grand Rapids, campaign manager for Vandenberg, walked to the speaker's platform and announced that Vandenberg had released the Michigan delegation. The results of a poll taken after the action were: Hoover, 1; Taft, 2; Willkie, 35.[47]

---

[46] On the previous ballot, Maine, having started on the second ballot with 9 votes for Willkie, finally brought in her 4 remaining votes for Willkie, making it unanimous; but on the sixth ballot, these 4 votes decided to switch back to Taft. As Maine voted just prior to Michigan, the Willkie strategists conferred to determine if it would be wise to have Maine pass so as not to show a loss just before Michigan and other states voted. Stassen thought it wise to do this, so Weeks suggested the action to Bob Verrill, chairman of the Maine delegation, who, when Maine was called upon, then passed the delegation.

[47] Mary Earhart Dillon, *op. cit.*, pp. 165-66, has written that the Michigan "break" came as the result of the payment of a political debt to John Hamilton by Frank D. McKay, then the national committeeman from Michigan. Dr. Dillon asserted that in 1936 Hamilton was influential in terminating some bad publicity McKay was receiving from the Hearst papers. "Therewith, McKay promised to give aid when called upon. 'You have a large credit in my bank,' he told Hamilton. Now after the third ballot in the 1940 Convention Hamilton decided it was time to make use of this credit, and so he sought out McKay and told him he wanted the Michigan votes for Willkie as soon as Vandenberg released the delegation. 'But,' replied the Michigan politician, 'I am in a hell of a fix. Mrs. Vandenberg has just sent me a note saying to turn the votes over to Bob Taft.' 'Well,' said Hamilton, 'that is just too bad. But I have to have those votes. You owe me a great deal more than you owe the Senator's wife.' The reminder of a political obligation was effective. McKay agreed to deliver the votes."

In a letter to the author dated July 21, 1952, Mr. McKay wrote: "Mary Earhart Dillon's quotation . . . is entirely incorrect. . . . Arthur Vandenberg was interested in Taft and a considerable number of the delegates from Michigan felt that way in case Vandenberg withdrew. . . . When we arrived in Philadelphia some days in advance of the convention the delegates talked over the matter informally and they were all quite satisfied Vandenberg had not made much headway and undoubtedly would withdraw early, and so instructed me to meet with some of the Taft directors in a confidential meeting at the Union Club. I did so, and after we went into the

The spectators in the galleries cheered wildly! The Pennsylvania delegation had gone into caucus to determine whether or not to remain with James; "News of the Michigan switch fell on them there like a bombshell, for 29 diehards had just voted to stick with James and let the other 43 go to Willkie." Minnesota gave Willkie 1 vote more than it had on the fifth ballot; Missouri increased her contribution to him by 5; New Jersey boosted his total by giving him the entire state delegation of 32 votes for the first time. Nebraska passed,[48] but Oregon, after a poll that resulted in 3 votes for Taft and 7 for Willkie, threw all 10 to Willkie. Pennsylvania passed temporarily and the balloting continued. Utah and Vermont placed Willkie within 15 votes of the nomination. Virginia then cast 16 votes for Willkie and made the total 502, or more than enough for the nomination. It was all over! Martin recognized former Senator David A. Reed, who cast Pennsylvania's entire 72 votes for Willkie.[49]

---

consideration of their request for the support of Mr. Taft upon the withdrawal of Vandenberg and before I had an opportunity to call our delegates together the early edition of the Detroit Free Press ran a big streamer across the front page stating that the Michigan delegation had just made a deal . . . to go for Taft. This irritated the Michigan delegates considerably and placed them in a more receptive mood to go to Willkie. John Hamilton had nothing to do with Michigan going to Willkie. Sam Pryor was doing Willkie's undercover work and Willkie was likewise doing much himself by contacting delegates on the telephone. . . . I never asked, nor did John Hamilton, ever intercede with the Hearst newspapers on my behalf. I do not now recall any bad publicity they were giving me in 1936. The quotation alleged to have been made by me, 'you have a large credit in my bank' — is pure bunk and did not happen. . . . I did not know, nor never had met Mrs. Vandenberg up to that time, nor did she ever at any time send me a note of any kind, nor did I at any time say, 'I am in a hell of a fix.' John Hamilton never has mentioned to this day Mrs. Vandenberg's name to me. . . . Our delegates had decided to swing to Willkie as soon as Vandenberg withdrew on the day prior to the beginning of the Convention."

A sentence in the Vandenberg diary reporting that Taft had made a checkup on the Michigan delegation that had convinced him that the delegates would vote for Willkie when released tends to bear out Mr. McKay rather than Dr. Dillon. Arthur Vandenberg, Jr., *op. cit.*, p. 7.

[48] *Proceedings,* p. 311. A few minutes later, the Nebraska vote was announced as 6 votes for Taft and 8 for Willkie. This change of vote, however, was not recorded and the secretary announced the results of the sixth ballot as 998 votes for Willkie with 2 delegates absent. *Ibid.,* p. 319. The error has never been rectified; the nomination was not unanimous. See a letter to the *Chicago Tribune,* August 20, 1951, p. 18, from the Rev. Fred Hall, delegate from the Third Nebraska District to the 1940 convention.

[49] Reed thought that he was voting in time to put Willkie over the number required for the nomination. This was caused by the confusion

John Bricker moved that the nomination be made unanimous, but Martin allowed him only to change the Ohio vote to Willkie. The clerk finished the roll as Martin accepted the various last-minute switches to the Willkie bandwagon. Governor Bricker, in the midst of the wild shouting, then moved that the nomination be made unanimous. The motion was seconded by J. Russel Sprague[50] of New York, who thanked the delegates for supporting Governor Dewey; by David S. Ingalls of Ohio, who said that Taft promised to join earnestly and sincerely in electing Willkie as the next President; by Senator Thomas; and by Governor James. Chairman Martin read a congratulatory message from Herbert Hoover and thanked the delegates on behalf of Willkie, with whom he had just talked on the telephone. Governor Stassen then obtained the floor to express his sincere appreciation of the fair way in which the participants of the convention had conducted themselves. He moved that the convention be recessed until the following afternoon. It was 1:57 A.M. on Friday, June 28.

On the following day, the convention reassembled to select a running mate for Willkie. Harold Knutson nominated Congressman Dewey Short of Missouri for Vice-President, and W. S. Moscrip, also of Minnesota, nominated Senator Charles L. McNary for the post. In the balloting, McNary was the overwhelming choice of the convention, receiving 890 votes to 108 for Short. Actually, McNary had been chosen by Willkie, Pryor, Bridges, and a few others early in the morning after the convention had adjourned. Some weeks earlier, Willkie had promised Governor Baldwin that he would support him for the Vice-Presidency, but this pledge now had to be abrogated in order to give the ticket the conventional balance. Baldwin took the news with a smile, and Joe Martin was asked to extend the invitation to McNary. McNary, who had returned to Washington, quickly agreed to the proposal.

Democrats were quick to point out that McNary had supported TVA and the SEC, agencies Willkie had criticized so forcefully, and that he had voted against all of the measures which aided European nations or made America more adequately prepared for war. More-

---

resulting from the change in votes by Oregon. Actually, Pennsylvania delegates had not voted unanimously for Willkie!

[50] On June 12, J. Russel Sprague had been elected national committeeman by a vote of 55 to 37 over the incumbent, anti-Dewey Kenneth Simpson, who then worked for Willkie's nomination. *New York Times,* June 13, 1940, p. 1.

over, Willkie had staunchly advocated reciprocal trade, while Mc-Nary had always been a protectionist. Therefore, some individuals thought that the Republicans could have found a more satisfactory running mate for the meteoric Hoosier, and that McNary's selection represented a blunder.[51] To call this choice a blunder ignores the realities of our party system. Factionalism is one of the forces that limits the selection of the vice-presidential nominee, and the McNary nomination was thoroughly consistent with the loose, confederate nature of American parties. Moreover, it fit the pattern of 1940, for only a party thoroughly entrenched in power can afford the luxury of a single-ideology ticket. The Republican party had been out of power eight years, and was philosophically split just about as Willkie and McNary were. To be sure, this would have made for doubtful party responsibility and immature party government if the ticket had been successful. But campaigns are not congressional governments in action, and the Republicans in Philadelphia needed a ticket that would appeal to many anti-New Deal emotional symbols. They were given such a ticket. Willkie was, as President Roosevelt stated on several occasions, the strongest candidate the GOP could have chosen in 1940, and McNary, with his extensive experience in the Senate as a party regular, strengthened, rather than weakened, the Republican slate.

At 4:30 in the afternoon, a rain-soaked, confetti-covered Wendell Willkie, accompanied by Mrs. Willkie, was introduced to the convention by Chairman Martin. He told the delegates that he had just come to thank them, that he had made no pledges or promises, that he expected to conduct a crusading campaign to bring unity to all classes for the preservation of freedom. In conclusion, he cried: "So, you Republicans, I call upon you to join me, help me. . . . We cannot fail if we stand together in our united fight!" Willkie's expression, "you Republicans," piqued some members of the Old Guard. They had nominated for the Republican presidency a man who had voted for Democrats just two years earlier, and they had hoped that he was thoroughly in the GOP. Now the seeds of suspicion opened again.

But the people didn't notice. Willkie put on an impressive performance. Marquis Childs wrote that it was perhaps *the* high

---

[51] For additional information on the political differences that existed between Willkie and McNary, see a speech given by John W. Boehne, Jr., Democrat from Indiana, in the House of Representatives, *Congressional Record*, vol. 86, p. 13938 (76th Cong., 3rd Sess., July 3, 1940).

moment of the entire Willkie campaign as the candidate stood bathed in spotlights amid the cheering throngs on the floor.[52] No one was challenging the generalities of speech. The crowds were united in spirit, and there was an American dream — an unknown, an underdog, an Indiana businessman who had made good — on the threshold of the American presidency. After Willkie smiled and waved to the galleries, he said, "I think I'll go home and sleep for a week."

The Willkie nomination was loudly hailed by those Republicans who were looking for a fresh and magnetic personality and by those who were engaged in business, finance, and advertising.[53] Willkie had been selected in spite of his big business background,[54] in spite of his former membership in the Democratic party. The press throughout the free world hailed the news with rejoicing. In Britain, Lord Beaverbrook's *London Daily Express* commented: "Aid for us ceases to be an issue in American politics. Both sides are for it!" In the United States, the large northern newspapers almost unani-

[52] Marquis Childs, *I Write from Washington* (New York, 1942), p. 200.

[53] John Chamberlain evaluated the nomination in terms of the party and Willkie as a person. He wrote: "At Philadelphia the candidacy of Senator Robert Taft stood for party government as against rule of the party by a dominating personality. But the nomination of Mr. Willkie, ex-Democrat, meant that party government had become less important to a majority of the delegates than choosing an effective personality, a man with charm to compete with F.D.R. Such a personality is bound to lead under any circumstances; he may work in harmony with the party, but the terms will be set from above. And with the Republicans and the Democrats standing more or less on identical platforms, the case for party government must inevitably seem weak to the voters: It is the man that counts." "Candidates and Speeches," *Yale Review*, 30 (ns) (September, 1940), 51.

[54] Few people, at that time, appreciated what an outstanding feat Willkie had accomplished. Harold Laski, in *The American Presidency*, stated: " . . . The first four presidents of the United States almost nominated themselves, and, among their successors, there was hardly a candidate for the nomination who was not a person of considerable political consequence. One feature, indeed, is constant. No presidential candidate in the whole record has been a business man. The vocation, clearly, is a full-time one; and the qualities which make for business success make, also, against the possibility of nomination. . . . Business men have played a not inconsiderable part in the convention as king-makers; but it is a curious fact that in a civilization perhaps more dominated by business than any other, they have had to surrender the hope of being king. . . . The business man . . . is likely to be important in negativing ambitions the realization of which would not be regarded with favor by the big interests. But, on the record, he must be the power behind the throne; he cannot hope to occupy it." Harold J. Laski, *The American Presidency, An Interpretation* (New York, 1940), p. 48.

mously applauded the selection of the convention. The business and financial community was more than pleased, but astute observers realized that Willkie would have to have the support of more than the press and the business world. Alf Landon had had both elements with him in 1936 and had suffered an ignominious defeat. Organized labor leaders, other than John L. Lewis, were not enthusiastic about a corporation leader for President, but liberal Republicans hoped that their candidate could force a significantly large defection from the Democrats among the independent and middle-class vote to carry the election. Willkie had no legislative record following the Old Guard line on labor, national defense, and social legislation, and it was hoped that his own discussions of liberalism would induce enough members of the skilled and semi-skilled classes to support him to return the GOP to power.

First, however, the American people wanted an explanation. They wanted to know how and why a former Democrat, an avowed candidate only seven weeks before the convention, and a tycoon of big business without previous political experience could capture the nomination of a major political party. The answers came from foes and friends alike. Senator George Norris, who was Willkie's most vociferous opponent in the Senate, claimed that Wall Street touched a button and the already existing utility machine, nationwide in scope and obeying "its master's voice," flooded the nation with propaganda for the nomination of Willkie.[55] He declared: "Willkie is Insull the second. He is head of a great utility empire. The power trust . . . gave him his nomination." Many Democrats, and particularly Congressmen Rankin of Mississippi and Patrick of Alabama, made these same charges again and again during the summer of 1940. In refutation, Styles Bridges announced in the Senate:

> Probably the most absurd and most self-evident wrong statement made on this floor is the assertion that the Power-Trust, so-called, engineered or had any part in Mr. Willkie's nomination. I have personal knowledge of efforts by his own business associates to dissuade him from running, on the ground that his nomination would make the utility industry a political football in this campaign. More than that, I have personal knowledge of strong influence brought to bear by interests closely identified with the utility industry to stop his nomination. The whole industry was paralyzed with fear of the political repercussions against it should

[55] *New York Times*, June 29, 1940, p. 3. See also the *Congressional Record*, vol. 86, p. 19244, and pp. 19250-261 (76th Cong., 3rd Sess., Sept. 27, 1940).

Wendell Willkie, a utility executive receive the nomination. . . . Wendell Willkie was nominated in spite of and not because of the power interests. Anyone with a realistic view-point of the selfish interests of the utility groups should realize that.[56]

The charges and countercharges, however, raged in and out of Congress during the rest of Willkie's life. In a vein of charges similar to those of Senator Norris, Dr. Harry Elmer Barnes and C. Nelson Sparks later wrote that Willkie obtained the Republican leadership through the pernicious influence of Ogden Mills Reid, publisher of the *New York Herald Tribune,* and Thomas W. Lamont, chairman of the board of J. P. Morgan and Company. Barnes and Sparks, in their respective works, claimed that the publishers and financiers of America backed Willkie at the insistence of these men after an elaborate dinner held at the Reid home for the purpose of exploring the foreign policy views of Taft and Willkie. At the dinner, Willkie pledged his support to all-out aid to the Allies, while Taft remained silent. As a result, the observers concluded, Reid and Lamont used their very significant influence to obtain the nomination for Willkie. Dr. Barnes subsequently told a group of historians at an annual meeting of the American Historical Association in Chicago: "It is doubtful if any man was ever nominated for the Presidency on the basis of less popular knowledge and approval. There were at least a dozen or more persons in the famous 'smoke-filled room' in the Chicago hotel where Warren G. Harding was chosen for the nomination in 1920. Two men decided that Mr. Willkie should be the Republican nominee. . . . These men were Ogden Mills Reid, . . . and Thomas W. Lamont. . . ."[57]

---

[56] *Ibid.,* p. 19644 (Oct. 2, 1940).

[57] Dr. Barnes continued: "Some time before the Convention, Mr. and Mrs. Willkie and Senator and Mrs. Robert A. Taft were invited to a dinner party at the home of Mr. Reid. No suggestion had been made to Senator Taft, at least, that this was more than a social gathering. He was surprised to find Mr. Willkie present. After dinner, Reid and Lamont put Mr. Willkie and Senator Taft through an inquisition as to their views on aiding the allies, especially England. Mr. Willkie expressed full agreement with the Roosevelt policy, but Senator Taft remained firm in his anti-interventionist stand. This he did, even though it had become apparent to him that he and Mr. Willkie were being decisively appraised as to their qualifications for the Republican nomination. From this time onward, Reid and Lamont worked vigorously for the Willkie nomination." Harry Elmer Barnes, *Was Roosevelt Pushed Into War by Popular Demand in 1941?,* Discussion of paper read by Professor Dexter Perkins before the American Historical Association, Chicago, December 29, 1950, p. 10. Sparks' version of the story is essentially the same. He mentioned that Lord Lothian, then am-

Literally scores of other opponents of Willkie took essentially similar positions during the 1940 campaign. Nearly all of the charges were stated in generalities, however, and, at best, they illustrated only that persons of influence in finance and the mass media supported the Commonwealth and Southern president. The demand for Willkie at the convention was certainly the product of a well-organized publicity campaign; the financial interests of the nation undoubtedly encouraged the boom with outright donations. But to assume that the support of the *Herald Tribune* and the Wall Street contributions accounted for the nomination of Wendell Willkie in 1940 is to ignore the situation which existed in the party, the Willkie personality, and the era in which the nomination took place. Other variables that influence nominations were certainly of

bassador to the United States from Great Britain, and Mr. and Mrs. John Pillsbury of Minneapolis were also present. He stated that ". . . Willkie, who later on in his campaign was to challenge President Roosevelt for war mongering, on the occasion of the Reid dinner, *went 'all out for war.'* " Sparks also wrote of Taft: "Retaining his calm, outwardly, Taft observed that he could add nothing to his remarks on the subject that he had not expressed on the floor of the Senate. . . ." and that "The next morning, the *New York Herald Tribune* editorially announced itself unequivocally for Wendell Willkie." Sparks, *op. cit.,* pp. 12-13. There is a discrepancy in the Sparks report in that he dated the meeting at "the week before the convention opened," whereas the *Herald Tribune* did not declare for Willkie until the convention was in session.

On February 21, 1941, Senator Danaher of Connecticut told the Senate that Willkie had pledged support for "all-out" aid to Britain at a pre-election dinner at the Reid home. *New York Times,* February 28, 1941, p. 10. Informed of the assertion, Willkie replied: "The story is quite humorous. Last Spring . . . I did attend a private dinner party, at the home of Mr. and Mrs. Ogden Reid. There were present some twenty-five persons of diverse international, political, and economic views. There was a very lively and interesting discussion. I did say at that dinner party, as I have said many times both publicly and privately, before my nomination, during the campaign and since, that I believed it imperative that the United States give all possible aid in the way of military and naval equipment, airplanes, etc., to the British. . . . The suggestion that there was any pledge in return for support is amusing when it is recalled that one of the honored guests was a leading candidate for the Republican nomination for President who was and is opposed to my views on international policy. I was just a guest. . . ." *Ibid.,* March 1, 1941, p. 4. Another account of this dinner may be found in the *Chicago Tribune,* January 13, 1952, p. 12.

Senator Taft, in a letter to the author, wrote that he recalled the dinner at which he differed with Willkie, and that quite a discussion followed. He stated that he did not know if this meeting led to the support of Willkie by Lamont or the *Herald Tribune,* but that they probably were already strongly in Willkie's corner. The discussion, Taft thought, may have made their views more definite.

more importance. Sam Pryor, rejecting the Norris-H.E. Barnes-Sparks thesis, declared: "Such a position is incorrect. Lamont and Reid had no influence at the Convention. Willkie was nominated by the 'inside' people of the Republican Party at the Convention, not by the 'outsiders.' It was men like Halleck, Baldwin, Stassen, Weeks, and Simpson, not the Oren Roots and Russ Davenports, who influenced the delegates. It was the 'inside strength' that won for Willkie."[58]

Harold Stassen confirmed this view in a description of his own work at the convention on behalf of Willkie: "The principal point of discussion on the floor was a matter of convincing other delegates that their candidate was not going to win the nomination, and that Willkie would win."[59]

This was the point in the decision-making process where the telegrams, letters, and petitions undoubtedly had a marked influence on the nomination. Many of the delegates arrived in Philadelphia pledged to particular candidates. After a few ballots, when it was apparent that the battle had narrowed to Taft and Willkie, the delegates had to make a choice between the two, and all evidence pointed to the fact that thousands of persons wanted their representatives to support the utility president. Publicists had been writing for three years about the vacuum of leadership within the GOP, and Willkie filled this vacuum with a refreshing and dynamic personality. Though he was a newcomer to national politics, he had vigorously opposed the New Deal for eight years. The millions of Americans who deprecated "politics" as such could support this man, whose organization seemed to be so amateurish and whose mannerisms were so atypical.

The delegates reflected, in a limited way, what they observed to be public opinion — not the public opinion of the galleries, for this action was antagonistic as well as enthusiastic, but the public opinion expressed in messages from their friends at home and also the public opinion crystallized by the fall of France.[60] The delegates were cognizant of the enthusiasm for this man who was not

---

[58] Interview with Mr. Pryor.
[59] Letter from Harold E. Stassen.
[60] D. W. Brogan wrote: ". . . although there are many forces behind the . . . nomination of Mr. Wendell Willkie, he would not have sufficed to batter through the barriers of tradition and professionalism had not Hitler's armies broken through the line of the Meuse." "The American Election," *The Political Quarterly*, 11 (October-December, 1940), 322.

only popular but who was also aware of the seriousness of the world situation, and the majority of them, deluged by the flood of messages, decided to submit to the very real and tremendous pressures.[61] All of the evidence indicates that Republican partisans, at the convention and at home, had been convinced that Willkie would be the strongest candidate to represent the party in 1940.

Finally, it should be remembered that Willkie probably would never have received the Republican nomination in 1940 if Taft, Dewey, and Vandenberg had been willing to cooperate in stopping him by pooling their pledged votes on one of the early ballots. The refusal of these candidates to unite, plus the inability of the Old Guard within the party to dominate the convention, created a situation that was exceedingly favorable to the political phenomenon which actually took place.

The results of the Republican convention of 1940 were, therefore, paradoxical indeed. The party of Harding, Coolidge, and Hoover, over the objection of its congressional wing and many local bosses, accepted a former Democrat, a corporation president, and political maverick as the result of a popular uprising of the nonpolitical components of the party's rank and file assisted by a relatively small band of floor leaders. The delegates before whom the Republican party was proclaimed to be the "peace party" nominated the only contender who could be labeled an "interventionist," and the convention, which met for the sole purpose of providing alternatives to the New Deal, selected as the titular head of its entire organization, the only man who agreed openly with many of Roosevelt's domestic reforms and much of the President's foreign policy.

---

[61] Thomas E. Dewey told friends and newspapermen that leading bankers and industrialists used economic pressures to swing delegates pledged to him to the Willkie bandwagon, and Charles H. Griffiths, member of the New York State Republican executive committee, said he had received more than five hundred telegrams of the "or else" type urging support for Willkie. He said that many of the messages came from "substantial persons" known to him. *PM*, July 3, 1940, p. 11.

4 CRUSADE, 1940

After the convention, Wendell Willkie held a late conference with those who had managed his floor campaign, Governor Stassen, Governor Baldwin, and Samuel F. Pryor, in addition to Representative Martin, the chairman of the convention. A few minutes later, he left for a weekend of rest aboard the yacht of Roy W. Howard of the Scripps-Howard newspapers. The following Monday, Willkie resigned his position with Commonwealth and Southern and made plans to sever relations with his other business affiliations.

Meanwhile, the Republican National Committee, at the request of Willkie, conferred upon a subcommittee of eleven of its own members and the nominee the power to unite the various factions within the organization into a well-coordinated unit capable of winning the election. At a meeting held at the Bellevue-Stratford Hotel, this subcommittee was authorized to appoint the various officers necessary to lead the campaign and handle the problems of organization and finance. Walter S. Hallanan of West Virginia was appointed chairman. Other members included William F. Knowland of California, Samuel F. Pryor of Connecticut, Ezra R. Whitla of Idaho, Werner W. Schroeder of Illinois, Grace B. Reynolds of Indiana, Harrison Spangler of Iowa, Sinclair Weeks of Massachusetts, William Stern of North Dakota, Mrs. Worthington Scranton of Pennsylvania, and Frank O. Horton of Wyoming. Henry P. Fletcher, general counsel of the national committee, was appointed as a twelfth member in an advisory capacity. The group included several individuals who had openly opposed Willkie during the convention. The *New York Times* referred to it as an "appeasement program . . . regarded as necessary by the Willkie group because of the newness on the national political scene of most members of the intimate Willkie circle."[1] The selection of these persons was a perfunctory gesture to all shades of Republican opinion so that complete support of the Willkie-McNary ticket could be obtained.

Willkie suggested that the campaign organization be supervised by a three-man board or triumvirate consisting of a campaign manager as chairman, the Republican National Chairman, and a personal representative of the candidate.[2] Hallanan expressed approval of the idea, but the plan was discarded at the suggestion of more experienced political advisers. Therefore Willkie announced the formation of a personal advisory committee, with Harold Stassen as chairman, to cooperate with him and the national committee. Others selected were Halleck, Martin, Representative J. William Ditter of Pennsylvania, chairman of the Republican Congressional Campaign Committee; Senator John Townsend, Delaware, chairman of the Senatorial Campaign Committee; David S. Ingalls of Cleveland, Ohio, preconvention manager for Senator Taft; Ruth Hanna McCormick Simms, New Mexico, preconvention Dewey manager; Governor Baldwin of Connecticut; Governor Ralph Carr of Colorado; Oren Root, Jr., of New York, volunteer organizer of the first Willkie Club; Mrs. Ruth DeYoung Kohler, Wisconsin, a former Chicago newspaperwoman; and Paul Kruesi, chairman of the Tennessee delegation to the convention.[3] This, again, was an endeavor by Willkie to obtain support from individuals some of whom had not originally favored his nomination,[4] but the committee was never active or effective.

---

[1] *New York Times*, June 30, 1940, p. 2.

[2] Raymond Moley described another plan by which Willkie planned to dispense with the traditional national chairman and to place his party machinery in the hands of a committee of five. Charles Evans Hughes, Jr., was to be the moderator on the committee, which was also to include Russell Davenport, while "political interests were to receive a salutation by the appointment of John Hamilton. . . ." Moley proposed that Willkie obtain the advice of Will Hays, former chairman of the Republican party, on the matter. Hays persuaded Willkie to abandon the plan. See Moley's *27 Masters of Politics* (New York, 1949), pp. 49-50.

[3] *New York Times*, July 3, 1940, p. 1.

[4] On July 9, 1940, ten additional persons were added to the advisory group. They were: John E. Jackson, New Orleans; William Stern, Fargo,

Exercising his prerogative as the successful candidate, Willkie decided to ignore his pledge to keep John Hamilton as party chairman and chose in his place Representative Joseph W. Martin. Martin at first refused, then told party leaders he wanted "to go down to the Cape and think it over." He declared to friends: "I don't want the job. I just want to elect a Republican Congress." While in Massachusetts on July 4, however, he was urged by Helen Reid, Alf Landon, Colonel McCormick, and several others to accept the position in order to unite the party and bring congressmen into the campaign. Finally, he agreed that if "the boys in Washington" approved, he would accept. Republicans in Congress were enthusiastic about the prospect of having the House leader supervise the campaign, so on July 9, Hallanan announced to the press that Martin was to be the new chairman and that Hamilton would remain with the committee as executive director.[5] After disclosing the Martin appointment, Hallanan said:

It has been a refreshing experience practically without precedent in national politics, to have the nominee for the Presidency sit around the table with the national committee and discuss the many problems incident to the organization of the campaign.

Wendell Willkie has cooperated splendidly with the committee and we have cooperated with him to bring about the result we are striving for. . . .

He won the complete confidence and affection of this committee by his honest effort and completely candid dealings in our problems of working out the Republican organization set-up.[6]

There were many Republicans however, who could not agree that

North Dakota; E. G. Bennet, Ogden, Utah; Howard Lawrence, Grand Rapids, Michigan; Kenneth F. Simpson, New York; S. M. B. O'Hara, Pennsylvania; Roger Straus, New York City; Thomas G. Mutter, Charleston, West Virginia; William King, Chicago; and Thomas J. Paolina, Providence, Rhode Island. *New York Times,* July 10, 1940, p. 12.

[5] Interview with Joseph Martin. Martin received no salary as chairman and manager of the campaign. Hamilton was allotted $15,000 a year for salary and $10,000 for expenses.

[6] *New York Times,* July 10, 1940, p. 12. The reorganization of the national committee was an additional product of another meeting between Willkie and other party leaders which was held to unite the various factions which had engaged in the preconvention struggle. The table of organization of the national committee as announced by Hallanan was as follows: Vice Chairmen: Samuel F. Pryor, Jr., Connecticut; Walter S. Hallanan, West Virginia; Mrs. Elsie Fitzsimons, Rhode Island; and Mrs. Grace B. Reynolds, Indiana.

Chairman of the executive committee: Sinclair Weeks, Massachusetts.

Members of the executive committee: J. Russel Sprague, New York;

Willkie had "won the complete confidence and affection" of the committee by his candid dealings in working out the Republican organizational setup. Certain individuals considered the removal of Hamilton to be a stupendous error of political judgment. Hamilton was extremely popular with the regular organization Republicans, he had worked diligently to rid the party of its 1936 debt, and he also had done much to obtain the nomination for Willkie in Philadelphia. As the campaign developed, it became evident that Joe Martin could not do justice to both his position as national chairman and his obligations as minority leader of the House of Representatives. That Willkie eventually realized that it would have been wise to have retained Hamilton is revealed in a letter written by Hamilton in which he stated: "I have in my files letters from many of Mr. Willkie's personal friends written during the Fall of 1943 and the Spring of 1944 to the effect that Mr. Willkie had told them his failure to appoint me was the greatest political mistake he had ever made. Added to that I have a letter from Mr. Willkie making that direct statement."[7]

On the other hand, in 1940 a substantial case could be made for the replacement of Hamilton. Willkie could not foresee the many organizational difficulties which were in store for him, and the appointment of Martin had its merits. Martin represented strength among the congressional Republicans who constituted Willkie's weakest link with the party. Martin also placed the candidate in the graces of many local leaders over the country in spite of any irritation they felt about Hamilton's replacement.[8] It must be remembered that though Hamilton had performed great services for the party, he was also publicly identified with the Republican organization at its lowest ebb from 1936 to 1940; he was, no matter how unjustified the thought and despite his attempts to liberalize the party from time to time, identified with Hoover and Landon in the

Robert Burroughs, New Hampshire; Daniel E. Pomeroy, New Jersey; Daniel O. Hastings, Delaware; Mrs. Worthington Scranton, Pennsylvania; David S. Ingalls, Ohio; Mrs. Bertha Baur, Illinois; Harrison Spangler, Iowa; Mrs. Horace Sayre, Oklahoma; William Knowland, California; Ezra Whitla, Idaho; Mrs. Chris Carlson, Minnesota; Mrs. Deall Utquhart, Washington; B. Carroll Reece, Tennessee; and Harvey Jewett, South Dakota. Treasurer: C. B. Goodspeed, Illinois. Secretary: Harold W. Mason, Vermont. General Counsel: Henry P. Fletcher, Rhode Island.

[7] This personal letter from Hamilton to Dr. Henry Evjen is reproduced in "The Willkie Campaign; An Unfortunate Chapter in Republican Leadership," *The Journal of Politics*, 14 (May, 1952), 246.

[8] Interview with Joseph Martin.

minds of many of the apolitical independent voters at whom Willkie intended to aim his campaign. This latter fact is crucial in evaluating the decision. It might be added that alleged charges of a personal nature which subsequently came to Willkie's attention also suggested that he seek a new chairman. In any event, a change in committee leadership is only rarely unwise politically. The appointment of a new national chairman always gives a campaign an air of freshness, and in this case, since Hamilton was kept on the active staff, the talents of both party leaders were obtained. It is probably true that local party leaders throughout the country were dismayed or even angered by Hamilton's demotion, but it is doubtful that this affected the political outcome of the election. The possibility of winning that Willkie inspired with this appeal to voters from all parties could have infused only enthusiasm in any political realist. The principle of party responsibility may have suffered as a result, but neither Willkie nor the rank and file of the voters was concerned with such a probability in July of 1940.

In his first few days as a candidate, Willkie made plans concerning his campaign. He applied for membership in the National Republican Club, met Dewey for the first time, flew to Washington for a short conference with Senator McNary, and gave occasional advice to his followers. He instructed the party to observe the proposed legal limitations on contributions by refusing offers of money in excess of $5,000 from any one individual[9] and by rejecting all corporate gifts. "The more one-dollar and five-dollar ones, the better," he said. He then asserted that he would make no appointments to public offices or to the diplomatic service of the United States in exchange for contributions. He maintained that he intended to enforce the provisions of the Hatch bill in limiting the expenditures of the Republican party in 1940 to $3,000,000 whether Congress passed the bill or not. He also stated that he had made no pledges, direct or indirect, about appointments or official acts in the event that he should be elected.[10] He naïvely told reporters that he was determined to present his problems during the campaign in

---

[9] In terms of the 1936 contributions, this limitation would have meant a loss of $1,366,000 to the party. *Ibid.* Actually, it meant nothing of the sort; large individual contributions were distributed over several members of each family. For example, the $203,780 given to the Republicans in 1940 by the duPonts was contributed legally by sixty-four members of the family. Overacker, *op. cit.*, p. 719.

[10] Makey, *op. cit.*, p. 263.

speeches that he had personally written. "I have never in my life delivered a speech which I haven't written myself and I am not going to change my habits now." With that statement, he left New York for Colorado for a vacation he eventually called "the most strenuous rest in my life."

Willkie's supporters laid tentative plans for the campaign. Eastern headquarters were opened under the direction of Samuel F. Pryor to supervise the campaign in seventeen states in the eastern and border states. A midwestern headquarters, under the command of Stassen and Hamilton, was to be set up in the Chicago area to plan the campaign for the remainder of the country. Headquarters of the Democrats-for-Willkie group were in New York, but they were not formally opened until August 12. The Willkie-for-President Clubs, under the direction of Oren Root, remained as a separate unit run from a twenty-room sixteenth-floor suite at 100 East Forty-second Street, the headquarters from which the unsuccessful campaign of Dewey had been directed. Oren Root stated, "It is the intention . . . to establish State-wide Willkie club groups to cooperate with the Republican State organizations. There is a probability that Democratic Willkie clubs will be set up as a separate wing of the organization."

The Willkie Clubs, of which 560 had been recognized by the Associated Willkie Clubs of America by July 15, were financed by a twenty-five-cent dues payment for membership in the clubs. The dues collected were then spent on local activities by the various clubs.[11] The agency authorized by Willkie and the national, state, and county committees to solicit contributions was called the United Republican Finance Committee. Under the direction of F. Trubee Davison, it was organized into two hundred divisions consisting of more than seven thousand volunteer workers. Willkie's personal headquarters were in the Hotel Commodore under the guidance of Henry J. Taylor, an advertising expert; Robert L. Johnson, editor of *Promenade;* and Fred Rahter, Willkie's secretary.

In Colorado Springs, Willkie got little rest. He was besieged by visitors and requests for speeches and visits. He was happy about Joseph Martin's acceptance of the national chairmanship: "I feel

[11] By the end of July, over seven hundred Willkie-for-President Clubs had been formed. *New York Times,* July 18, 1940, p. 7. For a suggestion that political parties institute a similar system of fund raising, see "Toward a More Responsible Two Party System," *American Political Science Review,* 44, Supplement (September, 1950), p. 70.

like a member of the Northwest Mounted Police: I got my man."[12] During the first week he made an address in Denver and held conferences with many friends and former foes within the party. The following week, the Democratic National Convention opened in Chicago. In his keynote address, Speaker Bankhead reminded the delegates of the ill-fated speculation of the 1920's. When asked for a comment on Bankhead's speech, Willkie said:

I found myself in complete accord with Speaker Bankhead in his condemnation of the speculative orgies of the Nineteen Twenties. I always have thought that such speculation was to be condemned, whether it was in the securities of utility companies, vending machine companies or took the form of gambling in foreign exchange, such as German marks. I am proud that I had absolutely nothing to do with that phase of American economic life. I have devoted a substantial part of my time during the past seven and one-half years to protecting the investments of the people against the assaults of their own government.[13]

When he heard that Franklin Roosevelt would be his opponent in the forthcoming election, Willkie declared: "I'm deeply gratified at the chance to meet the champ. It ought to be a great campaign. We will have presented to the voters of the country the issues which have been created by the New Deal and advocated for the New Deal by the author and ablest advocate of that philosophy and the directing force of the New Deal practices. In this election the voters themselves will have the opportunity to pass upon the doctrine of the indispensability of one man and the sanctity of our two-term tradition."

The renomination of President Roosevelt resulted in "a flood of offers of support" for Willkie from disgruntled Democrats. Prominent among them were Senator Edward R. Burke, Nebraska conservative who had been defeated for renomination in the primary election; former Governor William H. ("Alfalfa Bill") Murray of Oklahoma; former Senator James A. Reed of Missouri;[14] Stephen

---

[12] *Newsweek,* July 22, 1940, p. 17. Evjen, *op. cit.,* p. 246, wrote that Martin later confessed to friends that he left Washington to "hide out" from Willkie in order to avoid being asked to take the national chairmanship. Dr. Dillon, *op. cit.,* p. 179, stated that "Probably no one realized better than Martin the seriousness of the mistake of his appointment. It was in fact the second major blunder of the campaign."

[13] The quotation above is a composite of quotations by the *New York Times,* July 17, p. 1, and Makey, *op. cit.,* p. 272. There is a slight discrepancy as to Willkie's exact words in response to reporters' questions on this point.

[14] Representative Coffee, Democrat of Washington, stated on the floor of

F. Chadwick, former National Commander of the American Legion; Vance C. McCormick, Democratic national chairman in 1916; President Hamilton Holt of Rollins College; Irvin S. Cobb, humorist, who enrolled as "a high private in the rear ranks of the Incurable Democrats Willkie-for-President Club"; and John J. O'Connor, former Democratic representative from New York and one-time chairman of the Rules Committee in the House of Representatives.[15] A week later, Alfred E. Smith, Democratic nominee for President in 1928, formally announced that he would take another "walk" in 1940, and that his support would be given to Willkie. Smith contended: "The Democratic party should be defeated this year to rid itself of the minority block of New Dealers controlling it and return to the principles of Thomas Jefferson." Judge Samuel Seabury also endorsed Willkie. He called him the choice of the "plain people" as against the "machine politicians."[16]

In order to have a "nucleus around which the independent groups and the anti-third-termers can coalesce," Willkie created a committee of four anti-New Deal Democrats to organize a national independent Democrats-for-Willkie movement to support his presidential campaign. The committee included Lewis W. Douglas, John W. Hanes, and Alan Valentine, preconvention leaders of the Democrats favoring Willkie, and Mrs. Roberta Campbell Lawson of Tulsa, Oklahoma.[17] Valentine emphasized the independent nature of the organization and asserted that it would be free of any formal association with the Republican National Committee or state and local Republican organizations — or even the Associated Willkie

the House of Representatives: "Ever since Reed failed of nomination as Democratic candidate for President several years ago he has been doing his best to elect a Republican to office." *Congressional Record,* vol. 86, p. 14519 (76th Cong., 3rd Sess., July 22, 1940).

[15] *New York Times,* July 23, 1940, p. 1, and *Newsweek,* July 29, 1940, p. 17. O'Connor announced that he had sent letters to more than two thousand Democrats in various parts of the country urging them to support Wendell L. Willkie for President. *New York Times,* July 26, 1940, p. 11.

[16] *Ibid.* Seabury had been a potential Democratic candidate for the presidency in 1932 after his "brilliant exposé of Tammany rule shocked an indifferent New York as it had never been shocked before and caused independent Democrats throughout the nation to regard him as a new Woodrow Wilson." Roy V. Peel and Thomas C. Donnelly, *The 1932 Campaign, An Analysis* (New York, 1935), p. 43.

[17] *New York Times,* July 23, 1940, p. 1. President Roosevelt remembered Hanes and Douglas as "amiable and honorable young men. . . . But in the administration it had been observed that their minds ran in terms of dollars rather than in terms of humanity." *Ibid.,* July 28, 1940, sec. 5, p. 3.

Clubs. "The movement is one hundred per cent Democratic," he said. One of the purposes of the organization was to distribute information about the method by which Democrats could vote for Willkie while casting their ballots for Democratic candidates for state and local positions. The official slogan of the Democrats-for-Willkie group was "Country Before Party — No Third Term."[18]

While some Democrats and many other individuals throughout the nation were rallying to the Willkie cause, the candidate continued his strenuous vacation. He conferred with Governor George Wilson of Iowa on farm problems. He toured sugar-beet farms and a sugar plant with Governor Carr, and held conferences with George N. Peek, the AAA's first administrator, Claude M. Baker, president of the International Typographical Union, Colonel Robert R. McCormick, publisher of the *Chicago Tribune*,[19] Representative Charles Halleck, and many others. To add to this burden, Willkie received over fifty thousand congratulatory messages while in Colorado Springs. The press was always waiting for a newsworthy comment; as a result, significant copy ran pretty thin.

Gallup polls showed that Willkie was extremely popular with the voters. In the middle of July, forty-seven per cent of the people polled by the American Institute of Public Opinion claimed that they would vote for Willkie, while ten per cent of the people were undecided. Some indication of the basis for the popularity was also given to Gallup. More than half of those who thought he would make a good president said it was because he had been a successful businessman and a good executive — the publicity campaign by the public relations experts had produced results. However, "only a handful" of the voters polled said they were for Willkie because he might be able through his business experience to rearm the country more rapidly than the New Dealers. Willkie's chief point of popular appeal, in addition to his business ability, was his personality. Those who opposed him cited, in about equal proportions, his political inexperience and his connections with Wall Street and the utility industry.

---

[18] *Ibid.*, August 13, 1940, p. 12. Leo Casey, publicity director of the New York World's Fair, resigned his post to become publicity chief of the Democrats backing Willkie. *Ibid.*, August 11, 1940, p. 30.

[19] Colonel McCormick tried to get Willkie to take a more isolationist stand in regard to aid to the Allies. See Jack Alexander's article, "The World's Greatest Newspaper," *Saturday Evening Post*, 214 (July 26, 1941), 88.

Meanwhile, the second Hatch Act was passed on July 19, 1940. As a result, the combined fund-raising endeavors of the state Republican organizations and the Republican National Committee were immediately terminated. For the public, Willkie stated that he "did not believe in an expensive campaign," that "the combined total expenses of the Republican party, the Willkie-for-President Clubs, and the independent Democratic movement would be under $3,000,000 the limitation set by the Hatch Act," and that he was definitely in favor of the Act. Henry P. Fletcher, general counsel to the Republican National Committee, however, asserted that there should be a decentralization within the party in regard to campaign contributions. He pointed to the loophole in the Act by which the Republican organizations throughout the nation could escape from the limitation. Local heads of these organizations could then interpret the Act as allowing each independent nationwide organization to spend up to the three million dollar limit. Willkie tried to prevent such publicity, for he believed that it would injure the spirit of the campaign which had been so carefully nurtured. He maintained that he hoped to keep the total expenditure of *all* the national groups supporting him down to about two and one-half millions of dollars.[20] Willkie, of course, proved to be something less than clairvoyant. When the campaign was over, the declared expenditures of the various national Republican organizations were slightly more than five millions of dollars and this was less than one-third of the total amount of money raised and reported for the Willkie cause.[21]

Willkie, it was apparent, was planning an unorthodox campaign.

---

[20] On the floor of the Senate, Sherman Minton made the following comment: "I do not want to reflect on my old-time friend and schoolmate, Wendell Willkie. Of course, I know that Mr. Willkie has given out a statement that he will obey the Hatch Act. Everything is 'hunkydory' with Willkie. He is not going to take any money except up to a certain limit, and that is all within the law. That is Mr. Willkie; that is Mr. Puritan in politics. But then comes Mr. Fletcher, who shows how to get around the law Willkie is endorsing. That is Mr. Practical in politics. So what that looks like to me is a Dr. Jekyll and Mr. Hyde act." *Congressional Record,* vol. 86, p. 15024 (76th Cong., 3rd Sess., Aug. 5, 1940).

[21] Overacker, *op. cit.,* p. 713. The Democratic total was slightly below $6,000,000. Miss Overacker noted that many of the expenditures of local groups were not included in these figures and that there "unquestionably" was some duplication in compiling the amounts reported. The totals admittedly are not accurate but Miss Overacker asserted that they represented the closest approximation to the total cost of a national campaign which had ever been made available.

In addition to voicing his intention to keep expenses down, he made, during the early stages of the campaign, little pretense of his lack of difference with the President on certain facets of the New Deal foreign policy. He again asserted his belief that democracy was seriously threatened by the totalitarians, and, ignoring the Republican platform, he stressed his support of all possible material and moral aid to Great Britain. He criticized, however, the President's "recklessness and restraintlessness" in dealing with the foreign powers. Courting the Italian vote in New York, he deplored Roosevelt's "stab in the back" indictment of Mussolini, which he contended was not within the province of a president. He declared that a president should act as a "deterrent" to warlike gestures instead of leading their expression. The Gallup poll released early in August showed Willkie ahead of the President in twenty-four states possessing a majority of 304 to 227 votes in the Electoral College. Gallup stated, however, that Roosevelt held a nationwide popular lead by virtue of the large pluralities given him in the southern states in comparison to the relatively small pluralities for Willkie in northern and eastern states. Only Montana and Washington in the far Northwest were clearly in the New Deal column, but the Republican lead in Wisconsin, Minnesota, North Dakota, Wyoming, Connecticut, and Rhode Island was so slim that a shift of slightly more than one per cent in these states would give a majority of the electoral votes to the New Deal. The survey, which was the first state-by-state poll conducted after the Democratic National Convention, indicated that neither the Democrats nor the Republicans possessed sufficient "regular" party members at that time to capture the presidency. Gallup commented: "Whichever party wins the election next November will probably owe its victory to the so-called 'independent vote.' "[22]

[22] *Ibid.*, August 4, 1940, p. 2. Gallup estimated, as the result of the survey, that one voter in every five considered himself free of regular party allegiance. In response to the question, "In politics do you consider yourself a Democrat, Republican, Socialist or Independent?" the answers were: Democrat, 41 per cent; Republican, 38 per cent; Independent, 20 per cent; and Socialist or other, 1 per cent. It is interesting to note that most of the independent voters were living in the crucial states of the East and the Middle West; they did not constitute a large portion of the voters in the South. Perhaps of more importance to Willkie was the fact that more than half of the independent voters were in a relatively low income group, earning from $20 to $40 a week. Gallup stated, "Every Institute measurement in the last four years has indicated that this is the income group which may do most to decide the next election." *Ibid.*

Willkie and his organizations went after this independent vote. In New York two new organizations were formed for Willkie: The Manhattan Campaign Committee for Willkie and McNary, under the chairmanship of Joseph Clark Baldwin,[23] and the First Voters League, directed by Robert Rosthal, who had headed the First Voters League for Roosevelt in 1936. The Associated Willkie Clubs organized a speakers bureau with Democrats comprising thirty-five per cent of its personnel, and Oren Root was certifying new Willkie Clubs at the rate of thirty a day. Willkie was impressed by Root's work, and the young lawyer sat in on the conferences held with party leaders in Colorado Springs. Even at this early stage of the campaign, this inclusion of Root annoyed some of the more experienced party leaders who felt that too much of the campaign was being conducted beyond the control of the formal party organization. This was just the beginning of intermittent friction between the Willkie Clubs and the party regulars in many localities throughout the nation, and before the campaign was concluded, Willkie asked John B. Hollister to be Root's adviser in an effort to bridge the gap and reduce the quarreling between the two groups. Other irritations, such as inadequate handling of campaign business, and Willkie's off-the-cuff pronouncements on issues, indicated the confusion under which the campaign began. This was not the last time dissension was apparent in 1940 in the Republican ranks, but in August, the nominee had not as yet accepted the nomination, and the people of America were still eagerly waiting to hear what this new champion of the minority party had to present as an alternative to the New Deal.

Willkie left Colorado and returned to Rushville to accept his nomination. The time spent in the West had been no vacation at all. Not only did Willkie have insufficient time in which to coordinate his thoughts on the policy of the campaign, but he was already physically and mentally tired. Harold Stassen, in reviewing the intellectual inconsistency of the campaign, attributed it to Willkie's "exhausted condition following this Colorado Springs period when he . . . had no opportunity to become rested and poised for the final hard drive."[24] Sam Pryor put it even more strongly: "Col-

---

[23] *Ibid.,* August 12, 1940, p. 8. This group, sponsored by the Republican county committee, included Democrats and independent voters. It was the seventh committee formed for Willkie in Manhattan alone.

[24] Letter from Harold Stassen.

orado Springs was the worst possible place for Willkie to have taken that vacation. He was completely out of touch with the real party leaders. All the 'screwballs' in the United States visited him while he was out there. He was mentally fagged out before the campaign started and he didn't recover from it until the day he died. He should have gone up to the Maine woods for a complete rest, and have seen no one."[25]

Willkie went back to Elwood, Indiana, to make his acceptance speech on August 17.[26] Though the town's facilities were inadequate to accommodate the crowds and confusion, it was elaborately decorated; large pictures of Willkie ornamented every lamppost, and flags floated from the downtown buildings. At Callaway Park, which was once a meadow through which Willkie drove a neighbor's cow each day, space was made to park thirty thousand automobiles and to seat nearly two hundred thousand people. Three hundred stands and concessions were granted for the park. Forty-five trains brought thirty-four thousand persons from the Manhattan area, and a "Willkie Motorcade" of two hundred fifty automobiles from New York drove to Elwood to hear the Willkie speech. Thousands of other people journeyed to the small Indiana town from all over the nation. Homer Capehart, Indiana senator and radio manufacturer, was the general chairman of the Elwood Willkie Notification Committee which paid all of the expenses for the celebration. The press had for weeks been publicizing the oration and predicting that the definitive word of opposition to the New Deal would be voiced by the candadate in this address.

Willkie and his advisers remained in Rushville until August 17. On that Saturday morning, with the temperature hovering above ninety degrees, the party took a special train to Elwood for the ceremonies. A short program was given for Willkie on the steps of the high school from which he was graduated. Later, amid the

---

[25] Interview with Samuel Pryor.

[26] Senator Joseph F. Guffey of Pennsylvania stated on the floor of the Senate, "The reason for Mr. Willkie's going to Indiana for his acceptance speech was perfectly clear. He wanted to get away from his New York setting. He did not desire to be associated in the mind of the people either with Wall Street or with Fifth Avenue. Yet practically all of the newspapers, including the *New York Times*, were ready to aid him in what amounted to a deceit upon the people. You were willing that he should set up props as a background for this speech which would give the voters an altogether erroneous impression. . . ." *Congressional Record,* vol. 86, p. 17576 (76th Cong., 3rd Sess., Sept. 5, 1940).

cheers of thousands of supporters, the nominee rode through the city in an open car to the park.

At the formal ceremony, after the invocation, Representative Halleck introduced Joe Martin, who officially notified Willkie of the nomination. Martin said, in part:

An unbossed convention listened. A deliberative group of delegates acted. You became the nominee of a convention which elected you in the traditional American way. . . .

This campaign of 1940 is vastly more significant and important than an ordinary election contest between two political parties. It is a contest between the forces of constitutional government and liberty and those influences which are moving steadily toward government by men instead of by laws. . . .

The Republican party rejoices that in you it has provided the nation with a man who is preeminently qualified to meet the requirements of this critical period. It rejoices that your nomination has been enthusiastically acclaimed by Independents, Jeffersonian Democrats, Progressives, Liberals and Republicans alike. You are not the hope of one political party; you are the hope of a majority of the American people.[27]

Thereupon, Wendell Lewis Willkie, his face already covered with perspiration, rose to accept the nomination. He called upon Americans of every political and religious faith to help him lead the cause. He said that party lines were down,[28] as evidenced by the nomination by the Republican party of a liberal Democrat who had changed his party affiliation. He dedicated himself and the party to "the principles of American liberty" and pledged himself to fight the campaign on the basis of those principles rather than on a program of personalities, jealousies, and hate.

Willkie then enunciated the issues. He advocated preparedness for defense and explicitly asserted the necessity for some form of selective service. He came out strongly for aid to Great Britain, stating his agreement with the President that the material resources of the United States should be extended to "the opponents of force." He criticized the Chief Executive's conduct of foreign affairs, however, and cried that Roosevelt had "dabbled in inflammatory statements and manufactured panics." He said that the President's attacks on foreign powers had been "useless" and "dangerous," but a few minutes later promised that if the Republicans were victorious

[27] New York Times, August 18, 1940, p. 32.

[28] For an article asserting that party lines were not down during the 1940 campaign, see Henry Steele Commager's, "Party Strife: Sign of Health," in the New York Times Magazine, October 6, 1940, p. 3.

in November, the United States would "out-distance Hitler in any contest he chooses in 1940 or after," that America would regain prosperity and become strong, and that *when* Hitler was beaten, it would be "on our own terms, in our own American way."

He told the vast audience that the New Deal administration had preached the doctrine of division labeled the "I pass" doctrine, which had no confidence in the future of America. He then made his appeal for the votes of those who supported the New Deal reforms: "I believe that the forces of free enterprise must be regulated. I am opposed to business monopolies. I believe in collective bargaining, by representatives of labor's own free choice, without any interference and in full protection of those obvious rights. I believe in the maintenance of minimum standards for wages and of maximum standards for hours. I believe that such standards should constantly improve. I believe in federal regulation of interstate utilities, of securities markets, and of banking. I believe in federal pensions, in adequate old age benefits, and in unemployment allowances."

In the field of agricultural policy, Willkie again sanctioned the New Deal. He advocated cooperative buying and selling, the full extension of rural electrification, and an equalization of the lot of the farmer with that of the manufacturer. He said: "If this cannot be done by parity of prices, other means must be found. . . ." However, a few minutes later, he stated that the farmers were victims of the New Deal's plan of economic rehabilitation because "many of them are forced to subsist on what is virtually a dole, under centralized direction from Washington."

Wendell Willkie then asserted what was to be his principal appeal during the campaign: that if elected, he would usher in a period of unlimited productivity, restored prosperity, and re-employment by private enterprise. The investor would no longer be afraid to invest his capital and businessmen would no longer be fearful of expansion. Restrictions on small business would be lifted, obsolete industrial machinery would be replaced, the unemployed would go back to work, the nation would be strong, and therefore, free! It was in this section of the acceptance speech that Willkie unleashed his most successful criticism of the Roosevelt administration, but he advocated nothing specific to implement the solutions to the problems he condemned. Essentially, Willkie was declaring that he would do a better job, with less waste, and with fewer dollars. In conclusion, Willkie called for a series of debates with the President on certain defined issues, and demanded an end to division among the American people, an elimination of the exploitation by pressure groups, and a resurgence of liberty and unity in the United States.

Evaluations of the address followed party lines closely. The press reported it with some enthusiasm; Arthur Vandenberg called it "one of the greatest in our generation"; and the leaders of the Democrats-for-Willkie issued a joint statement insisting that the speech was a liberal platform enunciated by a leader all Democrats opposed to a third term could follow. The Democratic position was summed up by Representative Ludlow of Willkie's home state of Indiana, who asked: "I'm wondering how any issues can be raised in this year's campaign since Mr. Willkie's speech . . . seems to indicate that he stands for about the same things as President Roosevelt. Where is the fellow who wants a change going to go?" Norman Thomas, who had long been pleading for a thorough alternative to the capitalistic "catch-all" philosophies of the two major parties, remarked: "He agreed with Mr. Roosevelt's entire program of social reform and said it was leading to disaster." Actually, the difficulty with the Willkie speech was primarily with the candidate's delivery and with the fact that the millions of listeners, with their minute differences of expectations concerning the political candidate, would not have been satisfied by any address. Those who wanted clear alternatives were disappointed by Willkie's philosophical similarity to the New Deal; unconvinced liberals saw a blurring of political conviction; fence-sitters found neither originality nor conclusive reason for a change in administrations. In reality, Willkie sincerely endorsed the reform legislation that was too well entrenched for any nominee of a major party to overthrow. He was both too obstinate and too honest to alter his views of what he regarded as desirable programs, and he shrewdly bargained for independent votes by sanctioning the New Deal statutes while rebuking their administration. To be sure, the candidate immediately invited charges of inconsistency and "me-tooism," but he was gambling for seven million votes with a promise to restore the confidence of Americans in each other and in themselves. Instead of an alternative to the New Deal programs, Willkie proposed an antidote consisting of a new leader who was partially out of intellectual and political accord with both the Republican and Democratic parties but who temporarily had the support of one party and desperately needed the help of a segment of the other. In spite of his obstinacy, his amateur assistants, and his lack of political tact and awareness, Willkie rightfully expected to get this assistance, for as E. E. Schattschneider has written: "All who oppose the party in power are made to feel a certain need for concentrating their support behind the party most likely to lead a successful opposition."[29]

Harold L. Ickes, at the time Secretary of the Interior, was selected by President Roosevelt to reply to Willkie's speech of acceptance. He bitterly castigated Willkie for once opposing the reform legislation which he now endorsed, for trying to prevent the success of the TVA, and for placing the preservation of private utilities above service to his country.[30] He called Willkie, "The rich man's Roosevelt" and "the simple, barefoot Wall Street lawyer." In regard to Willkie's challenge to Roosevelt to engage in a series of debates, Ickes replied: "One cannot challenge the President of the United States to go about the country barnstorming, . . . without laying himself open to the charge that he is indulging in cheap bravado. . . . The President cannot adjourn the Battle of Britain in order to ride the circuit with Mr. Willkie. . . ." Ickes accused Willkie of inconsistency, of going to Elwood to escape the stigma of Fifth Avenue, of being a Morgan affiliate, and a member of Tammany Hall. He declared that Willkie's "current party" contained the "loudest and bitterest of those who protested against farm relief; work relief; collective bargaining; fair wages and hours for labor; taxation based on ability to pay . . . and measures necessary to check excessive concentration of control over other people's savings and other people's lives."

Senator Bridges issued a formal rebuttal to reporters. If anything, it was even more vindictive than the Secretary's address. He called Ickes a "Hitler in short pants" and "a common scold puffed up by high office." He asserted that Roosevelt withheld information from the nation on the subject of foreign policy, that the President had slept while Hitler armed, and that the Roosevelt family had not upheld the dignity of the office of the presidency of which Ickes spoke. The "Smear Campaign" of 1940 had begun.[31]

---

[29] *Party Government* (New York, 1942), p. 82.

[30] *Supra,* p. 56.

[31] *Ibid.,* p. 15. Peter Odegard observed: ". . . the serious tone of both Mr. Roosevelt's and Mr. Willkie's acceptance speeches has unfortunately not been maintained, but it would not be a political campaign without some billingsgate. We need not, therefore, be too disturbed when 'Honest' Harold

After the Elwood address, Willkie set up an informal general headquarters in Rushville. It was a repetition of the Colorado Springs period; occasional trips for speaking engagements, conferences with leaders in various fields, and frequent press interviews. Willkie was asked to comment on nearly every action taken by Congress or the President, and during the latter part of August, two issues arose that illustrated Willkie's refusal to compromise his opinions for partisan expediency. On the first issue, the granting of over-age destroyers to Great Britain, he went along with the Administration; on the second, the Overton-Russell Amendment to the Selective Service Act, Willkie opposed a large segment of his own party.

In August of 1940 the United States had about two hundred old four-stack destroyers in "mothballs." Since the previous May the government of Britain, whose fleet of destroyers had been reduced to sixty ships, had been asking for a portion of these inactive United States vessels. In the United States, polls indicated support for the request. William Allen White, a convention supporter of Willkie who had formed the Committee to Defend America by Aiding the Allies, asked the immediate transfer of sixty of one hundred sixty-two of the ships that were being rehabilitated for recommissioning. White and a group of journalists[32] bought full-page advertisements in various newspapers throughout the nation to promote the deal, and also succeeded in persuading General John J. Pershing to lend his influence in support of the gift. In addition, White made an attempt to get the support for the transfer from Willkie because President Roosevelt did not think an arrangement to trade destroyers for the use of British bases could be made unless Willkie would agree not to make a political issue of it.[33] Archibald MacLeish also mentioned the matter to Russell Davenport and asked him to persuade Willkie to withhold criticism. Willkie stated that his position in favor of aid to Britain was well known but that he could not be expected to assume the responsibility for any specific steps taken

---

Ickes calls Willkie a 'simple barefoot Wall Street lawyer' running for office as a 'rich man's Roosevelt' or when Senator Bridges replies by describing Ickes as a 'Hitler in short pants.' " Odegard, *op. cit.,* p. 88.

[32] The group included Barry Bingham, publisher of the *Louisville Courier-Journal;* Herbert Agar, the editor of that paper; Walter Lippmann; Joseph Alsop; Robert S. Allen; Frank R. Kent of the *Baltimore Sun;* Geoffrey Parsons, chief editorial writer of the *New York Herald Tribune;* Russell Davenport, and a number of others. *Newsweek,* August 12, 1940, p. 11.

[33] Drummond, *op. cit.,* p. 453.

which had to be measured against a background known only to Administration leaders.

On September 3, 1940, the destroyer transfer was announced to Congress as an accomplished fact. The agreement gave fifty American destroyers to England in exchange for a ninety-nine-year lease on bases in six British possessions in the Western Hemisphere. Willkie had given his private approval through William Allen White only to the aid per se, and had agreed not to make a campaign issue of the matter.[34] He felt compelled, however, for partisan reasons, to attack the method by which the deal was negotiated. He told reporters: "The country will undoubtedly approve the program to add to our naval and air bases and assistance given to Great Britain. It is regrettable, however, that the President did not deem it necessary in connection with his proposal to secure the approval of Congress or permit public discussion prior to adoption." Some of Willkie's advisers thought he should take a stronger position, so on the following day, he called the agreement "the most arbitrary and dictatorial action ever taken by a President."[35] This was all he could do and still remain consistent in his belief that Britain's welfare deserved material aid from America. His criticism obtained page-one publicity, but it was clear that the destroyer-base exchange was popular. The President was building confidence; Willkie could only follow his action and build phrases.

A second issue which caused Willkie some embarrassment also arose during the latter part of August, 1940. He had supported selective service legislation to enlarge the armed forces long before the Republican convention. While the Burke-Wadsworth conscription bill was being debated in Congress, an amendment designed to give the President power to "draft industry" was also passed. Willkie immediately condemned the plant-seizing plan as a "cheap trick" by two New Deal senators, Overton of Louisiana and Russell of Georgia, authors of the bill, to "sovietize" the country. He asked that the President publicly justify the legislation, and claimed that proposals of that type caused the ruin of France. The response from the Democrats in Congress was both derisive and immediate,

---

[34] Sherwood, *op. cit.*, p. 215.

[35] Dr. Herbert W. Briggs, an authority on international law from Cornell University, argued that the exchange was illegal. See his article "Neglected Aspects of the Destroyer Deal," in the *American Journal of International Law*, 34 (October, 1940), 569-87.

particularly in the Senate, where sixty-nine senators, including nine Republicans, had supported the bill. Senator Russell declared:

It seems that Mr. Willkie has about divorced himself from the political party he recently married, at least insofar as the members of that party who voted against conscription of men, and he disagrees with those of his party who voted for the utilization of the industrial resources of the country. He has therefore placed himself in direct issue with every Republican member of this body on one or the other of these questions.[36]

Senator Lee, Democrat of Oklahoma, chided the Republican nominee for his statements. He said:

I should not be surprised if Mr. Willkie should accuse me of wanting to set up a dictatorship; but when he accuses the Senator from Vermont (Mr. Austin), when he accuses the Senator from New Jersey (Mr. Barbour), when he accuses the Senator from Kansas (Mr. Capper), . . . when he accuses the Senator from California (Mr. Johnson), when he accuses the Senator from Pennsylvania (Mr. Davis), when he accuses the Senator from Massachusetts (Mr. Lodge), when he accuses the Senator from North Dakota (Mr. Nye), when he accuses the Senator from Minnesota (Mr. Shipstead) and when he accuses the Senator from New Hampshire (Mr. Tobey) of wanting to sovietize this country and set up a dictatorship, it seems to me that he is going a long way to protect his dollars which are too sacred to be used to defend the country against aggression.[37]

When Willkie realized that he had contradicted some of the party stalwarts, he tried to clarify his position. He told reporters: "There has been some confusion about the amendment. . . . Under the provisions of the Selective Service Bill, persons register and individuals are selected for service by a uniform rule. No government official can reach down and draft John Jones. By the terms of the amendment, one man can commandeer a plant or facility deemed necessary for defense. If a bill should be introduced providing that an industrial plant might be selected to be taken by the government by rule, as in the case of men, instead of the arbitrary act of one man, I would be for it." The explanation was insufficient and the Democrats continued to make an issue of the candidate's independence. Ed Flynn, chairman of the Democratic National Committee, stated that the Republicans in Congress would never support Willkie if he were elected. Joe Martin immediately sprang to the nominee's defense. He asserted: ". . . We may differ with Mr. Willkie on an amendment, but I think the country wants Congress to do some thinking of its own. . . . I want to assure Mr. Flynn there is no

---

[36] *Congressional Record,* vol. 86, p. 1717 (76th Cong., 3rd Sess., Aug. 30, 1940).

[37] *Ibid.*

difference between Mr. Willkie and the Republican membership in Congress concerning the fundamental issues in this campaign or before the country at this time. . . ."[38]

President Roosevelt refused to become involved in the heated exchange over the amendment. Republican sources, for the most part, realized that Willkie had placed himself in an untenable political position from which to attract the independent voter, but they defended his statements on what they considered to be haphazard legislation. The amendment was finally modified to prevent arbitrary seizures of property, and the entire conscription act was passed by Congress on September 14 and signed by the President two days later.

The Gallup poll released at the end of August showed that Willkie was still leading the President in electoral votes, but that the Republican nominee had lost four states, three of them in the West, since the previous survey.[39] Willkie still maintained the favor of twenty states and forty-nine per cent of the individuals polled. Gallup also found that Willkie's "most important single problem" was to win more votes in the lower and middle income levels of the population. He added: "No student of politics can pretend to understand the campaign without full knowledge of the sharp division of sentiment which has sprung up in American politics along class lines."[40]

Early in September, as Willkie saw that he was losing favor in

---

[38] Statement by Martin inserted in the Appendix of the *Congressional Record*, vol. 86, p. 18419 (76th Cong., 3rd Sess., Sept. 13, 1940) by Representative Daniel A. Reed of New York. The Republican senators who voted against the amendment, and thus in support of Willkie's beliefs were Danaher, Connecticut; Gurney, South Dakota; Hale, Maine; Reed, Kansas; Taft, Ohio; Vandenberg, Michigan; White, Maine; and Wiley, Wisconsin.

[39] The four states were Oregon, Idaho, Wyoming, and Connecticut. The electoral vote was 284 for Willkie and 247 for Roosevelt.

[40] The Institute poll revealed the following class stratification:

	For Roosevelt	For Willkie
Upper Income Group	29%	71%
Middle Income Group	47%	53%
Lower Income Group	66%	34%
On Relief	75%	25%

The upper group in the Institute's estimate was comprised of voting families earning more than fifty dollars a week. They represented about one-sixth of the voting population. The middle group earned between twenty and fifty dollars a week and constituted forty-eight per cent of the voting population. The lower group, comprising thirty-six per cent, were those earning less than twenty dollars a week, including persons on relief. In 1940, as in nearly every election, the middle group held the balance of power.

the West, he released the plans for his first two-week trip through eighteen states to the Pacific Ocean and back — a trip to cover nearly seven thousand miles. Willkie was also aware that he had to increase his popularity among those in the lower income groups who had supported Roosevelt in the two previous elections. The nominee's determination to gain in favor in all states, and to win a majority of the votes from people of all classes was eventually to make him the most widely traveled presidential aspirant in American history.

CAMPAIGN AWEIGH

During the first few days in September, Willkie occupied his headquarters in Rushville, making plans for his formal tour of the West beginning with a trip through Illinois and his first major speech from Coffeyville, Kansas, the city in which he had taught history before the first World War.

In the East, the campaign organizations were beginning to function in high gear. Oren Root announced that his organization was ready to begin a nationwide distribution of "Willkie Worker Kits" for which 25,000 requests already had been received.[41] The kits were designed to make active political campaigners out of the thousands of individuals who ordinarily would have taken no part in the campaign as such. Root stated, "The Willkie campaigners . . . will be unlike the well-known electioneers of bygone elections. Instead of petty officeholders, ward captains, and the party 'faithful' they are housekeepers, factory workers and others of every shade of political belief." In addition, the United Republican Finance Committee started a general drive for contributions in New York to raise additional funds for the Republican nominee. Robert B. Murry, Jr., secretary of the committee, announced that he had enlisted the support of 7,900 volunteer workers for a house-to-house canvass.

Though thousands of people were actively talking, evaluating, and supporting Willkie throughout the nation, the leader in Rushville was still conducting what was essentially a one-man show. It was the very fact that much of the work was not being supervised by the "well-known electioneers of bygone elections" that was causing reverberations within the ranks of the Republican organization.

---

[41] The kits contained a pledge card to be signed by ten persons agreeing to vote for Willkie, campaign buttons, pamphlets entitled "Willkie, the Man," and directions for campaigning.

Newsweek reported "one of the key men in the GOP high command" as complaining, "I'll be darned if I know who's running this campaign,"[42] and there were increasing numbers of others who deplored the fact that the amateurs were so influential in the Willkie camp, and that much of the advice of experienced campaigners was ignored.

Moreover, there was a general lack of coordination on all levels. Already weak in the far West, Willkie had hoped that McNary would appease liberals devoted to regional loyalties and the public-power theories. During the entire month of August, however, the candidate had only once talked with the Oregon senator. The acceptance speech at Elwood contained no mention of McNary, and McNary himself did not campaign publicly for the national ticket until the latter part of August, when he accepted the vice-presidential nomination in Salem, Oregon. He frequently told associates that he would allow Willkie to "carry the ball and set the pace."[43]

Luther Huston, a staff writer for the *New York Times,* observed that this was precisely what Willkie intended to do if it suited his personal strategy: "All the evidence indicates . . . that Mr. Willkie intends to pitch the tone of the campaign, set the pace for it, and provide the dynamics of it. He will make the issues. Probably he will not attempt to line up the Republicans, as such, behind anything. He may have in mind what trying to line up the party and pay heed to the old guardsmen did to Alfred M. Landon in 1936. The thought probably has occurred to Mr. Willkie that the Republicans want mostly to win and that if they had not been motivated by that desire he never would have been their candidate."[44]

Willkie, however, realized by this date that though he would run his own campaign, he needed the help of every Republican from whom he could obtain support. Therefore, he called a meeting of eighty party leaders from twenty-one states which was held in Rushville on September 6.[45] After a luncheon, the nominee discussed organizational plans to ameliorate the increasing friction between

---

[42] *Newsweek,* September 16, 1940, p. 17.

[43] *Ibid.,* September 2, 1940, p. 14.

[44] *New York Times,* September 1, 1940, p. 8.

[45] Though Sinclair Weeks, Sam Pryor, David Ingalls, Harold Stassen, and many organization Republicans were at the gathering, Homer Capehart, who had managed the entire acceptance celebration in Elwood and who resided in Indianapolis, was not invited. Interview with Senator Capehart.

the Republican National Committee, the Associated Willkie Clubs of America, and the Democrats-for-Willkie group. Willkie informed the visitors that he realized that his election depended largely on successful work by the established party machinery, and he therefore urged each national committeeman and state official on his return home to assemble the county, ward, and precinct leaders in order to plan an intensive effort to register and bring to the polls every possible Republican voter. He also told the politicians present that if he were elected, all patronage would go to the regular Republican organization members rather than to the independent groups which had been established under the leadership of Root and Davenport.[46] The candidate, rapidly becoming aware of his additional political obligations, also made a plea for the election of Republican senators and congressmen. Unfortunately, through an oversight, no state chairman or member of the national committee was asked to speak, and a few of them were piqued. Nevertheless, the meeting on the surface gave the appearance of success. Leaders in the East returning from Rushville expressed approval of the outcome of the gathering. All groups pledged cooperation and as an indication of the new accord, Oren Root made a September 7 address in Maine under the auspices of the regular Republican organization.

Willkie again devoted his hours to planning, rejecting unwanted support, commenting on current issues, and refuting Democratic charges. He had been embarrassed late in August and in September by the public support of the German-American Bund, the Italian Fascist organization, the American Communist party, Father Coughlin, and Mrs. Dilling.[47] The Republican nominee repudiated the entire group and with particular reference to Coughlin, he stated bluntly that he was against any man or organization "opposed to certain people because of their race or religion." "I am not only not interested in his support — I don't want it."

Willkie managed to iron out his differences with Joseph N. Pew, Jr., the Pennsylvania Republican leader toward whom he had been cool after the national convention, and to persuade the oil magnate to take an active role in the forthcoming campaign. He

---

[46] Personal letter from Frank D. McKay.

[47] Stone, *op. cit.*, p. 354. Willkie's acceptance speech had been highly praised in *Social Justice*, the weekly magazine of the Coughlinites. After Willkie's repudiation, Coughlin said he endorsed neither Willkie nor President Roosevelt. *New York Times*, August 28, 1940, p. 12.

tried to keep alive the enthusiasm created during the previous months. He gave countless interviews and praised his campaign workers, but across the nation an undercurrent of apathy, antipathy, or, in some cases, merely inactivity gradually rose to the surface in a discussion of a "slump" in the Willkie campaign. Reporters observed this public indifference and wrote that the crusade was leveling off, that Roosevelt, gaining favorable attention with the destroyer deal, the selective service preparations, and the "total defense" appropriations, placed Willkie in a position where he could merely follow the President. In addition, the disparity between Republican members of Congress and the nominee on such issues as the Overton-Russell Amendment and New Deal measures was looked upon as burdening the campaign for the party as a whole. The charges, made by organization Republicans, were that (1) the Willkie staff was inadequate; too many important people were slighted, while inexperienced publicists dictated policy; (2) the research aides were incapable and unimaginative; (3) Joe Martin was engrossed with congressional matters and was therefore unable to fulfill his function as national chairman; (4) Willkie himself had talked too much and had concentrated on minor issues; (5) some evidence of fear and defeatism was apparent among the staff members surrounding the candidate; and (6) the voting public was receiving a blurred image of the candidate and his potential policies if elected.[48]

In the haste and confusion of a campaign, however, such intangibles are at best difficult to remedy, and Willkie chose to ignore the criticism. On September 9 he told reporters the campaign was going splendidly and indicated his determination to assert his views on any issues regardless of adverse reactions. But on the following day, he came out against a House amendment to the Burke-Wadsworth selective service bill which would have delayed the draft until after the election in November. The amendment had been sponsored by Hamilton Fish and approved by 140 House Republicans, including Martin. Henry Wallace, the Democratic vice-presidential candidate, had been calling Willkie the "appeasement candidate," and undoubtedly Willkie wanted to repudiate such

---

[48] See Raymond Moley, "Is Willkie Slipping?" in *Newsweek*, September 16, 1940, p. 68. James Farley stated that, generally speaking, slumps do not affect the final outcome of elections because majority choices are made as soon as the conventions have adjourned. *New York Times*, September 11, 1940, p. 24.

charges, but congressional Republicans were furious at being left out on a limb, and many avowed that they would break away from Willkie in order to run their own campaigns.[49] At the Rushville meeting, Willkie had pledged support to his congressional colleagues, and five days later he had rejected their stand. Edward J. Flynn, the Democratic national chairman, challenged: "What I want to know from Mr. Willkie is how he is going to explain that he can't do anything with members of his own party in the event of his election when he can't do anything with them before the election. . . . Practically all of his party are voting against what Mr. Willkie announces he is for."

Willkie was forced into action. He held a conference in Indianapolis with McNary, Martin, and Stassen at which he convinced them that the Fish amendment should be eliminated in conference committee. It was the sound move, politically. Nearly all of the defensive measures advocated by both Willkie and the President were popular with the voters. On the other hand, the meeting removed an additional facet of the Roosevelt foreign policy from the list of clear alternatives between the candidates, and it served to point up the differences between Willkie and the congressional Republicans. Two days later, when the conscription bill passed both houses, seven Republican senators supported Willkie's position and ten refused to follow the nominee. In the House, only 46 of the 134 Republicans voting on the bill favored the measure, but the Fish amendment was defeated.

As Willkie made plans to campaign in the West, a number of organizational developments occurred. Chairman Martin selected eleven party leaders to be his regional aides;[50] a meeting of the eastern regional conference of Republican women leaders released plans to visit every registered voter in the nation "to take the party

---

[49] *The Nation*, September 21, 1940, p. 235.

[50] Senator Styles Bridges was appointed regional aide for the New England states; Joe Talbot for Connecticut and Rhode Island; David Ingalls for Ohio and Tennessee; Representative Leo Allen for Illinois, Iowa, Michigan, and Indiana; Harry Darby for Nebraska, Kansas and Colorado; Representative Dewey Short for Missouri and Arkansas; Herbert Hyde for Oklahoma and Texas; John E. Jackson for Louisiana, Mississippi, Alabama, Florida, and Georgia; Representative Frank Horton for Wyoming, Idaho, and Montana; Representative Harry L. Englebright for California, Oregon, Washington, and Nevada; E. C. Duncanson for Minnesota, Wisconsin, North Dakota, and South Dakota; and Representative J. William Ditter, chairman of the national Republican congressional committee.

to the people" under the leadership of Miss Marian Martin, head of the women's division of the national committee; and Stacey Beebe, executive assistant to Oren Root, announced that the Willkie Clubs would disband on November 5. This latter statement was considered necessary to alleviate the fears of Republican party workers that the clubs might encroach on the territory of the party organization. Willkie was visited by a number of labor union chiefs from Illinois and Ohio, by several farm leaders, churchmen, businessmen, and by Senator McNary. The candidate was gratified by the results of the Maine election which showed more than sixty per cent of the vote going to Republican candidates — a 7.2 per cent increase over the congressional majorities of 1938. He was disappointed, however, to hear that Mayor LaGuardia of New York had formally declared his support of President Roosevelt.[51] The Gallup poll also showed that labor was still for President Roosevelt by a 64 per cent to 36 per cent margin, but also that one worker in eight was undecided.[52]

On September 12, as Willkie departed from Rushville on his seven-thousand-mile trip to the Pacific Coast and back, he promised a fighting campaign. The following day he entered northern Illinois to make four speeches. He was heartily cheered in the Chicago Loop district, but the stockyards workers to whom he spoke were completely unenthusiastic. In Cicero he criticized boss rule, municipal corruption, and the national debt, while pledging a defense program so great that no dictator would dare strike the United States. During the day he also addressed 15,000 Negroes in the American Giants baseball park. Nearly a million people had seen him in less than eighteen hours. But when the candidate ended his day in Chicago and its suburbs, he was so hoarse that he could barely speak. It was a tragic beginning to a lengthy and strenuous tour; his advisers were afraid that he would be unable to continue, and called in a throat specialist who remained with the train throughout the entire trip.

---

[51] LaGuardia said to reporters, "I prefer Roosevelt with his known faults to Mr. Willkie with his unknown virtues." He then scored Willkie as a utility executive more interested in the profits of his bondholders than in the welfare of large numbers of consumers. He attacked the Republican nominee for having joined Tammany Hall and pointed out that a majority of the Democrats in New York City had not found it necessary to join that organization.

[52] The AF of L workers favored the President, 62 per cent to 38 per cent for Willkie. Three-fourths of the members of the CIO polled were against Willkie.

Willkie made some startling blunders. He used language that affronted his listeners, and made flippant remarks that Representative Sabath called "expressions utterly unfitting and unbecoming to a presidential nominee." In Joliet he asserted that Roosevelt had "telephoned to Hitler and Mussolini and urged them to sell Czechoslovakia down the river." Lem Jones, Willkie's press secretary, explained later that the candidate had "misspoken" and that what he had meant to say was that the President had urged a settlement at Munich and that the pact there "agreed to sell Czechoslovakia down the river." Before a crowd of 9,000 persons in Peoria, Willkie also corrected his statement. Nevertheless, the Democrats pounced on the error, and Cordell Hull immediately issued a lengthy denial in which he charged that Willkie's assertions indicated that he was "grossly ignorant of the history of the last few years." Actually, Administration leaders had, on occasion, claimed credit for Munich. In 1938, shortly after the pact had been signed, Harry Woodring, then Secretary of War, went on the air with Sumner Welles to claim that President Roosevelt had saved the peace of the world.[53] Willkie's charge concerning the telephone conversation, however, was groundless, and the fact that he had made the statement at all followed him, through his opponents, for years after the incident had taken place.

Willkie's continual improvisation in speeches was a constant cause of worry and confusion on the Willkie train. His impromptu statements often necessitated other remarks that placed ideas out of sequence, while his failure to read his speeches before he delivered them meant that they were frequently ineffectively delivered. Nevertheless, in Iowa Willkie made several short talks to crowds that were described as "uniformly enthusiastic." He declared that the President had "appeased the democratic world into destruction," and that a vote for Roosevelt would send American soldiers into a European war. He repeatedly challenged the President to a public debate, and as the campaign continued, Roosevelt's "silent treatment" became increasingly irritating. In Kansas City Willkie was kept under wraps on the orders of his doctor. Alf Landon, the only outsider allowed to visit him, called to assure him that "despite New Deal propaganda, the Republican campaign has not lost any ground."

At Coffeyville, in his first major speech, Willkie finally effectively

---

[53] *Propaganda Analysis,* October 15, 1940, p. 7.

centered an address on one specific issue which he called "the preservation of democracy." He declared that the President had lost faith in the American people and predicted that if Roosevelt obtained re-election, the nation would be placed under a totalitarian regime before 1944. He attacked the President's defense methods, his subterfuge in foreign policy, his lack of democracy, and his failure to delegate defense authority. He chided Roosevelt for his elaborate pretense that he had been "drafted" for a third term, and for pretending that he was too busy to campaign. The *New York Times* called the address "in some respects the most telling speech that the Republican candidate has yet made."

In mid-September, the Willkie train turned south. In Missouri, Oklahoma, and Texas, the candidate asked for Democratic votes. He traveled through New Mexico and on to Arizona, where he addressed the largest political crowd ever assembled in the state. He was introduced by Old Guardsman Clarence Budington Kelland as "a man selected by Divine Providence to lead America in this difficult period." He told the 15,000 people assembled that the Republicans, if elected, would "revitalize" the national economy. Then, playing on local economic issues, Willkie revealed the extent to which the forces of Republicanism had compromised his beliefs on tariffs as he promised never to lift the restrictions on Argentine beef and mutton.

In California, remembering Charles Evans Hughes and the campaign of 1916, Willkie paid frequent tribute to Hiram Johnson as a true liberal, despite the fact that his views stood in sharp conflict with Johnson's in the field of foreign affairs. In Los Angeles, San Diego, and San Francisco, he spoke to tremendous, enthusiastic crowds. Republican leaders saw a definite gain in Willkie sentiment. Stassen called it a "pick-up after a lag," and Oren Root hailed the California speeches as the end of the lull in the campaign. A Gallup poll, taken during the lull, however, showed an astonishing drop in the number of voters favoring Willkie. In August, he had led the President in electoral votes. By the middle of September, Roosevelt had captured a majority of the interviewees in thirty-eight states, leaving Willkie with only 78 electors and a prediction of less than forty-five per cent of the popular vote. Eleven per cent were still undecided, however, and about a third of the voters in each party indicated that they were not firm in their convictions as how they would vote in November. The only really heartening news from the East was that the *New York Times,* which had supported Roosevelt in 1932 and 1936, came out in a three-column editorial in support of Willkie.

Up in Portland, Oregon, Willkie spoke on the public power issue. To many people it seemed like the candidate did an about-face. He said that he favored the completion of the Bonneville and Grand Coulee Dams, that the power generated in connection with such projects should be sold for the benefit of the people, and that the people of the areas affected should decide whether that power should be distributed through privately owned distribution systems or publicly owned public utilities. The only hint of the old Willkie of the TVA fight was his statement that ". . . if you want to take over the private utilities, that is your business. . . . But you should do it by the determination of fair values so that capital will not be driven out of this area." Willkie's speech prompted Raymond Clapper to comment: "Although Willkie won his spurs fighting T.V.A. and the extension of public-power projects, it does not appear that he is trying to win the election on the same issue. On the contrary, the policy that Willkie outlined at Portland . . . dovetails with current public-power developments."[54]

In Seattle, Willkie promised to take business out of the "dog house." He said that the ending of the curb on enterprise was the only way that the United States could avert economic collapse. He again promised to complete the big dams, and pledged to the Northwest the use of the power from the projects for the benefit of the people. He told the 30,000 people assembled that the reasons for unemployment were the shortage of employers, the red tape forced upon employers, the inefficient and unscientific tax structures, and the constantly changing New Deal policies. Unfortunately, Seattle was not the completely appropriate place in which to make such statements. There were many job vacancies in the city at the time in lumber, airplane manufacturing, and naval construction. Such errors of judgment were typical of the lack of coordination and research aboard the Willkie train on which nearly all of the speeches were written. Willkie's principal speechwriters rarely had an opportunity to discuss the material with him, and their work was always revised by Russell Davenport. They were turning out speeches so rapidly that they had little chance to check facts or consider subtleties of crowd appeal.

---

[54] *Congressional Record,* vol. 86 (76th Cong., 3rd Sess., Sept. 24, 1940).

The candidate began his swing back to the East. In Butte, Montana, he scored the President for once making a statement that had resulted in a fall in the price in copper which in turn produced a reduction in pay for the workers of the industry. He then stopped denouncing Franklin Roosevelt, but condemned his advisers as "unscrupulous, cynical schemers, intelligentsia, disbelievers in democracy, anxious to hold on to their power." At one stop, a tomato struck a newspaperman beside Willkie. "That's the only kind of argument I get from the other side," the nominee remarked. On the whole, however, the campaign was improving in the response that the candidate was obtaining from his audiences. A new Gallup survey showed that though the President still was in the lead (with 51 per cent of those with opinions approving a third term), Willkie was at this point 25 per cent stronger among the independent voters than Landon had been four years earlier.

In North Dakota, to the nearly 15,000 persons who gathered to hear him in Bismarck, he charged the Roosevelt administration with wasteful spending and failure to build an adequate national defense. Later, he commented on Thomas Corcoran's resigning his job in Washington to devote his time to the Roosevelt campaign, "I don't think the President wants to be a dictator, . . . but I wouldn't say that for the group around him."

On to Nebraska went the Willkie train. In his major speech on farm policy, written by W. W. Waymack, editor of the *Des Moines Register's* editorial page, and by Representative Clifford Hope of Kansas, Willkie promised to help the farmers by pushing trade, calling an economic parley of growers, industrialists, labor, and consumers, and by continuing the AAA. He claimed that he would improve the program, however, by expanding the home market, reviving foreign trade, and by administering the farm policy more simply.[55] He also asserted that he had been for rural electrification since 1933 and that he thought that it ought to be developed and

[55] *New York Times*, September 27, 1940, p. 13. Henry Wallace retorted that he had no reason to doubt Willkie's sincerity, but that ". . . if the Republican nominee should be elected with a Republican Congress, no matter how he feels about the farm aid, his hands would be tied by his fellow party-members in Congress." Wallace pointed out that about 75 per cent of the Republican congressmen had voted against the New Deal farm measures. He also cited the fact that the New Deal's program of rural electrification had brought electricity to four out of every ten farm homes in comparison to the one out of ten rural dwellings that had had electricity in 1930. He stated: "This increase has occurred . . . not because private

extended.[56] His general conclusion was that the economic welfare of the United States could not come to or from one group alone; that prosperity depended on a united and a coordinated effort.

Willkie concluded his western tour with an impressive speech before 15,000 persons in the field house of the University of Wisconsin in Madison. He answered hecklers from the audience with enjoyable humor, and "gradually rose to an oratorical form that astounded the correspondents, who were only now discovering that Willkie doesn't talk, he likes to argue."[57] Unfortunately, the talk was the only major address of his tour that was not broadcast and it was Willkie's finest exhibition. Before the evening was over, he had his audience, made up largely of students, applauding enthusiastically.

During the entire journey through the West, in scores of brief talks from the platform of his train and from temporary stands created for the events, Willkie made many vague general promises concerning the economic future. He specifically said, however, that he would expand the Social Security Act; continue the Wagner Labor Relations Act and the Wages and Hours Act; give a Cabinet position to the Northwest; continue soil conservation, rural electrification, farm credit, commodity loans, and crop insurance; provide a job for every man and woman in the nation willing to work; and continue relief for all persons who could not find work. In less responsible flourishes of oratory, he promised that his crusade would result in "a new America with a higher standard of life than we have ever dreamed of before." In his final speech at the Republican state convention in Yonkers, New York, he pledged to 45,000 cheering partisans, "a new world!" Willkie was extremely fatigued, but his determination, courage, and brute strength kept him going in an effort to talk directly to anyone who was willing to listen. It is pos-

utility companies have shown an initiative in rural electrification but because government has led the way in developing rural power lines despite obstruction in many States by utility holding companies." *Ibid.*, p. 14.

[56] Senator Norris, on the floor of the Senate, declared that Willkie had always fought the REA, that he had testified before a state commission (in Michigan) on behalf of favorable applications by the Consumers Power Company of Michigan (which erected spite lines to make a rural electrification project impractical in areas where it had refused to erect lines before), and that if Willkie favored rural electrification, he should tell the people when he had been converted. *Congressional Record,* vol. 86, p. 19249 (76th Cong., 3rd Sess., Sept. 27, 1940).

[57] *Time,* October 7, 1940, p. 14.

sible that no candidate, not excluding William Jennings Bryan, ever waged so relentless a campaign.

The President continued to ignore the Willkie endeavor. He attended official functions, inspected defense establishments, urged peace, and hailed the growing national defense while other Administration leaders launched the main attack on the Republican candidate. Paul McNutt, speaking before 5,000 people at the New York World's Fair, asserted that "the Republican candidate is a man without a party" and asked, "how can a man run the country when he can't run his own party?"[58] He said that political leadership meant inducing others to help rather than ordering them to do so as in the business world. Henry Wallace attacked Willkie's labor stand and his associates. He said again that he did not question the "evidential good intentions" of Willkie, but charged that they were of little value against a record of "dishonest dealings" with labor by other Republican leaders and the Commonwealth and Southern Corporation. He asserted that Ernest T. Weir, head of the National Steel Corporation and treasurer of the Republican party, had taken a prominent part in resisting the attempt by organized labor to obtain free collective bargaining. He quoted

[58] This charge was frequently leveled at Willkie by the Democrats. The *New York Times* attempted to refute the charges in an editorial: "This line of argument is unfair to Mr. Willkie and misconceives the real nature of the situation. Complete control even of their own party in Congress is an achievement that has been granted to few Presidents in history. . . . [Here the *Times* printed a lengthy discussion of Roosevelt's inability to control his party on several major issues.] When Willkie becomes President he will have more influence. . . . Congressmen feel the importance of presenting a united front to the outside world on certain foreign policies; party members may go far to support a foreign policy of the President for that reason alone. . . . The President by virtue of his office has powers of many kinds by which he can influence Congressmen of his own party.

"It is true the record of Republican Congressmen on foreign policy has been far short of glorious. Many of them fought the revision of the Neutrality Law and even opposed some of the earlier defense appropriations asked for by the President. But it is fair to ask whether this represented anything more than the traditional partisan belief that it is the duty of an opposition to oppose. . . .

"There is no reason to suppose, in short, that Mr. Willkie, if elected President, would be any less able to lead the Republican party in Congress on either domestic or foreign policy than Mr. Roosevelt has been able to lead the Democratic party. Mr. Willkie might, indeed, be more successful not only in leading his party but in keeping it united." (The *Times* concluded that some congressmen will always be independent, but that the great bulk will usually go along with the policy of their leader in office. Many others will support any President if the external crisis is sufficient to demand unity.) *New York Times*, October 14, 1940, p. 18.

from *Fortune* magazine, which characterized Weir's treatment of labor as "appalling," and wanted to know why Weir was chosen for such an important office and why he was campaigning for Willkie. He also pointed to a decision of the United States Circuit Court of Appeals ordering the Consumers Power Company, a subsidiary of Commonwealth and Southern, "to cease intimidating its workers."[59]

The Republican forces were, however, beginning to open their final month's drive. National Chairman Joseph W. Martin declared that the brakes would be removed in the East in October; Franklyn Waltman, the national publicity chief, issued constantly increasing amounts of material for the nation's press painting Willkie as a courageous, fighting leader; and leading Republicans, including Senator Taft, castigated the New Deal with facts, figures, and phrases.

At the end of September, no one quite knew what the reaction was to the nominee's tour. Democrats continued to spread the word of a "slump" in the Willkie public standing, while Republicans were discounting such talk as a "whispering campaign" or as factless information. Nevertheless, objective observers were inclined to believe at this point that the candidate had practically no chance of upsetting the President. There was, indeed, a defeatism manifested everywhere except in the candidate himself and his immediate advisers. Dorothy Thompson and Walter Lippmann, both Willkie boosters in June, came out in favor of the re-election of the President.[60] Marquis Childs reported that there grew up among "Martin's flock in the House, an antipathy toward Willkie . . . almost greater than their hatred of Roosevelt."[61] Conservative Republicans over the nation wondered what type of candidate had been selected in Philadelphia. The Willkie campaign had hit rock bottom. For an additional week it remained there, but a new era

---

[59] *Ibid.*, p. 38.

[60] Miss Thompson had luncheon with Willkie earlier in the day she endorsed the President. The GOP standard-bearer tried to dissuade her, but she refused to withhold her endorsement of Roosevelt. She gave as her reasons: "[The President's] experience, his prestige in the democratic world, her faith in his ability to 'be a very great man in an emergency,' her belief that he has 'the confidence of the rank and file.' Said she: 'Mr. Willkie might also in time come to have that confidence. I think he would. But he does not have it now. He would have to win it and in winning it some of his supporters would be his greatest liability. Roosevelt has it, and time is of the essence.' " *Time,* October 21, 1940, p. 18.

[61] Childs, *op. cit.,* p. 205.

and an even more pugnacious Willkie were in the offing. There was still a month remaining in this fabulous "crusade."

WILLKIE'S CHALLENGE

Willkie went into the final month of his campaign with a determination to obtain eight million votes more than his predecessor, Alfred M. Landon, had been able to capture. To Willkie, this meant a personal appeal to as many people as he could possibly reach with every proposal he could sanction regardless of any planks in the Republican platform and in spite of the actions of Republican congressmen. He was confident that he could count upon the sixteen million voters who had supported the Republican party in 1936 to support it again in 1940. Therefore, he rejected the idea of campaigning on a "back to the 1920's" program, and concentrated on proving to the people that he represented progressive, intelligent, constitutional, and prosperous leadership which could advantageously be allowed to supplant the President. It is erroneous to assume, as some did, that Willkie did not have fundamental beliefs which he desired to present to the people. As an ambitious and successful businessman, he believed in free enterprise with a modicum of governmental supervision to prevent coercive monopolies; he believed in efficiency; and he believed in a prosperous United States. He also believed in most of the New Deal reforms, and his greatest task was to convince former Roosevelt voters that his beliefs were not incompatible with what they had come to expect from governmental administration.

It was obvious, however, that he was not running solely against a program or an administration. He was opposing the shrewdest politician who had ever held the American presidency, and it was, therefore, necessary to inspire in the people more than a conviction that he would be a satisfactory intellectual substitute. He had to create in them a faith in his ability and his integrity — a belief that he would be a superior replacement who would insure a greater period of prosperity and peace during the 1940's. In October, Willkie, by his own volition, chose to enter some of the most thoroughly entrenched Democratic areas in the nation in an effort to inspire that faith in himself and undermine the confidence in his opposition.

He began in Detroit, heart of industrial unionism, and found it, indeed, a difficult city in which to gain new votes. During the huge parade sponsored by the local groups supporting his candidacy, a cantaloupe, a telephone directory, a heavy ash tray, a wastebasket, a chair, and a bedspread were thrown at him at various times. To the Motor City crowds, he pledged that he would preserve the defense board, and that he would retain men like Knudsen, Hillman, Stettinius, and "other sound businessmen" with whom he was certain that he could work. He went on to Pontiac where the workers in the General Motors plant booed his statement that the New Deal barred prosperity. He became furious when an egg hit his automobile and splashed on Mrs. Willkie's dress, but he continued with his caravan. In Flint, before 3,000 white-collar workers, he received a warmer reception, and concluded his speech saying: "Please, please listen to what I have to say; you must not close your minds; listen to me on the radio, listen to the arguments on the other side, then decide how you want to vote. . . ." In Lansing, the crowds on the Capitol lawn were friendly, and Willkie was gratified by the greeting; in Grand Rapids, in his main address of the day, he told his audience that production was the key to a prosperous America. He asserted, "I know how to make jobs. I want to make American industry dynamic again."

The receptions for the Republican candidate were so varied, so partisan, and so filled with tension, while the Willkie courage and personal enthusiasm were so apparently genuine that *Time* stated: "There had never been anything like it. Maybe there never would be again. Only those who were actually on the scene knew what it was like. Wendell Willkie's tour of the U. S. was not a mere campaign. It was an extraordinary phenomenon almost certain to make a notable exhibit in the museum of political history. Its ups and downs were not reasonable. They were a fantastic form of political melodrama."[62]

The following day, Willkie decided to invade the "toughest, most Democratic factory areas of Toledo." As his automobile traveled through the industrial areas, he was heckled constantly. In front of the Auto-Lite Company, where strikers had once fought with National Guardsmen, workers held up signs lettered: "Win *What* with Willkie," and "Roosevelt Forever." He told his antagonists, "Boos don't hurt me. . . . All I ask is a square shake."

In Cleveland, the crowds of from 150,000 to 200,000 gave Willkie a tremendous ovation, but the hurried delivery of his address

---

[62] *Time,* October 14, 1940, p. 26.

indicated his fatigue and the pressures under which he had been campaigning. Willkie charged that "politics" in the defense effort imperiled America. He asked for more aid to Britain, even if it was necessary to sacrifice some speed in our own air force build-up.

Though he criticized the Administration for failing to defend America properly, he also shouted, ". . . the American people do not want war and have no idea whatever of joining any conflict, whether on the Atlantic or the Pacific. They are determined to keep America at peace." This particular statement prompted none other than Hamilton Fish to declare: "I can say without any reservations that the Republican members of the House of Representatives are unanimously for Mr. Willkie in his efforts to keep America out of war and will back him to the limit."[63]

Willkie traveled on to Pittsburgh, where he received a huge reception. Before more than 35,000 persons at Forbes Field, he presented a seven-point plan for labor which he asserted would help produce a rise in America's total economic prosperity. He promised to strengthen the existing Federal Conciliation Service, to decentralize the activities of the federal government in the labor field,[64] to encourage the states to strengthen their procedures for the settlement of labor disputes, to maintain fair minimum wages and enforce the law in both the North and the South, to preserve maximum hour legislation, to extend social security to many groups who were not covered at the time, and to include representatives of labor in the councils of the government. He also asked labor to clean the racketeers out of their organizations and promised a *man* from labor's ranks as his Secretary of Labor after he was elected.[65]

---

[63] *Congressional Record,* vol. 86, p. 19748 (76th Cong., 3rd Sess., Oct. 3, 1940). Representative Sabath of Illinois thought that both the Republicans were contradicting themselves. He stated in rebuttal, "The gentleman from New York states that Mr. Willkie in a speech . . . assures the voters he will, if elected, keep the country out of war. But how does this compare with his boast and bragging about what he is going to do to Hitler if elected? . . . The gentleman from New York states that he is speaking for the Republican membership in Congress. Though I dislike to question my colleague, I doubt very much that any considerable number of those 40 Republican Members who once stated Mr. Willkie's nomination would be a public calamity would be willing to stultify themselves now by saying too much." *Ibid.*

[64] For opposition to this plan, see Daniel Tobin's statement in the *New York Times,* October 6, 1940, p. 43.

[65] Willkie's speech was made to an audience made up largely of male workers. Thus, the statement at the time was well received. However, Frances Perkins, then Secretary of Labor, reported in her book, *The Roose-*

The speech, for the most part, went off very well, and it was said, unofficially, to have gratified both William Green and John L. Lewis.

On the journey through Pennsylvania, Willkie spoke to 25,000 people in Harrisburg, and made several talks from his train at Lancaster and Coatesville. An egg and several other missiles were thrown at him on the trip. The candidate told his audiences, "This is symptomatic of the class divisions and distinctions and bitterness and hatred that have been brought into American life in the last seven and a half years." In Philadelphia, however, Willkie was given a magnificent ovation. The courage, determination, and stamina of the man continued to astonish the correspondents and his advisers. The *New York Times* declared: "Even such professional cynics as newsmen knew that no mere love of office or appetite for acclaim could drive a man to the punishment Willkie was taking daily — not the boos, but the grinding strain of the campaign. . . ."

In Washington, Joe Martin thought that the congressmen should evidence some support of their candidates. On October 7 the Republican members of the House of Representatives unanimously commended Wendell L. Willkie and Senator McNary "for the splendid work they are doing in presenting the American cause to the country." The campaign needed such a lift, for the latest Gallup poll, taken during the latter part of September, showed the Republican popularity constantly decreasing. From 78 electoral

---

velt I Knew, that "The President, listening to the speech on the radio, was quick to catch the blunder. Although the audience of men applauded loudly . . . women in the United States, including Republican women, were pained and insulted." She added that the President thought the speech was excellent until Willkie made the remark about a male Secretary. Roosevelt then said, ". . . why didn't he have sense enough to leave well enough alone. Why did he have to insult every woman in the United States? It will make them mad, it will lose him votes." After the speech was concluded, Miss Perkins reports the President as having stated: "He's sure to make other boners as time goes on. . . . If we don't do anything to break the spell, I'm pretty sure he will talk himself out of enough votes to carry me without much effort." See Frances Perkins, *The Roosevelt I Knew* (New York, 1947), pp. 116-17. Willkie never decided just which *man* from labor's ranks he would have selected had he been elected. At another time, however, Willkie mentioned to friends that if he became President, he would like to have in respective positions: professional diplomat Norman Armour as his Secretary of State; John W. Hanes, corporation executive, as his Secretary of the Treasury; Paul G. Hoffman as Secretary of Commerce; Sinclair Weeks as Secretary of War; and Clifford Hope, Representative from Kansas, as his Secretary of Agriculture.

votes, Willkie's total had dropped to 32.[66] The situation seemed hopeless, but the Hoosier candidate refused to give up. Martin attacked the survey as "preposterous," and said that it had been taken before the candidate's recent "upswing." The odds still looked sizable, but Willkie continued to fight. He drove up to New Haven, Connecticut, where he gave 40,000 people a six-point program to revive business. In Bridgeport, he stressed his friendliness toward labor and scored the national debt. Here he charged that if the President was re-elected, there would be no social security benefits, for the government would be bankrupt. In Providence, Rhode Island, Willkie again spoke of labor's rights, the continuation of relief, the powerful nation that would result from a Republican victory, and added that he "looked forward constantly to the day when international tariff barriers would be reduced." In Boston, the Hoosier called the New Deal regime "Irresponsible Government" and criticized the President for pretending that his inspection trips of defense projects were nonpolitical.

While the nominee was blasting the New Deal in the East, Thomas E. Dewey spoke for him in upstate New York, and a galaxy of GOP stalwarts, Herbert Hoover, Alfred Landon, Senators McNary, Vandenberg, Taft, Brewster, Nye, and Wiley, Representatives Fish and Dewey Short, and Governors Sprague of Oregon and Stassen of Minnesota were actively campaigning for him in the West.

Surveys revealed that much of the Willkie voting support lay in protest groups rather than in positive endorsements of qualities in Willkie himself. The candidate's promises of future achievements were making no impact, and his advisers demanded that he make his attacks on the President more violent. Until this time, Willkie had tried to keep the campaign on a relatively high level, though the Republican and Democratic underlings had made it one of the worst smear campaigns that the nation had seen for some years.[67]

[66] The six states still remaining in the Republican column were Nebraska, Kansas, Maine, North Dakota, South Dakota, and Vermont.

[67] For an extensive account of the "smear" tactics in the 1940 campaign, see Hugh Bone's *"Smear" Politics, An Analysis of 1940 Campaign Literature* (Washington, D.C., 1941). The *Nation*, which was highly partial to the President during the campaign, said the campaign of 1940 would go down in history as one of the ugliest on record, and added: "In place of issues the Republican Party was forced to resort to devices, and they were not pretty . . . although Willkie himself was undoubtedly honest in his repudiation of such tactics." *The Nation*, November 9, 1940, p. 435.

He had presented to an American people accustomed to hearing of the glory of the United States a case for hard work ahead, a statement of the nation's weakness in time of crisis, and a record of its past mistakes. He had denied the validity of class division to workmen who had fought battles for industrial recognition, and he had attempted to take votes from the President in the regions where the people were most reluctant to give up the New Deal. It did not appear to be clever politics.

Other things also needed improvement. The campaign train, the last car of which was called "The Squirrel Cage" by reporters, was badly disorganized, and Willkie was not always placed in contact with local Republican leaders when he entered a state or city. Willkie had not ignited emotions with his emphasis on domestic issues, and his few differences with the Roosevelt foreign policy were not clear in the voters' minds. As a result, some of the Republican professionals insisted that he return to the Republican platform, brand the Democratic party as the "war party," and frighten the American people with statements that Roosevelt's election would mean death and destruction for American boys.

Willkie succumbed to these demands because at this stage something different had to be tried, and because the campaign had become so virulent that he had lost some of his earlier perspective. He was particularly irritated when The Colored Division of the Democratic National Committee in New York issued a scurrilous five-page mimeographed document which (a) underlined Wendell Willkie's German ancestry, (b) quoted Adolf Hitler as saying, "Negroes are lower than apes," and (c) asserted that Willkie had been nominated "by the Hitler formula" with the calculating support of Isolationist Senator Arthur Vandenberg, anti-New Deal Congressman Charles Halleck, and Harold Stassen, "the Governor of the 'German' State of the Union — Minnesota." The document also quoted Harlan Miller, columnist on the Boston Traveler, as saying that Willkie's favorite remark under emotional stress was: "You can't do this to me — I'm a white man." The unjustified attack infuriated Willkie and other thinking people as well. Democratic Chairman Edward J. Flynn, Charles Michelson, the President's press secretary, and Julian David Rainey, head of the Democratic Colored Division, disowned the circular, stating that it had no authorization, but Rainey eventually admitted that it had been written by a subordinate who had mimeographed it without his knowledge.

The change in tactics and the severity of the "smear" campaign produced an angered Willkie who struck at the "high professions and low performances of the New Deal." He began dramatizing himself as he had not since the convention days as he lashed out at nearly everything Roosevelt did on both the domestic and international scenes. The Willkie who had scattered his fire on too many issues at a particular time now concentrated on three which he considered most valuable in obtaining votes: the place of capitalism in the national life, the inability of Franklin Roosevelt to cope with the world's problems, and the possibility of war.

A new Gallup poll released on October 15 showed that Illinois, Indiana, Wisconsin, and Michigan had shifted to Willkie, and that he had gained in Ohio. But in New York, Ernest Weir, the chairman of the Republican national finance committee, said that businessmen had not made good on preconvention promises of financial support for the Willkie candidacy, and that, as a result, the campaign had been handicapped. Though Weir complained of a lack of financial aid for Willkie, no Republican could bemoan the press support given to the GOP nominee. A survey made by *Editor and Publisher* showed that Willkie had more than three-fourths of the nation's newspapers behind him. In terms of circulation, one analyst estimated that only one-eighth of the daily newspaper circulation supported the President for re-election; eleven daily papers in the North sanctioned the Roosevelt third term, and even in the South there was much opposition to the Democratic nominee.[68] In contrast, more than seven hundred daily newspapers had declared their support of Wendell Willkie. When the *St. Louis Post-Dispatch* and the *Springfield* (Massachusetts) *Daily Republican* came out in support of Roosevelt, however, they were considered to be the most significant losses to Willkie, for both of them had opposed Roosevelt in 1932 and 1936, and deserted the Republican candidate in 1940 only after much deliberation.

Several days after the *Post-Dispatch* repudiated him, Wendell

---

[68] See I. F. Stone's article in *The Nation*, November 16, 1940, p. 467. The eleven large papers favoring Roosevelt were the *Springfield* (Massachusetts) *Republican*, the *Daily News*, *Post*, and *PM* in New York, the *Philadelphia Record*, the *Camden Courier-Post*, the *Chicago Times*, the *Post-Dispatch* and *Star-Times* of St. Louis, the *Kansas City Journal*, and the *Los Angeles News*. For additional information concerning newspaper support of Willkie, see the *New York Times*, August 24, 1940, p. 28, and August 31, 1940, p. 28. For a study of the Republican rural press campaign of 1940 by Ralph D. Casey, see *The Public Opinion Quarterly*, vol. 5, pp. 130-33.

Willkie entered St. Louis to speak on foreign policy and receive the greatest ovation of his entire campaign. The citizens of Missouri, spurred on by a "Committee on Enthusiasm" headed by James W. Irwin, assistant to Edgar M. Queeny of the Monsanto Chemical Company, dropped more than 10,000 pounds of confetti and threw 50,000 serpentine streamers on a Republican parade headed by the nominee.[69] At night the candidate told 27,000 people who crowded the St. Louis Arena (while 7,000 more stood outside) and a nationwide radio audience that Britain needed arms, not an expeditionary force, that production was the key to both peace and war, and that Roosevelt failed to see this truth. Then he shouted to his listeners: "We do not want to send our boys over there again, and we do not intend to. If you elect me President, we will not. . . . I believe if you elect the third-term candidate they will be sent."

Back in Washington, President Roosevelt accused the Republicans of "systematic and deliberate falsification of fact," and said that he would openly reply to them in a series of five speeches. In Springfield, Illinois, the burial place of Abraham Lincoln, Willkie continued to flay the President and throughout the nation he seemed to be picking up momentum. Before the 10,000 people gathered in Springfield he declared: "Neither Roosevelt nor myself are [sic] great men. We are but the results of accidental circumstances that have brought us to the fore, respectively representing certain causes. . . . [Willkie then declared that the President favored State Socialism, and added] I sometimes really think he is not conscious that that is what he is doing. And I will accept his spasmodic remarks from time to time in favor of another system as sincere. But sincere or not that is what his policies lead to. State capitalism or . . . complete centralized government dominating the complete economic life of the people. That is the issue."

Willkie's alternative to "socialism" was "a peaceful revolution

---

[69] An editorial in the *Post-Dispatch* for October 25 described the welcome given Willkie and added: "Visiting correspondents were astounded, and news of the enthusiastic welcome was sent all over the country, to the delight of hopeful Republicans everywhere. Now the whole story comes out, and the explanation is not entirely a Willkie avalanche, but a smooth-working publicity machine and a judicious investment in confetti and serpentine." Twenty-five distributing depots were set up along the parade route and at each was stationed a group of individuals responsible for a number of fifty-pound bags of confetti and serpentine, and for the recruitment of persons to properly throw the paper.

and return to free enterprise, an enlightened capitalism free from the ancient evils of exploitation." He called upon all those who opposed socialism to join him, adding: "Private initiative made America. If you individually will exercise private initiative in this campaign and crusade to save America, private initiative can save America. Lincoln . . . had an expression for it and with that I leave you. 'We will nobly save or meanly lose the last best hope on this earth.' "

Out in California, Hiram Johnson, who had twice left the Republican party to support President Roosevelt, endorsed Willkie on the third-term issue. Senator McNary, speaking in Missouri, attacked the "Town Tammanys" and asserted that the AAA fostered rural machines in an effort to use the program for partisan ends. In New York, Al Smith released plans to give addresses at Willkie rallies in Boston, Chicago, Philadelphia, and Brooklyn. Alfred M. Landon, in a radio speech, warned that the President might try to remain in the presidency for life, that a third term would mean the Republic's doom, and that Roosevelt had attacked freedoms in the same way as had the European dictators.

The October 18 Gallup poll revealed that Willkie's electoral vote had jumped from 32 to 117, and the *New York Times* featured an editorial: "Mr. Willkie on the Upswing." October 23 was proclaimed "National No-Third Term Day" by the Republicans and more than one thousand rallies were planned for the occasion. There was fairly unified organizational support for this movement throughout the country, and many congressional leaders as well as local leaders regained their enthusiasm.[70] As a result, by the middle of October millions of Republicans again felt the contagion of possible victory. The Anti-Third Term Association, with offices in Manhattan, collected funds for billboards and literature to be spread throughout the country. The Citizens Information Committee, with headquarters in Chicago, was a nationwide organization of business executives and professional people who sponsored

---

[70] Henry Dorris, writing in the *New York Times,* however, observed that over the entire period of the campaign, the demonstrative enthusiasm of congressional Republicans was limited: "An examination of the *Congressional Record* since August bears out the assertion that the minds of members have been far more on their own campaigns than on the struggle of President Roosevelt and Wendell L. Willkie for control of the executive branch. . . . In the latter days of the 1936 Congress there was far more 'whoopin it up' for Alfred M. Landon than the present *Record* discloses for Mr. Willkie." *New York Times,* October 19, 1940, p. E7.

"pep-and-money-raising" luncheons and chain-telegram programs to increase the number of individuals contributing money and action to the Willkie campaign. The group supported radio programs, newspaper advertisements, campaigns within minority groups, and helped pay miscellaneous expenses. The People's Committee to Defend Life Insurance and Savings was principally a bankers' group, operating from Locust Street in Philadelphia, which distributed much anti-New Deal material and leaflets stating that savings and life insurance would be more dependable if Willkie were elected. In Manhattan alone were located the headquarters of the Women Workers for Willkie; the American Writers for Willkie; the Non-Partisan Willkie League of New York, Incorporated (Jewish Division); the Democratic Businessmen for Willkie; the Garment Workers for Willkie; We the People; First Voters League; and the Committee of Ten Million Businessmen, Professionals and Farmers.

Louise Overacker, reporting on campaign expenditures after the election, added the names of additional organizations that spent more than $10,000 each in Willkie's behalf, *in addition to the formal state organizations and the many state finance organizations.* She listed the National Committee to Uphold Constitutional Government, the Clearing House for National Interests, the Associated Willkie Clubs of America, the Democrats-for-Willkie, the Maryland Committee, the Willkie War Veterans, the Jefferson Democrats of California, the Pro-America Committee, the Willkie Magazine Fund, the No-Third Term Committee, the Independent Willkie Advertising Campaign Committee, the Women's National Republican Club, and the National Committee of Physicians.[71] The activities of the various groups pledging allegiance to Wendell Willkie and the GOP were undoubtedly more extensive than had ever been undertaken on behalf of any candidate prior to 1940.

The candidate himself continued to barnstorm the country. The crowds along the way seemed to get larger and more enthusiastic at each train stop. When Willkie returned to Chicago on October 22 for a speech in the Chicago Stadium, he was hit by an egg, but such things were now no longer important. Thousands of people, many of whom had given up in despair only a month ago, were now joining the Willkie bandwagon every day. Before the enthusiastic crowd, the nominee recalled that he had voted for Roosevelt

---

[71] Overacker, *op. cit.,* p. 709.

in 1932 on the basis of the platform, but asserted that none of the 1932 promises to reduce taxes and unemployment, revive business, and cut government costs had been kept. He followed with a ringing declaration: "If his promise to keep our boys out of foreign wars is no better than his promise to balance the budget, they're almost on the transports!"

The following day in Boston the President again tried to stem the tide by saying, "I repeat again, that I stand on the platform of our party: We will not participate in foreign wars and will not send our army, naval, or air forces to fight in foreign lands outside of the Americas except in case of attack."

Willkie would not accept the President's pledge. On his way back to New York, speaking in Harbor Creek, Pennsylvania, he again doubted the President's promise of peace, again asked him to justify his abandoning of the 1932 platform, and asserted that the third-term candidate "offered not one single argument why he should be permitted to violate" the sacred tradition. When Willkie, who never did learn to take advantage of his microphones, reached New York, his voice was a hoarse whisper. He recklessly told the audience attending the *Herald Tribune* Forum: "I predict again tonight that if the present Administration is restored to power for a third term, our democratic system will not outlast another four years!" Some voters admired Willkie's persistence, sincerity, and his new techniques, while others saw only a frightening lack of restraint in the candidate's charges. Nevertheless, off-the-record talks with leaders of both parties revealed a unanimous belief that Willkie had made steady gains during the previous two weeks, but that such gains would have to continue and even increase to carry the election.[72] Willkie attempted to sustain the trend. The spotlight of the campaign, however, was temporarily focused on another individual.

On October 25, one of the most phenomenal developments of any campaign took place when John L. Lewis, head of the CIO, endeavored to settle an old score with the President by throwing the support of labor to Wendell Willkie. In caustic terms, Lewis censured Roosevelt's "personal craving for power" and declared that the President's motivation and objective was war. He predicted a world of troubled peace, the demobilization of millions of men, and the eventual loss of foreign markets if Roosevelt obtained re-election. The burly labor chief then recommended Will-

---

[72] *Newsweek,* October 28, 1940, p. 7.

kie. He reviewed the candidate's promises and aims — including the promise that Willkie would give labor full representation in his administration, and added that if the Republicans were elected, there would be "a reasonable hope" that three previously anti-CIO steelmakers (Eugene Grace, Tom Girdler, and Ernest T. Weir) would soon sign collective bargaining contracts with the steel workers union. Lewis concluded with a dramatic pledge to resign as head of the CIO if Roosevelt won the election.

The broadcast, reported to have cost $55,000 for the thirty minutes, was supposedly financed by the national committee of Democrats-for-Willkie, though it was later revealed that it was paid for by William Rhodes Davis, who had, according to Marquis Childs, widely advertised Nazi connections.[73] In any event, this fact was not publicized at the time, and the principal question was whether or not the speech would have the desired effect of bringing labor into the Willkie camp.[74] At the time the speech was made,

---

[73] Willkie later said that he would have rejected the offer if he had understood it. Joseph Barnes, *op. cit.*, p. 222; Childs, *op. cit.*, p. 206. According to Childs, Davis agreed to pay for the broadcast, but that there was an "exchanging [of] checks at a furious rate to insure that no one individual would be listed as giving more than five thousand dollars" in violation of the Hatch Act. After the campaign, Willkie told Childs that he had never heard of Davis before being informed that he (Davis) would sponsor the Lewis broadcast, *op. cit.*, p. 207.

Lewis had visited the President in the White House earlier in the month. He had a number of grievances against Roosevelt, including the President's failure to consult labor leaders on the national defense program, the failure to reappoint J. Warren Madden to the National Labor Relations Board, the alleged "emasculation" of the Wages and Hours Law by administrative redefinition of white-collar workers (who were exempted), and the Administration policy with respect to awarding defense contracts to violators of the National Labor Relations Act, the Walsh-Healey Act, and the Wages and Hours Law. *New York Times*, October 16, 1940, p. 15.

Sherwood stated that the President welcomed a battle to discredit John L. Lewis more than the campaign against Willkie, "so indistinct a target." Sherwood, *op. cit.*, I, 236.

[74] Irving Bernstein, writing in the *Public Opinion Quarterly*, after a careful study of the repercussions of the Lewis speech on selected areas and specific labor leaders, concluded after the election that: "Over the country the Roosevelt vote showed no more than a normal decline from 1936 and in some instances it rose. It was only where the election was extraordinarily close that Lewis' slight influence [estimated at 2 or 3 per cent — "a pathetically small figure," by Bernstein] was decisive in terms of electoral votes. It is quite likely that Willkie carried Michigan because of Lewis, for the election was won by 6,926 votes in a total of 2,072,908, and the decline in Flint, which was substantially over the state-wide decline, probably provided the margin of victory. There is also the very slight possibility that Lewis

the possibilities of it were enormous and awful. If the CIO vote could have been captured, it would have insured a Willkie victory; if the news concerning the financial support had been exploited, the Democrats could have repudiated Willkie's stand on aid to democracy in Europe. The truth of the matter is that Willkie did not know Lewis was going to endorse him until the address was given, but there can be no doubt that, at this tense moment of the campaign, when winning seemed so desperately important, he welcomed the support. Though Hamilton had warned the candidate that the American Federation of Labor and several Republican governors would be offended by Lewis, Willkie considered the CIO leader's offer of support to be a "fortunate windfall." It was, nevertheless, a situation filled with dangerous repercussions. Several CIO groups immediately reaffirmed their allegiance to President Roosevelt, though Philip Murray and Harry Bridges remained silent. Secretary of State Hull called the Lewis war charges "baseless," and Senator Norris asserted that Lewis had denounced the President only because he had failed to receive a Cabinet position. Willkie, who until this time had had little in common with John L. Lewis, praised the labor leader for his contribution to "unity."

During the last week of the campaign, Willkie remained in New York and the middle Atlantic area making three or four speeches a day. Frequently departing from his prepared scripts, he repeatedly charged that if the President were re-elected, American boys would soon be on the transports. He buttressed this charge with the promise that under his administration, aid to Britain would be given only with the knowledge and consent of Congress and the public instead of through the "slick legal shortcuts" that had been used by the President.

The attack seemed to be paying off. The Gallup poll released on October 27 showed that the Republican nominee had picked up New Hampshire and that Willkie's electoral count now stood at 121. Democratic leaders became alarmed and President Roosevelt invaded New York to tour the five boroughs and make six important speeches. The GOP nominee, not to be outdone by the President's final drive, submitted to the people a six-point program to place housing on an efficient basis in America. He proposed slum clear-

---

carried Indiana for Willkie. Irving Bernstein, "John L. Lewis and the Voting Behavior of the C.I.O.," *Public Opinion Quarterly*, 5 (June 1941), 245. Bernstein did not document his hypothesis concerning Willkie's victory in Indiana.

ance, land use planning, and improved housing as a governmental function but only as a supplement and a stimulant to private enterprise and initiative. In response to the President's famous Madison Square Garden address which emphasized the opposition to national defense from Republicans in Congress,[75] Willkie declared that Roosevelt could not "pass the buck" on the issue of defense by seeking to place the blame on a small group of Republicans in Congress whose role it was to oppose. "The Democratic party was in control," he shouted, "and if it had had a leader who knew how to lead it, America today would not be defenseless!" Gallup reported that the nationwide trend of sentiment toward Willkie first shown in surveys in mid-October had continued at an accelerated pace into the final week of the election race. Willkie had narrowed the contest to the point where Gallup thought the undecided vote would determine the outcome of the election.

On Saturday, November 2, both Franklin Roosevelt and Wendell Willkie concluded the major portions of their campaigns. The President in Cleveland asked for a vote of confidence, hit "home dictators," and expressed regret that he had not been able to campaign in the West, South, and other places far distant from Washington. He criticized the forces represented by communism on one hand and the forces of reaction on the other. He asserted: "The first purpose of our foreign policy is to keep the country out of war. And at the same time . . . we seek to keep foreign conceptions of government out of the United States." He then reviewed the achievements of the New Deal and expressed confidence in its bright future. He also made his sole reference to the third term when he asked the people for four more years, but concluded, "then, when that term is over there will be another President and many more Presidents. . . ."

Wendell Willkie spent his Saturday night before 23,000 roaring enthusiasts in Madison Square Garden. He pledged the unification of the nation, called the preservation of democracy the outstanding

---

[75] Robert Sherwood called the President's Madison Square Garden speech one of the most equivocal of Roosevelt's career. It was, however, the speech in which the President hit upon the phrase "Martin, Barton, and Fish" which he used so effectively to chide the Republicans. Sherwood added: "Willkie said later, 'When I heard the President hang the isolationist votes of Martin, Barton and Fish on me, and get away with it, I knew I was licked.' (I must say that I doubt that statement; it was a virtue of Wendell Willkie's that he never knew when he was licked.)" Sherwood, *op. cit.,* I, 233.

issue, and stated his belief that the people would rise to win the "Battle of America." He again endorsed social security, relief, and old-age pensions, but predicted that there would be more jobs when he was elected. He scored the attempted packing of the Supreme Court and again denounced the whispering campaigns trying to connect him with intolerance, claiming he had always defended the rights of civil liberties of all people, regardless of race, creed, or color. He shouted: "I will pledge to you . . . a unity that you have not had in the last eight years. . . ."

The respective national chairmen, Edward J. Flynn and Joseph W. Martin, both predicted victory in the Tuesday election. Many columnists thought the election result was in doubt, but others thought there might as an electoral landslide possibly going to either candidate. The *Chicago Tribune* poll gave Willkie 280 electoral votes but predicted a close popular contest, while a poll conducted by *Pathfinder* magazine, edited by Emil Hurja, predicted a landslide four-million-vote majority for Willkie and a 353-178 electoral vote victory for the Republican. George Gallup found 52 per cent of the people favoring the President but the electoral vote in doubt. "To attempt to predict the winner on the basis of a 52-48 split," he said, "requires one to go beyond the figures and to ignore the known margin of error in all survey work. That error in Institute surveys in recent elections has averaged four per cent, state by state." Alan Valentine, one of the leaders of the Democrats-for-Willkie movement,[76] predicted that 21 to 26 per cent of the Democrats outside the South would bolt to Willkie. The *Fortune* survey, however, which proved to be the most accurate of all, and which ironically was sponsored by the magazine from which Russell Davenport had resigned to work for the Willkie cause, predicted a Roosevelt victory. In the survey which the magazine concluded on October 31, Roosevelt was shown to have slightly more than 55 per

---

[76] Several months after the election, Valentine was among those who no longer supported Willkie when he took a stand on increased aid to Britain. Valentine, in 1941, opposed any change in the Neutrality Act and spoke against the Lend-Lease Bill. In 1950, he again obtained national prominence when he was selected by President Truman to be head of the Economic Stabilization Agency. In this position, he championed "voluntary controls" and vetoed an immediate thirty-day freeze on all prices as proposed by Michael V. DiSalle, chief of the Office of Price Stabilization. DiSalle's plan was more acceptable to the Administration, however, so Valentine resigned in January, 1951, and President Truman appointed Eric Johnston as ESA director.

cent of the popular vote — a sufficient margin, if properly distributed, to sweep him into his third term of the presidency.

Top Democrats privately agreed that Willkie had proved to be the most formidable and disturbing candidate the Republicans could have nominated, and that he would have easily defeated any other candidate except Roosevelt. The Hoosier candidate campaigned right down to the wire. He characterized the contest three days before the election as "a horse race with the trend toward me." As the campaign came to an end, a strange optimisim came over the Republicans. Those who three weeks earlier had just about given up in despair suddenly thought that Willkie had a good chance to be elected. More than two and a half million persons had heard his 550 speeches directly, and more than twelve million had seen the candidate. Many of the minor mistakes of the crusade seemed to dissolve into insignificance as the election approached and all of the many hues of Republicanism stood united behind this candidate who, like the President, was many things to many people.

On the Monday before the election, Willkie made three nationwide addresses during the day and two in the evening. At midnight, in a huge radio rally, Al Smith, Joe Martin, Joe Louis, and Clare Boothe endorsed him from New York, and John L. Lewis, Hiram Johnson, Raymond Moley, Senator Taft, Stassen, Lewis Douglas, Charles Halleck, and many others spoke from sections of the country. Willkie's final address emphasized that "the free way of life can be preserved in America only if we become a united people. . . ." Thus, the crusade was concluded. Willkie had traveled 19,000 miles in fifty-one days. He had conducted a unique campaign typical of an amateur in politics. Because he was a businessman, the money "had flowed like water" into propaganda channels.[77] Much of it was completely uncoordinated so that the waste and duplication were excessive. Because the candidate was an amateur, scores of blunders and offenses had been committed. Willkie personally had ignored local and state workers; he had made conflicting statements on both foreign and domestic policy; he had contradicted the congressmen he sought to lead; and he had permitted discord between the regular party organization and his independent groups. In some areas, a rapidly recuperating party organization had been again demoralized by the authority assumed by members of these ad hoc groups who naïvely tried to escape the stigma of "politicians." Con-

---

[77] Interview with National Chairman Martin.

sequently, party veterans were shunted away from campaign leadership and bitter struggles ensued.[78]

A certain amount of such inefficiency and discordant activity is inevitable in any close campaign. It is forgotten if the candidate wins and new vistas of patronage, influence, and policy-making are in the offing after the election. But if the candidate loses, responsibility has to be fixed, and it invariably falls upon the titular head. On November 5, 1940, however, much of the antagonism had seemingly abated and Willkie was a tired but confident man — still the only acknowledged leader of one of the two great American parties. The action of fifty million Americans would determine whether he was to become the Chief Executive or be relegated to the unemployed leadership of the opposition — and whether he had been able, in four months of exhausting campaigning, to convince the voting public that he should replace the man who had occupied the presidency during the previous eight years.

---

[78] Evjen, *op. cit.*, stresses these points.

5 LOYAL OPPOSITION

On November 5, 1940, more than forty-nine million American voters went to the polls to select a President. This number represented the largest turnout for any election to that time. Early in the evening when the returns indicated a trend toward Willkie, Franklin Roosevelt was distraught, but as later figures reversed the trend, he regained his composure.[1] In New York, Willkie heard the results in his suite in the Commodore Hotel. Shortly after midnight he gave a short speech of enthusiasm to 1,500 supporters who had gathered for a victory celebration in the hotel's ballroom, and at 1:55 he went to bed still refusing to concede the election. The following morning, after studying the election results, he dictated a congratulatory message to the President and made a broadcast to the people in which he thanked them for support and promised to work for unity in the defense effort, in sending aid to Britain, and in the removal of antagonisms in America. Party leaders, the Democrats-for-Willkie, and most of the nation's press echoed the candidate's pledge of harmony.

Final tabulations of the vote indicated that Roosevelt had received 27,244,160 votes to 22,305,198 for Willkie.[2] The GOP nominee had

---

[1] Burns, *op. cit.*, p. 452.

[2] Willkie obtained 5,625,615 votes more than Alf Landon, though Roosevelt's total vote decline was only 507,437 from 1936. In the 1940 election, other candidates received the following votes: Norman Thomas, Socialist, 99,557; Roger Babson, Prohibitionist, 57,812; Earl Browder, Communist,

polled more popular votes than any Republican presidential candidate in history! He had cut the President's 1936 margin of victory in half, but he had garnered only 82 electoral votes compared to 449 for Roosevelt.

Though in the immediate post-mortems on the election, some Republican leaders declared that Willkie could have won if he had created more enthusiasm among active party workers by cooperating more fully with the established Republican organization, there was little indication that Republicans had stayed at home, that they had not campaigned vigorously, or that they were disappointed in their candidate's efforts. Instead, commentators who analyzed the outcome of the election agreed that two relatively distinct elements were probably most significant in determining the results: the traditional *class* voting patterns[3] that existed even before the campaign — reinforced by the stereotyped conceptions of New Dealism and Republicanism — and the frightening international situation.

The few voting behavior studies that were made of the 1940 election confirmed these opinions that, to a large degree, people did cast their ballots along class lines. Though Willkie repeatedly

---

46,251. *Historical Statistics of the United States, 1789-1945* (Washington, D.C., 1949), p. 288. In addition, the *New York Times* listed 14,861 votes for Aiken, the Socialist Labor candidate, and 413 scattered votes. Willkie defeated the President in Colorado, Indiana, Iowa, Kansas, Maine, Michigan, Nebraska, North Dakota, South Dakota, and Vermont. The total popular vote for Willkie was larger than that of Thomas E. Dewey in 1944 or 1948.

[3] This factor was prominent in the findings of Lazarsfeld, Berelson, and Gaudet, who conducted periodic polls among a select sample in Erie County, Pennsylvania. See *The People's Choice: How the Voter Makes Up His Mind in a Presidential Election* (New York, 1948). Sam Lubell, in his article, "Post Mortem: Who Elected Roosevelt?" in the *Saturday Evening Post,* 213 (January 25, 1941), 9-10 ff., came to the same conclusion. Lubell wrote: "The little fellow elected him, because there are more of the little fellows and because he believed Mr. Roosevelt to be his friend and protector. . . . It was a class-conscious vote for the first time in American history. . . . Two striking features about this 'economic voting' stand out. First, wards and precincts falling into the same economic strata yield virtually the same results; there are almost no freak reversals. So sharp is the cleavage that the campaign could hardly have changed any appreciable number of votes. If the election was close in the total popular votes cast, it also was peculiarly decisive in that there seems to have been little wavering between economic groups. The second striking feature is that in city after city the dividing line, where the great Roosevelt pluralities dwindle to a close squeeze and finally merge into slight leads for Willkie, falls across roughly the same incomes." See also Max Lerner, "The Education of Wendell Willkie," in the *New Republic,* 107 (October 26, 1942), 536.

stressed that he would keep the progressive economic reforms of the New Deal and improve their efficiency and administration, he could never clearly specify just how he would create more jobs and more production. The "economic expansion" promised by Willkie had a vague meaning to many voters, but the term often aroused suspicions of monopoly and exploitation, while the "restrictions on private enterprise" that he pledged to eliminate meant little to the salaried and wage-earning millions whose votes were necessary to insure a Republican victory. These people of the lower middle class, who only eight years after 1932 were not yet thinking in terms of protecting their property holdings — a motive that a dozen years later made them more conservative[4] — were uncertain about Willkie, the former corporation president, whose bright promises of legislation for a new prosperity contradicted the negative record of his party in Congress. To the man in the street — or the man at the lathe — the New Deal meant security on his job, and a feeling that decision-makers within the party were concerned about his needs. At the same time, the fact that the Republican party had opposed social security, the Wagner Act, workmen's compensation, unemployment insurance, and a host of other measures was constantly impressed upon him by Democratic spokesmen. Willkie's pledges to improve and continue New Deal programs were appealing, but his assurances were not convincing enough to reverse a voting pattern in 1940; he activated nearly six million new voters, but the President's cushion of votes from 1936 was too great. Willkie made practically no inroads into Roosevelt's strength among labor, the Negroes, the lower economic classes, or among the avowed liberals, and it is doubtful that anything he could have done in 1940 would have substantially affected this vote. As Lubell wrote: "The election was not decided on the issues he debated, but on forces long at work — economic status, nationalities, birth rates. . . ."[5]

There were, however, several other important influences on the outcome of the 1940 election. Citizens all over the land voted with the distressing European situation in mind, and there can be no doubt that this consideration aided the President. Roosevelt himself

---

[4] This is, to be sure, a controversial argument, and it was admittedly only one of many variables of the 1952 situation. It is well argued in Eric Goldman's article, "Liberals in Trouble," *Saturday Review of Literature,* October 8, 1955, pp. 9-10 ff., and in Sam Lubell's *Revolt of the Moderates* (New York, 1956).

[5] Lubell, *Saturday Evening Post,* January 25, 1941, p. 10.

stated in July that if the war were over before the election, Willkie would be elected. By November, in spite of Willkie's charges that Roosevelt was both an appeaser and a warmonger, the positions of the candidates with reference to defense mobilization, aid to Britain, and the determination to remain out of actual combat seemed to be essentially the same, and the President was the more experienced of the two in international affairs. As the campaign developed, and Willkie's charges became more emotional, confidence in the President's calm as the result of this experience loomed larger in the voters' evaluation of the candidates. The whole frightening atmosphere also weakened Willkie's arguments concerning New Deal economic controls and the unbalanced budget; people were willing to put up with economic restrictions in order to meet the new threat from abroad. Moreover, Willkie's statements on international policy were made in the face of his endorsements by isolationist and Fascist groups in this country and the contradictory record of his Republican colleagues in Congress. The question of how much influence the America-First advocates had on Willkie was never answered during the campaign, but Henry Wallace and other Democratic orators across the nation repeatedly declared that Hitler, Mussolini, and their cohorts wanted Roosevelt defeated. The emotional impact of such charges upon voters has been verified in several different elections. Actually, the final statistics of 1940 indicated that quite apart from economic status, Willkie indeed did receive the isolationist German and Italian votes, while the areas populated by citizens from nations endangered by the Axis powers — the Poles, Czechs, Norwegians, Danes, Swedes, and Jews — voted heavily for the President.

Evidence also indicates that regional issues may have influenced the result of the election. Willkie did not win a single state in which public power was related to the economy. He also lost every large city except the GOP stronghold of Cincinnati, though he ran well in Protestant rural areas which had been Republican for generations before 1932. But again, as was true of Landon in 1936, he was forced to compete for the votes of large groups of people who had been benefited by the New Deal programs, and the conclusion to be drawn is that though Willkie was a dynamic candidate capable of recapturing Republican votes in some areas and of activating thousands of new voters throughout the country, where the war and social services of the government were considered important, voters remained in the New Deal camp.

Both candidates in 1940 had mass appeal; both met the image-expectations of their supporters. But the inexperienced Willkie, roaring back and forth across the country without recognition from his opponent, inevitably offended certain groups and made little blunders that emphasized his inconsistencies. His extravagant promises also served to stress the differences between his own position and those of his conservative associates who, in 1940, detracted from his appeal to the independent voters he tried so hard to convince. The fact that the differences in philosophy between Willkie and the congressional Republicans were so apparent has led some Republicans to argue that Willkie's entire campaign technique was a mistake — that he was too independent — that he would have been more successful if he had cooperated more fully with the Republican organization and if he had followed the party line more closely.[6] But in view of the available evidence on the election, it is doubtful if such a campaign would have made a substantial difference in the final result. Willkie was up against the master-politician of the century, and in spite of his opponent or the era, he polled a record number of Republican votes — probably more than any party regular could have obtained. There are no data to indicate that organizational conservatives did not support the Republican ticket. On the contrary, the Republicans spent heavily, had exceptional

---

[6] Perhaps the most positive exposition of this view may be found in James L. Wick's volume, *How Not to Run for President* (New York, 1952). Wick wrote: ". . . the candidate does not win doubtful votes by claiming he is for the same policies as his opponent. . . . The Presidency would have been Willkie's if he could have held his August 3 Gallup poll electoral vote. . . . He lost the election when his Elwood and Coffeyville speeches were devoted largely to 'areas of agreement.' . . . In 1936, nothing that Landon could have said would have changed the result. In 1940 . . . the 'ins' had the edge, but a decisive number — perhaps enough to swing the election — were on the fence and willing to be convinced, and Willkie . . . could win them only by talking fundamental Republicanism," pp. 7-11. On page 27, however, Wick concedes that Willkie frequently contradicted himself and that these contradictions were recorded. In addition, Wick ignores the fact that the "fundamental Republicanism" of 1940 did not differ much from the Republicanism with which Landon failed in 1936. The same forces were still in operation. Basically, however, Wick's book is written solely in terms of winning elections. He did not really understand Willkie's intense belief (tempered during the final weeks of the campaign) that Britain had to be saved and that peace had to be preserved after the war by an international organization. Nor did Wick understand Willkie's strong drive for social reform (to be sure, not evident in much of Willkie's pre-1941 business career) that forced the 1940 candidate to endorse large segments of Roosevelt's program and to spend the remainder of his life trying to revise some of the "fundamental Republicanism" of his party.

organization backed by inordinate enthusiasm, and an overwhelmingly pro-Republican press. In the final analysis, however, to the multitudes of voters who are vigilant only for a short time in November, the election was a contest between Roosevelt and a capable but unorthodox opponent, between the New Deal and Republicanism, and in a time of crisis these voters chose to remain with a philosophy and a man they knew rather than elect an inexperienced businessman-politician from a party still thought to be out of step with the times.

After the election, many of Willkie's colleagues advised him that his smartest move would be to retire into aloofness and silence, but by the Saturday following the election, he had received more than thirty thousand telegrams and letters urging him to remain active in public life and requesting that he maintain his leadership of the opposition by refusing any federal position in the Roosevelt administration.[7] At the time, Willkie was uncertain about his role in the GOP. He believed that he had been nominated because he "fitted the times" but that he had little proclivity for party organization. He nevertheless felt that the Republican party needed "revitalization," a more humane and social approach to the national problems, and he wanted more "young blood" in the party in order to eliminate "certain symbols" which he believed had to go if future opposition to the New Deal was to have any effect.[8] Therefore, on the night of November 11, he presented his famous "Loyal Opposition" speech over the combined radio networks of the nation.

[7] *New York Times,* November 11, 1940, p. 1. These requests were not aimed at an impossibility. Frances Perkins reported in her volume, *The Roosevelt I Knew,* p. 117, that after the election, the President said to her, "You know, he [Willkie] is a very good fellow. He has lots of talent. I want to use him somehow. I want to offer him an important post in the government. Can you think of one? I want it to be an independent job. I don't want him to be a member of the cabinet or anything like that. I don't want him right around with us. I want him to do something where the effort is nonpolitical but important. But I'd like to use him, and I think it would be a good thing for the country, it would help us to a feeling of unity." Miss Perkins then suggested Willkie for the chairmanship of the Defense Labor Board, which preceded the War Labor Board, and the President concurred. Therefore Steve Early invited Willkie to the White House, where Roosevelt offered him the position. Al Smith was also to be asked to sit on the Board. Before refusing the job, Willkie called Smith and both men agreed the President was handing them a "hot potato," so they both declined to accept. Willkie told reporters that although he wasn't against doing something in the service of his country, he didn't propose to take on anything so controversial as a position with the Defense Labor Board.

[8] *New York Times,* November 9, 1940, p. 8.

He declared that American unity could be forged only between ideas of the vigorous, loyal, and public-spirited opposition and the practices and policies of the Administration; he rejected a one-party state, but warned the Republicans not to fall into the partisan error of opposing things just for the sake of opposition. "Ours must not be an opposition against," he shouted, "it must be an opposition for — an opposition for a strong America, a productive America." Willkie then reasserted the principles for which he had fought — a government of freedom, of service, and of protection — and recommended steps for a less restrictive economy and a unified foreign policy. In conclusion, he told his followers that it was appropriate for them to continue their thousands of organizations if they felt so inclined ("I hope you do continue them"), but that he did not want them continued in his name lest "this great cause be weakened by even a semblance of any personal advantage to any individual."[9]

Willkie's speech elicited a mixed response. Republicans such as Vermont's internationalist Senator Austin, Representative Wadsworth of New York, and Senator Vandenberg of Michigan indicated that they were in substantial agreement with the address. Kenneth F. Simpson, New York County Republican leader called it "a magnificent challenge to America." "I will be proud," he said, "to continue the fight under his leadership until we achieve a final victory with Wendell Willkie in 1944." Joe Martin was only slightly less enthusiastic. After terming Willkie's speech "a patriotic address," he stated: "I believe . . . he is on honest and sound ground when he says democracy needs a strong opposition party . . . that will uphold the President on matters of defense and other matters in the interest of the country, but that will not hesitate to oppose him when in its judgment, his policies are not in the interests of the people."

Senator Hiram Johnson, however, declared that he believed Congress should reassert itself and should thoroughly examine all Administration measures. "The idea of unity is a holdover from the hysterics of the last few months. Real unity doesn't mean that men in Congress should abandon their convictions!" Finally, it was shrewd Senator Taft who stated that though he favored the general principles enunciated for the party by Willkie, insufficient time had elapsed since the elections to plan any definite action for the future. "It's too soon," he remarked, "to talk about 1944 now. We have a

[9] *Ibid.*, November 12, 1940, p. 1.

Congressional election before then, in 1942." Concerning the policy suggestions made by Willkie, the Senator added: "The exact position of the Republican party on these specific issues will have to be worked out later."

From most Republican leaders, there was ominous silence in reference to the "Loyal Opposition" speech, and from others, open criticism. Crusty Clarence Budington Kelland, Republican national committeeman from Arizona, at a Lincoln Day banquet several months later spoke for many organization Republicans when he asked: "What, then is a loyal opposition, to whom and to what must it be loyal, and what can and must it oppose? Does patriotism demand . . . that we should strangle our principles, our honest beliefs, and be loyal to the New Deal? . . . The two words do not stand together. They do not make sense. . . . There can be loyalty and there can be opposition, but not in the same phrase."

Unfortunately for Willkie's political future, many of the accolades given to him for fostering unity with his address came from Democrats, while the talk opened wounds among many staunch Republicans who had fought most enthusiastically for him prior to the election. Among many supporters at the time, the theme of the talk was considered only a minor splinter that kindled the incipient opposition to the candidate, but at a later date, Sam Pryor asserted that he thought the address was *the* event which initiated Willkie's decline as the real leader of the Republican party.

On November 13, Oren Root made an announcement which "was not received with any great show of jubilation among Republicans in Congress," stating that the 10,000 Willkie Clubs would continue as an organization and hold a reunion the following month. The same day, Joe Martin let it be known that he planned to resign as chairman of the Republican National Committee in January. Thus, the party was immediately faced with two problems of "unity" within its ranks, as regular factions of the party bitterly opposed the continuation of the Willkie Clubs at the same time that they surveyed the field of eligible candidates for the national chairmanship. The forces supporting Senator Taft of Ohio wanted either former Representative John Hollister of Cincinnati, Taft's ex-law partner, or David S. Ingalls, Ohio national committeeman. Older members of the executive committee of the national committee preferred Walter S. Hallanan of West Virginia because he was not attached to any faction or candidate. Some of Willkie's friends suggested

Bruce Barton, who had been defeated for a senatorship in New York, but Willkie himself made no public announcement of his own personal preference.

To deal with the problem of party unity, Sam Pryor made some telephone calls and tried to heal the breach among the leaders of the party organization and the independent groups in the East. He then announced that "the Willkie Clubs, the Democrats-for-Willkie and the Republican party, all of us, are united in spirit. I am certain that a practical approach to the problem of establishing an opposition that will be strong and vigorous will be worked out." But it was only a few days later that Alan Valentine announced that the Democrats-for-Willkie had formally disbanded and that "the future status of each state and local organization rests with them as they were formed independently of the national committee." This, of course, was in the tradition of ad hoc groups of opposition party members who join a movement as a reform group because of an axe to grind or because of enthusiasm for a rival candidate. Such groups are quickly formed — usually as a calculated technique of the campaign — and they are abandoned as rapidly if the candidate is not victorious.

The selection of a new national chairman, however, was a problem that plagued the Republican party for several years. David Lawrence suggested that Willkie assume the position in order to (a) have a powerful voice in the party leadership; (b) acquire a closer familiarity with national affairs; and (c) develop party leadership in conferences that would eliminate policy contradictions — both inside as well as outside of Congress. Joe Martin thought Willkie would be a splendid chairman, and some of the former candidate's friends urged him to accept the position. Followers most closely allied with Willkie, however, realized that the duties of this position "would work against his interests if he planned to seek the Presidential nomination in 1944," and they quashed the move. Other prominent Republicans mentioned for chairman in December of 1940 included Halleck, Dirksen, Stassen, and Governor Carr of Colorado, but Alf Landon wanted Martin to retain the post, and this idea was strongly favored among Republicans who foresaw a party split on the chairmanship issue.

During this period, Willkie vacationed in Florida. He interrupted his rest on two occasions, once to fly to New York to address 3,600 people at a public dinner, and, two weeks later, to address the

Gridiron Club and the Willkie Club reunion. On this second trip, he convinced Martin to remain as national chairman until March so that the field could be carefully considered before his replacement was named; he declared to newsmen that the new man must be a "good liberal, forward-looking fellow with energy, drive and capacity." "Reactionaries are definitely out," he stated, as Martin nodded agreement. The Willkie Clubs, on the same day, decided to keep their national organization under another name in order "to encourage the exercise of good citizenship . . . and to encourage competent men and women to seek public office. . . ."[10]

Meanwhile, in Chicago, Republican chairmen and other party officials from ten middle western states held a two-day conference designed to produce a better understanding and closer cooperation among Republican organizations in future campaigns. Ben L. Berve of Illinois asserted: "We don't want the national Republican organization to think we are trying to take control of the party, but we do believe that, because of the Republican strength shown in the Middle West in the last election, the initiative in such a movement should come from this region." At the meeting, some of the members discussed the behind-the-scenes sniping at Willkie, designed to take him out of the 1944 picture, that was already under way. Magazines reported that "Old-line Republicans" were inspiring editors to write stories about a list of states in which Willkie's vote was below that of governors and senators, and about the necessity of allowing Republican leadership to fall to those who had been elected. Speculation concerning others who might have made a better race than Willkie included the fact that he had followed an independent rather than the Republican platform during the campaign — that he had substituted his personal philosophy for that of the party on many issues — that in his post-election "Loyal Opposition" address, he had not mentioned the party by name or himself

---

[10] The Willkie Clubs, however, never achieved these lofty aims. They were quietly disbanded late in 1941. Schattschneider, in his *Party Government*, wrote: "Republican experience with the Willkie Clubs in 1940 showed the dangers of duplicate organization; . . . It is hard to imagine that one such organization could be restricted to local politics while a parallel organization occupying the same area confined its efforts to national politics. Political organizations are incurably multifunctional. Once a political army able to carry a municipal election has been created, who is going to forbid its advantageous use in state and national elections also? . . . Local party machines, like local public utilities, are natural monopolies. Duplicate party organization is wasteful, leads inevitably to cutthroat competition. . . ." Schattschneider, *op. cit.*, p. 148.

as its nominee.[11] Stalwart Republicans all over the country skepti-
cally looked to Willkie to prove that he could maintain actual as
well as titular leadership of the party. They waited for him to demonstrate that he had the patience and the understanding of American politics that would enable him to unite the leaders of the party
on a common ground of party position on crucial issues, and they
expected him to blend the amateurs into the regular organizations
to produce a healthy party.

To Wendell Willkie in Florida in December of 1940, the personal
alternatives seemed relatively clear. He could become the true
leader of the opposition and scrupulously promote the welfare of the
Republican party; he could subjugate his personal ambitions and
work to unify the nation — possibly forfeiting his party leadership
for the role of a world statesman in a time of crisis — or he could
attempt the almost impossible task of maintaining his Republican
party leadership while trying to unify America behind a Democratic
President. In 1940 the choice belonged to Wendell Willkie, and he
naïvely and characteristically chose the third and most difficult role.
The choice was naïve in that he simply didn't understand the
mechanism of party organization and its incompatibility with a
concept such as "loyal opposition." It was characteristic in that
having reached the conclusion that the survival of democracy and
freedom in the world hinged upon victory in Britain, Willkie stub-
bornly risked his political future to support his belief. The initial
decision that aid to Britain was the first objective of a loyal opposition had lifelong implications for him for it foreshadowed a bitter
battle with the isolationists within the Republican party, a consequent position in support of a bipartisan prosecution of the war
effort, and an eventual championship of postwar collective security.
When Willkie later took each of these positions, none was politically
expedient, and each produced a battle for people's minds. Inevitably in these battles, Willkie's ideas seemed to be too progressive,
too far afield to his former supporters. And because he resolutely
resisted all attempts to temper his principles in foreign affairs, he
quickly discovered a substantial bloc of his party vociferously opposed to him. Irving Stone wrote of him: "He bears the distinction
of being [the only candidate ever to run for the Presidency and be
defeated] . . . who, a few weeks after the election, was being
patted enthusiastically on the back by his erstwhile opponents and

[11] *New York Times*, November 17, 1940, sec. 4, p. E3.

kicked in the rear with equal enthusiasm by his erstwhile friends. A month before the election the Democrats were denying that Wendell Willkie had ever been a Democrat; a month after the election the Republicans were denying that he had ever been a Republican."[12]

The events leading up to this situation began early in 1941 when President Roosevelt informed the nation of his plans to provide the materials with which to defend democracy both in the United States and in Europe on a "lend-lease" basis. On January 10, 1941, "H. R. 1776, a bill further to promote the defense of the United States," was introduced in Congress by Representative John W. McCormack (Massachusetts), the Democratic floor leader. Republican isolationists immediately condemned the measure as a destructive, undemocratic, unconstitutional, and legislative monstrosity. Landon assailed the bill as a step toward war, and Congressman Hamilton Fish, asserting that the bill would have to be amended, rewritten, or scrapped, said that the Republicans in Congress would oppose it almost unanimously. Nevertheless, Willkie endorsed the lend-lease proposal with a time limit on the President's power. Stating that the measure had to be considered in relation to the world situation and the perils confronting the United States, he asserted that he sanctioned the grant of power to the President contained in the bill because democracy could defend itself from aggression only by giving these extraordinary powers to the Chief Executive. He urged a thorough debate on the measure, a time limit on the period the President's powers were to remain in effect, and expressed the hope that the debate would be confined to the merits of the bill and not assume a partisan aspect.[13]

Considering the commitments previously made by Republican leaders on foreign policy, however, nonpartisan debate confined to the merits of the measure was manifestly impossible. Alf Landon told a reporter: "There is no essential difference between Mr. Willkie's position and Mr. Roosevelt's position which is to go to war if necessary to help England win. If Mr. Willkie had revealed it before the Republican National Convention he would not have been

---

[12] Stone, *op. cit.*, p. 342.

[13] *Ibid.*, January 13, 1941, p. 4. The text of Willkie's address was also printed in the *Congressional Record* as an extension of the remarks of Senator Chan Gurney of South Dakota in the Senate and by Representative Kenneth F. Simpson of New York in the House. See the *Congressional Record*, vol. 87, pp. A102, A138-A139 (77th Cong., 1st Sess., Jan. 14, 16, 1941).

nominated, and if Mr. Roosevelt had revealed it before the election, he would not have been reelected." Most congressional Republicans, however, were reluctant to express their opinions publicly on the Willkie-Landon clash of views, particularly at a time when Republican unity was so necessary during the forthcoming legislative session. Newspaper polls of congressmen revealed that Willkie's statement would change few, if any, votes, owing to the fact that so many legislators felt that having so recently been a Democrat, Willkie was "hardly considered the head of the Republican party."[14] Senator Capper, a member of the Foreign Relations Committee, agreed with fellow-Kansan Landon, declaring: "Certainly neither President Roosevelt nor Mr. Willkie indicated to the voters that we were headed for war . . . I am for giving all the help we can to Britain . . . but the lend-lease plan goes too far." Taft came out flatly against the measure, and Senators Wallace H. White, Arthur Vandenberg,[15] and Henrik Shipstead, other Republicans on the Foreign Relations Committee, declined comment, though Shipstead added to his "no comment" that he did not care what Willkie said. Hamilton Fish asserted that Willkie, as a private citizen, was entitled to make any statement he liked, but he added: "He is not speaking for the Republican party and he certainly is not speaking for me."

Nevertheless, Senator Warren Austin of Vermont said he thought the Willkie statement was excellent, and both Senator Chan Gurney of South Dakota and Representative Kenneth Simpson publicly endorsed it. There was no doubt that Willkie had enlarged the ideological split in the Republican party, and the dispute had several reverberations. Connecticut's former Governor, Raymond Baldwin, who was rumored to be Willkie's choice to succeed Joe Martin as national chairman, was now generally considered to be out of the running. The isolationist element from the Midwest seemed to be stronger in the party ranks than ever, and Willkie's hold over the party organization was diminished.

Actually, because lend-lease was nationally popular, Willkie had

---

[14] *New York Times,* January 13, 1941, p. 4.

[15] Vandenberg later wrote in his diary: "If America 'cracks up' you can put your finger on this precise moment as the time when the crime was committed. . . . I had the feeling, as the result of the ballot was announced, that I was witnessing the suicide of the Republic. . . . I do not believe we are rich enough to underwrite all of the wars of all the world. I fear it means the ultimate end of our democracy." Vandenberg, *op. cit.,* pp. 9-11.

millions of supporters but they were more outside the ranks of Republican leaders than within. William Allen White wrote: "Again Wendell Willkie had revealed his statesmanship. He is with the President. . . . Mr. Willkie is not the leader of Congress, but he is the leader of 20,000,000 Republicans and both the President and the Congressional leaders must reckon with Willkie. He has taken a position to which he can summon his party." Other editors throughout the country expressed similar sentiments, and Willkie himself received more than eight hundred telegrams and scores of telephone calls after he had stated his position. Nearly all of the messages expressed approval of his action.

Meanwhile, Willkie, again moving dramatically, told reporters that he was going to England during the week of January 19 to look over the situation. He repeated his concern over the possible menace to the American way of life should the Nazis be victorious, and added that he worried more about the effect of a British defeat on the United States than about any threat of an armed invasion of the United States. Before he left, he also informed Hamilton Fish, in response to an invitation to testify before the House Foreign Affairs Committee on the lend-lease bill, that he would be "very glad" to appear before the committee as soon as arrangements for his trip were out of the way.[16] On January 19 he conferred with President Roosevelt and Secretary of State Hull, and received from the President a personal note of introduction to Winston Churchill. After the conference, Willkie again advocated the passage of lend-lease, but insisted that the Congress keep its hands on the purse strings and that a provision be inserted into the bill providing for periodic reporting of information to Congress. He concluded emphatically that if the Republican party became the isolationist party it would never regain control of the United States government.

A Gallup survey taken during January revealed that 62 per cent of the November Republicans and 74 per cent of the Democrats approved of the lend-lease bill in principle. Throughout the country, however, the opponents of the bill seemed to have impressive support and the battle of words concerning the bill and Willkie's position continued to rage in the newspapers, among members of fringe groups, and within the Republican party. General Hugh S. Johnson

---

[16] Willkie was accompanied on his trip by John Cowles, president of the *Minneapolis Star-Journal,* and Landon K. Thorne, New York banker. Willkie paid all of the expenses. Upon his return, he eventually appeared before the Senate Foreign Relations Committee.

castigated the measure in his daily column; the Scripps-Howard newspapers and the Hearst press, strong Willkie supporters during the campaign, assailed the legislation,[17] and the arch-isolationist *Chicago Tribune* dramatically and bitterly read Willkie out of the Republican party: ". . . if Mr. Willkie has not already picked up his hat it should be handed to him. He should no longer be consulted in the national party organization, should have no place in its councils, and should neither give nor be asked advice. He was a Republican by name for less than a year and that period was much too long. The party will take leave of its late standard bearer with the hope that it will never again see him or he it."[18]

On the other hand, the *Chicago Daily News* defended Willkie and disagreed with Landon, asserting that it was "precisely because Willkie's views were known, and coincided with the views of a majority of Republicans, that he won the nomination over his faint-hearted rivals"; the paper lauded the 1940 nominee as "a man of principle and courage and conscience . . . a leader to be relied on."[19] The *New York Times* summarized the situation accurately in a review of the news: "Mr. Willkie's endorsement of the President's aims . . . has undoubtedly bolstered his claim among . . . Republicans as the real leader of the party. But on the same issue, he undoubtedly has lost the active support of some Republicans who insist they cannot politically defend democracy by going over to what they contend is a virtual totalitarian regime."[20]

The lend-lease measure was also bitterly condemned by the Communist party, the American Youth Congress, and the Mothers' Crusade, which was led by Mrs. Elizabeth Dilling. The Paul Revere Sentinels and the Women's Neutrality League hanged a two-faced effigy of Roosevelt and Willkie to the British Embassy gate, and John T. Flynn and General Robert E. Wood of the America First Committee spoke out vigorously against the bill and Willkie's support of it. Isolationists Norman Thomas, Colonel Lindbergh, Father Coughlin, together with party stalwarts of all complexions, including Senators La Follette, Nye, and Wheeler (who called Willkie "the intrepid Trojan Horse of the Republican Party") spread their acrimonious views across the nation's newspapers. Many more

---

[17] Roy Howard, however, later changed his mind. *Time,* March 10, 1941, p. 59.

[18] *Chicago Tribune,* January 18, 1941, p. 16.

[19] *Chicago Daily News,* January 17, 1941, p. 8.

[20] *New York Times,* January 19, 1941, sec. 4, p. 10E.

legislators, however, agreed with the view of George Aiken of Vermont when he said: "Any damned fool could see that Lend-Lease might lead to war, but this was the chance that had to be taken if Britain and democracy were to be saved."[21]

At Republican party headquarters, there was a noticeable slackening of activities as the national organization tried to avoid taking sides in the struggle between the Willkie and Landon-Taft factions. No "handouts" were given to the press for several weeks as staff members waited to see which group would control public sentiment. The Republicans in Congress were unified in favor of cutting nondefense outlays of the government to the bone and a balanced budget on all nondefense items, but beyond these principles, GOP policy was only a blur. Joe Martin was caught in a crossfire of the party factions that again created a vacuum of congressional leadership.

During this period of the "great debate" of 1941, Willkie went to England to observe production and see what he could of the social, economic, and military conditions within the country.[22] Politically, the trip was imaginative if a trifle superfluous. It bolstered British morale and put an end to many of the whispered charges that Willkie was pro-Nazi. Marquis Childs called it "the most brilliant stroke he had made since Philadelphia . . . ,"[23] but it was quietly looked upon by many congressional Republicans as unnecessary cooperation with Franklin Roosevelt which weakened Willkie's relations with his own former supporters. Fifteen years later, prominent Republicans still talked of "that trip to England for the President" as one of the principal incidents in Willkie's decline as a party leader.

While Willkie was in England, his friend and early supporter, Representative Kenneth Simpson of New York, died of a heart attack only twenty days after he entered Congress. H. J. Schwamm, leader of the Seventh Assembly District in New York, immediately proposed Willkie for the Simpson post, and the *New York Sun* also advocated the nomination in an editorial.[24] Willkie, however, real-

---

[21] Interview with Senator Aiken.

[22] It was rumored in Washington at the time that Willkie would become the next ambassador to the Court of St. James; the talk was groundless and immediately denied by the 1940 candidate.

[23] Childs, *op. cit.,* p. 214.

[24] *New York Times,* January 30, 1941, p. 20. The *Sun* stated that Willkie was in the paradoxical position (not unprecedented in American life, however) of being the titular leader of the opposition party and yet being without office or without any official responsibility. The *Times,* in commenting

izing that being the junior member of the New York delegation to
the House of Representatives carried no status of party leadership,
quickly cabled from London that he was "not interested" in
Simpson's position.

Meanwhile, Chairman Martin called a meeting of the Republican
National Committee in Washington on March 24, at which he said
he would present his resignation as chairman. He stated that he
would take no personal part in the selection of his successor and
then named the men who had been mentioned for the post: former
Governor Baldwin of Connecticut, Harold W. Mason of Vermont,
J. Russel Sprague of New York, Werner W. Schroeder of Illinois,
Dudley A. White of Ohio, John Hollister of Ohio, David Ingalls of
Ohio, Charles A. Joan of North Carolina, Kenneth Wherry of
Nebraska, Arch N. Bobbitt of Indiana, and Representative Everett
M. Dirksen of Illinois.

During the same week, Republican leaders from sixteen midwestern states met in Omaha, Nebraska, to discuss party policy and
questions. Before the parley began, there was an indication that
Wendell Willkie's status and his stand on lend-lease would be among
the chief topics of conversation. However, Martin's secretary, Robinson McIlvaine, attended the meeting and publicly stated: "There
is no place in the Omaha meeting for discussion of the lease-lend
bill. . . . This thing is not being handled on a party basis. There
are Republicans who favor the bill . . . and some who are against
it." Nevertheless, Gilbert E. Carpenter of Omaha, national committeeman from Nebraska, told reporters: "A lot of [the boys] want
aid to Britain, but they don't want to go too far. I'm not quite sure
Willkie is 'betraying' the party and I don't want to say so until I'm
sure he is. But you can quote me as saying that Willkie is not going
to get a grip on the party organization. You can bet your bottom
dollar on that. He was a Democrat before he came into the party
and I'm not so sure he still isn't a Democrat." Ben L. Berve, Illinois
state chairman, publicly implied that a "gag" had been put on the

upon the editorial, stated: "Mr. Willkie's personal dilemma illustrates a
defect in our political system. In Great Britain the leader of the opposition
party is also its leader in Parliament, with the powers and responsibilities of
that position. Our own geographical limits on candidacies, both constitutional and traditional, and Congress' self-imposed seniority rules, are major
reasons why we are not utilizing in an official and continuous way the talents
and experience of many able men, including in addition to Mr. Willkie, a
whole list of ex-Presidential candidates — Herbert Hoover, Alf Landon, John
W. Davis, James M. Cox and Al Smith."

meeting by Martin because the official remarks of the meeting were limited to discussions of party organization and finance. In spite of the suppression of criticism, it was clear that a majority of the state chairmen at the meeting favored a watchful waiting attitude before accepting Willkie as the real head of the party, and they tacitly rebuked him by asserting that if and when Martin resigned as national chairman, they would do all they could to make certain that an experienced political organizer rather than an "amateur" was named to the post. Moreover, in another move clearly directed at Willkie, they unanimously passed a resolution expressing confidence in the Republican delegation in Congress, in Martin as minority leader of the House and as national chairman, and in Senator McNary as minority leader in the Senate, but making no mention of Wendell Willkie.

On the same weekend that the Midwest state chairmen met in Omaha, the Young Republican National Federation gathered in Des Moines. Here again, a revolt against the leadership of Willkie was threatened by two resolutions submitted to the conference, one by a delegation from South Dakota criticizing Willkie,[25] and the other by Norton Briseth of Minneapolis criticizing the Willkie-for-President Clubs.[26] However, Chairman Martin again issued a statement that he would regret it if the Young Republican Federation members seriously considered any resolutions attacking Wendell Willkie. Before the meeting was concluded, the group voted to support aid to Britain but issued an accompanying statement in favor of limiting the efforts lest the United States be drawn into the conflict. All efforts to revolt publicly against the leadership of Willkie were defeated, but a resolution was passed which opposed the fostering by the Republican party of any independent organizations such as the Willkie-for-President Clubs. The clubs were urged, instead, to join the Republican party organization.

[25] The South Dakota resolution stated in part: "The defeated Republican candidate for President has seen fit to travel to England, purporting to be there as a private citizen, when in reality, he is there as the alleged leader of 22,000,000 Republicans who no longer consider him qualified to speak or gather information for them."

[26] Briseth's proposition asserted: "In the last campaign the young Republican League and the Republican party were deliberately sabotaged by a candidate of the Democratic faith on the Republican ticket whose campaign was epitomized by two words, 'me too.' The party was further submarined by devices to play down the Republican party — deluding people and trying to get them to vote for a candidate through devious means such as 'all-

On February 10, Wendell Willkie arrived home from England.[27] He predicted peace for the United States through help for Britain, and expressed his belief that the withholding of aid probably would involve America in war. He told reporters that he had found the British to be a united people without an element of defeatism. Almost immediately, Willkie went to Washington to testify before the Senate Foreign Relations Committee. Before a packed chamber in the Senate Office building, Willkie made a reality of the national unity on foreign policy which he had stressed during the campaign. In a prepared statement he urged the adoption of the lend-lease bill, the release to Britain of all our bombers not needed for training purposes and from five to ten American destroyers every month. He warned that "no man can guarantee" that aid to Britain would not involve the nation in war, and he also declared that nobody could say yet whether Britain would win. If she were defeated, he predicted, the United States "will be in a war a month afterward." "This country," he stated, "must decide whether or not to withdraw into itself or to recognize the interdependence of world ideas."

During the question period which followed the prepared statement, Willkie adroitly handled the loaded questions asked of him, and those individuals who remember only a misinterpreted phrase from the testimony would do well to read the entire record. When Senators Guy Gillette, Bennett Clark, and Gerald Nye questioned Willkie concerning the Republican platform and his statements during the campaign, chairman of the committee Walter F. George assured Willkie that he did not have to answer. But Willkie declared that he did not want to evade the queries for fear that someone would misconstrue his answers and endanger national unity. He did, however, say that he did not want to "rake over old coals." Nye, nevertheless, continued to question Willkie about remarks he had made on specific dates during the campaign. A short exchange was recorded as follows:

SENATOR NYE:

> One more assertion of yours, that of October 30: *"On the basis of his"* — that is, Roosevelt's — *"past performance with pledges* to the people, you may expect we will be at war by April, 1941, if he is elected."

party,' 'key-clubs,' . . . and dozens of others, all of which dissipated concerted Republican effort and made voters lose confidence in the party."

[27] This date was earlier than that on which Willkie had planned to leave Britain. The trip was shortened in response to a cablegram from Secretary of State Cordell Hull, who wanted Willkie to testify in favor of lend-lease.

Mr. Willkie:

You ask me whether or not I said that?

Senator Nye:

Do you still agree that that might be the case?

Mr. Willkie:

It might be. It was a bit of *campaign oratory.* I am very glad you read my speeches, because the President said he did not.

Senator Nye:

That is all.[28]

Willkie's answer caused laughter throughout the committee room. As he frequently explained later — and as the testimony in italics above shows so vividly — the words "campaign oratory" were made in reference to his somewhat extravagant prediction based on his view of President Roosevelt's past record. But because Willkie's opponents chose to interpret the words in application to all of Willkie's own pledges, the phrase lived long after lend-lease became a reality. Each time Willkie later advocated a controversial measure or supported an idealistic principle, "campaign oratory" was hurled at him as an irrational undermining of his position. Actually, Willkie, during the testimony, did little more than confess an honest overstatement of his views of his opponent, something of which nearly all political orators are guilty. As Schattschneider has written:

Party orators, in the heat of an election campaign, abandon themselves to fantastic exaggerations of the unanimity and resolution of the parties and magnify the differences between them. An insight into the nature of American politics may be gained by observing that the rhetorical and declamatory fury of party pronouncements does not decline with the diminution of the real differences between the parties . . . by a well understood convention of American politics, the extravagant language of party orators . . . deceives almost no one.[29]

Senator Nye, at the time, however, was not interested in "well un-

---

[28] Verbatim testimony of Willkie in *New York Times,* February 12, 1941, pp. 4-5. Italics added. Senators Harrison, Connally, and Hiram Johnson asked no questions at the hearing.

[29] E. E. Schattschneider, *op. cit.,* p. 91. William Allen White wrote of the incident: "I think one of the most courageous things any man has ever said in public life was Willkie's 'campaign oratory' statement. It was not discreet, but it was deeply honest. Only three times in public life have I seen such honesty. The pretension that a candidate's utterances are omniscient when everyone knows he is talking damned nonsense is one of the large reasons why the American people lose faith in democracy." Cited in Joseph Barnes, *op. cit.,* p. 254. Barnes himself wrote of the phrase: "It ended up, like George Washington's cherry tree, one of those legends that grows steadily stronger with every proof of their untruth." *Ibid.*

derstood conventions of American politics," and he had made his point. From this day on, antagonists of Willkie used the phrase as one of their most effective weapons in knocking the 1940 presidential candidate out of the political ring of 1944. The misinterpreted and regrettable little phrase, "campaign oratory," plagued Wendell Willkie, the political amateur, to his dying day.

On February 12, 1941, when Republicans gathered together in many parts of the United States to pay tribute to Abraham Lincoln, they were violently split on the issue of foreign policy. In Harrisonburg, Virginia, Senator Taft declared that "Mr. Willkie does not and cannot speak for the Republican party." Taft saw "no justification in precedent or principle for the view that a defeated candidate for President is the titular leader of the party," and asserted: "I happen to disagree with Mr. Willkie's views on foreign affairs and so do a large majority of the Republicans of the nation.' The policy of peace for America and aid to Britain to the extent consistent with peace is not only a definite, positive policy, and an American policy but it is the policy adopted by both parties and both candidates in 1940."

In other cities, Senator Gerald P. Nye called Willkie's endorsement of the lend-lease bill a "betrayal of the G.O.P.," and Congressman Hamilton Fish charged that Willkie was beating the war drums more furiously than the interventionists and war-makers of the Democratic party. In Arizona, Clarence Budington Kelland informed the titular head of the Republican party that he had not been elected Vice-President on the Democratic ticket and asserted: "The Republican party must not compromise. It must be a party of negation and this negation must state 'Thou shall not destroy this republic.' "

On the other side of the ideological fence, Willkie, in New York, addressed more than 2,000 persons at the Waldorf-Astoria. He called for cooperation to achieve national unity, adequate and speedy aid to Great Britain, and a "positive doctrine" for the Republican party. Though he criticized Roosevelt's domestic policy, he challenged his followers to support the President and abandon isolationism. He asked them to aim toward a higher fate than compromise, negation, and death. In Washington, as the principal speaker in the capital, Thomas E. Dewey finally came around to Willkie's position and endorsed lend-lease "in a form that Republicans can support," and Raymond E. Baldwin, former Governor

of Connecticut, cautioned the party not to "oppose just for opposition's sake, or to be 'agin' something just because the Administration is for it." William Allen White stated that Willkie was "just
dead right" on foreign policy, and Leverett Saltonstall, then Governor of Massachusetts, said: "I, for one, — and I feel that I am in
good Republican company — am fully with the President in his call
for us to go the limit as an arsenal for democracy."

The situation was similar all over the country; civil war had
broken out within the Republican party. Observers believed that
a test of strength between the two factions was likely when a new
national chairman was named in March. However, it was the
very fact that the intraparty dispute had erupted so openly which
caused analysts to predict that Joe Martin would be re-elected
despite his desire to step down. Martin, as an individual power in
the party, had been the one person who had tried most vigorously
to prevent the cleavage from developing, and he was respected by
leaders on both sides of the argument.

A few political pundits drew an analogy between Willkie's situation and that of Theodore Roosevelt from 1910 to 1912, but it was
obvious that Willkie had neither a tight grip on a large section of
the party machinery nor "the knack for the type of painstaking
organizational work among the state, county and local leaders" to
make such a comparison successful. Under the American system
of nominating presidential candidates, a large popular following is
not enough to capture control of a major party.

For a brief period in March of 1941, a local situation in New
York City seemed to indicate that Willkie would make a fight for
organizational control. In the congressional election in the famous
Seventeenth "silk stocking" District of Manhattan, Willkie, together with Tom Dewey and Mayor LaGuardia, stumped and
spoke for Joseph Clark Baldwin in his race against liberal Democrat Dean Alfange and the American Labor candidate, Eugene
Connolly. Baldwin was an avowed supporter of aid to Britain, and
when he polled 23,252 votes to 16,690 for Alfange and 3,985 for
Connolly, Willkie was gratified. He called it a blow to the isolationists, and Baldwin credited the victory to assistance "principally
from Wendell Willkie, who is leading the fight in our party for
national unity on foreign policy." *Time* commented: ". . . Willkie
had done what enemies said he could not do — buckle down to the
hard drudgery of machine politics to help elect Republicans who

stood for the things he believed in. From being on the edge of repudiation by the party two months ago, Wendell Willkie last week was in a stronger position than he had been since the early days of the 1940 campaign."[30]

The March, 1941, Gallup poll indicated that Wendell Willkie probably had achieved a wider degree of popularity with the rank and file of American voters than he had at any time during the presidential campaign. In a survey taken after Willkie returned from England, persons were asked if they had changed their opinions since the election. Twenty-two per cent of those polled liked Willkie better, 14 per cent liked him less, but 64 per cent had not changed their opinions.

	WILLKIE VOTERS per cent	ROOSEVELT VOTERS per cent
Like Willkie better	14	31
Like Willkie less	24	7
No change in opinion	64	62

When asked whether they thought Wendell Willkie would have made a good President if he had been elected in November, 60 per cent of the voters (85 per cent of the Republicans and 39 per cent of the Democrats) answered "yes."[31]

The Republican, a magazine published by the Young Republicans, also released a poll in March, 1941, which indicated that Willkie was still the top man in the party.[32] The magazine sent questionnaires to more than 7,000 Republican senior organization leaders, Young Republican leaders, and women Republican leaders. The result of the poll indicated a wide diversity of opinion on the type of leadership and the kind of program that those surveyed believed the party should follow. On the issue of foreign policy, the editors concluded that the rank-and-file Republican leaders were still rugged individualists who had not yet agreed on a common policy, and that the final catalyst on issues had to be supplied by leadership. Party workers were then asked what party leader's personal choice for national chairman should be respected. Nearly half of those questioned did not answer this question, indicating either that they did not care or that they had no particular choice. Among those who did answer, however, the results showed that Willkie was the overwhelming first choice of the Republican local

---

[30] *Time,* March 24, 1941, p. 18.

[31] *Public Opinion Quarterly,* 5 (June, 1941), 313-14.

[32] *The Republican,* March, 1941, p. 10 ff. Slightly more than ten per cent of those polled had replied by the time the March issue of the poll had gone to press.

leaders. He received 51 per cent of the votes cast; the East was for him 76 per cent and the far West 62 per cent. Chairman Martin was in second place with 16 per cent.[33]

When the House version of the lend-lease bill came up for a vote in Congress, it had no difficulty in passage. On February 8, the vote was 260-165, with only 24 of the 162 Republicans voting for the measure.[34] The bill embodied nearly all of Willkie's suggestions for limitations: power to rescind the lend-lease authority by concurrent resolution, a presidential report to Congress at least every ninety days on his actions under the bill, and a limit on the dollar value of defense items to be transferred. On March 8, when the Senate passed the bill, 60-31, twenty-one amendments were slapped down; eleven minor modifications were accepted, and Willkie's recommendations were left intact. Only 10 Republicans voted with the Democrats for passage, however, and Willkie had failed to convert such Old-Guard stalwarts as Capper, Johnson, Taft, Vandenberg, and Nye.[35] Oddly enough, when the final vote was taken in the House of Representatives, nearly two-thirds of the Republicans recorded themselves in favor of the bill.[36] This represented, if nothing else, a victory for popular opinion over partisanship, and credit for the change had to be given to Willkie. In his column, David Lawrence wrote: "Mr. Willkie incurred the lasting antagonism, no doubt, of a small number of isolationists in his party, but the record vote in the House is a sufficient vindication for what he did. The future of Mr. Willkie in the political arena may be uncertain, but there can be no doubt that he saw sooner than did the other leaders of his party the direction in which public opinion was moving."[37]

Wendell Willkie, together with Will Hays, was also responsible, in March, for Joseph W. Martin's agreement to remain as national chairman providing he was given a manager to take care of the "grass-roots" organization for which he did not have time. At the meeting of the national committee held in Washington, Martin

[33] Others mentioned were Dewey, 7 per cent; Hoover, 7 per cent; Stassen, 3 per cent; Landon, 3 per cent; Taft, 2 per cent; Vandenberg, 1 per cent; Not Willkie, 2 per cent; 8 per cent of the votes were scattered.

[34] *Congressional Record,* vol. 87, p. 815 (77th Cong., 1st Sess., Feb. 8, 1941).

[35] *Ibid.,* p. 2097 (March 8, 1941).

[36] *Ibid.,* pp. 2189-90 (March 11, 1941).

[37] *Ibid.,* p. A1240 (March 12, 1941). An extension of remarks of Charles A. Plumley of Vermont.

submitted his resignation, but it was unanimously rejected. In view of the party dissension during the preceding three months, the committee members attending the meeting displayed a surprising amount of harmony.[38] It was reported that there was "general agreement" among the committeemen that Wendell Willkie should be regarded as the titular head of the party, and several of the members of the committee even lauded Willkie for having supported the administration foreign policies which had found such strong favor with so many of the rank-and-file party members.[39]

As was normal at such meetings of the national committee, there was some talk of presidential candidates for 1944, and one spokesman, who had talked with Willkie several days earlier, reported that the former nominee was "not interested in running for the Presidency again in 1944." When Willkie was contacted concerning this statement, he confirmed the remark and added: "Civilization is facing one of its crucial moments. Talk of party politics and candidacies is completely out of place in either party. I am not the slightest interested at this time in the candidacy of any one for any office in 1942 or 1944. Such talk is pure nonsense. The sooner partisan politics is adjourned and talk of candidacies and petty ambitions discontinued the better off every one will be."[40]

Thus Willkie, temporarily at least, tried to eliminate partisan politics from his personal agenda. His political activities consisted, for several months, of making speeches advocating a greater degree of international cooperation by the United States. There were

[38] It would have been asking too much, however, to expect that all wounds reopened by Willkie's outspoken advocation of Roosevelt's foreign policy be healed. Arthur Sears Henning, in the *Chicago Tribune* (which pummeled Willkie constantly from 1940 to 1944), wrote: "Beneath the surface of the proceedings simmered party division on the war program and dissatisfaction with Wendell Willkie. . . . A complimentary reference to Mr. Willkie in Mr. Martin's speech elicited no applause. . . . R. B. Creager, Texas committeeman, came armed with a resolution commending Mr. Martin's vote against the dictator bill, which was a shot at Willkie. Friends of the chairman persuaded Creager to withhold it. . . ." *Chicago Tribune,* March 25, 1941, p. 15.

[39] Cyrus McCormick, the New Mexico committeeman, told reporters that "nobody can avoid the fact that Willkie was our last nominee and that, as such, he is the boss of the Republicans." *New York Times,* March 24, 1941, p. 1. Apparently such unity behind Willkie was the order of the day. In Indianapolis on March 21, Joe Martin had told a conference of Republicans from several of the western states that Wendell Willkie had a "strong hold on members of the party" and would continue to be a "strong factor in building up the party." *Ibid.,* March 22, 1941, p. 8.

[40] *Ibid.,* March 24, 1941, p. 9.

rumors, promptly denied by both men, that an agreement was being effected by friends of Willkie and Thomas E. Dewey to exchange support of Dewey for the New York governorship by Willkie in 1942 in return for the New Yorker's support for the Hoosier for the presidential nomination in 1944. Again Willkie denounced such reports, saying, "This is no time with the world in flames, to engage in the nonsense of talking about candidacies. . . . In no event would I enter into such an alliance. I don't believe in political trading."

In April, Willkie joined a law firm, closed his personal headquarters in the Commodore Hotel, and spoke in widely scattered cities at least once, and often twice, a week. He had received more than 280,000 letters in the six months after the election. Everywhere he went he found the tremendous enthusiasm for his pro-Britain statements tempered by isolationist pickets, vociferous charges, and name-calling. In Pittsburgh, on April 25, he first demanded that lend-lease supplies be convoyed across the Atlantic, and this became his principal plea for the remainder of the summer. Though his opponents were vicious in their denunciation of him, he continued his appeals. In Chicago in June, before 23,000 people, he shouted: "It has been said that in the last election the American people were not given a fair chance to express their views on foreign policy. . . . President Roosevelt's foreign policy was well known. . . . Frankly, I think one of the principal reasons I was chosen . . . was because I had been more emphatic and consistent than any of the other candidates in urging all-out aid to Britain. . . . My conception of what constitutes effective aid to Britain has changed. . . . Now it is painfully obvious that production is not enough. . . . It is now our job not only to produce the goods necessary for her survival but to deliver them by whatever means will be most effective."[41]

Thus, Willkie took a position in advance of the President, and far ahead of most of his Republican colleagues. After six months of 1941, though he held no office and belonged to no committees, Wendell Willkie was one of the most admired, most hated, most feared, and one of the most influential and controversial citizens of America. He had proved to be a good loser, and polls indicated that he was still popular with the voters. Ostensibly and undoubtedly honestly, he was not campaigning for 1944, but neither was he

---

[41] *Newsweek,* June 16, 1941, p. 19.

adverse to his position as a potential candidate — though he was unwilling to follow the isolationist Republicans to preserve that status. He told a reporter: ". . . if I could write my own obituary and I had a choice between saying I had been an unimportant President or a person who had contributed to saving democracy at a critical moment, I'd prefer the latter."[42]

Willkie believed that the New Deal had the correct foreign policy, but neither the administrative ability nor the proper philosophy to implement it in a capitalistic democracy. The Republican party, on the other hand, as represented by some of the congressional leaders, had the wrong foreign policy, but within its liberal element, had the talent and ability to produce a strong and prosperous domestic economy. "The party," he said, "that comes to represent the right foreign policy and the right domestic policy and contains within its membership administrative ability will inherit the earth. I hope it will be the Republican party. But no liberalism anywhere can survive a loose fiscal policy."[43]

The loose fiscal policy was the principal target of the Republicans in Congress. Joe Martin declared that the chief duty of his forces was to "audit the bewildering sums" spent on defense. But the GOP had few alternatives and the number of congressmen opposing the administration programs dwindled sharply after basic defense enabling acts were once approved. And when the Senate passed the seven billion dollar appropriation requested by Roosevelt to finance aid to Britain and her allies, only four Republicans, Langer, Butler, Nye, and Thomas of Idaho, voted against the sum. Henry Dorris of the *New York Times* wrote that the only Republican strategy seemed to be to trust in God and keep its powder dry while awaiting a break that would return the party to power. Defense measures dominated the legislative picture, and the consensus among the legislators' constituents concerning defense was such that Republicans were bereft of any healthy criticism which might have been furnished by an opposition party in more normal times.[44]

In June, 1941, a Gallup poll which asked whether Roosevelt's foreign program had gone too far or not far enough produced 17 per cent of those who had voted for Willkie in 1940 who replied,

---

[42] Elizabeth R. Valentine, "A Defeated Candidate Remains a Leader," *New York Times,* June 1, 1941, sec. 7, p. 5.
[43] *Ibid.*
[44] *Ibid.,* March 30, 1941, p. 6E.

"Not far enough"; 34 per cent who said, "Too far"; and 49 per cent who thought the President's course had been "About right." When the results were totaled on the "Not far enough" and the "About right" groups, 66 per cent of the 1940 GOP voters were supporting the national policy. In effect, this survey showed that among those polled, Willkie had two-thirds of the Republicans with him. The *Chicago Daily News* commented: "If the party is going to be split on the issue, it will be the fault of a minority, including a little group of disgruntled congressmen and senators."[45]

Thus, the American people — Republican partisans included — were overwhelmingly in support of the Roosevelt-Willkie stand on foreign policy. In the achievement of this consensus, Willkie had indeed divided his party and alienated powerful individuals within it. But he had also prevented the rise of anyone else who might have seriously impeded the defense build-up.[46] The significance of his activities was later noted by Walter Lippmann when he wrote:

"Historians will say, I believe, that second only to the Battle of Britain, the sudden rise and nomination of Willkie was the decisive event, perhaps, providential, which made it possible to rally the free world when it was almost conquered. Under any other leadership but his, the Republican party would have turned its back upon Great Britain, causing all who still resisted Hitler to feel that they were abandoned."[47]

[45] *Chicago Daily News*, May 28, 1941, p. 16.
[46] See Barnes, *op. cit.*, p. 242.
[47] *Ibid.*, p. 250.

6 ONE FOREIGN POLICY AND ONE WORLD

As the first session of the Seventy-seventh Congress drew to a close in the summer of 1941, most Republican legislators were still voting negatively on measures involving further commitments in European affairs, and half-heartedly for appropriations after such issues had been settled. But in July, when the President announced that the United States would insure the delivery of supplies to Britain and that American troops had occupied Iceland, Willkie called on Roosevelt to assure him of the fullest support from himself and the "overwhelming number" of the Republican rank and file. After the conference, Willkie also added that he also favored the establishment of similar American military bases in both Ireland and Scotland.[1] For this suggestion, he was denounced by both the American Friends of Irish Neutrality in New York, and by an official spokesman of Nazi Germany; on the floor of the House, Representative Robsion of Kentucky called Willkie "one of the most vociferous interventionists in the country," and condemned him for glibly passing over his previous promises to the American people as "campaign oratory."[2] Other isolationists bitterly asserted

[1] *New York Times,* July 10, 1941, p. 1. Arthur Krock wrote that he had learned on the best authority that these were Willkie's ideas and not trial balloons of the President. *Ibid.,* July 11, 1941, p. 14.

[2] *Congressional Record,* vol. 87, pp. 6142 (77th Cong., 1st Sess., July 14, 1941). On July 17, Senator Nye read a lengthy article to the Senate from a magazine called *The Insurance Examiner* entitled "Wendell 'Just Cam-

that America was on the brink of war as a direct result of the Roosevelt-Willkie leadership in the aid-to-Britain campaign.

Willkie's position was that the primary issue was not war versus peace, but a debate over the means of maintaining freedom — the freedom under which "tomorrow's peace will become fruitful." He declared that as the foreign situation developed, the nation might be compelled to make other moves, but that the sole criterion on which these actions had to be judged was whether they would provide free lives for the future generations of Americans. Willkie frequently repeated his warning to Republicans that if the party played no role in the preservation of this freedom and continued to present itself to the American people as the isolationist party it would never again gain control of the government.

Two manifestoes issued by separate GOP groups, however, ignored Willkie's admonitions and demanded a noninterventionist policy. The first was issued from the summer camp of former Governor Frank O. Lowden of Illinois and signed by fifteen elder statesmen of the party including Alf Landon, Herbert Hoover, Hanford Mac-Nider, Charles Dawes, Robert M. Hutchins (then president of the University of Chicago), and Henry P. Fletcher, former Republican national chairman. The document asserted that "The American people should insistently demand that Congress put a stop to the step-by-step projection of the United States into an undeclared war," and charged that the lend-lease bill had been followed by a series of belligerent moves that were leading the nation to war. The Republican veterans saw the war — as the result of the Anglo-Russian alliance — no longer as a clear-cut issue between liberty and democracy, and they discounted the Axis threat to the United States.[3] Hardly had the ink dried on this statement when, on the following day, a Republican caucus in the House of Representatives, meeting at the request of fifty noninterventionist members, reaffirmed the pledge of the 1940 platform that the party was firmly opposed to involving the United States in a foreign war, and condemned "all executive acts and proceedings which might lead to war without the authorization of the Congress."

---

paign Oratory' Willkie Gets Insurance Company Directorship with British Hook-Up." The article alleged that Willkie was closely affiliated with the directors of British insurance companies and that in the United States he was associated with a group who were interested in an all-out effort by the United States to save Great Britain and to make the United States pay for it. *Ibid.*, pp. 6260-61, July 17, 1941.

[3] *Newsweek,* August 18, 1941, p. 17.

Both manifestoes were heartily endorsed by the *Chicago Tribune,* the America First Committee, and by Charles A. Lindbergh,[4] but they were condemned by the Fight for Freedom Committee, the Committee to Defend America, and the Council for Democracy, who issued a joint statement against leaders who would block national unity with party issues. Wendell Willkie remained silent on these proclamations, but the *New York Herald Tribune* repudiated the edict of the fifteen Republicans as a "hopelessly unrepresentative . . . document redolent of old grudges, designed to create divisions . . . among whose sponsors not one today can speak for the party," and then criticized the caucus resolution adding that "many Republican members of Congress were reacting as if the duty of an opposition is to place imagined partisan advantages above the national interest."[5]

All of these exchanges between such well-recognized and dedicated Republican representatives were merely symbolic of the party division during this period. Willkie's position was the focal point of charges and countercharges — of conflict and hope — and of a fluctuating, confused public opinion which he tried to lead. In July, Gallup found that his popularity pattern established earlier in the year had remained constant. Nationally, Willkie was liked better by 20 per cent of those polled, less by 19 per cent, while 61 per cent of the people had not changed their opinions. Among Republicans, however, 38 per cent of the interviewees liked Willkie

---

[4] The position of Lindbergh as the isolationists' chief drawing card during this period had temporary political implications. In Minnesota, rural non-interventionists outside of the Stassen organization began talking of native-son Lindbergh as a Republican candidate for the Senate to run against internationalist Senator Joseph H. Ball. Friends of Lindbergh thought he would do better, however, by awaiting a nationwide grass-roots movement for the Republican nomination for President as an anti-war candidate in 1944. *Ibid.,* September 15, 1941, p. 16. This movement was inadvertently stopped by Lindbergh himself when, in Des Moines, Iowa, in September, he charged that the three "most important groups which have been pressing this country toward war are the British, the Jewish, and the Roosevelt Administration. . . ." Al Smith immediately charged Lindbergh with "anti-semitism"; Willkie said he was "shocked at the race prejudice," and called the statement "the most un-American talk made in my time by any person of national reputation." Thomas E. Dewey accused the flier of "an inexcusable abuse of the right of freedom of speech," and even John T. Flynn, chairman of America First in New York, called the speech "stupid." Flynn feared that the address would give the interventionists a chance to launch an "all out smear" against the isolationists on an extraneous issue. *Ibid.,* September 22, 1941, p. 16.

[5] *Ibid.,* August 18, 1941, p. 17.

less than they had in November, 1940, while only 9 per cent thought more of him.[6]

During the summer, while Republicans split over men and issues, Willkie made one or two speeches every week in his effort to force the United States to take a more aggressive foreign stand. On one of these occasions in August, he attended a Vermont sesquicentennial program in Montpelier as a surprise visitor. Harold Stassen, as the main speaker, scored the "overlapping and confusion of defense agencies" and suggested a single director of defense. When asked to speak, Willkie complimented Governor Wills, whose position on the international situation, he said, reflected "the growing sentiment of the progressive wing of the Republican party, as does also Governor Stassen's." Then he added: "And here's a tip for you Republicans up here in Vermont. From now on, men like Governor Wills, Governor Stassen and myself are going to dominate the Republican party."[7]

Alfred M. Landon saw an ominous evil in a Republican party dominated by those favoring the President's foreign policy too completely, and in a major broadcast entitled "The Roosevelt-Willkie Program," he declared:

There is an obvious attempt being made these days to smother political debate in this country. The national administration accuses the minority of playing partisan politics when it fulfills its duty of questioning and exposing, for discussion and debate, the record of that administration. This attempt to eliminate all opposition has reached the point that the row now is not over the question of whether the administration is doing wrong but that we who think the administration is making mistakes may not even debate it. . . . It makes no difference to this war group that the opponents to war policies are standing on the platform pledges of both parties to the American people in the last campaign.[8]

Landon then quoted newspaper articles predicting that both Roosevelt and Willkie would support only interventionist candidates in the 1942 congressional elections, articles in which Willkie was quoted as having said, "The people should have the opportunity in every senatorial and congressional election next year for a clear-cut expression of opinion on . . . foreign policy. In districts represented by isolationists we should put the strongest candidate in

---

[6] *Public Opinion Quarterly,* 5 (Winter, 1941), p. 666.

[7] *New York Times,* August 31, 1941, p. 21.

[8] *Congressional Record,* vol. 87, p. A4389 (77th Cong., 1st Sess., Sept. 2, 1941). Landon's speech was inserted into the *Record* by Senator Arthur Capper of Kansas.

the field we can get regardless of his party label or economic views.
. . ." As a result, Landon was apprehensive about the future of
the two-party system if Willkie should prevail in the Republican
party. He asserted: "A healthy situation in popular government
. . . requires the benefit of criticisms by the minority. Mr. Roosevelt and Mr. Willkie would destroy this situation and deprive the
country of the benefit of debate by its representatives in Congress
regardless of party. . . . Thus, fighting to preserve democracy in
the world, we lose it at home. However, the Republican party
still belongs to the people, and as long as that is the case I think
we will have a successful political program."[9]

The press predictions proved to be accurate. In mid-September,
Willkie's associates announced that he would take an active part
in the off-year elections of 1942 in an effort to make the Republican
party stand for "internationalism," that he would spend his spare
time campaigning for the nomination and election of those Republicans who had supported the Administration foreign policy, and
that he would remain silent in campaigns where Democrats supporting Roosevelt's foreign policies were fighting Republicans who
opposed them.[10] Willkie's friends made it clear that the 1940
nominee opposed many of the New Deal domestic policies and that
he would attack them during the campaign, but they also reported
that he was convinced that if the Republican party turned to isolationism there would be room for a powerful new party in the
country.[11]

That Willkie's influence was still significant for or against congressional candidates was implicit in the results of a survey of
presidential timber conducted by the American Institute of Public
Opinion in September. Examining the choices of those polled in
both parties, respondents put Willkie at the top of the list in
preference to Secretary of State Cordell Hull, Thomas E. Dewey,
and Vice-President Henry A. Wallace. Others mentioned, in their
order of frequency, were: Fiorello LaGuardia, James A. Farley,
Senator Robert Taft, Senator Arthur Vandenberg, Federal Security

---

[9] *Ibid.*

[10] *Chicago Tribune,* September 14, 1941, p. 13.

[11] *New York Times,* September 14, 1941, p. 1. At a later date, Willkie
thought seriously about forming a third party but in 1941 he frequently
said that any man with a claim to political leadership should exhaust every
avenue within his party before seeking another method of achieving his
objectives. Willkie did just that from 1941 to 1944.

Administrator Paul V. McNutt, and Herbert Hoover. Of the top five candidates, all supported the Administration's foreign policy or were engaged in prominent national defense activity.[12]

Several days later, Willkie endorsed the renomination of Fiorello LaGuardia in the New York City primary election, despite the fact that the mayor had vigorously opposed him in 1940. LaGuardia was opposed by John R. Davies, an isolationist who had injected foreign policy into the mayoralty race, and therefore Willkie announced his desire for the election of the reform mayor. On September 17, Willkie also attacked as "wholly unrealistic" the attitude which former President Herbert Hoover had advocated three nights earlier. Hoover had urged that the United States adopt a waiting policy while Hitler's Germany destroyed itself. At a China Relief Rally, Willkie asserted that American isolationism was responsible for a portion of the world as it existed in 1941 and that America now had an obligation to right its previous wrongs.

Such statements continued to obtain negative reactions from many of his Republican colleagues in Congress. Senator Taft declared that "it is unfortunate that Mr. Wendell Willkie should attempt to read out of the party those who disagree with him on foreign policy," and added that he saw no reason for Republicans to make an issue of international policies in the off-year elections of 1942. Taft maintained that foreign policy was not usually considered a matter of partisanship and that the congressional votes on the question had cut across party lines. In the House of Representatives, Congressman Harry Sauthoff of Wisconsin inserted into the *Record* an editorial from the *Sioux Falls* (South Dakota) *Argus-Leader* which compared Willkie's pre-election record with his subsequent action and concluded: "Some persons still maintain that the voice of Willkie will be a dominant one in Republican councils in the future. It won't be. He is through, and Republican Congressmen have no occasion to worry about his opposition in the ranks of their own party. He now belongs — where his heart has always been — to the Roosevelt Party."[13] September, 1941, was not a time when Wendell Willkie was through in the Republican party, nor was it a time when his future success could be predicted.

In October, President Roosevelt expressed his belief that the Neutrality Act passed in 1939 should be revised. The night before

---

[12] *Ibid.,* p. 45.

[13] *Congressional Record,* vol. 87, p. A4714 (77th Cong., 1st Sess., Sept. 29, 1941).

the President assembled the first bipartisan conference to discuss the revision, Wendell Willkie publicly called upon the members of the Republican party to assume leadership of public opinion and fight for outright repeal of the Act. This was more than the President had had the courage to request, for it was his opinion that only "piecemeal" revision could be effected.[14] Roosevelt wanted the ban on arming merchant ships removed and also requested that Congress give "early and earnest consideration" to the correction of a section of the law that kept United States ships out of the ports of nations at war. Willkie's action proved both embarrassing and helpful to the Administration when he advocated outright repeal and he became what Arthur Krock called "the follower who got ahead of his leader." He tried to activate a strategy that he had advocated all along — that of taking a constructive, progressive policy out of the hands of the President in order to credit the Republican party with a more vigorous leadership in the defense of America.

Congressional Republicans would have none of it, however, and the move again served only to deepen the cleavage within the GOP, for though Willkie was the titular head of the party, he was also a private citizen — one of the many Republican voices representing a party out of power. Essentially, the party was groping for both program and leadership, and there was little evidence that Willkie influenced any great number of congressmen who were not already supporting him. Turner Catledge wrote that observers in Washington believed that the Republican position and confusion on foreign policy during this period were traceable to three factors: conviction, opportunism, and jealousy; conviction in that much of the criticism of the New Deal was based upon high principle and sincere belief; opportunism in that many Republicans expected a reaction similar to 1920 to be produced by the contemporary

---

[14] *New York Times,* October 12, 1941, sec. 4, p. E3. Roosevelt's opinion was probably based upon the fact that one month earlier the Selective Service Extension bill had passed the House by the narrow margin of one vote — 203-202. Though the Democrats had voted 189 to 70 in favor of the measure, the Republicans had voted 135 to 21 against the bill. Democrats from west of the Appalachian Mountains and north of the Mason-Dixon line voted with the Republicans against the extension. Administration leaders feared that an attempt to repeal the Neutrality Act might return the control of Congress to the Republicans in the 1942 off-year elections, and that the GOP would then stymie Roosevelt's foreign policy as decisively as the Republicans had stopped President Wilson's program in 1918.

international emergency, and therefore felt that if the United States could avoid war, the GOP would be in a desirable position politically when the reaction occurred; and jealousy which simply settled around Willkie and his activities.[15] During the 1940 campaign, the congressional Republicans had been Willkie's weakest link, and his advice and threats to them during 1941 did little to endear him more strongly to them — not only because they could not accept what he said, but also because they did not like the author of the statements. Willkie was, of course, aware of this bitterness, but because he was sensitive to remarks that he was already making a race for the Republican nomination of 1944, he had not, up to this time, endeavored to translate his views into legislative action.

Late in October, however, in a sudden move which irritated the leaders of both major parties in Congress, three Republican senators, Styles Bridges of New Hampshire, Warren Austin of Vermont, and Chan Gurney of South Dakota, aided by behind-the-scenes planning and timing of Willkie, introduced an amendment providing for complete repeal of the 1939 Neutrality Act.[16] To support the move, Willkie released a lengthy statement signed by 124 men and women described by the 1940 candidate as having been "honored by the Republican party" in the past. The signers, including Governors Saltonstall, Stassen, and Blood (New Hampshire) were recruited from the entire nation but the majority of them were from the eastern states.[17] This "Willkie manifesto"

---

[15] *Ibid.*, October 12, 1941, sec. 4, p. E3.

[16] *Ibid.*, October 21, 1941, p. 1. The amendment was to the already House-approved armed ship resolution which would have repealed only a portion of the Neutrality Act. Opponents of the bill called it the Willkie Amendment. During this period, Governor William H. Wills of Vermont thought that much of the confusion among party leaders could be resolved by a gathering of the top leaders, and he wrote a publicized letter to Chairman Joe Martin asking him to call "an immediate extraordinary caucus" of the national committee, governors, congressmen, and former presidential aspirants to work out a party line and "achieve unity on foreign policy." Martin was noncommittal, but Landon, McNary, and Governor Sewall of Maine were immediately against it, and most congressmen thought that little could be gained from it. Actually, much of the opposition of the isolationist wing was to Wills personally. His reputation with them had declined when Willkie had predicted that he would be one of those to dominate the party in the future. An unnamed Republican leader reportedly rejected Wills' proposal saying "party policy isn't made by some Johnny-come-lately from a ten-cent state." Willkie thought the suggestion was "interesting and helpful" but nothing ever came of the letter. *Newsweek,* October 27, 1941, p. 19.

[17] *Chicago Tribune,* October 22, 1941, p. 4.

stressed the desirability of a foreign policy "designed to encompass the destruction of totalitarianism by whatever means necessary," and spelled out the ways in which the Republican party might play an important part in the achievement of these objectives.[18]

Willkie's action was widely applauded as a bold and courageous move by newspaper columnists in the east, but polls of congressmen showed them to be furious at Willkie's endeavor to dictate the party's policy. When the Senate held hearings on the bill, Alf Landon, Hamilton Fish, and John T. Flynn, in addition to many other opinion leaders, testified against all-out repeal. Former Senator David A. Reed of Pennsylvania reportedly told committee members: "Willkie is just a stooge for President Roosevelt. He and the Republicans with him are completely out of step with the majority of the party."[19]

Moreover, on the floor of the Senate, Taft accused Willkie and a number of senators of advocating a war policy,[20] and Senator Nye

---

[18] Clarence Berdahl, "Political Parties and Elections," *American Political Science Review,* 37 (February, 1943), 73.

[19] *Chicago Tribune,* October 23, 1941, p. 3. One of the most vigorous speeches against the 1940 nominee was given in the House of Representatives by Mr. Lambertson of Kansas. He quoted Willkie's campaign speech in Brooklyn saying that we must stay out of war, and then asserted: ". . . that speech was made by Wendell L. Willkie, now clearly recognizable as the Dr. Jekyll and Mr. Hyde of American politics — the Republicrat or or Demorep of the contemporaneous scene. . . . What has happened to Wendell L. Willkie, the great Republican liberal, who joined the Republican Party after serving as a Democratic captain in New York City? Where has Mr. Willkie been? Who has been feeding him the red, raw meat of war? . . . Did a few handshakes with the dukes and earls he met in England change his mind? . . . In light of Mr. Willkie's publicly expressed principles before and after election, it appears he was engaging in a sham battle. And in doing so he was perpetrating a fraud on the American voting public. . . . Only yesterday, Mr. Willkie . . . completed the final act of his right about face. We read in the papers . . . that more than 100 prominent Republicans agree with him that the Neutrality Act should be repealed outright. The warmongers of the Nation hail this statement issued by Mr. Willkie . . . as proof sufficient that we have now achieved national unity. Unity for what? If this is unity it appears to me that it is unity for an immediate shooting war. . . .

"Frankly, as an elected Republican, I disavow Wendell Willkie as the leader of the Republican thought. . . . Wendell Willkie is America's No. 1 warmonger. . . . The President is going too slow to suit him. . . . We do not follow Mr. Willkie in this. . . . Mr. Willkie has reached eminence as a private citizen. The voters of the nation saw fit to continue him in that capacity. He cannot commit the Republican party. . . ." *Congressional Record,* vol. 87, p. 8441 (77th Cong., 1st Sess., Oct. 23, 1941).

[20] *Ibid.,* p. 8493 (Oct. 28, 1941).

bitterly criticized the integrity of "Sir Echo" Willkie for repudiating his campaign determination to keep America out of war unless the United States were attacked.[21] Right-wing columnist George Sokolsky, in a widely syndicated article, pointed out that Willkie's attempt to needle the President into a more vigorous war policy accomplished two things: first, it split the Republican party wide open; and second, it forced many isolationist and middle-of-the-road Americans to choose between Roosevelt and Willkie on foreign policy. Sokolsky concluded that they would choose President Roosevelt, "the man of responsibility."[22]

On November 2, a group of House Republicans organized an effort to read Wendell Willkie out of the party. Several congressmen, including Charles Halleck of Indiana and Dewey Short of Missouri, led the anti-Willkie move by pledging opposition to the Administration's effort "to involve this country in an undeclared war."[23] The aim of the anti-Willkie forces was to make Representative Joseph Martin the party spokesman and then to make the Republican party the standard-bearer of peace. Representative Short said that he and the group opposing Willkie believed that more than eighty per cent of the House Republican membership would support the resolution reading the 1940 presidential candidate out of the party. He added: "We've tried to restrain ourselves. We have shown more restraint than I thought was possible. We have no fault to find with the fact that Willkie is an interventionist as long as he speaks for himself. But now he seeks to tell lifelong Republicans what to do. He has helped Roosevelt put the United

---

[21] *Ibid.*, p. 8519 (Oct. 29, 1941).

[22] *Ibid.*, p. A5234 (Oct. 30, 1941). Read into the *Record* by Congressman Lambertson. Sokolsky also stated that Willkie's list of supporters was not representative. He had 27 of the 104 members of the national committee; 9 Republican state chairmen and co-chairmen of the 104; 6 of the 20 Republican governors; none of the party elders, and no former chairmen of the Republican National Committee. Sokolsky wrote: "Statistically, his list shows a maximum strength in the party of 25 per cent. In influence it is no greater. . . . If Wendell Willkie wishes to prove that his leadership is realistic and effective, why does he not ask that the Republican National Committee meet and endorse his proposal? Why does he not request a caucus of the Republican Senators and Representatives to meet and endorse his position? These men and women are elected to represent the party. They are its accredited leaders."

[23] *Chicago Daily News*, November 3, 1941, p. 5.

States in war and now with Roosevelt's blessings he is smashing the Republican party wide open."[24]

Willkie's reply was a demand that the GOP purge itself of isolationists and become the party of aggression against Hitler. He reportedly felt that the sooner the entire question of isolationism within the Republican party was fought out, the better it would be for the country.

To this suggestion came an immediate reply. On the floor of the House on November 5, Dewey Short violently condemned Willkie for his whole attitude on foreign affairs. The speech, which lasted twenty minutes and was applauded for a minute by the Republican side, came soon after reports that Republican House leaders had been trying to dissuade him from pressing a demand for a House Republican conference to expel Willkie from the party. Assailing Willkie as "We-Win-de-War Willkie, . . . belligerent, bombastic, bellicose, bombinating, blow-hard who couldn't be elected dog-catcher," Short again asserted that the 1940 nominee was "unfit to lead any party," and urged his fellow Republicans to repudiate him.[25] This vehement address had been cleared with Joe Martin and with Representative Englebright of California, the minority whip. It was reported that they had cautioned Short with the statement: "Give him [Willkie] enough rope and you won't need to worry."

When Willkie was informed of the attack, he stated that the Representative from Missouri talked like "many men when they represent a dying cause such as isolationism, . . . I hope he and other isolationists, both Republican and Democrats, keep right on talking. . . . It's all very helpful. His personal references remind me of the bad boy who, when he runs out of arguments, begins to make faces."

The *Chicago Daily News* reported that the movement by the isolationists obtained the active support of a comparatively small number of Republican congressmen, but that the feeling among them was bitter.[26] Though the Republicans in Congress who agreed with Willkie's views on foreign policy did not actively refute Short

[24] *Ibid.* Short and his associates also claimed the support of a large but unidentified group of local leaders in the country. Short was interviewed by United Press correspondent Lyle C. Wilson.

[25] *Congressional Record,* vol. 87, p. 8813 (77th Cong., 1st Sess., Nov. 6, 1941), and the *New York Times,* November 7, 1941, p. 11.

[26] *Chicago Daily News,* November 5, 1941, p. 9.

at the time, Representative Paul W. Shafer of Michigan placed in the *Record* a pro-Willkie editorial from the *Battle Creek Enquirer-News* which concluded: "As to Mr. Willkie . . . the question is not whether he's helping or hurting the Republican party but whether he's talking sound sense." New York columnist Mark Sullivan was also quoted to the effect that Willkie's utterances with respect to what the nation faced showed a clarity of thought rare in either party.[27] The Republican state committee of Massachusetts publicly expressed complete approval of Willkie's position in supporting Roosevelt's policy of all-out aid to the nations fighting Germany, and similar resolutions, not so strongly expressed and coupled with criticism of the President's leadership, were also adopted by the Republican state committees of Connecticut and Rhode Island.[28]

On November 13, the repeal of the Neutrality Act of 1939 was voted by Congress, but it was opposed by a large majority of the Republicans in both the House and the Senate.[29] The amendment, which actually repealed sections two, three, and six of the original act, permitted the arming of merchant ships and the entrance into combat zones and belligerent ports by American cargo vessels. Republican Senators Austin, Ball, Barbour, Bridges, Gurney, and White were the only members of the GOP in the upper chamber to favor the bill; eventual advocates of postwar international leadership, such as Senator Vandenberg and Senator Tobey, voted against the measure.[30] Willkie's efforts and his manifesto had little

---

[27] *Congressional Record,* vol. 87, p. A5345 (77th Cong., 1st Sess., Nov. 6, 1941).

[28] *New York Times,* November 29, 1941, p. 7. In the Middle West, Willkie's position was supported by such party leaders as former Illinois National Committeeman Hill Blackett, Illinois State Treasurer Warren Wright, and Congressman Everett Dirksen; Minnesota's Harold Stassen and Senator Joseph Ball; South Dakota's Senator Gurney; and North Dakota's National Committeeman William Stern and Lynn U. Stambaugh, National Commander of the American Legion. See Berdahl, "Political Parties and Elections," p. 74.

[29] The breakdown of the vote was as follows:

HOUSE OF REPRESENTATIVES				SENATE			
Yea		Nay		Yea		Nay	
Dem.	Rep.	Dem.	Rep.	Dem.	Rep.	Dem.	Rep.
189	22	53	137	43	6	15	21

See the *Congressional Record,* vol. 87, pp. 8680, 8891 (77th Cong., 1st Sess., Nov. 7, 13, 1941).

[30] Several years later, Senator Vandenberg privately admitted that Willkie had provided the impetus for the bipartisan foreign policy and that the

effect on the party members, though the amendment would have failed in the House if twenty-two Republicans had not voted for it. The point is that on the eve of America's entrance into World War II, less than twelve per cent of the congressional Republicans were willing to support an aggressive policy against Hitler.

With the coming of war, the complexion of the controversy over foreign policy took an immediate turn for what seemed to be an era of divorcement from partisan politics. Two days after the attack on Pearl Harbor, National Chairmen Ed Flynn and Joe Martin exchanged telegrams concluding an agreement that was described by the Democratic committee as "the most complete adjournment of domestic politics since the formation of a two-party system."[31] In addition, Martin called off a scheduled meeting of the Republican state chairmen and declared: "Let us publicly proclaim our support of the Administration in an irresistible effort to win the war. . . . We can at the same time with full consistency uphold the great principles for which our party stands." Most of the isolationists who had opposed the programs for extended aid to the European countries fighting Hitler supported Martin in his plea for unity.

Wendell Willkie, who was immediately suggested for a number of administrative posts in the government, was gratified to discover that his formula for national unity would now materialize. Asserting that "all remembrance of past differences over international policy must be forgotten," he proposed that those who had opposed the President's international policy be given positions of importance and responsibility. The 1940 nominee then projected his thoughts into the future and declared that the United States and its people had to insure that, once the war was brought to a successful conclusion, the nation would regard itself as belonging to the world community. He maintained that America could no longer hide behind high tariffs; that it could not live alone; that in war or peace, isolationism would forever be a repudiated doctrine. "We must never forget," he stated, "what we are fighting for. We are fighting for the elimination from this world of narrow nationalism

---

loyal opposition advocated by the 1940 candidate facilitated the party harmony necessary to obtain approval of the United Nations Charter. Dillon, *op. cit.*, p. 260.

[31] Berdahl, "Political Parties and Elections," p. 75.

and isolationism, which are the breeders of war and of economic degradation and of poverty."[32]

In reference to the war and to the Republican party, Willkie told one correspondent that "If Hitler wins, nothing matters. If Hitler is crushed, the power will go to those who led the fight to defeat him. . . . The Republican Party will be impotent unless it plays its part in leading the fight to crush Hitler."[33]

In December, 1941, *The Republican* magazine released the final results of a complete survey of 9,554 GOP leaders which showed that Willkie was still the most popular leader in the Republican party. The poll included 4,219 county and township leaders, 2,625 women, and 2,710 Young Republican leaders, though only twenty-one per cent of the senior members, eight per cent of women, and fourteen per cent of the Young Republicans responded. Willkie was the first choice of forty-two per cent of all those who answered the question: "If you were to vote today for a Republican for President, whom would you prefer to vote for?" Willkie was more popular with the women and Young Republicans, and the editors concluded that if those groups had responded in as large numbers as the county and township chairmen, assuming that the trend established would have carried through, Willkie's vote would have indicated an even greater degree of popularity. The 1940 nominee's two closest contenders were Senator Taft and Thomas E. Dewey. On a regional basis, Willkie's popularity had increased in the South and in the far West, but had declined in the Midwest; there had been no change in the East since the previous poll taken by the magazine.[34]

---

[32] Francis Brown, "National Unity, A Willkie Formula," *New York Times Magazine* (December 14, 1941), sec. 7, p. 11.

[33] Henry F. Pringle, "What's Happened to Willkie?" *American Mercury,* 54 (January, 1942), 49.

[34] *The Republican,* December, 1941, p. 14. A breakdown within the various groups and the other candidates was as follows:

	COUNTY CHAIRMEN	WOMEN LEADERS	YOUNG REPUBLICANS	TOTAL FROM ALL GROUPS
	per cent	*per cent*	*per cent*	*per cent*
Willkie	38	47	40	42
Taft	20	27	11	19
Dewey	16	9	20	15
Hoover	9	5	5	6
Vandenberg	5	2	3	3
Martin	3	1	3	3
Stassen	2	..	3	2
Green	2	..	1	1
Scattering	5	9	14	9

Thus, Wendell L. Willkie concluded a stormy year in which he had been praised and condemned repeatedly for his frank and courageous convictions. He had helped the nation rally to the support of the Administration's foreign policy with fidelity rare in its annals, but he had also alienated many of his own party members in his personal campaign to aid democracy in Europe. Despite the opposition to Willkie, the polls indicated that he was still the preferred leader of the legions of voters who considered themselves members of that vague entity called the Republican party; the polls also indicated, however, that for all of his labor, his popularity was on the wane.

The adjournment of politics for the duration of the war, proclaimed after the bombing of Pearl Harbor, turned out to be only a recess. On January 4, 1942, Joe Martin appointed Clarence Budington Kelland as the new publicity director of the Republican party, and Kelland's first statement was a demand for the right and the obligation of Americans to "engage vigorously in politics" even in wartime.[35] Kelland, who had been appointed without Willkie's knowledge,[36] said that the Administration would be criticized whereever necessary, and added: "Politics is good in time of peace; in time of war politics is indispensable. When political unity comes in at the door, human liberties go out of the window. It is political unity which has plunged this world into war."[37] Observed the *New York Herald Tribune*: "The Republican party has faced a lot of

---

[35] *New York Times*, January 5, 1942, p. 1.

[36] During this period Willkie participated in many activities outside the political arena. He was in great demand as a speaker, toastmaster, corporation executive, and special pleader for civil liberties. He was active at receptions for various Allied governments in exile and elected chairman of the board of the 20th Century-Fox Film Corporation. In addition, he attracted much attention by defending, without charge, William Schneiderman, secretary of the Communist party in California, before the United States Supreme Court. For a more detailed account of this activity, see the *New York Times*, November 29, 1941, p. 1; January 17, 1942, p. 9; November 10, 1942, p. 20; 320 U.S. 118; Barnes, *op. cit.*, pp. 321-23; and Dillon, *op. cit.*, pp. 303-7. When, on January 18, President Roosevelt appointed Donald L. Nelson as chairman of the War Production Board, with full power to mobilize American industry and labor, this move was commended by Willkie as necessary but belated in that Willkie had called for such a single director of national production eighty-seven times during the campaign and thirty-seven times during 1941. There was talk during this period of an important war job for Willkie, but Harry Hopkins was never enthusiastic about a really high position for Willkie, and Willkie always rejected anything less. See Robert E. Sherwood's *Roosevelt and Hopkins*, II, 46.

[37] Berdahl, "Political Parties and Elections," p. 75.

hard luck in its day but Mr. Kelland is just too much."[38] The pre-Pearl Harbor isolationist papers, however, thought Kelland was representative of the predominant attitude of a majority of the party members.

From the Democratic camp, a few days later, Chairman Ed Flynn, one of the original participants in the truce between the parties, charged in a nationwide radio address that the Republicans were "not as much interested in the war as . . . [in] controlling the House of Representatives." "I naturally feel," he declared, "that no misfortune except a major defeat could befall this country to the extent involved in the election of a Congress hostile to the President."[39] Willkie immediately assailed Flynn, and said that in the fall elections he hoped he would find the least partisanship possible.[40] Declaring that he was "greatly distressed" to read Flynn's remarks, he called for an abandonment of "the route of pure partisanship . . . a route . . . which imperiled the United States in the year preceding the outbreak of its war with the Axis." He said, "Each party . . . should be selecting men now who have the daring and the imagination to tell the truth and the whole truth unaffected by partisan bias, bitterness, or propaganda."[41] A week later, in Boston, he criticized both the New Dealers for their labor policy and the Republicans who desired a passive course for their party. He declared:

> I do not intend in the formation of my opinion to be chained by a need to oppose, any more than to be rendered innocuous by a need to acquiesce. But there are [Republicans who] . . . counsel that the Republican party should not develop an affirmative program at this time. It should await the inevitable reactions from this war. . . . They recall the throwback to intense nationalism which followed the first world war. . . . And they believe, therefore, that the Republican party will then come back into office on an inheritance of discontent. I have no faith in such a theory. . . . I would not have my party rely on the logic of luck or the calculus of expediency. I would not have the party of Abraham Lincoln merely "going along" when freedom itself is at stake.[42]

---

[38] *New Republic*, January 26, 1942, p. 115.

[39] Berdahl, "Political Parties and Elections," p. 75.

[40] Willkie believed in such a course so strongly that in January he had gone to see James Farley to try to work out a bipartisan plan for the support of candidates who had endorsed the President's foreign program. Farley told him that he was against any such agreement, and that the decision on such matters should be left to the voters. Joseph Barnes, *op. cit.*, p. 282.

[41] *New York Times*, February 4, 1942, p. 38.

[42] *New York Times*, February 13, 1942, p. 16. For a similar statement by

Nevertheless, it was hard for certain Republicans to shake the accusation that they were either negative or just going along. So many of them had voted against all attempts to prepare the country for combat that in 1942, when it became obvious how inadequately America was equipped, most of these prewar isolationists had confusing and contradictory records. As a result, they protested their patriotism on the one hand, and usually successfully blamed the Democratic administration for the condition of the national defense on the other. When Flynn made his statement about a Congress hostile to the President, Joe Martin accused him of seeking a one-party system, and of wanting to "liquidate" the Republican opposition. He asserted, however, that "Republicans will continue to give President Roosevelt one hundred per cent support to win the war. We will continue to put national safety above partisanship. Despite abuse or vilification . . . we will stand by the American right to offer any constructive appraisal or suggestion."[43]

This unity was the general theme of Republican leaders when they gathered at a meeting of the national committee in Chicago in April. There was no doubt about party support for the prosecution of the war, but maneuvering had been going on for some weeks concerning resolutions about what stand would be taken on postwar cooperation with other nations to maintain peace. Wendell Willkie, Senator Brooks of Illinois, and Senator Taft all had prepared resolutions to be submitted to the delegates for their approval. The Willkie resolution contained a declaration which pledged: "to undertake now and in the future whatever just and reasonable *international responsibilities* may be demanded in a modern world . . . to the end that our own liberty be preserved, that free institutions and a free way of life may be supported *in the rest of the world.* . . ." Willkie also telephoned a message to the delegates stating: "If the Republican party is to remain an effective instrument of party government, it must not only repudiate completely . . . the doctrine of isolationism but with courage and imagination must recognize that America must take its full part hereafter in world affairs and help lead the peoples of the world to peace and democracy." When Joe Martin was asked about the Willkie resolution, upon his arrival in Chicago, he replied: "Willkie spoke to

Willkie, see "Let's Look Ahead," in the *New York Times Magazine,* February 15, 1942, p. 5.
　[43] *Ibid.,* February 4, 1942, p. 38.

me several times about the resolution, but I haven't seen the text
. . . Willkie, of course, is head of the party and anything he sends
to our meeting will be given careful consideration."[44]

John D. M. Hamilton, Martin's predecessor, was represented at
the meeting through an open letter calling upon the national committee to take a united stand on the war. He said that the Republican party should be determined to end waste, inefficiency, and
unnecessary experiments in national socialism, but that only after
the electorate was satisfied with the GOP sincerity on the war effort
would the voters pass on other issues such as the need for keeping
the two-party system.[45] The Taft resolution followed Hamilton's
line of thought. It promised support to the President in the prosecution of the war and pledged the Republican party to eliminate
from the war effort complication, inefficiency, and unnecessary expenditures for nonwar purposes. But Taft wanted no committal on
foreign policy and his statement made no reference to *future* international cooperation. The Brooks resolution, which had been approved by the *Chicago Tribune* and Colonel McCormick, merely
called for a vigorous war effort and made no mention of postwar
plans. The submission of several other resolutions was rumored
and the day before the meeting opened, Willkie supporter Sinclair
Weeks charged that the multiplicity of resolutions was an attempt
to sidetrack the Willkie resolution. "We propose to fight any such
move. . . . This is a chance above all others for the Republican
party to take a clear-cut positive position on the great issues which
face the country today."[46]

The atmosphere was filled with tension and Chicago newspapers
predicted a "bitter factional fight" within the party. Martin tried
to drive the dispute underground by allowing no debate on the
resolutions after they had been read to the assembled committee,
and he referred them at once to the presumably pro-Taft subcom-

[44] *New York Times,* April 19, 1942, p. 21. The *Chicago Tribune* thought
otherwise. An editorial in the April 20, 1942, issue stated: "While custom
gives the party's last nominee for President the privilege of offering it his
advice, custom does not apply to Mr. Willkie. He is not a Republican. He
deserted the principles of the party that nominated him, even before the
election, and any advice he may offer can be considered only in the light of
the betrayal that that desertion involved. Courtesy may require that any
resolution Mr. Willkie offers be received, but his influence, fortunately, is so
slight that they cannot become a source of party dissension."
[45] *Ibid.,* April 20, 1942, p. 11.
[46] *Ibid.*

mittee for consideration. This subcommittee was then authorized to reject all of them if it chose. The subcommittee, however, approved Willkie's proposal and chose to ignore the *Chicago Tribune*. Then, to the complete surprise of most observers, and after an entire afternoon of discussion, the entire national committee accepted the subcommittee's recommendations by unanimously adopting a resolution that included Willkie's basic tenets in what was called a compromise plan but which was, in reality, a statement clearly indicating Willkie's victory. The controversial paragraph on which agreement was reached was a substitute for the paragraph submitted by Willkie, but it declared: "We realize that after this war, the responsibility of the nation will not be circumscribed within the territorial limits of the United States; that our nation has an *obligation to assist in* bringing about understanding, comity, and *cooperation* among the *nations of the world* in order that our own liberty may be preserved and that the blighting and destructive processes of war may not again be forced upon us and upon the free and peace-loving peoples of the earth."[47]   The committee incorporated some of Taft's suggestions into other sections of the entire statement of policy, but the Brooks resolution was ignored. In answer to several remarks that Representative Martin should resign because of his prewar position as an "isolationist," the committee adopted a motion made by Werner Schroeder expressing confidence in Martin's wise leadership and pledging continued cooperation.

Willkie hailed the declaration by the committee as an abandonment by the party of isolationism and a recognition of the necessity for the United States to assume a positive position in world affairs after the war. In a telephone conversation, he said: "The next job for Republicans to do is to see to it that in the coming primaries candidates are nominated not alone for Congress but for other positions of public influence who have the courage to declare and who believe sincerely these principles and their necessary implications. Thus, the Republican party can win and become a great force for liberal enlightened government."[48]

The *New York Times* called the resolution "the strongest and boldest statement of Republican foreign policy made in all these barren years since a Republican majority in Congress committed itself to opposition to every constructive proposal that was brought

[47] *Ibid.*, April 21, 1942, p. 13.
[48] *Ibid.*

before it. . . ."[49] The Republican-oriented *Saturday Evening Post* thought the party's stand "one of the most significant political events" of the decade, and declared that the resolution gave it hope that the Republican party would now begin to assume once more "its rightful place in the American political system."[50] Even Hamilton Fish, on the floor of the House, declared that he was in "entire accord" with the committee's declaration and hoped all Republicans in Congress would unite behind it.

The resolution offended other individuals in the party, however, and the positions of the principal contenders for leadership were significant. After the resolution was passed, Thomas E. Dewey was reported to have been for it all along, and he telegraphed J. Russel Sprague, national committeeman from New York: "Issues which split both Republican and Democratic parties before December 7 are now dead. Our complete unity of purpose to win the war overshadows every other subject. But we should not neglect our duty to demand and procure a more efficient conduct of the war and a firm declaration that, as Republicans, we shall help lead America in procuring a lasting peace after we have won the war."[51] *Newsweek* commented: "Dewey's position is still dubious. He straddled the issue of isolationism until after Pearl Harbor, when he came all-out for the war issue. Likewise, he straddled the issue of international policy at Chicago, but when the Willkie resolution passed, he telegraphed the committee his congratulations. . . ."[52] When Willkie saw the Dewey statement, he said: "I am puzzled. I am not sure from a reading of the wire whether he urged the committee to adopt isolation or for the United States to take a position of world outlook and cooperation."[53]

It was Senator Taft, however, whose position and statements indicated that isolation was not dead — that the Old Guard had not capitulated to Willkie. Taft thought that a majority of the members of the committee were reluctant to go on record on future American foreign policy, and he said so. He also differed with Willkie in his belief that the national committee had no power to commit the party to a postwar program. Unable to prevent the declaration, however, Taft then worked to make the statement as innocuous as

---

[49] *Ibid.*, April 22, 1942, p. 22.
[50] *Saturday Evening Post,* April 30, 1942, p. 18.
[51] *New York Times,* April 22, 1942, p. 18.
[52] *Newsweek,* May 4, 1942, p. 26.
[53] *New York Times,* April 22, 1942, p. 18.

possible, and after the committee's version had been published, he claimed to reporters that the teeth had been taken out of the original Willkie proposal. Nationally, the press and the public failed to interpret the news in this way, and Willkie was generally regarded as having strengthened his position in the party. Most committee members were so reluctant to have isolationism as an issue in the 1942 elections and were so afraid that Republican prewar isolationists might be attacked by both Willkie and the Democrats that they accepted a rewritten version of the original resolution. But, again, although a large segment of the Republican party — both officially and among the rank and file — endorsed Willkie and his display of leadership, in his hour of ideological triumph he unavoidably offended, repudiated, and discounted some of the major powers within the GOP.

This situation was intensified early in April, when, in spite of the prevailing opinion that Dewey was virtually assured of the Republican nomination for the governorship of New York, Willkie asserted that he thought that the race was still wide open, and that men such as Representative James W. Wadsworth, Irving Ives, Charles Evans Hughes, Jr., Robert Moses, Roger W. Straus, Joseph Clark Baldwin, and others were well qualified for the position.[54] Willkie was cool toward the Dewey candidacy because he was convinced that the District Attorney was deliberately evasive about the role the United States would play after the war.[55] The issue at the time was believed to be crucial to Dewey, for many observers maintained that no candidate on the Republican ticket could win in November without Willkie's endorsement. In May, before the Association of New York State Young Republican Clubs, however, Dewey called for cooperation of the United States with other free nations in establishing and maintaining a stable world and in preventing another world war after the peace was negotiated.[56] But even this move did not, at least for the time being, bring Willkie into Dewey's corner.

A week later, the *Times* reported that Dewey, in a speech before the Women's Republican Club of Putnam County, declared that he was opposed to Hamilton Fish for re-election to Congress "not for

---

[54] *Ibid.*, April 5, 1942, p. 40. Willkie's preferences were Ives and Wadsworth.

[55] *Ibid.*, April 22, 1942, p. 18.

[56] *Ibid.*, May 17, 1942, p. 1. The convention of the Young Republicans endorsed Dewey, took no stand on endorsing any candidate for the presidency in 1944, and adopted Willkie's resolution to the Republican National Committee.

his views," but because of the friends Fish had and the "misuse" they had made of his office.[57] Willkie agreed with Dewey that Fish had to be defeated, but he was deeply disturbed by Dewey's statement for he believed that Fish was unacceptable to the Republican party precisely because of his views. In Watertown, New York, the Hoosier demanded that all candidates for nomination on the Republican state ticket for the fall elections "forthrightly and directly, without evasion or confusion" publicly give their stand on all major issues, particularly on isolationism. Willkie also, by inference, assailed statements credited to Dewey for supporting a policy of economic self-sufficiency for the United States after the war. The 1940 standard-bearer maintained that such a doctrine, if carried out, would lead to high tariffs, intense nationalism, political isolation, and inevitable war; and that it had to be discarded if permanent peace was to prevail.

In response, Dewey claimed that he had been misquoted and that his opposition to Fish was "all-out" because of his views as well as because of his associates. Friends of the New York district attorney contended that his views were being deliberately distorted by his opponents within the Republican party in an attempt to block his nomination or to impair its value. At a meeting in Albany, GOP leaders would not officially discuss the Dewey-Willkie differences, but "in private conversation . . . before and after the meeting, no other subject was discussed."[58] Dewey had the support of Edwin F. Jaeckle, state chairman, and a reputed majority of the state delegates to the forthcoming convention, but a sizable number of upstate delegates were not enthusiastic about him. The principal difficulty for these people was that they had no other prominent candidate to support.

Several independent moves were made early in June to get Willkie himself to oppose Dewey for the New York governorship. Willkie squelched an early attempt by Sidney S. Baron, a publicity expert, by simply asking him to refrain from any further effort on his behalf, but other movements for Willkie persisted. Richard B. Scandrett, Jr., co-chairman of an organization called "Vote-for-Freedom," made a formal announcement on June 24 that he was starting a movement to draft Willkie for the Republican nomination for the governorship on the ground that the records of Dewey and Attorney

---

[57] *Ibid.*, May 24, 1943, p. 37.
[58] *Ibid.*, June 20, 1942, p. 1.

General John J. Bennett, Jr., the prospective Democratic nominee, "unfitted them for this position of leadership in time of war."[59] He declared that Willkie would be supported not only by his enthusiastic personal following, but that "even on the Republican ticket," he would be backed by David Dubinsky, president of the powerful International Ladies Garment Workers Union.

The movement produced opposition in some quarters. The New York Young Republican Club endorsed Dewey, and references were made to Willkie's attacks on Dewey as undermining the Republican party. William Fulton of the *Chicago Tribune* wrote that while Willkie claimed that his opposition was based on his belief that Dewey was not enough of an internationalist, Dewey's friends believed that Willkie had his eye on the presidential contest in 1944, and that if Dewey became governor of New York, he might be in a position to capture the 1944 nomination and send Willkie into a political eclipse.[60] Though this allegation proved to be accurate, Willkie at the time did not consider the New York gubernatorial position essential to his future. On June 17, he again announced that he was not a candidate for the post, and asserted even more strongly that he doubted he would ever again seek public office, since to do so might attach a "taint of self-interest" to the causes he was advocating for the United States.[61] He declared that his principal cause was the preservation of democracy in the United States, with particular reference to the rights of minorities.[62] Never-

---

[59] *Ibid.,* June 25, 1942, p. 1. Other leaders in the movement were Mrs. Helen P. Simpson, Mrs. J. Borden Harriman, Herbert Bayard Swope, and Stanley Rinehart.

[60] *Chicago Tribune,* June 24, 1942, p. 15.

[61] *New York Times,* June 18, 1942, p. 42. James Hagerty, *ibid.,* June 28, 1942, sec. 4, p. E7, stated: "Willkie . . . has repeatedly told friends that he would not run for Governor and has no desire to hold that office. . . . He does not regard the Governorship of New York, in his case at least, as a necessary stepping stone to the Presidency. Mr. Willkie has taken the position that the nomination should be kept open. . . ."

[62] *Ibid.,* June 18, 1942, p. 42. The address was made at a dinner at the Hotel Commodore attended by prominent Jewish and labor leaders who sought to establish a memorial colony in Palestine in honor of Louis D. Brandeis.

It should be recorded here that Willkie spoke splendidly and frequently for the cause of civil rights during this period, and, for that matter, during his entire life. In May, 1942, he said to a large audience: "On Bataan the Filipinos and Americans, fighting side by side, learned the real meaning of equality. We know now, in a way that we could never have known before, the real equality between races. We know too, that in the idea of equality lies the hope . . . of the future. The day is gone when men and women of

theless, the movement continued, and continued to pick up momentum.

The governorship race took on national significance. Pearson and Allen wrote that "Wendell Willkie is wrestling with the toughest decision of his political life. He must choose between taking off the gloves and wading bluntly into a powerful Republican office-seeker whose views he detests, or remain silent and permit himself to be elbowed out of party leadership." The columnists believed that Willkie sincerely did not want to run for governor, but that there seemed to be no other method of defeating the popular Dewey.[63] The editors of *Time* stated that "the future of the Republican Party was quite possibly at stake," and called the election "perhaps the most significant political contest of the year. They saw, in the behind-the-scenes maneuvers, a struggle for control of the party between the Old Guard and the followers of Willkie which would determine the GOP choice for the presidency in 1944. The Luce publication, in effect, called for a genuine "draft-Willkie" movement so that "the people could take a hand; could, perhaps, help the bosses pick the People's Choice as Governor . . . as chief of the Republican Party, as the next GOP Presidential nominee."[64]

All of the discussion concerning Willkie for governor was finally stopped, however, when Willkie apparently made up his mind to refuse any offer. On July 1 in Westport, Connecticut, he stated bluntly that he had no intention of becoming a candidate. He said that if he could just obtain party support for his principles, other persons could have every office in the United States as far as he was concerned. He then gave his party some enduring advice. He declared: "I am exceedingly anxious for the Republican party to win

---

whatever color or creed can consider themselves the superiors of other creeds or colors. . . . The day of equal peoples is at hand. Let us keep that aim shining before us like a light — for the people [of the world] and for the people of our own beloved land." *Time,* May 4, 1942, p. 12. On July 19, before several thousand persons representing the National Association for the Advancement of Colored People, in Los Angeles, he expressed similar beliefs and asserted a hope that the war was liberating the Negro. *New York Times,* July 20, 1942, p. 28. On the floor of the House of Representatives on June 26, however, John E. Rankin of Mississippi blasted Willkie for defending Schneiderman and for joining the Communists in their anti-Jim Crow fight "through which they are trying to stir up race trouble all over the country and especially throughout the South." *Congressional Record,* vol. 88, p. A2650 (77th Cong., 2nd Sess., June 26, 1942).

[63] *The Daily Illini* (University of Illinois), June 24, 1942, p. 2.

[64] *Time,* June 29, 1942, p. 15.

the fall elections. . . . But Republicans cannot win unless they choose candidates who by record and firmness and clearness of belief can attract votes from liberals, from labor, and from people with an enlightened view about the country's foreign policy now and in the future." In conclusion he asked the Republican party in New York to name a man who would hold the confidence of all the people to insure victory, but he did not endorse Dewey.[65]

During this period in which Willkie was alienating Dewey in New York, he was involved in political fortunes in other parts of the nation. In Iowa he supported State Secretary of Agriculture Mark Thornburg for the nomination as candidate for the United States Senate, but Thornburg's opponent, Governor George Wilson — veteran corporation lawyer and Republican politician who had the backing of the *Chicago Tribune* — won the primary. After the primary, the *Tribune* asserted that Willkie was the "real loser in Iowa," and that he had been "repudiated all over the middle west. . . ."[66] The *Mason City* (Iowa) *Globe-Gazette,* however, declared that the *Tribune*'s statement was a misrepresentation, and rebuked the McCormick paper for its stand by stating:

. . . it's a fair guess that the *Tribune*'s own intrusion into the Iowa campaign . . . was both more noticed and more universally resented than any part Wendell Willkie took in the campaign. Wilson himself would not list such uninvited support as one of his assets in the primary campaign. . . .

Any honest and disinterested observer of the Iowa scene would list the Willkie influence as just about the last . . . of a dozen factors entering into the contest. . . . The one greatest reason for Wilson's election was the feeling . . . on the part of a majority of Iowa's Republicans that Wilson would make the better . . . senator.

Just a year and half ago the voters of Iowa . . . gave [Willkie] a ringing endorsement. . . . That the *Tribune* hasn't changed its opinion con-

[65] *New York Times,* July 2, 1942, p. 23. The Willkie-for-Governor headquarters was not finally closed until July 29. *Ibid.,* July 30, 1942, p. 15. Representative Dewey Short inserted into the *Congressional Record* an editorial from *The Progressive* magazine which criticized Willkie for supporting those who were long-time advocates of intervention when Willkie himself during the campaign had criticized the President for those same interventionist views. The editorial concluded: "By his own definition of courage, imagination, and leadership, Mr. Willkie seems to have disqualified himself for public office. We hope so, and we hope the nation doesn't let him weasel out of his predicament by repeating his bland disavowal of all [six] 1940 speeches as more 'campaign oratory.' " *Congressional Record,* vol. 88, p. A2829 (77th Cong., 2nd Sess., July 6, 1942).

[66] See the editorial page of the *Chicago Tribune* for June 4, 1942.

cerning him during the intervening months would argue that perhaps Iowa hasn't either. . . ."[67]

From other sources, however, came evidence that corroborated the *Tribune*'s evaluations. The *Missouri Republican,* a semimonthly newspaper which circulated among the officials throughout Missouri, published the results of a poll with respect to Willkie's leadership and ability to speak for the Republican party in the state. Of the 765 persons who responded to the questionnaire (out of 5,000 who received the paper), an astounding 764 voted against the 1940 nominee's leadership.[68] Meanwhile, at the Indiana Republican state convention at Indianapolis, the platform adopted by the state convention did not follow the national program approved at Chicago in April. Instead, the Hoosier platform accepted the Taft position that, during the war, conditions changed so frequently that no individual or group could possibly formulate an adequate program for the future.[69] Finally, a Gallup poll illustrated the impact of the war on voters who were asked to identify presidential timber for 1944. General Douglas MacArthur was listed in first place; Willkie was second, followed by Dewey, Vice-President Wallace, and Donald Nelson, the war production chief. This was the first time Willkie had been supplanted as the favored candidate for 1944.[70]

These events notwithstanding, Willkie continued his fight to liberalize the Republican party independently of the party leaders in Congress. To a gathering of party workers, he declared: "Our party should be the friend and advocate of the workingman. Ours is the party of production, the party of plenty, whether in war or in peace. It has always been our aim to produce, for the American workingman, the highest standard of living in the world, not alone in dollars of wage, but in expansion and opportunity. Thus in so far as we have lost the workingman's confidence, we have lost our grip on our most basic purpose. We must regain that grip, we must redefine our deep purpose in terms of the world that lies ahead, and we must put forth candidates who have the confidence of the men and women who will build that world."[71]

In Connecticut, Willkie spoke in behalf of the candidacy of

---

[67] Editorial reprinted from the *Mason City Globe-Gazette* in the *Chicago Sun,* June 11, 1942, p. 8.

[68] *Chicago Tribune,* June 9, 1942, p. 3.

[69] *Ibid.,* June 19, 1942, p. 15.

[70] *New York Times,* May 20, 1942, p. 40.

[71] *Ibid.,* June 19, 1942, p. 24.

Raymond E. Baldwin for Governor. Demanding men of "fore-sight" for political posts, Willkie praised Baldwin for supporting him "despite opposition from many leaders of the Republican party" in his advocacy of the President's foreign policy, the over-age destroyer deal, the Selective Service Act, and the repeal of the Neutrality Act.[72] Disavowing any personal reasons, Willkie lauded Baldwin's courage and leadership, and said he was the type of man Americans needed all over the nation.

Speaking several weeks later in Chicago, Willkie said: "I'll go into the elections or into the primaries in the States as I see fit. . . . I can say now that if I was a citizen of Illinois I wouldn't vote for the reelection of Congressman [Stephen A.] Day. I want to see men elected to office who will see that barriers to international trade are broken down. We cannot have peace without economic cooper-ation and I want to see men elected who realize that. After the last war the Republican party was misled. I don't want to see the party today fall into the hands of the wrong leadership."[73]

When asked if he would support a Democrat against an isola-tionist of his own party, Willkie sidestepped the question by reply-ing: "I've made no decision on that . . . I'm a Republican and I expect to remain a Republican. Everything I do now has but one end, to bring the party to a realization of problems to be faced after the war."

Actually, though Willkie supported no Democrats, his attempts to eliminate the isolationists from the Republican party in pre-liminary skirmishes were completely unsuccessful. Hamilton Fish defeated his opponent, Augustus W. Bennett, by a margin of more than two to one in New York; Congressman Day and Senator Brooks were both victorious in the Illinois primary; and at the New York convention, all opposition to Thomas E. Dewey had disap-peared before the convention began on August 23. Prospects for Republicans generally looked favorable across the nation as primary results seemed to indicate that voters were more disturbed with the apparent inefficiency in the conduct of the war than by concern for postwar plans. As a result, the GOP expected to pick up at least thirty seats in the House and five seats in the Senate.

At the New York convention, Dewey was nominated unanimously for the governorship, and a three-point international relations plank

[72] *Ibid.,* June 28, 1942, p. 30.
[73] *Ibid.,* July 13, 1942, p. 13.

framed by Willkie was placed in the platform. At the time, however, Willkie was no longer thinking about the congressional or gubernatorial campaigns. Just prior to the convention, he announced that he would leave shortly on a semi-official flying trip to the battle fronts of Russia and the Middle East. The announcement was made from the White House after Willkie had lunched with the President and had talked for two hours with Secretary Hull and Soviet Ambassador Maxim Litvinoff. Willkie emphasized that the trip had been arranged on his own initiative because of his desire to become acquainted with the countries and the leaders with whom, he said, he believed the United States would cooperate in the future.[74]

The general attitude of New York party workers toward the trip was illustrated when Rolland B. Marvin of Syracuse, a prominent Willkie supporter in 1940, was rebuked as he offered a resolution at the New York convention wishing Willkie "Godspeed and success" on his mission, and praising him for his national leadership and contributions toward unity in the war effort. After a warm debate, Marvin's resolution was referred to the party's state executive committee, and shortly before midnight, the committee adopted a substitute resolution that wished Willkie Godspeed and success on his trip, but which assumed the credit for leadership in foreign relations and national affairs for the entire Republican party.

On August 26, 1942, Wendell L. Willkie, private citizen but personal representative of the President, left the United States for his trip around the world, and left the Republican party without its

---

[74] *New York Times*, August 21, 1942, p. 14. Willkie was accompanied by Gardner Cowles, director of domestic news for the Office of War Information, and Joseph Barnes, an OWI foreign propaganda supervisor. The government provided a bomber for the Willkie party. According to Sam Pryor, Willkie's request for permission to make the trip was granted because "Franklin D. Roosevelt, a skillful political strategist, had the brains to send the leader of the loyal opposition out to see the problem of the world situation first hand. Roosevelt believed the Administration would profit from it."

Willkie later wrote a complete account of his journey under the title *One World*. In several editions, well over one million copies of the volume were sold. Since the trip did not involve Willkie's relations with the Republican party to any great degree, it is not reported here. For thorough and highly contradictory accounts of public reaction to the journey, see Joseph Barnes, *op. cit.*, pp. 289-316, and Dillon, *op. cit.*, pp. 266-90. Needless to say, the publicity given to Willkie during the trip was extensive, but the copy often featured him as a traveling representative of the President rather than as a Republican leader.

titular head during an off-year election campaign. To Republican candidates for Congress, this was the ultimate omission which destroyed any remaining vestige of Willkie leadership within the national legislature. In a sense, this trip did much to summarize the man Willkie, his relation to his party, and his status within the political framework of the nation in 1942. The "One World" trip, next to the campaign of 1940, was the most dramatic event of Willkie's life. It publicized many issues of the war and attracted world-wide attention to the cooperation existing between the heads of America's rival parties. But the timing of the journey also epitomized Willkie's basic attitudes about American political life. As a courageous, almost thoughtlessly stubborn man arguing for a principle, he ignored his political colleagues and their personal situations. He had no orientation toward politics apart from the stand which he believed the party should take, no realization that differences of opinion among elected officials might reflect varied constituencies or political inheritances, and little appreciation of his position of responsibility to party members as titular head of the Republican party. As a result, the many Republicans who would have welcomed his support that never came — together with others who remembered his barbed remarks concerning their voting records — campaigned in 1942 on their own records, with their own defenses, and, in the words of one congressional leader, "sour on Willkie." Though he returned to the United States in time to endorse Clare Boothe Luce for a seat in the House,[75] Dewey for Governor of New York,[76] and Republicans as a collective group of candidates, Willkie was never again strong with more than a handful of congressmen. A high-ranking party official in the House explained: "Willkie be-

---

[75] Just before the election of 1942, the *New Republic* stated: "Clare Boothe Luce bears watching because she is a bona-fide advance agent of the New Republicanism. What she says in the congressional campaign is worth attending for hints of the coming opposition line. On the basis of what she has said so far, however, the line remains almost as hazy as it was in the last presidential campaign when Wendell Willkie was the lone star of the New Republicanism. Miss Boothe's 1942 campaign has been reminiscent of Willkie's 1940 effort." *New Republic*, November 2, 1942, p. 575.

[76] Many of Willkie's opponents charged that he deliberately chose this period to be out of the country so that he would not have to campaign for Dewey, whose nomination he had failed to block. This was untrue. The campaign simply was not particularly important to him at the time. In this, he was probably characteristic of the populace as a whole. Eventually Willkie gave Dewey a substantial endorsement "anticipating from . . . statements that Mr. Dewey . . . will give New York a liberal government."

came allergic to Republicans. He didn't consult them, work with them, or for them. After the campaign of '42, not five members in the House were willing to follow his leadership!"[77]

Actually, the campaign of 1942 was completely subjugated, both in news and in effort, to the conduct of the war. Nationally, it was based largely on a ten-point Republican manifesto drawn up early in October by Representative J. William Ditter, chairman of the Republican Congressional Campaign Committee, and approved by a caucus of 115 GOP representatives.[78] A mild statement, the document stressed efficiency in the war effort, eventual victory, the necessity to maintain the right of opposition, free enterprise, and individual freedom. During the final weeks of the campaign, however, the Republicans publicized and exploited the halting, uncertain way in which the Democrats were administering the war, and as prices went up slightly, they stressed the fear of inflation. GOP orators criticized the "big city machines" that still wielded power within the Democratic party, and declared to millions of people who had been isolationists before Pearl Harbor that the attempts to purge

[77] These statements were obtained in 1957 from congressional leaders whose names are withheld by request. A poll taken in June, 1943, of 180 House members placed the number at 13.

[78] Since this was the only general expression of party policy during this period, the points are summarized here:

1. The nation's war effort must continue unabated until complete decisive victory is won.
2. The Republican party opposes any attempts to negotiate a peace.
3. The U.S. is obligated to effect a world understanding for continued peace.
4. The Republican Party pledges constant vigilance to eliminate governmental inefficiency.
5. The Republican Party will continue to give the President loyal support in the war. The gravity of the situation requires the undivided effort of everyone.
6. The right and duty to criticize must be fully exercised.
7. The nation's peril must not be exploited by any individual or group for special gains.
8. Individual freedoms must not be permanently surrendered in the name of the war.
9. We shall insist that non-defense spending be reduced to essentials.
10. We oppose any use of the war effort as an encroachment on free enterprise. In winning the war, we must not lose the peace.

Shortly after this manifesto was approved, an amendment to an agricultural bill to raise farm price ceilings passed 99 to 53 in the House under pressure of farm groups. This violated point 7 of Ditter's statement and he exclaimed: "By God, we are caught on that one. There is no backing out of it. I hope we do better on the other points in the future or we've wasted a hell of a lot of time." *Time*, October 5, 1942, p. 21.

anti-interventionists were reflections on their patriotism. Voters reportedly disliked wartime censorship and the drain on their labor supply by large war-production centers; there also seemed to be a feeling among many middle-class voters that labor had not been required by the Administration to share proportionately in the sacrifices of the war. Moreover, rumors circulated that some people were making exorbitant profits out of the war, that Negroes were being discriminated against in the production and manpower build-up, and that the war was being run by a small administrative clique.[79] All of these intangibles combined to create both enthusiasm and optimism in Republican circles.

In opposition, the Democrats were on the psychological defensive. They stressed the fact that if Republicans assumed control of the Congress, such men as John Taber, Jesse Wolcott, Hamilton Fish, and Allen Treadway would dominate important committees and emasculate all liberal legislation. They pointed to pre-Pearl Harbor voting records to show that key Republicans voted wrong on crucial issues of domestic mobilization, and they defended their conduct of the entire war program. But the people seemed to be listening with only half an ear, and a light vote seemed likely. Party lines were obscured in many districts by the similarity of platforms that called for a swift prosecution of the war. In New York, Dewey pledged full support of the war, proposed a liberal five-point labor program, charged that reactionaries had taken over the Democratic party, and constantly castigated Tammany Hall. Newspaper columnists all over the country speculated that if he were elected by a large majority, particularly in view of the lack of assistance from Willkie, he would be placed in the very forefront for the Republican presidential nomination in 1944.

During this period, Willkie made daily news of his own from far corners of the world. From August 26 until October 14, his recommendations concerning military strategy, aims and objectives, and policies of the United States irritated Administration decision-makers and caused comment among governmental leaders throughout the flaming globe. Because he had not been informed of the forthcoming North African invasion, he called for a "second front" in both Moscow and China. The situation was confusing, for it was impossible for Allied leaders to know when Willkie was acting for

---

[79] See Irving Dilliard's article, "Can the Republicans Win?" in the *New Republic*, 107 (September 7, 1942), 276-77.

Roosevelt and when he was speaking as an American tourist. When Willkie heard of the criticism, he said: "I speak for no one else and no one else speaks for me. When I speak for myself I'm Wendell Willkie and say what I damn please." The confusion was exaggerated when President Roosevelt told correspondents that he had read the headlines concerning Willkie's appeal for a second front, but had not thought it worth while to read the news stories themselves. A number of reporters had drawn the clear impression from Roosevelt that he was irritated by Willkie's blunt appeal, and they wrote that he had disavowed Willkie as his personal representative. In a subsequent interview, however, the President declined to comment on Willkie's remarks, saying that any controversy was merely political. He said that everything was all right with the Willkie mission as far as he was concerned. Nevertheless, on October 12, in a speech discussing manpower and other issues, including the drafting of eighteen-year-old men, the President said: "I can say one thing about these plans of ours: they are not being decided by the typewriter strategists who expound their views in the press or on the radio. . . . The trouble with the typewriter strategists is that, while they may be full of bright ideas, they are not in possession of much information about the facts or the problems of military operations. We therefore will continue to leave the plans for this war to the military leaders."[80]

Whether these remarks were aimed at Willkie is not known, but he thought that they were and he became very angry. When Willkie was about to return to the United States, Stephen Early, Roosevelt's secretary, contacted Sam Pryor and asked him to ask Willkie to stop in Washington to report to the President. Willkie did this, issuing a statement that he had told the President "very frankly and candidly" of the things he had seen and heard during his trip through fourteen countries, and that his proposals had been made only after talking with high-ranking military officers of the United States, Britain, and Russia. He also told reporters that "Mr. Roosevelt had volunteered the statement that any reports that he had 'criticized' me or my activities while abroad were entirely erroneous."

According to Pryor, however, this was an understatement. He declared: "Willkie saw the President and they thrashed things out that night. Willkie really raised hell with Roosevelt. No one has

[80] *New York Times,* October 13, 1942, p. 5.

ever talked to 'F.D.R.' like Willkie did that night. This explains why Roosevelt was so cool concerning the trip when he reported to the press."[81] In any event, Willkie had made the trip, and a number of analysts found the response favorable. He had exercised his opportunity to criticize major policies while acting as Roosevelt's representative, and he had gathered public opinion behind a more vigorous prosecution of the war. On October 26, he made a nationwide broadcast concerning his tour of the world. Speaking to an estimated thirty-six million persons, he renewed his demand for a second front in Europe, expressed hope that an offensive would be undertaken in Burma, and warned the American people that the United States stood to lose half its friends abroad if it did not begin to do a more satisfactory job on the war. He declared that he had made the journey as a free agent and had become convinced that the world was so small that a Pacific charter and global planning were vital to the future. He asserted to his vast audience: "Winning the war is not enough. . . . to win the peace three things seem to be necessary — first, we must plan now for peace on a global basis; second, the world must be free, economically and politically, for nations and for men that peace may exist in it; third, America must play an active, a constructive part in freeing it and keeping its peace."[82] Finally, Willkie also spoke of freedom for colonial countries, America's effort in the war, and his observations of the countries he had visited. The statement, like so many of his speeches, prompted all types of response. Willkie's personal mail was tremendous and overwhelmingly favorable. The President, when questioned about the talk, said "there is not a controversy [between his view and Willkie's] in a carload of speeches," and many other Democrats endorsed parts of the address, while most Republican congressmen were only lukewarm toward it. Again Willkie had provided national stimulation to postwar planning before millions of listeners, but again he had made no advance within the leadership of his own party ranks.

Meanwhile, in the November election, the Republicans made sizable gains. The drama of the canvass was submerged by the long-awaited invasion of North Africa a few days earlier, and only twenty-six million Americans, half of the 1940 total, went to the polls on November 3. The GOP gained a surprising forty-four

[81] Interview with Mr. Pryor.
[82] Ibid., October 27, 1942, p. 1.

seats in the House and nine new members in the Senate, and the Democratic delegation was reduced to a record New Deal low. Kenneth Wherry defeated the great independent Senator Norris in Nebraska, Homer Ferguson beat Prentiss Brown in Michigan, and even Oklahoma went Republican as E. H. Moore outpolled Josh Lee. Senator McNary called the results "only a breeze compared to what will happen in 1944." In New York, Thomas E. Dewey, whom Willkie had endorsed only at the end of October, won a stirring victory with more than a 600,000-vote plurality to become the first Republican governor of New York in twenty years. And across the country, the elections of Bricker in Ohio, Stassen in Minnesota, and Saltonstall in Massachusetts, all of whom could be considered presidential aspirants backed by authentic voter support, were part of the GOP sweep.

The Republicans claimed that their victories reflected farm discontent with agricultural price control, dissatisfaction with confusion and inefficiency in Washington, and doubt about the competence of the high command. But George Gallup attributed the decline in the Democratic vote to the fact that so many Democrats were moving across the nation for war work, that many young Democrats were in the armed forces, and that the lower income groups were not particularly interested in the election. Professor C. A. Berdahl, after examining a variety of explanations, wrote: "As a matter of fact, it becomes extremely difficult, if not impossible, to draw any conclusions from the election except that the people were somehow dissatisfied, probably with the lack up to that time of any important military victory."[83]

In any event, few observers saw any strengthening of the Willkie forces in the election, though the *New Republic* conjectured that "It is conceivable that a few voted [against the New Deal] in the hope or expectation that Wendell Willkie would now assert actual as well as nominal leadership in the Republican Party."[84] Most analysts accurately saw the rise of new leaders as a threat to the 1940 candidate.[85] Raymond Moley summarized their views when

---

[83] Berdahl, "Political Parties and Elections," p. 80.

[84] *New Republic*, November 16, 1942, p. 638.

[85] Arthur Sears Henning, writing in the *Chicago Tribune*, October 11, 1942, p. 17, stated: "One of the most extraordinary aspects of this election canvass is the character of the Republican leadership. It has been furnished not by Wendell Willkie . . . but by Representative Martin, minority leader of the House . . . and by other Republican members of the House. . . ."

he wrote: "A dozen rival Republican leaders have suddenly appeared . . . most of them will not favor a Willkie controlled party. . . . The rank and file of the Republican organization will be opposed to Willkie. Probably Mr. Willkie will continue free-lancing with a big public following. He will be a public figure, not a political leader."[86]

Nevertheless, many eastern presidential Republicans demanded that the party chart a course that would utilize Willkie and his principles. Considering the statements of Republican leaders during this period, this is what the editors of the *New York Herald Tribune* must have meant when they wrote: "Let the party now demonstrate that it has learned by its blunders, and possesses the ability and the bravery to support the war effort wholeheartedly, and to place in key positions men sufficiently wise and farseeing to take command in a national crisis. If they do not give this proof . . . their victory will be an empty success leading nowhere. If they live up to their opportunities their march to power cannot be halted."[87]

In the days following the election, however, the Republican party gave evidence that it did not yet possess the unity to coordinate its collective thoughts with men of one farseeing philosophy. On November 12, National Chairman Joe Martin announced that he would resign his chairmanship in order to concentrate on his duties as minority floor leader in the House of Representatives. Thus, a meeting of the national committee had to be held to elect a new chairman, and St. Louis was selected as a site for a December 6 meeting. Within the three weeks of November, no fewer than fifteen different men were seriously mentioned for the job.

The most prominent aspirant was Werner W. Schroeder, the conservative national committeeman from Illinois, who had been

Mr. Willkie has taken no part in the campaign. He is not even in the country. . . . Mr. Willkie took himself from the political scene shortly after he found that very few people were interested in running him for the New York governorship nomination against Tom Dewey. Nationally, as the campaign wore on, he suffered a complete blackout. No Republican platforms so much as mentioned the name of the Republican titular leader. No Willkie pictures hung in Republican campaign headquarters. No Republican spellbinders conjured with the name of the Democrat the Republican party nominated for President only two years ago. The party seemed to be trying to forget what will be remembered as one of the most extraordinary episodes of political annals. Incidentally, the gossip among the politicians is that the President looks with favor on Willkie as his running mate for a fourth term."

[86] *Newsweek,* November 16, 1942, p. 44.
[87] *Ibid.*

chairman of the national committee's important committee on organization. Schroeder represented the Middle West center of strength in the party; he was acceptable to all wings of the party except the followers of Willkie; he was identified with no particular candidate for President; he had an excellent reputation as a fund raiser and party organizer; and he had just managed the re-election of C. Wayland "Curly" Brooks to the United States Senate. Schroeder also had been an isolationist, and as a result, the *Herald Tribune,* eastern Republican magazines, and Wendell Willkie were immediately opposed to his candidacy. Willkie denied any personal dislike for Schroeder, but stated: "Even if he thought right, he could not do right," because he was, as Willkie had once said, "under the aegis of the *Chicago Tribune.*" Schroeder was, nevertheless, favored by friends of Hoover and Senator Taft, so he decided to make a determined fight to obtain the chairmanship despite Willkie's opposition. Willkie had no personal candidate, though it was believed that Governor Ralph Carr of Colorado, who had been defeated for a United States senatorship, or Sinclair Weeks, the Massachusetts national committeeman, would have been very acceptable to him.[88] The United Press quoted Willkie as saying: "All I want is a fellow who by deeds and words really believes the declarations and principles of the Republican Party. I want a chairman who believes in these principles . . . regardless of whether he was an isolationist before Pearl Harbor. And I want a fellow who is a liberal on the economic front."[89] Because Schroeder could not fill these qualifications, it was obvious that the party was going to be split by another fight. Joe Martin asked Schroeder to withdraw from the contest for the sake of party unity, but the Illinois committeeman, who realized that the party workers who were more interested in jobs than in international policies were for him, replied that he would participate in "no compromise efforts." "I have enough votes to win," he said, "I am ready to go to bat. . . ."

---

[88] Others frequently mentioned were Rochester publisher Frank Gannett, who stated that he was ready to do anything to protect the country from the state socialism that the New Deal had tried to impose on the people, former Senator John G. Townsend of Delaware, Barak T. Mattingly of Missouri, J. Kenneth Bradley of Connecticut, John Hollister of Ohio, Harrison Spangler of Iowa, Clarence Budington Kelland, executive director of the national committee and national committeeman from Arizona, Alf Landon of Kansas, Fred Baker of Washington, Ralph Cake of Oregon, Ezra Whitla of Idaho, and Walter Hallanan of West Virginia.

[89] *Chicago Sun,* December 7, 1942, p. 4.

Nevertheless, the *New York Times,* as early as November 26, reported that the choice of successor to Martin had unofficially narrowed down to Alf Landon, John Hollister of Ohio, and Harrison Spangler of Iowa.[90]

Willkie did not attend the meeting in St. Louis, but he was represented there by Lem Jones, his secretary, with whom he was in constant contact by telephone; by his close friend, Sinclair Weeks; by J. Kenneth Bradley, national committeeman from Connecticut; and by others from the eastern delegations. Both Jones and Schroeder claimed 55 of the 106 votes available. All efforts for a compromise on the first day of the meeting failed, though new names such as Barak T. Mattingly of Missouri, Frank Gannett of New York, and John G. Townsend of Delaware were suggested to the committee. Robert Lasch, a correspondent, concluded that, "in simplified terms, this dispute may be stated as the question of what to do about Wendell Willkie."[91]

When the national committee met in a special session at two o'clock the following afternoon to ballot on the vacancy for national chairman, Ralph Cake of Oregon, a friend of Willkie, nominated, to the surprise of many observers, Frederick E. Baker, a relatively unknown thirty-five-year-old businessman from the state of Washington. Baker's nomination was seconded by Mrs. Worthington Scranton of Pennsylvania and by Dan Whetstone of Montana. Mrs. Bertha Baur, national committeewoman for Illinois, then nominated Schroeder, calling him a man of sterling character who had helped bring Illinois back into the Republican fold. Senator Taft also spoke briefly of Schroeder as the best qualified man in the field. Harrison Spangler of Iowa was nominated by Bourke Hickenlooper, and this nomination was seconded by Harold W. Mason of Ver-

---

[90] Hollister was really not qualified in that he was too closely identified with the future candidacy of John Bricker.

[91] *Ibid.* Sam Pryor believed that this battle would not have come up if Willkie had been more active in party functions when he returned from his trip. Mr. Pryor said, "I suggested to Wendell that he go out and raise money to help the party to hold the meeting and also to reacquaint himself with the party leaders so that he could have an important role in the selection of a new chairman who would be favorable toward him. Willkie, at this time, felt that he had the party solidly behind him; I knew that he didn't. Willkie stayed at home and did not help raise the necessary money, and Harrison Spangler, an anti-Willkie man, was chosen. Willkie should have worked vigorously at this point to elect a chairman who was in tune with him, but he didn't and his leadership was further impaired." Interview with Mr. Pryor.

mont, and Dr. O. F. Hume of Kentucky. Publisher Frank Gannett and Barak Mattingly were also nominated.

On the first roll call, with 99 votes cast, and a majority necessary for election, both Schroeder and Baker received 40 votes, Spangler was given 15 from, he said, people not supporting or opposing Willkie, Gannett got 3, Mattingly, 1, and 4 persons passed. On the second ballot, Baker obtained 43 votes, Schroeder's total fell to 38, Spangler's vote remained at 15, Gannett was given 4 votes, Mattingly, 1, and 2 delegates passed. At this point, a recess was voted by a rising vote, 58 to 38, and delegates filed out of the conference room. This was the time that Joe Martin went to work. Though the balloting was scheduled to be resumed at four o'clock, it was five before he arranged a compromise and Baker and Schroeder returned "arm in arm" to declare themselves for Harrison Spangler, who was then unanimously elected. Actually, Spangler had been in a favorable position from the beginning. The night before the balloting began, both Senator Townsend and Harold Mason had assured him that he was going to be elected. According to Spangler, Senator Taft was privately for him, and some representatives of both the Willkie and Schroeder camps asked him to remain as a possible compromise candidate.[92] Nevertheless, though he was a nominee acceptable to everyone, he aroused enthusiasm in practically nobody.

The Willkie forces considered his selection a victory because Schroeder had been defeated,[93] but Spangler had actually supported Taft at the 1940 Republican convention and he did so again in 1948. The *Chicago Tribune* called the election a "Blow to [the] Eastern Clique." "Nobody here," stated the McCormick publication, "has any thought that Harrison Spangler will be found among the Willkie backers in 1944."[94] And the *Tribune* ultimately was

[92] Interview with Harrison Spangler.

[93] *New York Times*, December 8, 1942, p. 1. When asked if the nomination pleased him, Willkie stated that he was satisfied, and said he had no comment because "a person should not boast after a victory." The *New Republic*, December 21, 1942, p. 819, put it more accurately: "The antiinterventionist wing — Taft, Colonel McCormick and the rest — saw the chairmanship go to a rabid foe of the New Deal. And the run of the Committee members, who regarded Willkie as a Roosevelt stooge, had the pleasure of slapping Willkie's ears back by electing a chairman who would not have been his first choice or his second choice or his third."

[94] *Chicago Tribune*, December 7, 1942, p. 1. W. H. Lawrence, in the *New York Times*, asserted: "The defeat of Mr. Schroeder can be considered a victory for Mr. Willkie. Even the *Chicago Tribune* called it that

correct. Though Spangler issued statements that he would steer a neutral course, and though he tried mightily to show deference to Willkie's ideas, the harmony[95] and neutrality were synthetic. The schism between the wings of the party was too great, and a national chairman, by the very nature of the characteristics that are necessary for the job, cannot be neutral in such a conflict of men and objectives. Shortly after he was elected, Spangler encouraged the Willkie followers when he stated that he realized that "we can't say the Atlantic and Pacific Oceans are moats around the country anymore," that he hoped "we do better than last time" when the new peace would be made, and that his efforts would be devoted to party organization rather than to policy-making. But he also said: "My job is to build up an army of voters in the United States to defeat the New Deal, and I don't think there are any votes in China or Mongolia or Russia that I can get for the Republicans."[96]

Late in 1942, one further incident arose that is significant today only in that it drew an interesting parallel between Wendell Willkie, the dynamic and distinctive Republican in an era when such men had no base from which to operate, and Dwight D. Eisenhower, the man who eventually provided such a center of power with its conflicting GOP wings. It also served to indicate just how courageous, idealistic, and, perhaps unrealistic — and how clairvoyant and removed from present and future policy of his party — Willkie was during this period.

Willkie was disturbed by the cooperation between the United States and Admiral Darlan, the French Vichy leader, who was recognized by General Eisenhower, then Allied Commander in Chief

in one edition Tuesday morning, though in subsequent editions it ridiculed any such suggestion. Later, thoroughly angry, it called for the creation of a new party." For additional information on the creation of this new "American Party" which the *Tribune* desired "to call to its standards all patriots, regardless of sectionalism or previous party affiliation, and to exclude from its ranks all traitors to American ideals," see the *New York Times,* December 3, 1941, p. 8, December 12, 1941, p. 28, and the *Chicago Tribune,* November 12, 1941, cited in Berdahl, *op. cit.,* p. 79.

[95] "T.R.B." in the pro-New Deal *New Republic* wrote that the compromise revealed "the line that GOP policy always takes. Spangler symbolizes Republican harmony — the harmony that in 1920 gave the nation . . . Harding, whose virtue was that he hadn't offended anybody. Spangler hadn't offended anybody either. Spangler and the Spanglerites will try to get somebody who hasn't offended anybody, as nominee in 1944. . . ." *New Republic,* August 16, 1943, p. 223.

[96] *New York Times,* December 9, 1942, p. 26, and *Time,* December 21, 1942, p. 22.

in North Africa, as head of the French government in North Africa. President Roosevelt described the move as a military expedient to save American lives, and stated that it was a temporary arrangement. Willkie intended to criticize the Darlan agreement on November 16, but he was dissuaded by a telephone call from Secretary of War Henry Stimson.[97] In a talk in Toronto, Canada, on November 25, however, he lashed out at any resort to expediency in international relations. He declared: ". . . the people must discuss and define their common purpose before the war is over or run the risk of having worked and sacrificed and suffered to win a war for no purpose . . . the moral losses of *expediency* always far outweigh the temporary gains . . . [and] every drop of blood saved through expediency will be paid for by twenty drawn with the sword."[98] Because President Roosevelt released his own explanation of the Darlan incident on the night on which Willkie had withheld his criticism, Willkie felt that he had been outmaneuvered politically and in December, after the immediate crisis had passed, he published his views in the *Christian Advocate,* the official newspaper-magazine of the Methodist church. The former nominee condemned the arrangements with Darlan and asserted, ". . . some of our leaders seem to forget that how we win this war may determine whether we win the peace"; and then added that America had "lost moral force" through the Darlan arrangement. "I have found," Willkie continued, "that, to the peoples of Africa, the Middle East, China and the whole Far East, freedom means the orderly abolition of the colonial system. It is not too much to say that this sort of freedom is their number one war aim. Lately they have begun to wonder whether it is also ours."[99]

The article prompted Senator Vandenberg to take the Senate floor and attack the critics of American collaboration with Admiral Darlan. In remarks obviously, though not nominally, directed at Willkie, the senator from Michigan said that Eisenhower was probably guilty of "false finagling with expediency," but added, "he is also guilty of saving American lives and of saving months of valuable time and of amazing bloodless victories in the winning of the war. If that be a crime I should like to sign his bond. He is out

[97] See Henry L. Stimson and McGeorge Bundy, *On Active Service in Peace and War* (New York, 1947), p. 543.

[98] *New York Times,* November 26, 1942, italics added.

[99] *New York Times,* December 6, 1942, p. 57.

where the shooting is. He is supported by our Chief of Staff and our Commander in Chief. He should not be shot at from the rear — and especially from the sanctuary of this safe home front."[100]

Both Vandenberg and Willkie had their followers and supporters — both had their personal reasons for taking an open stand on the Roosevelt-Eisenhower arrangement of expediency. This incident merely serves to illustrate, however, how opposition to the frank expressions of Willkie continued to be constructed, piece by piece, among Republicans in 1942. On the other hand, Marquis Childs saw in Willkie's action a healthy and desirable service, that of smoking out a secret Administration maneuver.[101] In any event, the episode showed that Wendell Willkie was not following a course of expediency with anyone during this period, that he was far removed from his Republican colleagues, and that inevitably his philosophical victories had been Pyrrhic indeed.

In 1942, the polls indicated that Willkie's popularity continued to decline. In June, fifty-two per cent of the Republicans favored Willkie over Dewey in a poll taken by the American Institute of Public Opinion. A November survey, however, revealed that forty-nine per cent of the people polled looked favorably on Willkie, but that thirty-eight per cent reacted unfavorably to him. In contrast, Dewey was better liked than any other Republican, with 53 per cent favoring him. Stassen, Bricker, and Taft followed the leaders.

During 1942, Wendell Willkie had tried to strengthen the weak spots that had been apparent in his list of presidential attributes in 1940. He had studied foreign affairs first hand, he had courted labor, becoming the attorney for the AF of L's International Ladies Garment Workers Union, and he had worked tirelessly for Negroes and the general cause of civil rights. By December, he was in great demand as a speaker, but politically he remained the captain of an obscure and disintegrating team. Many of the Republican leaders who were to be influential in selecting the GOP nominee in 1944 were openly opposed to him, and his actual strength among the mass of Republican and independent voters was a great unknown. He continued to be the crusader, speaking bluntly when his ad-

---

[100] *Ibid.*, December 16, 1942, p. 15. Secretary of State Hull, asked for a comment on the Willkie charges, suggested that before commenting on Willkie's position, it might be advisable to await a conclusion of the controversy between Willkie and Senator Vandenberg. *Ibid.*, December 18, 1942, p. 5. Admiral Darlan was assassinated in Algiers on December 24, 1942.
[101] *Look*, March 9, 1943, p. 14.

visers suggested a more cautious respectability. He declared that he could not keep silent at a time when no man should allow his personal destiny to stand in the way of whatever he could contribute to a better world.

In contrast, the other Republican hopefuls quietly minimized their controversies within the party organization. The Dewey strategy called for the New York governor to be inactive in the struggle over the chairmanship of the national committee lest anyone think that he was actively campaigning for the presidential nomination of 1944. On several occasions, he asserted that he would serve his full four-year term as governor but most analysts felt that if the party prospects were particularly favorable in 1944, he would accept a draft movement. On December 6, 1942, Senator Taft announced that he would not be a candidate in 1944, but that he would support Governor John Bricker. Similarly, Senator Vandenberg disqualified himself in a letter to Jay G. Hayden, Washington correspondent for the *Detroit News:* "I am not a candidate," he wrote, "and I shall not be a candidate for President at that Convention [1944]. In my opinion, the events of the next eighteen months will dictate our appropriate nominee. In my expectation, he will be found amid the new timber which is richly available for this leadership, and which will become more so as the war progresses."[102] Thus, at the conclusion of the year, the prospect of new personalities within the party coupled with a hostility toward Willkie as a person made a combination of circumstances that produced a completely unstructured party leadership. The principles adopted officially by the Republican organization belonged to Wendell Willkie, and he probably still exercised a veto over party policy, but it was clear that no individual could be recognized as the responsible chief of the GOP.

---

[102] *New York Times,* December 15, 1942, p. 1.

7 CRITICAL COLLABORATION

In the annals of the Republican party, 1943 was a year of political build-ups, trial balloons, intraparty maneuvers in the mass media, and speculation about the presidential nomination of 1944. Though the war was still the overarching responsibility of the nation, Republicans everywhere were convinced that no higher law decreed that the United States could not continue the war or negotiate the peace under leadership other than President Roosevelt's. Notwithstanding this unified conviction, however, several different opinions existed among Republican leaders as to ultimate objectives. In the February issue of *American Magazine,* National Chairman Harrison Spangler stated his views on the mission of the GOP.[1] Domestically, the aim of the Republican party was "to get the United States back on the tracks of constitutional government and away from totalitarianism and state socialism." The chairman saw the vote in the November election as a mandate to preserve the two-party system, to restore the independence of Congress, and to bring about economies in government spending for nonwar purposes. He agreed that every essential power had to be granted to the President for the prosecution of the war, but maintained that Roosevelt should be denied powers to socialize the country. The Republican party, Spangler wrote, had to stand for orderly supervision and regulation of the nation's economic life, but also had to

[1] "GOP's New Stand," *American Magazine,* 135 (February, 1943), 24 ff.

230

strive for an end to the bureaucratic hampering of decent industry and honest business. The party's duty was to open the door of betterment and opportunity, protect savings, encourage thrift, bring about harmony among capital, labor, and agriculture, and reverse the "bad thinking" that it was improper to acquire private property. Internationally, Spangler's Republicanism stood for collaboration with the Allies in a peace settlement without diminishing the national sovereignty or allowing unthinking idealism to bring the people of the United States down to foreign economic levels. He conceded that the responsibility of the country could not be confined to its territorial limits, but he also asserted that this responsibility did not extend to an impairment of the nation's identity.

Spangler's ideas summarized the position of the conservative elements of the party — the normalcy groups within the GOP. Patriotic and safe in their defense of "free enterprise" and "constitutional government," they found their leadership in 1943 in Governor Bricker of Ohio, and also, rather surprisingly, in Thomas E. Dewey. But it was Bricker whose cautious activity attracted most of the attention of the stand-patters within the party. He was a solid, budget-balancing governor who stood for the most popular concepts among his constituency. To reporters who asked for his views on foreign relations, postwar planning, social security, and even the problems of agriculture, he was consistently noncommittal. Bricker was opposed to the New Deal; he was a nationalist, but not an isolationist; and he also was, according to William Allen White, one of those Republicans who was "agin everything and for nothing. . . ." In his *Emporia Gazette,* White attacked Bricker as a man who was "trying to capitalize the tremendous discontent . . . to rally a majority in the election of 1944. In that election, he hopes to get by without saying anything, without getting on either side of the momentous questions of the hour — domestic and foreign." He concluded, "Bricker is an honest Harding. Thumbs down!"[2]

Among those who could not accept Wendell Willkie, but who wanted a more dramatic opponent for the President — one who fit the times — a mild movement was begun to advance the availability of several military heroes. Occasionally mentioned were Eddie Rickenbacker and Hanford MacNider, the former head of the American Legion who had been nominated in 1940. More prominently featured, however, was the campaign for Douglas

---

[2] *Time,* March 29, 1943, p. 13.

MacArthur, the nation's most publicized general at the time. In MacArthur, the pre-Pearl Harbor isolationists, the members of America First, and the adherents to the political line of the *Chicago Tribune* found a strong, brilliant, and devoted leader who could fulfill the demands of a President–Commander-in-Chief. Though MacArthur himself ignored his advocates, an active movement for the general was undertaken in May, and its unofficial headquarters was reportedly in the office of Senator Arthur Vandenberg. Jay Hayden, writer for the *Detroit News,* wrote that politicians by the score visited the Michigan senator early in 1943 to discuss the general's availability. Vandenberg himself privately endorsed Mac-Arthur among party leaders, but he made no public announce-ment of his action because he believed the spring of 1943 was too early to begin a serious move.[3] By December he managed to inveigle a special statement out of army and navy officials that no regulation would forbid the election of an officer to public office, but by this time the announcement from the Pentagon seemed to benefit Lieutenant Commander Harold Stassen as much as it did MacArthur.

Stassen, during this period, was closely identified with the liberals in the GOP. While preparing to go on active duty with the navy, he found time to write about political matters and international policy in such a way as to impress his talents, availability, and daring on the American public. He advocated a forthright Repub-lican party that would take a positive stand on pressing problems. He suggested a postwar program of public improvements in order to utilize manpower not used by private enterprise, economic floors below living standards in the United States, the measurement of public policies by individual dignity as much as by a material basis, agricultural price protection, the support of research, an improve-ment of social security, and an environment conducive to free enter-prise and individual initiative.[4] But the radical departure from majority opinion within the elected leadership of the GOP came with the young Minnesota governor's foreign policy. At a time when Republican congressmen were voting against a renewal of reciprocal trade treaties, Stassen advocated a concrete postwar pro-gram in which he envisioned a United Nations of the World with

---

[3] *Ibid.,* May 17, 1943, p. 23.

[4] Harold Stassen, "Wanted: a Forthright Republican Party," *Saturday Evening Post,* 215 (May 15, 1943), 12-13.

a unicameral parliament, a world council, a court, and military force to guarantee its decisions. He declared that isolationism was dead and that it was the duty of the Republican party to tell the people precisely what it was going to do after the war.[5] Ironically, such demands placed Stassen ideologically right beside Wendell Willkie on the spectrum of Republican thought, but they also indicated his decision to compete against Willkie for the endorsement of the liberal wing of the party in 1944.

The emergence of numerous candidates both left and right, however, illustrated the drama within an optimistic GOP in 1943 when opinion was in a high state of flux. Though Taft, Vandenberg, and Dewey had disqualified themselves from the presidential race, Willkie had lost control of the organization workers to such an extent that he was unable to capitalize on the discontent with Bricker's stand-pattism or the withdrawals from the race by more available Republican leaders. Instead of adding up to a clear field for Willkie, the situation produced a case of "The field against Willkie" in Republican circles.[6]

Across the nation and particularly within the key Republican states, the situation was the same. No candidate produced more enthusiasm than Willkie among the rank and file, but the leaders thought him too inconsistent, too visionary, and personally too inconsiderate. In Pennsylvania, to the Pew-Grundy machine he was anathema; in Illinois, Colonel Robert McCormick, with his frequent diatribes against Willkie on the front page of the *Tribune*, made the 1940 candidate a man without a party; in Ohio, Willkie seemed to be more popular than Bricker among the masses of citizens, but he simply didn't exist in the minds of the machine precinct workers. In New York, he had failed to make a deal with Dewey, and lost what control he had over the party organization. In Indiana, only four or five members of the GOP leadership were still Willkie supporters, and even in California, where Willkie had many friends, most of them were disappointed in his refusal to exercise partisan leadership. Said one supporter: "He's got to forget about the front page and talk cold turkey with the men who can nominate him."[7]

---

[5] *American Mercury*, 56 (March, 1943), 272 ff.

[6] *Chicago Tribune*, January 8, 1943, p. 17, quoting the *New York Daily News*.

[7] *Time*, January 4, 1943, p. 19.

Conversely, in several states Willkie still had ardent supporters high in the party ranks. Throughout New England and in the far Northwest, his adherents controlled the organizations. In addition, approximately forty per cent of the national committee was willing to accept his principles if not always his forceful methods. Willkie himself thought he could win the nomination by persuasion in spite of the hostility among the party leadership. During 1943, he spoke at many functions throughout the country, represented a multitude of clients, and occasionally went to Indiana for a rest. On such a vacation in January, he was invited by Ralph F. Gates, Republican state chairman, to be the Lincoln Day speaker before the Indiana General Assembly. The invitation aroused such a protest from county Republican clubs in the state that rival groups invited Colonel McCormick, Governor Green of Illinois, and Governor Bricker to speak in the state to balance the Willkie influence.[8] The apprehension was well justified, for when Willkie appeared, he was at his oratorical best. He declared: ". . . of the more than two billion people on the earth, the overwhelming majority have awakened. They fervently desire education, political emancipation, and the opportunity to raise their standards of living. . . . This should be a challenge to Republicans. For the Republican party is the party of production. It should be the party of expansion as well, and of dynamic industrial evolution."[9]

On the following day, Willkie addressed seven hundred party and business leaders of the arch-conservative Indiana Columbia Club — many of whom had been openly hostile to him — and called for a renewal of lend-lease and reciprocal trade treaties. He accused the Democrats of stealing these ideas from regular Republicans. Reciprocity, he maintained, was invented by James G. Blaine and advocated by William McKinley and William Howard Taft. "Let's reappropriate our own," Willkie told the stalwarts, "and use it as a base from which to move forward." After the formal address, he assailed Vice-President Wallace and complimented Chairman Gates for his splendid job of organization in the previous election. He called the GOP "the vital thinking party" in

---

[8] *Chicago Sun,* February 9, 1943, p. 9.

[9] Joseph Barnes, *op. cit.,* p. 335. Willkie also told the legislators that the political thinking of the nation and of the world would be determined in the Middle West. K. M. Landis, II, in his syndicated column stated that the 1940 candidate might have added that the political future of Wendell Willkie be included in the statement. *Chicago Sun,* February 17, 1943, p. 8.

the country. "Why be on the defensive," he shouted, "against a party that is a combination of northern political machines of the worst type and southern oligarchies that don't even allow Negroes to vote?" When he had finished, the club members rose and applauded wildly. One anti-Willkie leader was heard to say: "By golly, I believe that guy has become a Republican since Elwood. And I'm for him."[10]

On February 28, the *Indianapolis Star,* in a copyrighted dispatch from its Washington correspondent, produced the first report of the year that Willkie would be a candidate for the Republican nomination in 1944. The paper stated that Willkie's name would be entered in thirteen state primaries for the selection of delegates to the Republican national convention. Everett C. Watkins, the paper's correspondent, said Willkie's candidacy for the nomination "may be taken for granted without any formal announcement from him."[11] Many Republicans in Indiana, however, wanted no part of Willkie's nomination. When the *Fort Wayne News-Sentinel* canvassed 1,693 Republican precinct committeemen and committee-women of Indiana's ninety-two counties concerning their choice for a presidential candidate in 1944, the results showed that only 11.9 per cent would support the 1940 nominee again in 1944. The preferred candidates among Indiana Republican leaders were Dewey and Bricker.[12] Representative Hamilton Fish of New York, after reading the results of the Indiana poll, sent out five thousand circulars containing excerpts from the Fort Wayne paper to the delegates and alternates to the 1940 Republican convention and to all Republican county chairmen in the United States. He said that the survey proved conclusively that it would be political suicide for the party to nominate Willkie again for President.[13]

Rolland B. Marvin, leader of the Onondaga County (New York) Republican organization, immediately came to Willkie's defense. Characterizing the *News-Sentinel* as "one of the most bitter-end reactionary isolationist newspapers in the United States," Marvin stated, ". . . if the country becomes convinced that the Republican organization is against Wendell Willkie and the principles for which he fights . . . [we] will find ourselves deserted by millions of Republican and independent voters. They admire and like Wendell

---

[10] *Ibid.*

[11] Cited in the *New York Times,* February 28, 1943, p. 36.

[12] Editorial in the *Chicago Tribune,* March 31, 1943.

[13] *New York Times,* May 5, 1943, p. 28.

Willkie."[14] Early in March, however, a Gallup poll again indicated
that Dewey remained more popular than Willkie with the rank-and-
file Republican voters.[15] The 1940 candidate still had many followers, but more people opposed him than any other aspirant to the
presidency.

This controversy over the desirability of Willkie as a presidential
candidate was heightened early in April when Simon and Schuster
published Willkie's story of his global trip under the title of *One
World*.[16] The book, which sold over a million copies, prompted
John Chamberlain to write:

I want to see Mr. Willkie go places in the American political future.
He is that rare person in politics, a man who won't take jobs except on
terms which will allow him to be true to his own best instincts. But no
man can aspire to the Presidency if the people get the idea that he is
more interested in the problem of Yakutsk and Chungking than he is in
the problem of Indiana. Mr. Willkie must somehow convey to the
American people that he is interested in freedom for China because it
has a close connection with the well-being of Rush County or Poker Flat.
He must convey to them that he is an internationalist because he is an
American, not because he is more interested in the cosmic than in the
local. Mr. Willkie is, of course, tremendously interested in the problems

[14] *Ibid.*, May 3, 1943, p. 11.
[15] *Ibid.*, March 7, 1943, p. 8. Each Republican voter questioned in the
Institute survey was asked to tell whether his attitude was favorable or
unfavorable toward several candidates named.
The results were as follows:

	FAVORABLE	UNFAVORABLE	NO OPINION
	per cent	per cent	per cent
Dewey	69	13	18
Willkie	49	43	8
Stassen	31	10	59
Bricker	25	10	65
Saltonstall	15	9	76

[16] For a review by Harold E. Stassen, see the *New York Times* for April
11, 1943. Stassen believed that Willkie did not sufficiently recognize the
dangers of Russian communism at the same time that he stressed the evils
of British colonialism. Lem Jones stated that this review was one of the
deepest hurts Willkie received because he regarded Stassen as a dear friend.
When he read the review, Willkie said, "If Harold felt that way, why did
he have to write it?" On May 6, the Council on Books in Wartime placed
the volume on its list of "imperative" books. Admiral Harry E. Yarnell,
United States Navy, (Ret.), a member of the council's War Book Panel,
presented Willkie with a citation declaring that the book marked "a definite
turning point, a new starting place, in our attitude toward international
affairs." "*One World*," he asserted, "is excellent reading, and more than
that, it is excellent Americanism." In accepting the award, Willkie told a
group of assembled book publishers, critics, and guests that his life had been
unbelievably full of satisfaction and that the recognition of his book was
the "richest satisfaction of all." *Ibid.*, May 7, 1943, p. 7.

of Rush County. But he must prove it. For internationalism is a two-way street.[17]

A month later, at the peak of the volume's popularity, the *New York Times* commented: "Mr. Willkie is getting tremendous personal publicity from his book . . . but it may be likely that in this project as in many others since his defeat in 1940 he is making more friends outside than inside the Republican party organization. And it is the 'organization' which nominates party Presidential candidates even if it is unable to elect them without the support of outsiders."[18]

Meanwhile, Willkie's political life was a series of speeches, endorsements, and defections. In South Dakota, he assailed the "get mine" attitude of those who were seeking special advantages from the government. He said that too many "arrogant men" within our society were making arbitrary demands on the people. In response to an invitation to enter the California primary in 1944 from Jerrold Seawell, president pro tempore of the California Senate, Willkie replied that he had not finally decided what he would do with reference to seeking the nomination of the Republican party in 1944. In Ohio, where he received an honorary Doctor of Laws degree from Oberlin College, he spoke facetiously to reporters concerning the presidential picture. "Ham Fish is against me, Gerald L. K. Smith is against me and I understand Landon is against me. If this keeps up I may be nominated in spite of myself." In a more serious mood, he said that the Republicans would have to put up a candidate who recognized that the countries of the world were interdependent and that the United States would have to play its full part in bringing about cooperation among all nations. Concerning the possible outcome of the election, he said: "In spite of all the talk you hear to the contrary, President Roosevelt still holds the 'Solid South.' Any Republican candidate can be expected to carry the Midwest agricultural states which have no large metropolitan centers. The election will be decided in Ohio, Michigan,[19] and the eastern states and possibly the Pacific Coast states."

---

[17] *Ibid.*, April 8, 1943, p. 21.

[18] *Ibid.*, May 9, 1943, sec. 4, p. 10E.

[19] *Ibid.* Paul W. Shafer, Congressman from Michigan, took the floor of the House of Representatives to castigate Willkie and remind the Michigan Republicans that Willkie was the leader who did not lead in 1942. He criticized Willkie for not campaigning for Republican candidates, for travel-

In June of 1943, three significant surveys were taken of the respective strength of the possible Republican presidential candidates for 1944. Representative Leo E. Allen of Illinois polled 180 of the 207 Republicans in the House of Representatives with the question: "If you were a delegate to the Republican convention and the convention was now in session, whom would you vote for as the man best qualified to serve as President and the most certain to win the election? Answer without regard for personal or friendly preferences." Governor Dewey received fifty-one votes from the legislators; Willkie ran fourth in the survey, behind Dewey, General MacArthur, and Governor Bricker.[20] *Pathfinder* magazine found the sentiment similar among the members of thirty-eight state legislatures who answered its questionnaire. On the basis of ballots returned by 35 per cent of the 3,523 legislators, Governor Dewey was favored by 29 per cent, Willkie by 25 per cent, and Bricker by 18 per cent.[21] Among the Republican voters, the Gallup survey in June also showed Dewey to be the most popular potential candidate. Interviewees who were asked, "Which one of these men would you prefer for President next year?" voted 37 per cent for Dewey compared with 28 per cent for Willkie.[22]

Meanwhile, however, it was reported that a movement was under way in Indiana to launch Willkie in the 1944 campaign as a favorite son. Mrs. Grace B. Reynolds, the Republican national committeewoman, and Lieutenant Governor Charles M. Dawson were said to be organizing the campaign with the support of Homer E. Capehart, Indiana manufacturer who later became a United States senator.[23] In addition, Willkie announced that he would challenge

ing around the world when he should have been working for the party, and for giving William Schneiderman, a Russian-born Communist, more help than he did his fellow Republicans. See the *Congressional Record*, vol. 89, p. A2811 (78th Cong., 1st Sess., May 27, 1943).

[20] *Ibid.*, June 12, 1943, p. 14. The results, in addition to Dewey's total, were as follows: MacArthur, 33; Bricker, 32; Willkie, 13; Taft, 11; Martin, 9; Stassen, 6; Warren, 6; Hoover, 5; Vandenberg, 4; Green, 3; Lodge, 2; C. Wayland Brooks, Charles E. McNary, James W. Wadsworth, James A. Farley, and Harry F. Byrd, one each. The *New Republic* cracked: "As for the votes for Jim Farley and Senator Byrd, we should have thought that the Republicans had plenty of similar characters of their own without raiding the Democratic preserves." *New Republic*, June 21, 1943, p. 814.

[21] *New York Times*, June 22, 1943, p. 10.

[22] *Ibid.*, June 27, 1943, p. 9. Others mentioned by percentage were: MacArthur, 15; Bricker, 10; Stassen, 7; Saltonstall, 2; and Warren, 1.

[23] *New York Times*, July 14, 1943, p. 20. Capehart was actually unenthusiastic. Willkie had never acknowledged the tremendous effort Capehart had put forth at the Elwood ceremony.

Colonel Robert R. McCormick to a "hammer-and-tongs" campaign for the Illinois preferential primary vote if the publisher would oppose him. This statement was made in response to rumors that McCormick might run in the Illinois primary for the Republican presidential nomination. Willkie asserted: "I certainly hope it is true. For then I could really make the issue clear — the greatest issue of the day — American relations to the rest of the world and liberal domestic policies."[24] When he could be reached for comment, Colonel McCormick scoffed at Willkie's challenge and declared: "I won't pay any attention to the story and advertise that joke . . . Mr. Willkie coupled his own name with mine just to get his name into the newspapers. . . . As things stand now, . . . any Republican nominee except Willkie can beat Roosevelt. . . . As for Willkie, I don't believe that at this present time he could carry a single State west of New Jersey — either in the primaries or the general election — but almost any other Republican could do it. . . . If the convention was held now, General MacArthur would be nominated by acclamation. . . ."[25] Informed of the rejection of his challenge, Willkie replied: "Just say I had a good laugh. I announced I would run in the Illinois primary . . . because I felt that we could face the issue of the nation's foreign and domestic policy squarely. That was the important thing."[26]

A week later, in Rushville for his summer vacation, Willkie met with his most loyal followers[27] to discuss future strategy, obtained more rest than he usually did on his Indiana trips, and made some

[24] The *Daily Illini* (University of Illinois), July 16, 1943, p. 1. At a meeting sponsored by the Republican Nationalist Revival Committee, a group organized with the announced purpose of helping to maintain the Republican party as the "nationalist party in American politics," a resolution was adopted urging McCormick to become a candidate in the Illinois primary. In its declaration of principles, the committee declared its opposition to Willkie. Former Representative P. H. Moynihan of Illinois was chairman of the group. See also the *New York Times*, July 2, 1943, p. 11.

[25] *Ibid.*, July 17, 1943, p. 1. The *Chicago Sun* reported that McCormick also thought that Governor Dwight Green and Senator Wayland Brooks, both of Illinois, could be classed as logical candidates. *Chicago Sun*, July 7, 1943, p. 7.

[26] *New York Times*, July 17, 1943, p. 1.

[27] Among those present were Sinclair Weeks, then treasurer of the national committee; Ralph H. Cake, Republican national committeeman from Oregon; Wilson Williams of Atlanta, Georgia; Mrs. Grace B. Reynolds of Cambridge City, Indiana, then national committeewoman from Indiana; and Frederick Baker of Washington, who had been defeated by Spangler for the national chairmanship the preceding year. *Ibid.*, August 29, 1943, p. 27.

remarks to the press concerning the Republican party. He stated that the Republican party, by eliminating some objectionable symbols such as isolationism, ultra-nationalism, and destructive criticism, could gain the confidence of the people and win the election in 1944. Asserting that he had carried on a continuous fight with Old Guard party members, Willkie then promised that he would continue to support the approach which he thought would win the election. He said that he could never run again for the presidency on any platform except one based on "liberal progressive ideas," and declared that international cooperation was certainly one of the planks of such a platform. He called for "the progressive element of the party" to assume control of its destiny — "in what may be its last chance to retain its power."[28]

Willkie's statements had all the earmarks of phrases aimed at a presidential nomination from one faction of the Republican party, but his assertions concerning postwar policy, as Turner Catledge wrote, "must have come as would a shower of red flags in a bull pen to the sizeable and powerful Republican group which has given up isolationism only 'for the duration,' if for that."[29] Catledge continued:

Mr. Willkie has been anathema to the Republican Old Guard ever since he humiliated them by grabbing the nomination at the Philadelphia convention in 1940. He will never be forgiven by the oldliners for that. But he has added to that humiliation lately by constantly confronting them with the challenge to come on out and take a stand on the international front. . . .

Mr. Willkie is at one and the same time one of the most important and one of the most troublesome elements in the Republican party. His importance does not stop at the fact that he was the party's most recent Presidential nominee and therefore still its titular head. It goes more to the evidence on every hand of his continuing appeal to a large number of the rank and file of American voters and to the further fact that he, of all possible candidates in 1944, has gone all-out . . . on the overwhelmingly important question of international policy.

Catledge noted that in the recent polls Willkie had run second to Governor Dewey, but he added that regardless of this, "Mr. Willkie still holds a predominating position in the Republican fold. The fact that all eyes in the party are trained on him . . . is proof enough of this. Even the old-timers concede that the first major

---

[28] *Ibid.*, August 12, 1943, p. 10.
[29] *Ibid.*, August 15, 1943, sec. 4, p. 3.

task before them is to 'stop Willkie,' and other prospective candidates are being appraised for their likely ability to do that."

Meanwhile, however, the eyes of the party shifted to policy planning. These efforts gave new indications of Willkie's impact on the thinking of party leaders concerning international policy, but without attribution to Willkie. At the annual Governors' Conference, held in Columbus, Ohio, in June, Governor Dewey urged the Republicans to take the lead in international planning, and Governor Bricker, though he refused at the meeting to speak out on issues, released a belated statement, the day after the conference ended, favoring participation in an international organization to preserve peace. Concurrently, more significant developments had been taking place in party planning for more than six months.

Early in January, Harrison Spangler, as the new national chairman, thought that the "brains of the party should get together to make a statement on foreign policy — to present a united front." At a breakfast meeting with Willkie at the Shoreham Hotel in Washington, Spangler made such a suggestion. Willkie, however, believing that Spangler's objectives were irrevocably different from his own, evaded a commitment to Spangler, and the national chairman left the breakfast "with the idea that Willkie was opposed to it."[30] Spangler was therefore surprised, a few days later, to hear of the formation of a planning group called The Republican Postwar Policy Association headed by Chicago lawyer Deneen Watson, who had managed Governor Dwight Green's race in the Illinois primary. The stated purpose of the Watson group, which according to Spangler was financed by money from Wall Street and the *New York Herald Tribune* to take over the Republican party, was to force the GOP to take a permanent stand against isolationism and in favor of international collaboration to keep the peace.

On May 3, seventy-five Republicans from twelve states held a meeting in Chicago to implement Watson's ideas. Included in the group were Dennison B. Hull, Chicago architect, and Mrs. Lorena Hahn of Omaha, former past president of the American Legion Women's Auxiliary. The members declared that the association, with Watson as chairman, would advocate an internationalist plank in the 1944 Republican platform to neutralize the President's strength in foreign affairs so that the GOP candidates could con-

---

[30] Interview with Mr. Spangler.

centrate their campaign against Roosevelt's domestic policies.[31] Watson opened an office in Chicago and announced that his eventual goal was a national organization with a paid director in each of the forty-eight states.[32] With publicity man Leo Casey, he journeyed throughout the nation trying to line up support for internationalism. Watson denied that he was supporting Willkie specifically, and Willkie deliberately kept his hands off the group, but if the RPPA had been successful, Willkie undoubtedly would have been the principal beneficiary.

In July the association held a convention at the Commodore Hotel in New York. Hull paid the bills because, he said, he did not want to have to choose between "the dead hand of bureaucracy, the liberalism that is not liberalism, as portrayed by the New Deal, and the Maginot Line of isolationism that . . . is an imaginary line, fraught with war . . . for generations to come." Senator Warren Austin of Vermont and Representative Charles Eaton of New Jersey were the main speakers. Supporters of Willkie dominated the proceedings and a five-point program opposing nationalism was adopted. After the meeting, Watson warned Spangler that Republicans needed a peace policy immediately. He denied that his association was trying to split the GOP, but he declared that unless the Republicans announced a policy, the party would surely be split in 1944. Spangler, however, ducked an argument with Watson at this point, for his plans for a two-day conference on Mackinac Island on the Michigan peninsula were already well developed, and he expected an acceptable party statement to come from this meeting. By October (when Watson originally had planned to hold a convention), the Postwar Policy Association had become inactive. The principles advocated by the group had indeed, for the most part, been adopted at the Mackinac Island conference in September. When Watson announced that the Association would no longer continue in existence, he also urged the nomination of Eric Johnston, then president of the United States Chamber of Commerce, as the Republican presidential candidate in 1944. Casey, the Association's publicity director, immediately stated, however, that Watson completely misrepresented the wishes of the rank and file of the outstanding Republican leaders who had supported the Association. He said that in his travels for the group he had found no sentiment

---

[31] *Newsweek,* July 19, 1943, p. 42.
[32] *New York Times,* July 28, 1943, p. 1.

for Johnston, but had found an overwhelming majority of the members ardently for the nomination of Wendell Willkie.[33]

The Mackinac Island conference grew out of Spangler's thought of bringing party leaders together to formulate some statement, but it was stimulated by Watson's extra-party association. In May, Spangler, Joe Martin, and Senator McNary selected the *forty-nine* partisans they wanted on the Republican Post-War Advisory Council, and on May 31, Spangler announced the appointments.[34] The Council included six members of the national committee, the chairmen of the party's senatorial and congressional campaign committees, twenty-four Republican governors, five senators, and twelve representatives. Wendell Willkie, the Republican's titular head and the party's chief exponent of international postwar cooperation, was not invited to attend the conference.[35] Nor were Herbert Hoover or Alf Landon, though Spangler asserted that "all Republican leaders" eventually would be consulted. Spangler emphasized that the group was chosen from the elected representatives of the party, but this statement brought a rebuke from the *New York Times:* ". . . This is not a convincing reason for using only incidentally some of the best material in the party. Mr. Willkie has stood out head and shoulders above all other leaders of his party during the last three years in the range and realism of his thinking on questions of international policy."[36] Other observers noted that the Council of Forty-nine was considerably weighted with pre-Pearl Harbor noninterventionists, but Spangler and Vandenberg, chairman of the Council's committee on foreign affairs, both vehemently denied that the committee was "stacked" against Willkie.

The Council, after weathering criticism of the selection process during the summer, met at Mackinac Island on September 6 and 7. In all of the advance publicity, Spangler stressed the fact that the

[33] *Ibid.,* October 14, 1943, p. 17.

[34] Though the group was known as the Committee of Forty-nine by the press, fifty participants were actually present. The extra person was Representative Charles A. Eaton of New Jersey, ranking minority member of the House Foreign Relations Committee, whom Spangler wanted but originally had not included. Eaton attended as an "adviser" because the chairman did not want to let the bars down to the scores of congressmen who wanted to be part of the committee.

[35] In a personal interview, Spangler told the author of this study that he did not invite Willkie for fear he would be turned down and because many working Republicans did not look favorably upon Willkie.

[36] *New York Times,* June 2, 1943, p. 24. The *Times* also lauded Hoover and Landon.

drafting of a program, rather than a discussion of personalities, was the purpose of the gathering. The one hundred-plus reporters, columnists, and correspondents who covered the meeting, however, were looking for more dramatic news, which turned out to be exceedingly scarce. As a result, irrelevant differences among the participants were exaggerated, and well-known techniques of parliamentary procedure were blown up as undercover maneuvers to control party policy. Actually, because nearly all obstreperous and outspoken intraparty critics had been excluded from the meeting, there was an understandable harmony which pervaded most of the proceedings. This is not to imply that there were no differences of opinion among the delegates. All shades of pre-Pearl Harbor attitudes on foreign policy were represented. By this time, however, there was general agreement on the necessity for some postwar cooperation among nations, and the internationalist thought advocated by the President and Willkie over a four-year period was widely accepted among the populace.

Thus, Tom Dewey, who originally opposed the meeting, carefully timed his arrival for the day after most of the other delegates had arrived, clothed himself in prevailing opinion and created most of the preconference news by advocating a postwar alliance with Great Britain in which he hoped Russia and China might be included. Dewey told reporters that making treaties or entering a group of nations promoting international action would not impair America's sovereignty. He replied to other questions with such obviously predetermined and personal answers that several GOP leaders were irritated. Senator Taft, hearing of Dewey's statement, said: "that was a fool thing to do,"[37] and charged that Dewey evidently had "swallowed whole the proposals espoused by Walter Lippmann."[38] Governor Bricker would not commit himself on Dewey's ideas, but Governor Warren stated that he would expand such an agreement to include more countries. Dewey, Bricker, and Warren all denied that they were candidates for the presidency at that time, but reporters wrote that "Dewey . . . became at once more attractive to groups within the party who want to spike Mr. Willkie's guns on post-war policies." Despite his protestations that he was not a

---

[37] *Time,* September 13, 1943, p. 25, and September 20, p. 19. The *Chicago Tribune* attacked the New York governor in an editorial entitled: "Tom Dewey Goes Anti-American."

[38] *New York Times,* September 6, 1943, p. 1.

candidate, many of the "old-liners," it was noted, placed him in the class of being a "hopeful" more than ever before.

After Spangler convened the meeting, he appointed two committees, with Vandenberg as chairman of the group on foreign affairs, and Taft as chairman of the committee on domestic problems. Though Spangler suggested that each committee simply adopt a statement outlining problems for future study and research, some of the governors wanted more specific statements. Subcommittees were therefore appointed and they worked far into the night stating and restating positions until they became satisfactory to both their own sympathizers and the congressional groups. The press reported that Taft and Vandenberg lost control to the state executives, and that criticism was circulating that too few of the members were participating in the actual decision-making process. It was reported, for example, that Senator Austin and Representative Eaton forced a foreign policy plank far more specific than that which Vandenberg had brought to the conference in his pocket, and that Governors Griswold, Warren, Langlie, and Hickenlooper forced Taft to reconsider his statements on labor and veterans.[39] Actually, during the entire proceedings there was little difference among the members on questions of principle. Most of the argument related to the language to be used in the publicized planks. The statement on foreign policy was approved almost without a change on September 7 in an executive session and Taft's final domestic statement — with two planks written by Warren and Hickenlooper — was quickly adopted.

The important product of the Council's meeting was the declaration on foreign policy and international relations. The final version was a collaboration by Senators Vandenberg and Austin with Chairman Spangler;[40] it pledged the Republicans to: "responsible

---

[39] Governor Warren criticized the labor plank, which did not even guarantee collective bargaining. When this guarantee was added, the committee approved the section. Stated Republican political scientist Dr. Wilfred Binkley, ". . . organized labor . . . will not be impressed by cautiously phrased platform planks perfunctorily approving collective bargaining." *Time*, October 4, 1943, p. 22.

[40] Governors Martin of Pennsylvania and Green of Illinois added sentences which called for wide acceptance of the principles of the document. Though it has never been widely noted, the moving force behind the declaration was Spangler. Following is an excerpt from a letter to the author from James P. Selvage, who was Spangler's assistant on the national commitee: "I know that he [Spangler] never received the credit that was his due in conjunction with the formulation of the Mackinaw Declaration. For weeks prior to that

participation by the United States in post-war cooperative organization among sovereign nations to prevent military aggression and to attain permanent peace with organized justice in a free world."[41] To be sure, this was a minimum statement that left a door open for retreat if necessary, but it was, as Willkie said in Providence, Rhode Island, where he was holding a round of informal conferences with industrialists and party leaders, "a move in the right direction." "In recognizing the necessity of post-war collaboration," he told reporters, "they appropriately express the thoughts of Republicans all over the United States."

Willkie's statement was undoubtedly accurate, and the press called the Mackinac declaration the greatest tactical advance made by the Republican party in years. Willkie's position had again been sustained, but observers saw more significance to the party in the emergence at the conference of the Republican governors group. Here were promising new leaders for the GOP — elected administrators who had proven their abilities to handle an executive position — and here were men, as one writer noted, who "brought . . . the appearance of having come more freshly from the people than did most of the 'Washington cabal' and the other leaders."[42]

Nevertheless, in the middle of September, 1943, Wendell Willkie indicated with reservations his intention to fight for the Republican nomination in 1944. Using *Look* as his vehicle, he stated his willingness to head the Republican party on a "liberal" platform. "If the Republican party intends to drive heart and soul for liberal objectives, such as I seek to outline," he wrote, "I shall give it my complete and undeviating service, whether as the convention nominee or as a worker in the ranks." Willkie declared that a liberal platform would contain five indispensable planks — on minority rights, efficiency in administration, a rebirth of *real enterprise,* absolutely

---

conference, Mr. Spangler went from Senator Austin to Senator Vandenberg to Senator Taft to Representative Eaton to Senator Taft to Senator Austin, and around again, getting their agreement upon what became the Declaration. The thing was 99 per cent in the bag and written before the Foreign Policy Committee convened at Mackinaw, and the harmony was attributable to only one man. . . . the Mackinaw Declaration . . . was, in truth, the beginning of the bipartisan foreign policy, fathered by Harrison E. Spangler who many of my friends continue to belabor as an isolationist."

[41] *Tennessee Republican Age,* February and March, 1944, p. 17. This entire issue is devoted to the results and achievements of the Mackinac conference.

[42] Turner Catledge, *New York Times,* September 12, 1943, p. E7.

guaranteed employment, [43] and a new foreign policy.[44] He called upon the Republicans to re-establish its great liberal traditions — to become again *"the great American liberal party . . . ,"* — and to see that the United States was made strong in economic as well as military terms.

The statement was both courageous and timely. Coming imme-

[43] Concerning Willkie's desire for "absolute guarantees," the *Philadelphia Record* commented: "The groans are from Hoover. That thud is Taft passing out." *Congressional Record,* vol. 89, p. A4297 (78th Cong., 1st Sess., Sept. 24, 1943.)

[44] *Ibid.,* September 21, 1943, p. 1. The article appeared in *Look,* October 5, 1943, pp. 25-31, and as an extension of the remarks of Charles A. Plumley, Representative from Vermont, in the *Congressional Record,* vol. 89, p. A4247 (78th Cong., 1st Sess., Sept. 22, 1943). In Willkie's words, a summary of the planks is as follows:

1. We must never forget that, while democratic government rests on majority rule, the essence of freedom is the protection of minorities. The Republican party has always advocated equal rights for all, irrespective of race, creed or color. Now, above all times, we must make these principles a reality. . . .

2. We must have efficient, well-managed, and economic administration. . . .

3. We must have a rebirth of enterprise — *real enterprise.* This is where the liberal element in the Republican Party has such an enormous role to play. Some of the talk we hear about "free enterprise" or "private enterprise" is just propaganda on the part of powerful groups who have not practiced real enterprise in a generation and have no intention of doing so. We must distinguish between enterprise and private ownership. A corporation may be privately owned and still be the worst enemy of free enterprise. Unfortunately, some of our big corporations are in this class, and the Democratic Party, despite noisy proclamations, has done nothing really effective about it. . . . Private ownership is not enough — we must have competition, invention, expansion, lower rates, lower prices of manufactured goods. Only thus can we create more opportunities, raise the standard of living and — most important — maintain real jobs for all. . . .

4. While a courageous government may hope to check somewhat the disastrous ups and downs of the economic cycle, we cannot hope to do away with them entirely. This means that *absolute guarantees must be provided by our society against unemployment* — and against want because of old age, injury or incapacity. . . . All forms of social insurance, including protection against unemployment, must be taken out of politics. . . .

5. Finally, the Republican Party . . . must take the leadership in formulating a new foreign policy, by which we and other nations can assure our future safety and promote our mutual interests. . . .

The *Philadelphia Record,* in reference to Willkie's comment on big corporations, stated: "Figure how that would set, say with Joe Grundy. . . . Can't you hear 'em saying in the Union League: 'Is that damn Willkie guy the same one that was head of Commonwealth and Southern?' " See the extension of remarks of Senator James M. Tunnell of Delaware, *Congressional Record,* vol. 89, p. A4297 (78th Cong., 1st Sess., Sept. 24, 1943).

diately after the Mackinac meeting from which he had been excluded, it demonstrated that Willkie was well aware that to win in 1944 he had to begin a grass-roots Republican movement of the people rather than depend on the Republican organization as it was then constituted. The whole tone of the article indicated that he was still out to capture votes from Roosevelt, that he was the one Republican leader who was willing to appeal to the masses of lower income groups, and that he wanted to capitalize on his previous Republican leadership in the international field. Again, as in his 1940 campaign, he was not explicit as to how all of his aims were to be achieved. In spite of this rather characteristic but understandable omission, however, Willkie's dramatic declaration was a shining example of candor among the vague but more politic equivocations of the other Republican aspirants. It was also a clear indication that he believed that he could make no inroads among the party hierarchy and that he would have to appeal again directly to the independent voters. There could be no doubt of his sincerity, for a more inexpedient course would have been difficult to chart. In writing the *Look* article, he again challenged the right wing of the GOP to preliminary battle. By demanding a platform based on liberalism, Willkie added to the injury of reform the insult of betraying the beliefs of many individuals in his adopted party.[45]

Early in October, Willkie went out West to keep several speaking engagements. When asked if the trip had anything to do with his possible candidacy in 1944, Willkie replied that he was not making the journey for his health. He obtained details on election laws in a conference with Governor Warren, and spoke to the Republican state central committee, labor officials, the San Francisco Press Club, and several other nonpolitical groups. After most of his talks, he received standing ovations from cheering crowds. Los Angeles correspondent Sidney L. James described the invasion of California as "very successful," and concluded: "If he has not completed the capture of California by the time he leaves San Francisco . . . this is my last flyer in political prognostication."[46] On his return trip,

---

[45] See "Willkie as Candidate," in the *New Republic*, October 4, 1943, p. 442. Governor Ralph Carr of Colorado, who had seconded the nomination of Willkie in 1940, told the *Portland Oregonian*: "I don't think that Willkie can be nominated . . . that Willkie himself believes he is a Republican [or] believes in the principles of the Republican Party. . . . He is a man of impulse." *Time*, September 27, 1943, p. 24.

[46] *Ibid.*, October 11, 1943, p. 19.

Willkie spoke to the leaders of the Council of State Governments meeting in Nevada. He impressed them with his party orthodoxy, and said that his future political plans included taking the stump in the New York race for Lieutenant Governor and in the New Jersey and Kentucky gubernatorial contests, "as a Republican and as a citizen."[47]

Willkie returned to New York and then to Maine for a vacation, only to have the respite shattered by an irritating political incident. Early in September, Grover W. Dalton, chairman of the Missouri Republican state committee, and industrialist Edgar Monsanto Queeny, together with thirty-four other nationalist Missouri Republicans, sent Willkie a list of nine questions to which they said they desired answers.[48] Asking for Willkie's "considered views" on whether the 1940 candidate thought the United States should become a member of a "world supranational state," on "absolute freedom of international trade," tariffs, the desirability of "flooding our country with alien individuals and alien ideas," and the "political and economic organization of one world," the letter was couched in obviously hostile terms.[49] The writers gave Willkie ten days in which to answer, but when Willkie received the questions the ten days were nearly over. He replied that he would be glad to answer the queries, but that his replies would have to be "off the record." This statement was patently not the desired answer, and several Missouri Republicans and newspaper correspondents declared that Willkie's position was of such public interest that any response should be publicized. To this demand, Willkie exploded that he was not going to be put "on the spot." Until October 11 the questions did not receive wide publicity. On that date, however, Representative Louis E. Miller, Republican of Missouri, demanded on the floor of Congress that Willkie reply to the questions and called upon him to make a clear statement of his postwar proposals so that Republicans could determine whether he favored United States subordination to a world state. The Missouri legislator, who had been a preconvention manager for Willkie in the 1940

---

[47] *New York Times*, October 4, 1943, p. 11.

[48] Joseph Barnes, *op. cit.*, p. 341, wrote that the questions were privately checked with Herbert Hoover. *Time* called the queries "have-you-stopped-beating-your-wife" questions. September 27, 1943, p. 24.

[49] For the complete text of the letter, see the *Congressional Record*, vol. 89, p. 8297 (78th Cong., 1st Sess., Oct. 11, 1943). A rebuttal to Dalton and his cohorts by another Missouri congressman, Wat Arnold, appears on p. A4639 (Oct. 14, 1943).

campaign, challenged Willkie to tell the public whether his "liberalism" was "true liberalism" or a left-wing "neo-liberalism" whose "ultimate phase would be a totalitarian state like Russian communism wherein all individual rights to liberty disappear except those bestowed or permitted at the pleasure of a despot."[50] Miller's request was widely circulated and the challenge was accepted.

Moreover, in addition to the letter from Dalton and the speech by Representative Miller, Willkie received a letter from Queeny, who had been another of his outstanding supporters and organizers in 1940, imputing to Willkie the general beliefs expressed by Thomas W. Lamont and other directors of Freedom House (a New York organization for the furthering of international understanding, of which Willkie was a director), and accusing him of sympathy with the "Union Now" movement headed by Clarence Streit, Washington newspaperman.[51] Willkie returned a blistering letter to Queeny accusing him of using the same methods of guilt by association that he alleged were used by the New Deal. He stated that he knew Lamont in the same way that he knew Queeny, and that he was influenced in his opinions by such men of wealth only in regard to the logic of what was said. Willkie then added:

> I never have been awed by great wealth such as yours, nor afraid of defending a Communist such as Schneiderman if I thought his cause was just. I wear my sovereignty under my hat. . . . Ed, let me give you a tip. If you want to pursue this . . . policy of strong condemnation by frail association, I also belong to the board of directors . . . of Town Hall. One of my fellow-directors is Mr. Norman Thomas, Socialist, and pre-Pearl Harbor isolationist. You can do wonders with that.
>
> But I'll not reciprocate. I do not assert that all isolationists are Socialists. I do, however, happen to believe that if isolationist policies were adopted by this country, we should eventually be forced to come to some form of socialism.[52]

Willkie decided to go to St. Louis and defend his position. When local Republican leaders began selling seats for the rally for fifty dollars each (to pay expenses and help clear away a campaign deficit), he refused to sanction the admission charge, and hired a hall with six hundred dollars of his own so that the general public would be admitted. Other aspects of the visit brought out the environment of animosity. At one of the luncheons in Willkie's honor, attended by one hundred fifty political and business leaders,

---

[50] *Chicago Tribune,* October 12, 1943, p. 20.
[51] *New York Times,* October 12, 1943, p. 22.
[52] *Ibid.*

Queeny introduced him as "America's leading ingrate," saying, "In 1940, I raised two hundred thousand dollars in his behalf and never got a thank you."[53] Willkie was furious, and when he rose to speak he shouted, "I don't know whether you're going to support me or not and I don't give a damn. You're a bunch of political liabilities anyway. The days are gone, which some of you want to bring back, when you could go to your plants and cause employees to tremble in fear of losing their jobs. Those days are gone forever and good riddance."

Though Willkie was visibly angered by the incident, the evening speech, given before 3,000 cheering people, was a vigorous, partisan address. Willkie demanded the removal of President Roosevelt and his whole administration from Washington in order to show the world that democratic government could be maintained in the United States. He asserted that the Administration was abusing its media of communication and he criticized the Roosevelt aides for distrusting the people and perpetuating themselves in power. Willkie then offered the citizens a domestic policy with five planks advocating the elimination of waste, the enforcement of antitrust laws, a nonpunitive labor policy, a productive agricultural policy, and a cooperative effort between industry and government. Though he refused to answer the nine questions submitted to him earlier, he said that "most important of all," was the absolute necessity of American participation, military, economic, and political, with the rest of the world. After discussing the future needs of an American foreign policy, Willkie concluded: "If the party selects from among its many able men . . . a man whose record leaves no doubt that he is qualified for the leadership of such a cause, I will, of course, support him. . . ."[54] The mass reaction to the speech was excellent, and for the press Willkie commented: "Missouri looks very good to me . . . I would say . . . a majority of the men and

---

[53] Wick, *op. cit.*, p. 31.

[54] *New York Times,* October 16, 1943, p. 8, or see "Willkie's Speech," *Life,* October 25, 1943, p. 34. The speech was broadcast over NBC and to save radio time, Willkie spoke so rapidly that listeners had difficulty in following him. The *Times* declared: "The outline and description fit the man Willkie like a pair of gloves." An editorial in the same issue on page 16 stated: ". . . certainly it can be and should be said that at this time, on the record he has made, on the merit of the causes he has led and so long as he goes straight ahead on the path which he has chosen, Wendell Willkie is head and shoulders above any other man in his right and title to that nomination."

women active in the Republican organization in Missouri go along with me. As far as the rank and file are concerned they are overwhelmingly for me."

As a result of the acrimonious incidents with the Missouri politicians and his enthusiastic reception by the general public, Willkie realized more than ever before that he had to double his efforts to obtain support at the grass-roots level, and that the only way in which he could prove that he had such support was through the state presidential primaries. Consequently, he traveled widely and frequently in an effort to swing local leaders back to his fold. He exuded confidence, for he believed that a bandwagon movement was his only hope of obtaining the nomination in spite of opposition from cliques within the state organization. He was not always tactful, however, and this often strengthened his enemies. For example, on October 19 he spoke in Washington at a meeting of first-term Republican congressmen and their guests. The address was supposedly off-the-record, but Willkie's remarks were so intemperate that they were leaked to the press. He declared that some of the young lawmakers had come merely to ask him embarrassing questions, and antagonized them saying: "I know you people are opposed to me. You don't like me. But I am going to be nominated whether you like it or not. Better get right with me. I am going to be your next President!"[55] Commented Lawrence H. Smith, House member from Racine, Wisconsin, ". . . Willkie is wooing the Republican party in a very peculiar manner. . . . He has been going around the country telling regular Republican groups he didn't care if he had their support or not. He has definite ideas as to a program and platform and stated if we didn't like it, he didn't want our support. He was tough about it all. He has his own ideas on the domestic front, the international front, and the Republicans can take it or leave it."[56] Smith concluded that Willkie had offended the young Republicans and had little support among them. National Chairman Harrison Spangler later revealed that letters written to him during this period indicated that some Republicans were alienated at practically every dinner that Willkie attended. The mail to national headquarters ran nearly nine to one against the 1940 candidate.[57]

---

[55] Wick, *op. cit.*, p. 32.
[56] *Chicago Tribune,* October 23, 1943, p. 5.
[57] Interview with Harrison Spangler.

Just before the 1943 elections, Willkie returned to New York and asked the citizens to support Governor Dewey by voting for Joe R. Hanley, Republican nominee for Lieutenant Governor. He credited Dewey with a "sound, clean, and able administration." Several days later, Willkie also praised the record of Walter E. Edge, New Jersey Republican gubernatorial nominee, who had been a United States senator and ambassador to France. Both Hanley and Edge won their contests, and the Republican pattern of victory was repeated in local and special elections over the entire northern part of the nation. Kentucky elected a Republican governor; Republicans won local battles in Pennsylvania; Connecticut went overwhelmingly to the Republicans; and known Republicans were victorious in nonpartisan California elections. When final tabulations were made, the GOP controlled twenty-six states with a population of nearly ninety million persons and an electoral college vote of 342. The party was actually approaching the strength it had in its peak year of 1928. Republicans were jubilant and many observers saw a deeper significance in the election as foretelling a GOP victory in 1944.[58]

In light of these developments, Willkie went to Wisconsin to line up a possible slate of delegates for the 1944 primary in that state and to talk with Republican leaders. For weeks before the visit, the *Chicago Tribune* and many other smaller anti-Willkie papers had been warning the people not to be swayed by Willkie's "campaign oratory" during the trip. Congressmen, minor party members, small-town businessmen, and local editors were quoted to the effect that Willkie was really a Democrat, that his words could not be trusted, and that he was not desired as a speaker in Wisconsin.[59] Nevertheless, in an address at a luncheon attended by four hundred Republican men and women in Madison, Willkie asked for the support of the Badger state "liberals" and criticized Senator Robert La Follette's isolationist views. "I hope you're with me in Wisconsin," he declared, "because I want a state like this

---

[58] Walter Lippmann wrote: "Responsibility of governing the country has been passing gradually but surely into the hands of the Republicans . . . and the question is one of men, not of principles. . . . [The Republicans] are going to win [the next election] as now seems not unlikely because the appointed time for a change has arrived and for no other reason." *Time,* November 15, 1943, p. 20.

[59] See the *Chicago Tribune,* October 19, 1943, p. 10; October 21, 1943, p. 10; October 27, 1943, p. 10; and November 1, 1943, p. 1 and p. 26.

with a great liberal tradition. But whether you're with me or not, I'm sticking to my policies."

Willkie spent two days in the Wisconsin capital but departed without welding a campaign organization. His followers, who included politically powerful John E. Dickinson of West Bend, and Milton R. Polland of Milwaukee, said that a Willkie slate would be formed at a later date. In Milwaukee the candidate warned Republicans not to be anti-labor. Speaking to Milwaukee County Republican party members, Willkie stated that there was no irrepressible conflict between labor and industry, that if the Republicans stressed the point because of "certain disturbances in the field of labor," it would "take the road that leads to defeat," and that he would fight "every step of the way against any such foolish course." He declared that there were many in the Republican party who believed that there was an "inevitable trend" toward a GOP victory in 1944 because of gains made in the off-year elections, but that he could not wholly agree. "I hope that it is true. It can be true. But it is not inevitably true. The Republican party must take stock and make itself worthy of winning in 1944." When Willkie left Wisconsin, State Senator Robert Robinson, Republican from Beloit, stated: "By all rules of politics, Willkie ought to be a dead dog, but he is able to stir up interest and support and opposition."[60]

Willkie returned to New York, and then headed South and West for speaking engagements. In Baton Rouge, Louisiana, he told a large group: "If Southerners would vote logically, I think I would come nearest representing their political beliefs. I am not so foolish to think I have any chance to carry Louisiana, even though I am conferring with members of the Republican organization here. . . . I know perfectly well I am going to see a lot of Democrats. And I think I come a lot closer to representing the views of most of these Southern Democrats than the present national administration does."[61]

---

[60] *Ibid.*, November 13, 1943, p. 2. In spite of all of Willkie's public statements that he was anxious to run in Wisconsin, he was actually exceedingly reluctant to make the race. Moreover, neither Dickinson nor Polland thought Wisconsin would be a fair test of his strength. Willkie went into Wisconsin because of demands by his financial backers in New York that he prove his strength in the Midwest. This decision was made at a meeting in February at the Ambassador Hotel in New York at which Willkie argued that an isolationist state was no place to make his initial primary bid, but at which he was told that the necessary money for his entire campaign would be contributed only if he could carry Wisconsin.

[61] *New York Times,* November 18, 1943, p. 1.

On many economic issues, this statement by Willkie may have been accurate, but with reference to civil rights, it was completely untrue. Willkie was the greatest Republican champion of Negro rights of his era, and he would have been as ambivalent as a Southern Democrat as he was among the conservative Republicans. In Dallas, Willkie declared that a main objective of his southern tour was to bring the South "into the Republican party in order to make it a party more representative of the nation as a whole." He told reporters that he felt the Republicans could win the 1944 election without the South, but that the party needed the South if it was to be truly national. On the following night in the same city, Willkie called for a return to the policies and program of Woodrow Wilson under which, he said, the United States would be controlled neither by overcentralized government, nor by big business, nor by big pressure groups of any sort.

Willkie's final major address of his November tour was given before one thousand members and guests of the Denver Chamber of Commerce. He declared that the Republican party must change from a philosophy of "negation" to one that was "affirmative and alive" if it intended to win the 1944 presidential election. He called upon the party to adopt a policy which extended the doctrine of "peace, freedom, and economic cooperation to all the countries of the world." Wendell Willkie was speaking like the candidate of 1940. On other fronts, however, forces were at work to depreciate his efforts.

While Willkie was traveling in Wisconsin, the South, and in the West, John D. M. Hamilton, the former chairman of the Republican National Committee who had become an attorney for Joe Pew's Sun Oil Company, made a tour of seventeen states throughout the nation — presumably to determine the accuracy of Willkie's assertion that he already had pledged to him 400 of the 1,058 votes at the 1944 Republican convention.[62] The *New York Times* reported that Hamilton was incidentally advising party leaders to support "favorite sons" if he found that votes claimed by Willkie were not actually pledged. The strategy then would be to deadlock the convention so that party leaders would name their own candidate as they had selected Harding in 1921.[63] Though Hamilton

---

[62] Dillon, *op. cit.*, p. 317.

[63] From Portage, Wisconsin, Willkie recalled the nomination of Warren Harding, and warned the Republican state delegations against nominating

denied the *Times'* report that the purpose of his trip was to block Willkie, he made statements that clearly indicated that he had never forgotten that Willkie had not accepted him as national chairman four years earlier. In Denver, he predicted that the party's nominee in 1944 would be chosen from among the twenty-four Republican governors, and remarked that the delegates to the convention would not "make the fallacy of being stampeded for someone their mature judgment would otherwise reject." Moreover, in California, where he was reportedly trying to persuade Governor Earl Warren to break any tentative pledge he had made to Willkie, Hamilton said: "Anyone who reads the polls knows that no man up to this time has captured the public imagination to the extent of as much as one-third of the vote. In view of this . . . it may not be out of place to note that the public agrees with Mr. Willkie's often-repeated phrase of the last campaign — 'There is no one indispensable man.' . . . The Republican Party has the finest group of Governors it has ever had. Irrespective of their personal ambitions, they should all be considered on their merits. . . ."[64]

Time reported that on his way home, Hamilton stopped off in Indianapolis and advised Republican leaders, in effect: "Get behind Tom Dewey for 1944. . . . No man would turn down the

---

"favorite son" aspirants. "I have been told," he said, "that Hamilton and Pew are seeking to create enough regional and favorite son candidates to prevent anyone else from securing a majority of delegates before the convention. I hope the reports that those tactics are being used will be proved untrue before it is too late." *New York Times,* November 12, 1943, p. 38.

[64] *New Republic,* November 29, 1943, p. 742, asserted: "Hamilton does not deny that Joe Pew is paying his bills . . . Hamilton's hosts are generally assuming they can rely on his backers for small things like expenses. Many of them have done so before. Pew and duPont [Lammot duPont] and some of duPont's friends who have been most active in the National Association of Manufacturers did their 1944 planning early. Pew, for example, contributed at least $5,000 in 1942 to every Republican state organization that needed money. That was most of them, and that kind of practice gave Pew and his friends a good-sized mortgage on the Republican Party in states like Nebraska and the Dakotas. It is going to be hard for those state organizations to refuse to come through for the Pew-duPont ticket while those gentlemen continue to hold the mortgage. . . ." This article also discussed the influence of the *Farm Journal* (a Pew publication) among rural voters, and the effort by certain Republicans to neutralize the foreign policy issue in the 1944 campaign. The magazine concluded: "If the Tafts, the Vandenbergs and the McCormicks maneuver so as to take the international issue out of the campaign, many think they will practically have taken Willkie out too."

Presidential nomination."[65] And when he returned to New York, the former national chairman told reporters that support for Willkie for the 1944 nomination was not nearly as strong as it had been represented. He said that after having talked with approximately one thousand persons, including the party leaders on all levels of government, he had concluded that Governor Dewey had strength in all communities he visited, but that the support of other candidates was "spotty." Hamilton admitted that Willkie was "the $64 question of today," but explained that "what is the question of today is not the question under conditions of June, 1944." Discussing the general political sentiment he had found on his tour, Hamilton concluded: "I have been active in national politics for twenty years and I never saw the Republicans so hopeful and enthusiastic as they are today. They feel they have the best chance of victory in years."

Another prominent Republican, Alf Landon, similarly stated: "The recent elections show that the American people are changing political horses as fast as they can." Three weeks later (and seven months before the Republican convention) Landon also made two accurate predictions: that Governor Thomas E. Dewey of New York would be nominated for President by the Republicans not later than the second convention ballot, and that Wendell L. Willkie, before June, was likely to slip almost completely out of the running.[66] Dewey refused to comment on Landon's statement, but when it was brought to Willkie's attention, he declared: "Predictions are hazardous. This much, however, is certainly true — that if Governor Landon's recent speeches . . . represent the thinking of the Republican party, then certainly someone other than myself should lead the party in 1944."[67]

Landon made his statement with reasonable assurance of accuracy because to his experienced political eye, all of the evidence of support and victory was clearly running against a renomination for Willkie. The political build-up for Tom Dewey, picturing him as

---

[65] *Time,* December 20, 1943, p. 20.

[66] *New York Times,* December 6, 1943, p. 1.

[67] *Ibid.,* December 7, 1943, p. 29. Landon had asked Republicans to refrain from endorsing the various international conferences, which Willkie had praised, until all the decisions which had been made by the foreign ministers and the other leaders of Russia, Great Britain, China, and the United States were made public. Willkie construed Landon's statement as a repudiation of the Administration's foreign policy and as a move backward to isolationism. *Ibid.,* December 12, 1943, p. E3.

"calm, neat, painstaking and deadly efficient," was in full swing
among the mass media of the nation. In spite of his denial that he
was a candidate, Dewey worked closely with shrewd Edwin F.
Jaeckle, the New York Republican chairman, and J. Russel Sprague,
the powerful boss of the Nassau County Republican machine.
Though Willkie and many critics regarded Dewey as an opportunist
who became an internationalist only after he had seen the tide of
public opinion flowing in that direction, his supporters countered
that Dewey had never been an isolationist, and that he had favored
both early military preparedness and the lend-lease program. Moreover, Dewey had boldly endorsed a postwar alliance with Britain,
Russia, and China, including a pledge to use force against aggres-
sors to prevent future wars. Dewey had also candidly advocated
increased trade, tariff reduction, the preservation of the Securities
and Exchange Commission and the Wages and Hours Act, plus
expanded social security. He also wanted the antitrust laws enforced more sensibly and more vigorously than they had been under
the New Deal. "In the last analysis," he declared, "the greatest
single need is for better management in government. . . . The government cannot do everything and it must recognize this fact above
all others. It must permit a basic freedom of action to its people,
remembering that the things that Government does are in response
to the will of the people. . . ."[68]

Such statements, together with what was often called Dewey's
"unassailable record as Governor," were given wide distribution by
the same papers and periodicals that had always supported Willkie.
Ideologically the Republican party did not necessarily become more
conservative during this period, it merely shifted its allegiance to
another candidate who looked almost as liberal, who subtly appropriated Willkie's most successful ideas, and who had fewer enemies
than the 1940 nominee. After the elections in 1943, a survey taken
in the House of Representatives showed that 89 of 206 Republicans
polled thought that Dewey was the best qualified GOP leader and
the one most certain to defeat the Democratic nominee. In this
poll, Willkie received only six votes. Ahead of him, the House
members ranked MacArthur, Bricker, and Taft.[69] Additional evi-

---

[68] *Time,* November 1, 1943, p. 15.

[69] *United States News,* November 12, 1943, p. 24. Willkie never regained
the lead in public opinion polls that he held early in 1942. In July, a Gallup
poll revealed that organized labor still supported President Roosevelt in
preference to Willkie, and that Governor Dewey was ahead of Willkie

dence that the trend was against Willkie appeared in December when his friend, Fred Baker of Washington, tried to get a comprehensive Willkie-inspired resolution adopted at a meeting of the Republican national, state, and county committeemen from eleven Western states in Salt Lake City. So afraid were the delegates that they might be labeled Willkieites, that they frustrated and stymied Baker and his suggestions; the program was finally defeated in the resolutions committee headed by Clarence Budington Kelland.[70] Back in New York, during this period, a national committee to draft Governor Bricker and General MacArthur for the 1944 nomination opened headquarters. John A. Schaefer, who helped establish the group, told reporters: "It is a purely voluntary movement among Republicans who do not see eye to eye with Wendell L. Willkie, and who accept the statement of Governor Thomas E. Dewey that he is not a candidate for the nomination."[71]

Meanwhile, out in California, the star of Governor Warren was rising. In his eight months as governor, he had set up a monetary reserve to meet the state's postwar problems, cut taxes, and made several progressive changes in the state's criminal procedures. Though he refused to discuss his political future with reporters, he had confided to Willkie in October that he intended to run in the California primary in order to hold the delegation together. This, too, was a blow to Willkie, for a popularity poll among California county committee members had revealed that he was stronger than either Dewey or Warren among the grass-roots politicians. Willkie felt that he was more popular on the West Coast than anywhere else in the nation, but he could not invade the province of a favorite son, and thus had to content himself with Warren's pledge that he was not, at the time, a serious candidate. Simultaneously, in Illinois, another new group became part of the inexorably expanding opposition. Representative Everett McKinley Dirksen told the press that thirty-six fellow congressmen from thirteen states had signed a peti-

---

among the rural voters. *New York Times,* July 30, 1943, p. 8. By the latter part of October, however, Willkie was again the second choice of Republicans, four percentage points behind Dewey. *Ibid.,* October 24, 1943, p. 12. Among ten thousand Negroes polled by the *Pittsburgh Courier,* a Negro weekly, 84.2 per cent favored Willkie for the GOP nomination in 1944. *Ibid.,* October 29, 1943, p. 16. In a popularity poll among county committee members in California, Willkie placed first ahead of Dewey and Warren. *Ibid.,* November 5, 1943, p. 11.

[70] *Time,* December 20, 1943, p. 20.

[71] *New York Times,* October 30, 1943, p. 9.

tion urging him to try for the Republican nomination. Though he denied that he was merely part of the Pew-Hamilton strategy to block Willkie, it was well known among the petitioners that 35 of the 36 opposed the renomination of the 1940 candidate. Few observers took the Dirksen move seriously, but it represented another facet of political reality with which the dwindling Willkie forces had to contend.

The final opinion surveys taken in 1943 revealed that Willkie led Dewey only in Massachusetts and Kentucky. Nationally, he was favored by 35 per cent of the Republicans polled and another 10 per cent were undecided. With Dewey still uncommitted, however, the party found itself split into pro-Willkie and stop-Willkie camps. David Lawrence, in a syndicated column, cautioned party leaders lest they "crucify" the GOP in an attempt to smear their titular head out of the presidential race.[72] Willkie's strength among the masses of voters was indefinite; he had embryonic organizations in more than half the states, and an office in New York which was preparing new campaign literature for him.[73] In addition, there were rumors that he would form a third party if he failed to obtain the nomination from the Republicans. Though conservatives realized that he would first wage an all-out battle for the nomination before risking the hazards of a third-party candidacy, they considered him sufficiently daring to take this unorthodox course that would split the party. As a result, the Democrats, who had begun to doubt their ability to win in 1944 after observing the 1942 and 1943 election results, regained hope.

At year's end, Willkie's enemies across the country violently resisted every effort of the Willkie forces to regain nationwide support. They denounced the candidate's aggressive international stand as a "me-too" New Deal position, and they attached his "campaign oratory" remark to nearly everything he said. In Congress and in the press, they again publicly questioned the method by which he had obtained the 1940 nomination. The conservative polemicists were out to demolish his political stature and they were determined to do a thorough job of it. It was in this setting that Wendell Willkie entered the final year of his life.

---

[72] *Washington Star,* December 13, 1943, p. A-9.

[73] See William Allen White's analysis in the *New York Times,* October 10, 1943, p. 50.

8 PARTY IN TRANSITION

Early in 1944, *The Republican* magazine released the results of a survey on foreign policy taken among 3,581 Republican county chairmen, district committeemen, district committeewomen, members of the Republican state central committees, officers of the Women's Federation of Republican Clubs, and Republican members of state legislatures. The poll revealed that the "average Republican leader" was willing to have the United States join a worldwide organization dedicated to keeping the peace and promoting economic cooperation. This average Republican, however, was against extensive disarmament after the war, the surrender of island outposts, and the "idea of Uncle Sam masquerading as an international Santa Claus."[1] Among the questions asked in the survey was one designed to measure the extent to which the local leaders were familiar with and approved of the foreign policy views of some of the party's prominent national leaders. Of the twelve national leaders included in the list submitted to those questioned, Willkie's views ranked third in the popularity behind — paradoxically — those of Dewey and Herbert Hoover. Moreover, a greater number of the leaders expressed disagreement with the views of Willkie than with the opinions of any other candidate. This opposition was greatest in the Midwest, but even in the East 22 per cent of the local leaders refused to be identified with the 1940 candidate.

---

[1] *The Republican*, January, 1944, p. 2.

Meanwhile, the Republican hierarchy was meeting at the Hotel Stevens in Chicago to select a site and date for the 1944 Republican convention. The national committee quickly agreed to June 26 in Chicago after the Willkie supporters withdrew their opposition to the Illinois metropolis. These leaders of the internationalist wing declared that Chicago was the center of isolationism and that Colonel McCormick undoubtedly would do all he could to pack the galleries with partisans hostile to Willkie. They finally agreed, however, that Chicago's central location would minimize the wartime travel of the delegates, and so they accepted the invitation to the Windy City. Private discussion at the meeting centered almost exclusively around the possible nominees. An Associated Press poll, taken secretly among the members, revealed that Willkie and Governor Dewey were tied in favor with twenty-one votes each. Governor Bricker ran third with the support of only five committee members, while other state leaders backed favorite sons or stated that they had not made their decisions on the presidential race at the time.[2] Most observers agreed, however, that should the issue come to a showdown, the scattered and undecided votes would probably favor Dewey over Willkie. Werner Schroeder, the anti-Willkie national committeeman from Illinois, asserted that the members really stood at least 75 to 12 against the 1940 candidate.[3]

While the national committee met in Chicago, Willkie made a nationwide radio address aimed at its members from a Metropolitan Opera Victory Rally in New York. In a short, cogent talk, he attacked the President's "recurrent seizures" of factories, mines, railroads, adding that the confusion in the Administration's domestic policy was a perfect illustration of the fallacy of one-man rule in a democracy.[4] The following night, from Montpelier, Vermont, Willkie also received some much needed support. Governor William H. Wills told the delegates over the Columbia network that it would mean suicide for the Republican party to allow a handful of bosses to stop the nomination of Willkie. "Wendell Willkie," he asserted, "is the only Republican certain to beat the strongest Democratic candidate." Wills then delivered a sharp attack against those whom he termed "the four-year locusts of Republican politics who clouded the victory crops raised in recent Republican victories in the states

[2] *Ibid.*, February, 1944, p. 2.
[3] *Newsweek,* January 10, 1944, p. 40.
[4] *New York Times,* January 8, 1944, p. 14.

and congressional districts." "This cloud has some leaders and some spokesmen. I do not have to tell you who they are: Alf Landon, John Hamilton, Joseph Pew, Senator Nye and Gerald L. K. Smith and of course, the metropolitan McCormick-Patterson newspaper axis. . . ." Wills then concluded:

> These political locusts of whom I speak had nothing constructive to say. They agreed on no candidates. They simply agree in their hatred of the outstanding Republican of our times — Wendell Willkie. For only Willkie packs a wallop in both fists. Roosevelt's right arm is in a sling labeled "domestic shortcomings." In a sling too, is the left arm of every Republican challenger except Willkie, and this sling is labeled "no foreign policy." No sling hampers Willkie. Both arms are free. Willkie's left glove is stamped "sound foreign policy," his right glove is marked "sound domestic policy." Up here in Vermont we stand for fair play. All we ask is fair play for a man who fights clean and in the open — Wendell Willkie.[5]

When the Republican National Committee met on the following day, those opposed to Willkie's nomination condemned the Vermont governor's speech as likely to cause disunity in the party, and six days later, over the same network, John D. M. Hamilton replied to Governor Wills, asserting that Willkie's managers had brought "undue pressure upon party leaders in every section of the country to pledge themselves to his cause before anyone else had a chance to be heard." "The intensity of this propaganda," Hamilton declared, "has been such that it is called the 'Willkie Blitz.' Certainly I did not find . . . the overwhelming demand for Mr. Willkie claimed by Governor Wills."[6]

All of the important candidates were represented at the national committee meeting, but Willkie and Dewey were most widely discussed. Ralph Cake, who was slated to become Willkie's campaign manager, announced that his candidate probably would enter the Oregon and Wisconsin primaries, and reporters agreed that Willkie's chance of receiving the nomination depended largely upon his success in the preferential races he entered. Anti-Willkie committeemen charged that Willkie was again trying to go over their heads, but that he was slipping. They felt that in view of the anti-Roosevelt trend evidenced in 1943 elections and the President's troubles with Congress in 1944, any strong Republican could capture as much of the independent vote as could the former Hoosier. Bricker forces, nevertheless, made little headway in Chicago; the Ohio governor

---

[5] *Chicago Sun,* January 9, 1944, p. 9, and *New York Times,* January 9, 1944, p. 14.

[6] *Ibid.,* January 16, 1944, p. 5.

was certain only of his state delegation. And though the Stassen supporters worked hard and apparently had no liaison with the Willkie men, there was also little national support for the Minnesota governor early in 1944. Governor Warren was mentioned only as a possible running mate for Dewey, and MacArthur sentiment among the committee leaders was nearly nonexistent. Thus, among the professionals in the party, Dewey looked like a certainty in spite of his refusal to commit himself. He had popular appeal, a good platform and radio personality, no fierce enemies, and a proven ability to get votes. His sole drawback, silence on national and international issues as they arose, was discounted. He really had not said "no" to a possible draft.

Willkie, however, was in a less advantageous position. He had committed himself and consequently had to continue to press for widespread endorsement. His close supporters, realizing that nothing would change the convictions of the top party leaders, noted that his opinions among the masses of the voters were known primarily on foreign policy, and they suggested that he make a major address on the domestic policy he advocated for the nation. Willkie agreed, and received his opportunity when a series of meetings devoted to questions affecting the home front were sponsored by the *New York Times*. Willkie's address, on the subject "Our Domestic, Economic, and Fiscal Policy in Relation to Our Well-Being at Home and Abroad," turned out to be another political bombshell. He advocated drastically increased taxes to help pay for the war while it was still being waged. Calling for the imposition of additional levies which would yield *more than double* the net of eight billion dollars that he said would be realized by the proposal already submitted to Congress by the President, Willkie conceded that the standard of living in the United States would go down for a time, but asserted that the postwar period would be more prosperous because it would not begin under a financial handicap. He declared: "So-called political experts tell you that the American people will never stand for a tough tax program . . . I do not agree with those so-called experts. Give the people an understanding of the issues involved and they will do their duty by their country, however incredibly painful it may be."[7] After the war,

---

[7] *Ibid.*, February 3, 1944, p. 1. A financial speech was originally suggested by John W. Hanes, who, at Willkie's request, even drafted an outline for the candidate's approval. Willkie, however, rejected the outline saying that a "lower the taxes" theme was unrealistic and did not agree with his

he said, the individual income tax, particularly in the lower and middle brackets, should be reduced. Willkie also advocated a postwar revision of corporation tax laws, the repeal of the excess profits tax, and the devising of ways and means of stimulating the flow of venture capital into new enterprises.

Republicans were appalled, and the reception of Willkie's speech in Washington was, according to Arthur Krock, "for the most part, dismal confirmation that the elected of the people firmly believe a display of this type of courage and candor by a Presidential candidate, even in wartime, is politically fatal."[8] Professional politicians privately stated that "no man can become President who proposes such things," and at his press conference, President Roosevelt stated that he "did not have the nerve" to support Mr. Willkie's taxation policy.[9] Walter H. Judd, Representative from Minnesota, placed a *Minneapolis Star-Journal* editorial praising Willkie in the *Congressional Record,* but congressmen did not openly discuss the proposal on the floor.[10] The nation's press, however, gave wide publicity to Willkie's plan and most papers expressed admiration for his candor in taking such an unorthodox position in an election year.[11] Within

---

thoughts. He maintained that the economy could easily absorb twice the taxation that was then levied. Hanes argued that such a proposal would kill Willkie politically, and that he would rather that he made no speech at all if this were the line he intended to take. Willkie adamantly replied: "Johnny, you said this was the time for a speech on taxation, and I am making it."

[8] *Ibid.,* February 4, 1944, p. 14. Krock wrote that the New Deal was living proof that a different formula was politically more successful. Raymond Leslie Buell, in a letter to the editors of the *Times,* praised Willkie for his courage, but concluded: "If the American people, fed by New Deal sedatives for the past eleven years, are not ready for Mr. Willkie's strong medicine, then the future of this land is extremely dark." *Ibid.,* February 18, 1944, p. 16.

[9] *Ibid.,* February 18, 1944, p. 16.

[10] *Congressional Record,* vol. 90, p. A976 (78th Cong., 2nd Sess., Feb. 23, 1944). The Minneapolis paper stated that the Willkie suggestion was much sounder financially than the Roosevelt program. The Cowles publication added: "On the central issue of stiff wartime taxes for all who can help bear them, the administration's position is what it has always been: to make this, for the majority and for political reasons, a soft war."

[11] Eugene Lyons, writing in the *American Mercury,* however, thought that the Willkie tax program was presented so late that it failed to present leadership to the Administration's opposition. He wrote: "In his budget message of January, 1943, President Roosevelt declared himself in favor of $16,000,-000,000 of additional taxation. There was no public comment on this from Willkie. Ten months later the Treasury proposed increased taxes of $10,500,000,000. No comment from Willkie. Hearings were then held by the Ways and Means Committee of the House and later by the Senate

the Republican party, however, the program did nothing more than frighten the politicians into intensifying their determination to find another nominee. In advocating higher taxes, Willkie offended the most powerful elements of the GOP — the businessmen from whom he had received support in 1940.[12] While he was running for the presidency that year, Willkie frequently spoke of initiative, incentive, and profits as the stimuli to achievement. In 1944, Willkie had great faith in the character of the American people when he submitted a program which would have placed the basis of that motivation solely on patriotism.

Almost immediately after he had concluded his New York address on taxation, Wendell Willkie started out on a three-week speaking trip across the country. He began his western campaign in Milwaukee by conferring with the slate of delegates pledged to him in the Wisconsin primary election. Admitting the difficulty of his race in the Badger State, Willkie declared: "Here is a Midwest State with an established leadership that holds views opposite to the views that I have on domestic and international affairs . . . I look upon this as a good State for me to make a test and I am anxious to make it. I believe that the rank and file of Republicans should determine who is to be the Presidential nominee. . . . Wisconsin is one of the most difficult States for me to make such a test. I deeply appreciate those who have pledged their support to me,

---

Finance Committee. Willkie did not appear before either committee, nor did he assert himself as the tax bill was on its way through Congress.

"A bill raising only $2,300,000,000 additional passed the House, then the Senate. It was not until this had happened, not until Republicans and Democrats in both houses had gone on record and the bill was beyond any major changes, that Willkie came out with a speech advocating increased taxes of 16 billions. This gesture, though productive of very extensive front-page publicity, was waste motion so far as practical influence is concerned.

"His belated statement was widely hailed as courageous. Yet the only thing that would have required courage . . . would have been the submission of a concrete program for raising those extra billions. Did he propose to obtain them from higher taxes on corporations; on the upper, middle, or lower income brackets; on sales? On all this Willkie was silent. He brought neither national nor party leadership to bear." "Notes on Wendell Willkie," *American Mercury,* 58 (May, 1944), 521.

[12] When Willkie went into Nebraska to campaign for convention delegates, one of the leaders of his opposition was Christ Abbot, a rancher, a director of the Burlington Railroad, one of the wealthiest men in Nebraska, and a candidate for delegate-at-large to the Republican convention in 1944. Abbot summarized the businessman's view of the Willkie proposals when he charged that Willkie's $16,000,000,000 tax program would paralyze food production and lose the war on the home front. *New York Times,* March 31, 1944, p. 14.

and I expect to come back in the middle of March to make a definite campaign."[13]

Willkie then went to Utah, where he addressed approximately 300 party members. His sponsors were GOP national committee members George T. Hansen and Mrs. G. A. Marr; his speech was made at a dinner given by State Chairman David J. Wilson and the central committee. After discussing the heritage of the Republican party, he repeated his proposal for increased taxes and said that though he realized that it was the accepted political formula for a candidate to tell the people that he was for every expenditure and against every tax rise, "someone must tell the American people the truth. That's just the kind of fellow I am. The Republican party has been talking about unsound financial practices for eleven years. Is it going to advocate unsound financial practices now? It has been talking about excessive deficits. What is it now going to do about them? The Republican Party can't win by dodging these basic questions."

In Twin Falls, Idaho, where he was introduced by National Committeewoman Mrs. Emma Clouchek, Willkie described as "illusory" and a "myth carefully cultivated," the assertion that President Roosevelt had such established relations with the leaders of other nations that his continuance in office was indispensable. In Boise, indirectly attacking both Roosevelt (for his silence on a fourth term) and Dewey, Willkie called for full frankness on political issues. "Don't trust any leader," he shouted, "take no man on faith. Make him tell you what he believes." When Willkie left Idaho, Governor Bottolfsen declared: "His straightforward manner made a good impression. I am sure he has made a lot of friends."[14]

In Seattle, in a brief talk from a train-stop, Willkie said with a smile: "I want to tell you confidentially that I am going to be

---

[13] New York Times, February 8, 1944, p. 34.

[14] Ibid., February 10, 1944, p. 34. Ezra R. Whitla of Coeur d'Alene, the Idaho national committeeman, ignored an invitation to meet Willkie at either Twin Falls or Boise. Willkie was met in Boise by Reilly Atkinson, the state chairman. Ray McKaig of Boise, the legislative committeeman for the Idaho Grange, issued a statement asserting that "the farmers of Idaho are overwhelmingly against Willkie. . . . Farm leaders and county organizations are distrustful of Mr. Willkie. . . . To put up a man for President on whom there is such a fight and whom so many farm leaders fear is, to say the least, not good politics. When people are paying to the limit on income taxes and business is staggering under the load . . . it is political stupidity for Willkie to say 'let's increase the taxes . . . more.' " Ibid., February 21, 1944, p. 9.

nominated for President of the United States on the Republican ticket." Later questioned on this point at a press conference, he replied that it was "just between friends." "You wouldn't expect me to say that I will not be nominated," he cracked. Willkie also told reporters that in traveling through forty states, he had been doing everything he could to help others mold the Republican party into an effective unit, but the next night in Tacoma, before more than 4,000 persons, after blasting the New Deal's attack on management, he also warned against Republican reactionaries, malcontents, and panderers of prejudice who might try to dominate its national convention, write its platform, and dictate its nominee for President. In Portland, Oregon, the following day, Willkie said that he would welcome a primary contest with Dewey. "That's the purpose of primaries," he added. "I would be delighted to have him or any other candidate file in Oregon. It is an appropriate method by which members of a party may express their choice of a Presidential candidate. I believe in primaries." In his Lincoln Day address, Willkie censured Roosevelt's policy of pitting labor leaders against one another and against business, and again declared that the Republican party should be the party that represented the growing social obligations of the time — the party to bring unity to America. On February 15, Willkie started for home. He and his supporters believed that the trip, up to this point, had been most successful. His receptions had been well attended, and most of the important party leaders in the area had welcomed him. Though he realized that there was a great deal of anti-Willkie sentiment being voiced throughout the country,[15] he had seen few manifestations of it on this journey. As a result, Willkie sincerely believed at this time that he would be the Republican nominee in 1944.[16]

Willkie returned to New York through Montana, the Dakotas,

---

[15] For remarks criticizing Willkie during this period, see the *Congressional Record*, vol. 90, p. 556 (78th Cong., 2nd Sess., Feb. 1, 1944). Dewey Short of Missouri inserted into the *Record* an editorial from the *Sioux Falls Argus-Leader* entitled "Willkie's Obvious Decline." See also in *ibid.*, p. A621 (Feb. 3, 1944), a statement by Representative Calvin D. Johnson of Illinois, and an editorial inserted by Hamilton Fish called "Dr. New Deal and Dr. My Deal," from the *Port Jervis* (New York) *Union-Gazette* in *ibid.*, p. A708 (Feb. 8, 1944). In Springfield, Illinois, on February 10, 1944, the "National Anti-Willkie Republican Club" was granted a state non-profit charter. The organizers listed as their purpose: "to register our protest with the Republican party that it should not nominate Wendell Willkie for President." *New York Times*, February 11, 1944, p. 17.

[16] Interview with Sam Pryor.

Minnesota, Iowa, and Illinois. He gave an address nearly every night, dined with governors, party professionals, and publishers, and talked with thousands of voters. When he arrived in Manhattan, he said that he was pleased by what he had seen and heard on his tour. All of the news which reached him was not so encouraging, however. Governor Edward Martin of Pennsylvania announced that the Republican organization of that state would oppose the efforts of Willkie or any other candidate to line up convention delegates in the state at the April 25 primaries. Commenting on Willkie's assertion that he would campaign in every state, Governor Martin declared: "We feel it is good, common-sense Americanism for the Pennsylvania delegates to go to the convention uninstructed so they will have an opportunity to talk with delegates from other states and in that way secure the strongest candidate."[17]

Disconcerting information also came from the Democrats. They were damning him with praise. Senator Claude Pepper of Florida, for example, after calling Governor Dewey a "coy candidate" and John Bricker a "Harding," praised Willkie for his "outspoken stand" in favor of international cooperation to maintain peace. Asserting that Willkie was unacceptable to the Republican Old Guard because of his courageous convictions, Pepper said that comparing the 1940 nominee with "these retreating, shifting, word-mouthing candidates" was like comparing a giant to pygmies.[18] To Willkie, trying to convince the members of the Republican party that he should be their recognized leader, this commendation was a kiss of death. The effect of such acclaim merely increased the anti-Willkie sentiment among those who already felt that the former Commonwealth and Southern head was too much like the President. That Willkie needed all the Republican support he could get was self-evident in a Gallup poll released on February 23 which revealed that Willkie received only one-third as many votes as Governor Dewey. Despite his strenuous speechmaking tour, only one-fifth of the people polled still wanted the 1940 nominee to be the presidential candidate in 1944.

In the state of New York, the selection of delegates to the Republican National Convention, which the Republican voters of New York were to approve on March 28, was completed by February 17. The process was completely controlled by the Dewey forces; at

[17] *New York Times,* February 16, 1944, p. 12.
[18] *Ibid.,* February 17, 1944, p. 11.

least eighty-five of the ninety-three New York delegates committed themselves to the Governor's nomination if he would yield to a draft movement. Dewey denied any desire to run, however, and though the nation listened to his every announcement, he concentrated his attention on state matters. In a widely applauded address, he demanded that the surplus funds of New York be saved for postwar reconstruction and veterans unemployment insurance benefits. Reporters noted that he was becoming less arrogant, more understanding and more tolerant. On February 23, he made a specific attempt to withdraw from the Wisconsin presidential primary election scheduled for April 4. In telegrams to the twenty-five delegates, Dewey stated: "I hope you will convey to those who have circulated petitions for delegates to the Republican National Convention using my name that I earnestly request that those petitions be not filed and I want to make it entirely clear that any use of my name meets my strongest disapproval."[19] The message caused some confusion in Milwaukee; some delegates dropped out of the contest but several others ignored the Governor's request and continued the campaign on the existing petitions. On the following day, Leo Egan, one of Dewey's supporters, qualified the telegrams, saying: "Governor Dewey regards himself as pledged not to seek the Republican Presidential nomination, but considers himself free to accept it if the national convention should name him as its candidate." In North Carolina, the GOP convention voted unanimously for a "Draft Dewey" resolution and in Detroit, a Dewey campaign was started among some of the state Republican leaders by U. S. A. Heggbloom, a Detroit attorney. In letters sent to party workers, Heggbloom urged Dewey supporters to get to work in Michigan before "Willkie carries off all the Michigan delegates."

Willkie's campaign was also reported to be gaining in momentum. Mrs. Reynolds planned to open a New York headquarters in the Grand Central Building, and she announced that there would be Willkie buttons and campaign literature in the 1944 campaign, but that there would be no Willkie clubs. She said that Willkie had a better chance to be elected President than he had four years earlier because "the country is ready for him now as it wasn't quite then." The advance organization early in 1944, coupled with the selection of a preconvention manager, was a departure from Willkie's 1940 tactics. By the end of February, Willkie had entered

---

[19] *Ibid.*, February 24, 1944, p. 1.

the Wisconsin, Nebraska, New Hampshire, and Oregon primaries; he had met nearly all of the twenty-six Republican governors who were potential favorite sons, and he expected to obtain much of their support on the second convention ballot. Of the governors to whom he had talked, he believed that only Dewey of New York and Green of Illinois were definitely hostile to his nomination.

On March 10, Willkie went into New Hampshire for one major address before the presidential primary.[20] At the polls four days later, Willkie captured six of the eleven delegates to the national convention, Dewey won two, and three others were unpledged. The *Chicago Tribune* reported that the results were a blow to the "Willkieites" because three candidates expressly pledged to the 1940 nominee were "soundly beaten."[21] This was an overstatement, but inasmuch as Willkie followers had predicted that their candidate would capture nine of the eleven seats, the New Hampshire vote was disappointing. Nevertheless, Willkie had obtained three times as many delegates as Dewey, and, on the surface at least, this was cause for rejoicing.

New Hampshire, however, was not the nation. A Gallup survey released in March revealed that Republican voters, limited in their choice of candidates to Willkie or Dewey, voted only 27 per cent for the 1940 standard-bearer. The poll also indicated that Governor Dewey had more to gain if General MacArthur, Governor Bricker, and Harold Stassen were to drop out of the race, and that though the New England area and the West Coast were the sources of Willkie's strength, Dewey was more popular in every section of the country.[22]

---

[20] *Ibid.*, March 10, 1944, p. 19. Willkie had visited New Hampshire in September of 1943. After this visit, a movement for a Willkie-pledged delegation to the 1944 convention gained much momentum. The impetus, however, had been dissipated in the intervening months by the death of Judge William Britton, former chairman of the Republican state committee and an ardent admirer of Willkie, and by the announcement of his successor, Harold K. Davison, that he believed that the New Hampshire delegation should be unpledged "due to the fact that our primary comes so early and before public sentiment has become crystallized for candidates, and even before the candidates are definitely known. . . ." *The Republican*, January, 1944, p. 17.

[21] *Chicago Tribune*, March 16, 1944, p. 17.

[22] *New York Times*, March 12, 1944, p. 30. The Gallup poll released on March 17, which was restricted to the state of Maine, however, showed Willkie had a two-to-one lead over Governor Dewey in that state. *Washington Post*, March 18, 1944, p. 9. In addition, when Governor John Bricker was a weekend guest at the home of Governor Leverett Saltonstall

Governor Bricker, during this period, presented an interesting example of the organization-oriented aspirant in search of delegations. Though he was an announced candidate for the nomination, he ignored most of the primaries and quietly but diligently traveled around the country discussing his brand of Republicanism and the forthcoming convention. Out of his seemingly patternless agenda there emerged in February and March a well-organized design to promote the Ohio governor's cause. While Bricker personally visited party leaders in Michigan, Missouri, New York, Connecticut, Pennsylvania, and several southern and western states, fourteen campaign lieutenants, each a political public relations specialist, fanned out across the nation, beating the drums for their conservative leader. Operating on the assumption that Dewey could have the nomination if he wanted it, but that a battle for delegates with Willkie might be fruitful if the New York governor declined the nomination, such men as Milo Warner, former national commander of the American Legion, Ed Schorr, the Ohio GOP chairman, Donald Hornbeck, ex-national president of the Young Republicans, and Charles Racine, former president of the Ohio bar association, conducted a "campaign of friendliness" among the leading machine politicians in nearly all of the states. Bricker was also well supported by the Hearst newspaper chain. Seasoned politicians considered it a very shrewd campaign.[23]

Willkie, meanwhile, was forced to turn his attention toward his thirteen-day campaign in Wisconsin. Earlier he had drawn up a statement stepping out of the presidential race because of his discouragement over the reaction to his forthright stand on foreign and domestic issues, but he destroyed the statement when he received a multitude of letters asking him to continue his work.[24] He believed the Wisconsin test to be the most crucial of all the presidential primaries. Isolationism was still alive among much of the heavily German population, and the state had been Dewey's in 1940. If he could win a majority of the twenty-four delegates from this area in which opponents believed him to be weakest, he would be off to a flying start against the New York governor. The drama was

in Newton, Massachusetts, on March 12, Saltonstall reportedly told him that the voters of the Bay State regarded him very highly as a man but that the majority of the delegates to the national convention were friendly to Willkie. *New York Times,* March 13, 1944, p. 25.

[23] *Newsweek,* February 14, 1944, pp. 46-47.

[24] See "Washington Calling," by Marquis Childs, in the *Washington Post,* April 8, 1944, p. 7.

increased by the entry of General MacArthur and Harold Stassen in the race, and by the fact that Wisconsin had an open primary — a situation which meant that voters of both parties could vote in the Republican column.

MacArthur's headquarters in Madison were in lawyer Lucius Squire's office, and the campaign was run by Victor Johnston. Stassen supporters were in the Hotel Loraine with Ralph Timmons in charge. Eighty-one-year-old acting Governor Walter S. Goodland endorsed Stassen but announced that he would not run for a convention seat. Heading Dewey's slate were Bernhard Gettelman, a Milwaukee soapmaker and state senator who had organized the Dewey forces in 1940 and had held the Wisconsin delegation almost intact for him up to the final ballot in Philadelphia, and Secretary of State Fred Zimmerman, who directed an intensive letter-writing and coffee-hour campaign from his own office. However, several Dewey supporters, including Vernon W. Thomson, the speaker of the state assembly, switched to Willkie in February because Dewey would not assert his availability.

Willkie entered Wisconsin on March 18 realizing that the national trend was moving strongly toward the Governor. Consequently, he traveled nearly 1,500 miles and made forty speeches in his effort to sell himself and his program to the voters of the Badger State. The entire two-week period was much like the closing days of the 1940 campaign: a powerful, dynamic, program-laden Willkie condemning the opposition and attempting to rally large but sometimes apathetic crowds to his bandwagon. When it was over, Willkie had made his views crystal clear, but Wisconsin voters preferred someone less candid.

Willkie's campaign began in Richland Center, Wisconsin, on March 18, and concluded in Superior, Wisconsin, on March 30. He campaigned against his Republican opponents as well as against President Roosevelt, and the speeches were uneven in quality. Politically, he made many mistakes. He was not always cordial to party workers upon whom he was dependent; he was uncompromising in his charges that his opponents represented reaction in contrast to his brand of liberalism; and most important, he bitterly criticized his own party members. No matter how valid his comments may have been, they smacked to party regulars of disloyalty to the party as a whole. In many cities he proposed programs of objectives, programs for farm production, and programs of postwar economic necessities. But near the end of the campaign, more and more frequently he thought it necessary to spend much time refuting his GOP opponents and the newspapers that had been so critical of his actions. In a political campaign a modicum of acrimony goes a long way.

In Ripon, Willkie gave an address that Marquis Childs said "may well become one of the vital documents in our political history." Childs then added: "In a moment of bitterness and dissension, of cynicism and indifference, Willkie has with simple clarity defined the dilemma of the Republican Party. And more than that, he has defined the political crisis of our time."[25] The theme of the Ripon address was that the Republican party, if it was to survive, had to stand up and speak out on the important issues before the nation. "A political party," declared Willkie, "can never stand still. . . . Those leaders of a party who insist on applying old formulas to present problems merely because those formulas worked in the past are damaging the party and will eventually destroy it. For they are standing still, whereas the world around them moves." Willkie warned that parties out of power had the constant temptation to indulge in a narrow and negative partisanship and to make every possible issue with the party in power. He declared that negative criticism of everything the Administration did would fail to gain the confidence of the people to whom it would look as if the leaders of the Republicans were more interested in gaining office than in the merits of the issues. He condemned men who were afraid to antagonize any large group within the party or outside of it because they were so eager to gain office, and said that this attitude destroys a party's vitality. Aiming his shafts at Dewey, Willkie asserted that a political party had the task of dealing openly and constructively with issues, that it "must not determine its convictions about these issues by the poll-taking methods." Willkie also criticized the Roosevelt administration, but the importance of the speech was in the forthrightness with which he spoke of the lack of clear alternatives given to the voters by conventional methods with which American presidential aspirants campaign for the nation's highest office.

[25] *Washington Post*, March 22, 1944, p. 11. Professor Dillon reported, however, that the speech was a "gloomy disappointment." "Willkie was tired and his throat was painful. Although some insisted that the script was good, the speech as delivered was one of his poorest." *Op. cit.*, p. 331.

In Green Bay, Willkie, "with more vehemence than he had previously shown in his Wisconsin campaign," again denounced his
rivals for the nomination. He charged that they were avoiding a
discussion of the issues, and that they were defaming him by a
smear campaign. He declared that if isolationists, "of the school of
thought represented by the *Chicago Tribune,*" prevailed at the
national convention, nominated the candidate, and adopted the
platform, Franklin Roosevelt would be re-elected for another four-
year term. In Appleton, Willkie defended his stand on the lend-
lease bill, repudiated the America First Committee, and denounced
those who were trying to prejudice the voters against him through
the use of lies. The pattern was similar throughout the entire
southern part of the state. In Manitowoc before 1,000 persons,
and in Sheboygan before 5,000, Willkie rebuked the "false leadership and political philosophy" of the followers of Colonel Robert R.
McCormick, and in Racine, he assailed Governor Dewey's "peace
plan" by asserting that an alliance with Britain alone would merely
result in more war. The former utility chief then added that the
reason he was not elected President in 1940 was that he had "had
to lug leaders . . . who opposed Selective Service and aid to Great
Britain." In Janesville, Willkie lashed out at those who opposed
international cooperation and who charged that if he were elected,
he would attempt to "boondoggle" the world and give away the
substance of the United States. "That is so foolish," he fumed.
"Certainly no one would expect Wendell Willkie to give away the
substance of the nation. I did not get where I am by being a nut."

Willkie spoke in Beloit, Burlington, Elkhorn, Kenosha, and
Evansville. When he spoke of his farm program, he told listeners
that he favored neither the New Deal regimentation of the farmer
nor the abandoning of the farmer wholly to the law of supply and
demand. He praised labor's contribution to the war effort and
proposed its adoption of a three-point program to democratize
itself. In the Milwaukee Auditorium, where he was introduced by
Walter J. Dunn, international representative of the Carpenters and
Jointers Union, AF of L, he recommended, as he had in 1940, that
a member of the President's cabinet should represent labor in its
contacts with the government.

In most of his Wisconsin speeches, Willkie spoke on a variety of
issues, frequently dividing his time between a condemnation of the
Roosevelt administration and a denunciation of groups within the

Republican party. By the time he left Milwaukee for his swing to the west and north, he spoke against certain Republicans at nearly every stop. In LaCrosse, Willkie quoted a statement made by General Edward Stuyvesant Bragg, a Wisconsin delegate to the 1884 Democratic National Convention, who, in advocating the nomination of Grover Cleveland for President, said: "We love him for the enemies he has made." He then added: "If I have no other reason to ask for your good will, I am entitled to at least some of your support for the enemies I have made. I have the most valuable list of enemies of any public or quasi-public figure in America."[26]

Farther north, Willkie braved a snowstorm to drive two hundred miles, speaking to capacity crowds in Menomomie, Chippewa Falls, and Eau Claire. In these cities, Willkie again attacked the Roosevelt administration but told his listeners that the real issue of the Wisconsin primary was the leadership of the GOP. In Eau Claire, after criticizing those who tried to win elections by remaining silent on the basic issues or by trying to capitalize on the discontent of those dissatisfied and unwilling to bear the burden of war, Willkie exclaimed: "I wouldn't accept the nomination of a party like that on a silver platter set with diamonds. . . . I don't want a delegate from Wisconsin unless they [sic] believe in me, and I want them all to make the Republican party stand up."

Willkie concluded his Wisconsin campaign in Superior. He had made forty speeches in thirteen days and was extremely fatigued. He told reporters that he would be satisfied if he won a majority of the delegates, but his supporters expected him to be more successful. Vernon Thompson, who headed the list of Willkie-pledged candidates for delegates-at-large, said he believed Willkie would win all twenty-four of the Wisconsin delegates.[27]

---

[26] New York Times, March 29, 1944, p. 19. Willkie said that false reports, accusing him of being a Communist one day and a capitalist the following day had been circulated by his enemies. "Obviously I am not a Communist because my strongest belief is belief in freedom," the aspirant asserted. "I recognize that a great experiment is going on in Russia and that Russia is a great and powerful country. My interest lies in preventing war between Russia and the United States." Concerning the accusation that he was a capitalist, Willkie declared: "I am not exactly impoverished but I have no financial or business connection that at any time affects my political thinking. No man who knows me ever suggests that he can control me. Anybody who knows me knows that I am a complete independent." Ibid., March 30, 1944, p. 15. These refutations illustrate the type of charges Willkie had to face and the level on which he was forced to campaign during the Wisconsin tour.

[27] Ibid., March 31, 1944, p. 15.

Actually, except for the heroic, challenging, and vigorous speaking by Willkie personally, the Wisconsin campaign was ineptly run. No local organization was developed, much of the publicity was written in New York, local leaders who were favorable to Willkie were not allowed to make the decisions which would have properly pitched the campaign to Wisconsin voters, and Willkie's advance organization in the field was practically nonexistent.[28] For the most part, the candidate carried the burden alone. In spite of all this, the country was, in a sense, obligated to Wendell Willkie for his campaign in March of 1944. At a time when all other Republican candidates refused to take a position on issues, foreign or domestic, Willkie made himself and his stand as clear as he was oratorically capable. He campaigned against both the Roosevelt administration and what he called the "Toryism of the Republican Party's Old Guard." At times, he also remembered he was attempting to obtain a nomination and invited his Republican opponents "to get in or get out" of the Wisconsin race.

Basically, however, Willkie's effort was wasted on Wisconsin because the political climate among its voters made his acceptance impossible. His words fell, for the most part, on deaf ears. The record of the Republican party in Wisconsin, as illustrated by the record of its representatives on the floor of the House prior to 1944, was one of complete opposition to the principles for which Willkie stood. During the period of preparedness, the Republican members of the House from Wisconsin voted unanimously *for* continuation of the mandatory arms embargo which prohibited all aid to the European democracies, and unanimously *against* permitting American merchant ships to be armed (although Germany declared its intention to remove Allied shipping from the seas), the reciprocal trade program, the Selective Service Act supported so strongly by the 1940 Republican nominee, and a year later, on the very eve of the attack on Pearl Harbor, the extension of the draft act. They opposed, again unanimously, the passage of the lend-lease bill, and they voted unanimously, or were paired, against the first seven-billion-dollar appropriation bill under the Lend-Lease Act after that Act had passed the Congress and was signed by the President.

Willkie's invasion of Wisconsin in the face of this overwhelmingly isolationist record illustrated the desperation of his primary test, the sincerity of his convictions, and the pressure upon him to

---

[28] Dillon, *op. cit.,* pp. 329-31.

prove his leadership. The question of just whom Willkie was to lead, however, was his perpetual dilemma. In 1940 he had discovered that New Dealers and many independent voters refused to desert President Roosevelt to follow him. Shortly after the 1940 election, it was abundantly clear that he was no longer the leader of a large group of the spokesmen for the Republican party in and out of Congress. It was this very fact that made the strongest argument against Willkie's candidacy for the Republican presidential nomination in Wisconsin in 1944. He simply was not the leader of a majority of the Republicans in that year. The party leaders had not only refused to vote as Willkie had suggested they vote, they had openly defied and opposed him. Moreover, Willkie's statements that the Republican party was the party of labor, world leadership, and progressive social actions were not consistent with the voting record of the GOP representatives, and there was doubt that Willkie could control or dictate any action that would make the congressmen change their thought.

If Willkie was to win the presidential nomination, he had to do it as an individual personality with a personal platform, not as a party leader. As a personality, Willkie was a powerful, courageous, and obstinate politician who had a program that urged heavier taxes rather than "economy" as a way to reduce indebtedness, who warned the farmer that he could never expect to go back to the "good old days" of unlimited production, and who called upon the people for sacrifice rather than capitalize on the distaste for the readjustments the war had made necessary. Willkie presented an admirable, and in some ways realistic, program of a type that traditionally had not been used to obtain votes in the United States.

Accordingly, as the primary election on April 4 drew near, observers were unable to ascertain just what effect Willkie's campaign had had on the Wisconsin voters. William K. Hutchinson, a staff writer for the *Washington Times-Herald,* wrote that Willkie was generally conceded to be a heavy favorite to win the primary simply because his opposition was so thoroughly split. Governor Dewey had tried to withdraw from the race, and Lieutenant Commander Harold Stassen and General Douglas MacArthur were both in the Pacific and had made no personal efforts to wage campaigns. Wisconsin State Senator Bernhard Gettelman, who, with 8 others on a Dewey-pledged slate of 24, had withdrawn at the insistence of the New York governor, gave Dewey 5 delegates, and most of the remaining posts to Willkie. Lester Bradshaw, the Wisconsin manager for Bricker (who was not entered in the Wisconsin primary), predicted 15 "certain" for Willkie and conceded that he might obtain 5 more. Democratic State Chairman Thomas King forecast a minimum of 15 delegates for Willkie, and other political analysts acknowledged the possibility that Willkie might surprise Wisconsin's experienced politicians by drawing heavily from Democrats voting in the Republican primary and thereby win a much larger portion of the total Republican delegation. Fred R. Zimmerman, the leading Dewey-pledged delegate who had refused to withdraw from the primary, however, was the only individual whose prediction was accurate. He bet a hat that Willkie, despite his heroic campaign against three noncontesting opponents, would not win a single delegate.[29]

Several days before the election, Willkie traveled to Nebraska to make a series of speeches for his candidacy in the Nebraska primary. His pattern of attack was essentially the same. In speeches in Lincoln, Hastings, Kearney, and Grand Island, he criticized President Roosevelt and his administration, warned the people against supporting those in the Republican party who were working deals and combinations to defeat him, and challenged the GOP to take a forthright course in domestic and foreign affairs in order to attract the independent voters. On April 4, while he was in Norfolk, Nebraska, he heard the reports of the Wisconsin primary election. As Governor Dewey accumulated substantial leads in district after district, Willkie refused to issue a statement and went to bed. The following day, in Omaha, he delivered a bitter attack on the Roosevelt foreign policy in an address he had written the day before the Wisconsin primary. After its conclusion, Willkie changed both his tone and topic completely as he said to his 3,000 listeners:

I wish I could speak to you from my heart tonight. I cannot, because there are too many factors that prevent it. If I spoke of what's on my mind, I would make too great a castigation of American politics.

I had been encouraged to believe that the Republican party could live up to the standards of its founders, but I am discouraged to believe that it may be the party of negation. It is apparent that the average citizen fails to realize the far-reaching effect upon him of what is going on in the rest of the world or to realize that a war anywhere has its effect upon him. I had been hopeful that the Middle West, in which so many moral causes have been started, would again find the leadership that is needed.

[29] *Newsweek,* April 17, 1944, p. 24.

. . . I want the Republican party to be the leader, not the follower, in cooperation with other nations so that the fires of war can be restrained. . . . Perhaps the conscience of America is dulled. Perhaps the people are not willing to bear the sacrifices, and I feel a sense of sickening because I know how much my party could do to make it worthy of its traditions.

Willkie then read the text of his formal withdrawal from the presidential race. He declared:

It has been my conviction that no Republican could be nominated for President unless he received at the convention the votes of some of the major Midwestern States. For it is in this section of the country that the Republican party has had its greatest resurgence. Therefore, I quite deliberately entered the Wisconsin primary to test whether the Republican voters of that State would support me personally and in the advocacy of every sacrifice and cost necessary to winning and shortening the war and in the advocacy of tangible, effective economic and political cooperation among the nations of the world for the preservation of the peace and the rebuilding of humanity. The result of the primary[30] is naturally disappointing and doubly so since the candidate who led the poll for delegates is known as one active in organizations such as the America First, opposed to the beliefs which I entertain.[31] As I have said many times, this country desperately needs new leadership. It is obvious now that I cannot be nominated. Therefore, I am asking my friends to desist from any activity toward that end and not to present my name at the convention. I earnestly hope that the Republicans will nominate a candidate and write a platform which really represents the views which I have advocated and which I believe are shared by millions of Americans. I shall continue to work for these principles and policies for which I have fought during the last five years.

Willkie's withdrawal was highly dramatic. The audience listened in silence and rose to applaud him as he finished. Many went to the stage to shake hands with him, and others lingered with puzzled expressions on their faces, obviously astonished at hearing that the 1940 nominee was stepping out of the contest. Almost immediately

[30] The final result of the Wisconsin vote was 15 pledged and 2 unpledged delegates for Governor Dewey; 4 for Stassen; 3 for MacArthur; and none for Willkie. On the basis of votes cast, the rout was even more complete. The top Dewey delegate polled 143,031 votes; the top MacArthur man, 76,811; the top Stassen delegate, 67,495. The leading Willkie candidate polled only 49,535 votes. Willkie's delegates ran last in every contest. *New York Times,* April 20, 1944, p. 36.

[31] Fred R. Zimmerman, Wisconsin Secretary of State, who, as a Dewey-pledged delegate-at-large candidate, led the field in the election, denied the Willkie inference that he was connected with organizations such as America First. *Ibid.,* April 6, 1944, p. 15.

after the meeting was concluded, Willkie and his party boarded a late train for New York.

In Washington, Joe Martin declared that he was still counting on Willkie to keep working for the party, and Governor Bricker, who eventually became the vice-presidential nominee in 1944, declared that Willkie had stimulated interest in the campaign by "freely and courageously discussing his conception of the issues that are facing us in this very serious situation." Senators Ball of Minnesota, Wherry of Nebraska, and Burton of Ohio all applauded Willkie and expressed a hope that he would continue to press his efforts to effect a change in the national administration in November. Senator Austin of Vermont remarked: "Many of the views which Mr. Willkie has advanced I have held for years. I hope there will be someone who will come into the field to take up the torch and carry it forward." Senator Reed of Kansas thought that the Wisconsin primary election indicated that Willkie had "talked himself to defeat." "Ever since his reference to his 1940 speeches as 'just campaign oratory' and his practically demanding a purge of Republican members of Congress, he has talked too much. . . . I think Willkie is a man with brains, energy, and ability," Reed concluded, "but that he is the worst case that can be cited of a man talking himself into an impossible situation and the Wisconsin returns show it." Senator Robert A. Taft asserted that Willkie had apparently recognized the inevitable. "It is unfortunate," he added, "that he allowed his natural disappointment to lead him to attack Republicans who disagree with him on foreign policy. Nevertheless, his withdrawal will produce a greater unity[32] of all Republicans behind the principles declared at Mackinac."

Editorial comment from the nation's press ranged from a statement in the *New York Times* that "Mr. Willkie's . . . withdrawal from the campaign takes out of the contest for the leadership of his party the candidate who . . . has been best fitted by experience, by ability and by conviction for the Republican nomination . . ." to a conclusion in the *Chicago Tribune* which said that "From

[32] Sidney Hillman, president of the Amalgamated Clothing Workers of America, and chairman of the Political Action Committee of the CIO, declared: "Yes, there is unity in the camp of reaction today. There is unity of the Tafts, the Hoovers and the Nyes with the old America First crowd and Gerald Smith. . . . They rejoice today because the Wisconsin primaries have consolidated their control of the Republican machine on which they hope to ride into power." *Ibid.,* April 9, 1944, p. 1.

today on Mr. Willkie can be dismissed as a minor nuisance. His power to harm the Republic, by denying its voters a choice of policies, has, by his own confession, ended."[33]

Political correspondents, who sought an explanation for Willkie's defeat,[34] blamed isolationism in several cases, but this argument was only partially correct in that it failed to take into account the total vote for Willkie and Stassen, which exceeded that cast for Governor Dewey. Luther Huston reported that the defeat of Willkie was regarded by many in Washington as a sweep of the political tides in the farm states against the Administration with whose foreign policy Willkie was too closely associated. In perspective, the explanation of the election would appear to be more political and personality-oriented than these analyses of issues. Willkie was defeated because of his own activities, because of the long-held hostility of Republican leaders toward the 1940 candidate, and because of the uncertainty of the masses of Republican voters about his attitudes on GOP domestic policy.[35] When Willkie spoke of issues, he spoke realistically but as an internationalist; when he spoke of the party, he analyzed its difficulties correctly but harshly. He was courageous, but he was impolitic. He opposed too many of those whose support he needed, and when the polls opened, the professionals and the antagonized turned out against him. More broadly, Willkie had failed, over the course of

---

[33] *Ibid.*, p. 17. The *Tribune* added that it would surprise no one if Willkie came out openly for Roosevelt. "The Republican party has never had his allegiance, nor do its members feel that they owe him any. He is the debtor, not they. If Mr. Willkie takes a walk, he will walk alone." In contrast to this statement, the *Times* asserted: "He [Willkie] will have his honor in due time, from all sections of that party. The Republicans are certain to find and to acknowledge, we believe, that to no other man in recent years have they reason to owe so deep a debt of gratitude for services performed." *Ibid.*, April 6, 1944, p. 22.

[34] Willkie told Raymond Moley that it was his opinion that the opposition of the county leaders was the most important factor in his defeat. See Moley's *27 Masters of Politics*, p. 54.

[35] Arthur Krock wrote that Willkie was not sufficiently "regular" for the Wisconsin voters, and that reports also indicated that these voters felt quite certain that he could not defeat the Democratic ticket. There was conflicting opinion on this point, however, and Ernest K. Lindley claimed that Willkie's withdrawal had removed the candidate whom most top-ranking Democrats regarded as hardest for President Roosevelt to beat. He wrote: "The political judgment of these Roosevelt supporters . . . was based on the elementary political precept that the strongest candidate is not necessarily the man best liked by the regulars of the party, but the man who can win the most marginal votes." *Newsweek*, April 17, 1944, p. 24.

three years, to perform his proper role in the leadership of his party. He had criticized and castigated, but he had only half-heartedly worked at party organization. He had, as he frequently stated, devoted his time to making the Republican party worthy of national and world leadership, but in the process he had made practically no attempt to heal party schisms through a compromise of conflicting interests. He had insisted that it was his way or no way, and he was unable to be the critic and the leader at the same time. He literally forced the GOP into policy declarations, but in doing so, he also forced its cautious leaders to look for some other individual who fit the times with less rancor, less vindication, and fewer enemies. The scoldings brought results, but coupled with Willkie's lack of patience and his lack of feeling for American grass-roots politics, the fruits of his labor were lost to him. The loss was serious, not only to Willkie, but to the country as well.

When Willkie arrived back in New York, he declared his intention to return to his law practice, but rumors were already circulating that he would accept a position in the Roosevelt Cabinet. His own views on this matter were disclosed in a letter to Marquis Childs dated May 10, 1944. With reference to a report that he would be offered the post of Secretary of the Navy, Willkie stated:

. . . obviously no one from the outside becoming Secretary of the Navy at this time, no matter how great his administrative skill or his wide knowledge, could possibly master the multiple ramifications of the Navy Department or the Navy and its activities short of several months. . . . The only objective the administration could possibly have (even if it is considering such a move, which I seriously doubt) in offering me the position would be for the political benefits. . . . If I had a notion that I was the only one qualified to serve as Secretary of the Navy, or in any other position, I would, of course, accept it if offered. Or if I really thought that such action on my part could unify the people, I would, of course, accept. Not believing either of these things, I would, of course, not accept. By the same token, the many suggestions that are made to me that I should in advance agree to accept some important position in Government under the anticipated Republican administration as a condition of my support of Mr. Dewey, or support him in the hope of some position, leave me equally cold. . . . I happen to believe these are critical times, almost determinative times."[36]

The rumors, Willkie's attitude notwithstanding, continued to persist, but they were only conjecture in view of the fact that he actually was not being considered for a Cabinet position by the

---

[36] *Congressional Record,* vol. 90, p. A5093 (78th Cong., 2nd Sess., Dec. 13, 1944).

President. This was confirmed in a letter to the author from Harold L. Ickes, then Secretary of the Interior, in which he stated: "The Republicans were already well represented there and my suspicion is that President Roosevelt would have felt doubt as to whether Willkie could play satisfactorily on a team. I would further suspect that the influence of Harry Hopkins, which was very great in those days, would have been against Willkie. Hopkins was not a man to let anyone get near the President, if he could prevent it, who might develop as much influence as he himself had. After all, Willkie was a very engaging character. . . ."

More realistically, in the political sphere during the spring of 1944 four courses were open to Willkie. He could attempt to organize a third party, but this was conceded to be an impossibility at so late a date. He could, as the *Chicago Tribune* had suggested he might, bolt to President Roosevelt, but this, too, was highly improbable because of his personal antipathy for the President and because it would have been contrary to all of his public and private utterances. His third alternative was that he could merely express disapproval of both parties through a series of speeches stressing issues or omissions — endorsing neither candidate without an explicit pledge. Finally, Willkie could support the GOP nominee. It was reported in April that most politicians were betting that he would follow the third course — which he did. Willkie felt as strongly as ever about his convictions concerning postwar policy, and he thoroughly believed that once the Allied armies had invaded Europe, a resurgence of support for his position would materialize. His effort, therefore, had to be aimed particularly at forcing the Republican party, and the now apparently invincible Dewey, into a positive commitment to international organization and worldwide cooperation. He could do this only by stating clearly what he thought should be America's position and endeavoring to coerce the New York governor into agreement with his declared principles under the threat of withholding an endorsement if his statements were ignored. This threat was considered to be significant because Willkie's personal following, in spite of his defeat in Wisconsin, was still estimated in terms of millions of voters. Correspondents believed that in a close campaign, his assistance to the GOP candidate would be of "necessitous importance." From all outward appearances, however, the professionals of the Republican organization realized no need of his support during the convention period. In the summer of 1944, therefore, all Willkie could do was to exert what pressure he could on the GOP platform and wait for the crisis of the campaign to bring the overtures for his endorsement. And with the abandon and frankness of a middle-aged statesman freed from the necessity of maintaining political availability, he wrote, negotiated, and waited.

9 FREE SPIRIT

Wendell Willkie went into semi-retirement for nearly two months. Early in May, he wrote letters to twenty newspaper columnists in which he stated his determination not to sit by while the peace of the world was again wrecked as it had been in the twenties. The purpose of the personal letters, which were not published until after his death, was to inform the newsmen of his intention to try to influence both Dewey and the Republican platform on the issue of international cooperation.[1] Two weeks later, in his first public appearance after his withdrawal from the nominating race, he attended a nonpolitical gathering of six hundred people at a dinner honoring Walter White on his twenty-fifth anniversary as secretary of the National Association for the Advancement of Colored People. Though Willkie made no political address, he contributed five thousand dollars from the Willkie Trust Fund, established with the proceeds from the sale of *One World*, to help finance the activities of the Association.

On June 12, the first of Willkie's series of seven articles on subjects due to be presented before the platform committee of the 1944 Republican National Convention appeared in many of the nation's newspapers. The articles were written at the request of six Republican papers in the hope that discussion concerning the various topics would be stimulated before the convention met.[2] Because

---

[1] Joseph Barnes, *op. cit.*, p. 364.
[2] The papers were the *New York Herald Tribune*, the *Boston Herald*, the

286

these articles represent the final expression of Willkie's thought, and because they are illustrative of his ideas stripped of any immediate political ambitions, they are invaluable to any understanding of his eventual impact.[3]

On the issue of "Federal Power and States' Rights," Willkie declared that a strong central government was necessary to prevent disruption of the economic and social structure by the variety of conflicting authorities and interests. He said that the problem was not the "worn-out issue of states' rights versus strong central government," but that of government administered under law. "Any national administration in a modern complex industrial society must exercise vast powers. The United States cannot be divided into forty-eight separate economic units. . . . And the more we move, as we must move, into the affairs of the world, the more this will be true." Willkie asserted that the solution to problems lay not in a weakened central government but rather in assuring the proper use of the power granted to that federal government. That meant, he said, local administration of numerous federal functions in their local application, and the substitution of government by law for government by caprice and unlimited discretion. Willkie called upon the Republican party to state clearly and fight for the issues involved in federal power and its proper use, but "not . . . in conjunction with those who use that mask to prevent social and political advance, or . . . others who . . . really seek to weaken the federal government to such an extent that the United States will be unable to play its appropriate role in the world. . . ." He concluded that to build such a government — strong centrally and just in its administration — would be in the finest tradition of the Republican party.

On the second problem, that of the American Negro, Willkie outlined the rights to which the Negro is entitled, and called upon the Republican party to commit itself unequivocally and specifically to federal anti-poll tax and anti-lynching statutes. He said that millions of Negroes distrusted the Democratic party which deprived them of their votes in Atlanta while it sought their votes in Harlem,

---

Minneapolis Star-Journal and *Tribune,* the *Des Moines Register* and *Tribune,* the *Portland Oregonian,* and the *San Francisco Chronicle.*

[3] The complete articles may be found in the *New York Times,* June 12-18, 1944, inclusive, or in a small pamphlet entitled, *An American Program,* by Wendell L. Willkie, published by Simon and Schuster in 1944.

that Negro leaders were alert and educated and sophisticated, and that the Negro asked only for the rights to which he was entitled. These rights, economic, educational, physical, and the rights of Negroes in the armed services, Willkie maintained, represented an obligation for the Republican party to fulfill, completely consistent with the principles upon which the party was founded.

On the topic of "Social Security," Willkie, who had originally gained national prominence in his fight against the New Deal, declared that "protection against old age, illness and economic misfortune must be a *right* for everyone." The former Commonwealth and Southern chief asserted:

A free economy, by its nature, entails a certain amount of fluctuation and risk. As a matter of fact, much of its strength and its very freedoms are directly related to its risks. But one cannot enjoy the freedoms of such a society without a minimum of economic security. Therefore the risks must be spread sufficiently to guarantee that all members of society are protected against the final economic disaster of going without the bare necessities of life. This is the function of the social insurances.

Willkie then demanded that complete medical care be available to all (within a plan sufficiently flexible to allow for experimentation and growth and respecting the value of the practicing physician's relationship to his patient), that there be enacted an adequate and uniform system of federal unemployment insurance, and that provision be made for America's youth so that the feeding, clothing, shelter, and medical care of children would no longer be determined by the income of the parents of those children. He insisted:

There is nothing new in providing men with minimum protection. When our society was predominantly agricultural, Abraham Lincoln's Homestead Laws offered to the people of the United States what was then necessary protection — land and a chance to build a home. Today when our society is predominantly industrial, the formulas must change. And all the resolutions for the preservation of the enterprise system will not do one fraction as much to preserve it as the assurance to men and women of the protections which they are rightfully demanding, protections which are basic to their time.

The Republican party should see to it that they get them.

Willkie's ideas on the "Economy of Demobilization" were significant in that he recognized, in 1944, that the aftermath of the war would bring a tremendous rise in western Europe of state ownership of resources and industries. Willkie asserted that to combat this trend, it would not be necessary for the United States to adopt similar controls, but he suggested that there be set up some type of cooperative mechanism which would act as a clearing house for information and constructive programs. This was a job for industry, labor, and government in order to spread the wide fluctuations of the economic cycle over the years. "But we must be realistic enough to acknowledge that the best efforts of private industry, even supplemented by such intelligent cooperation, will not always be enough. In addition the federal government must exercise a counter-cyclical influence against depression in order to preserve a reasonably high level of employment." Willkie called for an expanded economy, but warned: "The Republican Party cannot meet the need of the postwar period by merely passing resolutions in favor of 'free enterprise.' It must realize the inevitability and the justness of the people's demand for both protection and opportunity, and it must find the answers, answers which exist uniquely within a responsible enterprise system."

In writing on the topic of "Labor," Willkie admitted that there was considerable truth to the view of labor leaders that they had not had a fair break before the advent of the Roosevelt administration. He maintained, however, that there was nothing inherent in the nature of the two parties that cemented them into the roles which the labor propagandists had assigned them. He stated that the Republicans should acknowledge the necessary requirements for the protection of labor under conditions existent at that time and support the continuation and improvement of the federal Wages and Hours law. He urged the broadening of the base of social insurance, the repeal of the Smith-Connally act banning strikes, and the preservation of labor's right to strike. He asked labor to become responsible, to drive out its racketeers, to adopt democratic procedures, and account for its funds and activities both to the public and to its own membership. Finally, illustrating how well he understood the needs of the Republican party but also how far he had departed from a substantial wing of its membership, he emphasized: "The Republican Party must demonstrate visibly and tangibly that it appreciates the contribution of labor to our economic well-being. It must leave no doubt that it understands that labor has legitimate grievances, and justifiable aspirations toward a more secure place with larger participation in our modern industrial life."

Concerning the "Tariff and International Trade," Willkie said: "Certainly the pattern of our foreign policy will have to be fashioned to government supervision, allocations and perhaps even price fixing. For state-controlled economies [of the other nations of the world] can sell without regard to costs." He declared that it was indispensable for America to revise its tariff and cooperate in a policy of international currency stabilization in order to create an atmosphere conducive to the development and growth of a free economy in the rest of the world. He warned the Republican party not to repeat its error of the period following the previous war in which it had made it necessary for other nations to erect barriers against the United States.

In the final article through which Willkie attempted to influence the delegates to the Republican convention, he condemned the Roosevelt foreign policy as having produced "dislike, distrust and loss of prestige for the United States without achieving the intended political aims. . . ." He admitted that there had been sharp divisions within the Republican party concerning the extent to which it was desirable for the United States to maintain and develop relations with other nations, but he asserted: "surely the long debate, the events through which we lived before the war, and the war itself have made plain that American policy cannot be separated into two unrelated compartments, one labeled Foreign Policy and one Domestic Policy. The two areas of action are inseparable; what happens in either immediately affects the other." "Furthermore," Willkie declared, "we have learned conclusively that in the modern world the United States cannot survive militarily, economically or politically without close and continuing cooperation with the other nations of the world." The defeated candidate then made a plea that the peoples of the small nations be given a voice in shaping the world in which they were to live.

In discussing the "sovereignty" of the United States, Willkie said that the Republican platform should be clear and unambiguous, that it should not adopt narrow nationalistic interpretations of the term, and that it should not substitute quibbling words such as "integrity." "It should emphasize that our sovereignty is not something to be hoarded, but something to be used. The United States should use its sovereignty in cooperation with other powers to create an effective international organization for the good of all. History should have taught us," he wrote, "that we gain more by cooperating to protect the general interest than by working alone for some imagined separate interest."

This was the program by which Willkie thought the Republican party could be rejuvenated. Using his recommendations as a foundation, he wrote a proposed platform which was sent to the convention when it convened in Chicago,[4] but its reception was perfunctory and cold. Willkie did not personally attend the convention, for though he received an invitation to attend the meetings, he was not specifically invited to address the delegates. When reporters asked Harrison Spangler whether overtures had been made to Willkie to present his views on issues before the platform committee, he remarked that Willkie was in the same category "as any other person who may wish to appear before the Committee."[5] Herbert Hoover had been invited to address the convention and Alf Landon was a delegate from Kansas, but because "Willkie had practically seceded from the party," the National Chairman had deliberately refused to issue an invitation to the 1940 candidate to be on the stage.[6]

When the national convention opened in Chicago on June 26, it was obvious that the nomination of Dewey was assured. Most of the Willkie supporters, Weeks, Williams, Baker, Pryor, and Cake, had accepted the inevitability of the Governor's victory and had pledged their support. Among the delegates, a pervading spirit of harmony and optimism was present, and party leaders were determined to preserve it. The conclusions of the resolutions committee were so closely guarded, except from Dewey, that even Republican governors who were delegates could not get copies of the proposed platform to study.[7] Willkie, however, obtained a copy of a tentative draft which contained the foreign relations plank that was nearly identical to the final version submitted to the convention:[8]

---

[4] The platform may be found in the *New York Times,* July 11, 1944, p. 10, or in Wendell L. Willkie, *An American Program,* pp. 26-37. It was not until July 10, 1944, that the news of Willkie's proposed platform was released to the press.

[5] *New York Times,* June 16, 1944, p. 32. Dr. Dillon reported that Dewey used his authority as head of the New York delegation to block any effort to name Willkie to that body. *Op. cit.,* p. 346.

[6] Interview with Harrison Spangler. After the Wisconsin primary, Spangler specifically asked several close friends of Willkie if he would support the party's choice, whoever he might be. Willkie reportedly refused to commit himself, and Spangler decided not to give the unpredictable Willkie an opportunity to address the delegates. This was, of course, unique in recent party history.

[7] Wendell Willkie, "Cowardice at Chicago," *Collier's,* 114 (September 16, 1944), 11.

[8] According to Dr. Dillon: "All members of the Committee were pledged

We shall seek to achieve such aims (to keep America secure, to keep the Axis powers impotent to renew tyranny and attack, and to attain peace and freedom based on justice and security) through organized international cooperation and not by joining a World State. We favor responsible participation by the United States in post-war cooperative organization among sovereign nations to prevent military aggression and to attain permanent peace with organized justice in a free world. Such organization would develop effective cooperative aims to direct peace forces to prevent or repel military aggression. Pending this, we pledge continuing collaboration with the principal United Nations to assure these ultimate objectives. . . .

It (such organized cooperation) should promote a world opinion to influence the nations to right conduct, develop international law and maintain an international tribunal to deal with justiciable disputes. . . . Pursuant to the Constitution of the United States any treaty made on behalf of the United States with any other nation or any association of nations, shall be made only by and with the advice and consent of the Senate of the United States provided two-thirds of the Senators present concur.[9]

Not more than a few hours later, Willkie issued a statement denouncing the plan as ambiguous, subject to opposing interpretations, and capable of being used to throttle effective collaboration by the United States with other countries to maintain peace. He told the reporters who had been invited to his offices at 15 Broad Street that he chose this manner of making his views public because he had not been chosen as a delegate to the convention. Willkie likened the 1944 platform to that which the Republicans adopted in 1920, and added:

A Republican President elected under the proposed platform of 1944 could with equal integrity, announce that the United States would not enter any world organization in which the nations agreed jointly to use their "sovereign" power for the suppression of aggression. . . . The net result would be no international organization. No effective international force for the suppression of aggression. No peaceful world . . . we

---

to secrecy until after the scheduled reading of the platform to the convention . . . Senator Taft and others were determined that Willkie should be prevented from stampeding the convention into amendments of the platform by any adverse comments which he might issue in New York. Finally, Willkie turned to a distinguished newspaperman with a request for a copy of the release issued to the press. Upon the understanding that he would not use the release until after the platform had been read to the convention, a copy was given to him on Sunday evening preceding the opening of the convention. Whether Willkie misunderstood the agreement or willfully broke his promise could only be revealed by the man himself." *Op. cit.*, p. 347.

[9] *New York Times,* June 27, 1944, p. 13.

should speak in words forthright, clear and strong. We should demand the immediate creation of a Council of the United Nations as a first step toward the formation of a general international organization. . . . We should advocate the use of American sovereignty in cooperation with other powers to create a continuing international organization for the power of all with the power to uphold its decisions by force if necessary. . . . To use this leadership, for our own enrichment and that of mankind, will not be to weaken the sovereign power of the American people; it will be to widen it and make it more real.[10]

Willkie made it clear that his criticism was not of Senator Austin of Vermont, chairman of the platform subcommittee on foreign affairs, whom he termed "an able, forthright statesman," and whom, he said, he hoped his own statement would assist in obtaining "a better resolution."

Surprise at Willkie's outspoken declaration was evinced by most of his friends in Chicago, who said that they would issue a statement of their own which would endorse the party plank.[11] The *New York Times* reported that this was taken to indicate a definite break with Willkie. In addition, Senator Austin asserted:

It [the plank on foreign policy] is not ambiguous. It definitely stands for the employment or direction of military or economic reactions to prevent or repel military aggression. . . . It is for development of international law and establishment of a world court. There is no ambiguity about the use of the words "sovereign nations." It intends that sovereignty shall be used internationally to keep the peace. Mr. Willkie is mistaken in saying that if the policy were carried out it would result in no international organization. It does not support an international integrated

---

[10] *Ibid.*

[11] Russell W. Davenport, writing after Willkie's death, made a reference to this situation: "And in the end the party was his undoing. The motto for his life might be *'Et tu, Brute'*; for it was the desertion of self-styled friends and associates that hastened, if it did not actually cause, his death. He was not 'disillusioned' by these desertions; he was shrewd enough to know that few men are capable of sacrificing their own interests for the principles they profess. But he was practical enough to see that each defection from the cause merely added to the impossible load he was carrying. Immediately before and after the nomination of Thomas E. Dewey, when hundreds of professed One Worlders were yielding to the forces of political expediency, the tragic little scene was re-enacted almost every day: 'Why, so-and-so was one of the best friends I had in the world. He went all-out for the limitation of sovereignty. How can he do this now?' The complaint was not merely personal. It was the complaint of a giant dedicated to a cause which he recognized as greater than himself: a cause that was too big to carry all alone." "The Ordeal of Wendell Willkie," *Atlantic Monthly,* 176 (November, 1945), 71.

army. Its military resources are vested in a council with power to direct them in the right regions to the right places on the right occasions.[12]

Disagreement with Willkie was also voiced by Senators White of Maine, Ball of Minnesota, and Burton of Ohio, while Senator Taft, who had been chairman of the Republican resolutions committee, challenged "any adherents" of Willkie to press before the committee his protest against the foreign policy plank. "I'd be very surprised if the plank adopted by the Democratic platform committee suits Mr. Willkie any better than that of the Republicans," he added. Finally, Senator Arthur Vandenberg of Michigan, who was eventually to become the Senate's Republican spokesman for international cooperation, defended the proposed plank against Willkie's criticism. He said that he hoped it was "too late" for anyone to break down the efforts made to unite the Republicans "upon a program to preserve America and exert our national power for organized peace with justice in a free world."

Presumably Willkie would have been satisfied with the conduct of the Senate Republicans in their voting on international cooperation in 1946: to a large degree he had forced the party into a position from which it could not retreat. Vandenberg and public sentiment had developed his case, and in most respects, Willkie would have been gratified by the action taken by the United States in the establishment of the United Nations organization. In any event, Willkie should have realized that in view of his own defeat in Wisconsin the party would not accept the proposals he sent to Chicago. Moreover, if Thomas E. Dewey was to be the new Republican nominee, allowance had to be made for his desires and interpretations of foreign policy rather than those of the 1940 candidate.

When the Republican platform was submitted to the convention, it was quickly adopted without changes. Willkie's attack on the foreign-policy plank was unheeded. On the following day, Dewey was nominated on the first ballot to head the Republican ticket for the Presidency in 1944. Willkie sent the new candidate a message: "Hearty congratulations on your nomination. You have one of the greatest opportunities in history." Observers immediately noted that the telegram omitted any promise of support in the

---

[12] *New York Times,* June 27, 1944, p. 13.

campaign. When reporters asked Willkie about this message, he refused to comment upon either the platform or the nominee.[13]

After the Republican convention, there were constantly recurring reports that Willkie might be nominated for the United States Senate from New York to oppose Senator Robert F. Wagner. These reports, though never specifically repudiated by the 1940 candidate, were treated with scorn by Willkie's associates who said that they believed he would not accept the nomination "under any circumstances." Of more political significance were the efforts by supporters of both Dewey and Roosevelt to obtain Willkie's endorsement or at least to give the public a general impression that Willkie favored their respective candidates. Samuel I. Rosenman wrote that in a July 5, 1944, conversation with Willkie, the former Republican nominee had said that "he had been subjected to terrific pressure to come out for Dewey — pressure from Dewey himself, and from others who were house guests with him over the holiday; that the pressure on him from our [the Democratic] side was also substantial and was growing."[14] Endeavors to obtain Willkie's support for the Republican ticket were naturally more intense than the efforts made by the Democrats. Willkie's friends within the Republican party, including Baldwin, Pryor, and Weeks, requested on numerous occasions that he issue a statement in support of Dewey, and Dewey's personal effort to gain Willkie's support came just prior to the Dumbarton Oaks conference in August, 1944. In a campaign address, Dewey had expressed a fear that the small nations of the world might be discriminated against in any postwar international organization. Therefore, Secretary of State Cordell Hull invited the New York governor or a representative to confer with him over the details of the peace plan. Dewey decided to

---

[13] *Ibid.*, June 29, 1944, p. 1. Werner W. Schroeder of Illinois, an old Willkie foe, was elected to the post of vice-chairman of the Republican National Committee. Considering the fact that Governor Dewey probably approved the selection of Schroeder before the election, this action was viewed by observers as a move that would make it difficult for Willkie to support Dewey in the presidential race. In addition, Sinclair Weeks, a close friend of Willkie, was dropped as committee treasurer. Informed by reporters of the changes in party management, Willkie laughed and commented: "They're making it complete, aren't they?" *Ibid.*, July 1, 1944, p. 26. Weeks and Ralph Cake, however, were subsequently named to the fifteen-man Republican executive committee. *Ibid.*, July 6, 1944, p. 32.

[14] See Samuel I. Rosenman, *Working With Roosevelt* (New York, 1952), p. 465.

sent John Foster Dulles instead of accepting the invitation himself.[15] Just prior to the Dulles-Hull talks, Willkie was invited to Albany to present his views concerning what he thought the Republican stand should be, but he refused the invitation.[16] The attempt to contact Willkie began at midnight on August 20 when Elliott V. Bell, the New York Superintendent of Banks who had been one of Willkie's close advisers on the candidate's train in 1940, made a telephone call to him in the presence of Dewey from the New York Executive Mansion. Willkie, however, had retired, and the members of his home refused to disturb him. Dewey then sent Willkie a telegram which stated: "Foster Dulles and I have conferred extensively today and I should like to have the benefit of your views if you could join us at any time on Sunday . . . before Mr. Dulles goes to Washington. . . ." To this wire, Willkie replied:

. . . I shall be glad to meet Mr. Dulles on his way to the conference. . . . I wish I had known of your desire for my views prior to your original statement. [This was a reference to Dewey's statement expressing alarm over a possible world domination by the big powers.] For several years I have been deeply concerned about the ill fate of the small nations inherent in military alliances between any or all of the Great Powers. But I have been equally concerned that there should not arise among our Allies the notion that our party would in any way obstruct or endanger the success of an international conference.

I therefore made inquiry about ten days ago of the Washington authorities to determine if our Government intended to insist upon the protection of the position of small nations in the forthcoming Dumbarton Oaks conference. I was given strong affirmative assurances. Therefore, I had determined to await results before entering into any public discussions.

However, since . . . the discussions between the Secretary and Mr. Dulles are to be of a nonpartisan character, I shall be glad to give your representative, Mr. Dulles, freely of my views.[17]

On August 21, Willkie and Dulles discussed Willkie's views on foreign policy for an hour and a half. They agreed on all facets of a future international organization except the extent to which Congress would supervise the President in his use of any interna-

---

[15] *United States News,* September 1, 1944, p. 28.

[16] The *New York Times* reported that Willkie's refusal to make the trip to Albany was based on his desire not to be associated with the Dewey campaign: "Had he come here, his picture with Mr. Dewey would have been taken and sent all around the country and would have been interpreted as support of Mr. Dewey." *New York Times,* August 21, 1944, p. 8.

[17] *Ibid.,* p. 1. For a satirical account of all the activities which led up to the Willkie-Dulles discussion, see "Conference," in the *New Yorker,* 20 (September 2, 1944), 14-15.

tional armed force which might be created under a United Nations organization. Willkie wanted no legislative strings on the President's action. At the conclusion of the meeting, the two men issued a joint statement declaring that there had been a full exchange of views not animated by partisan considerations nor having to do with any candidacy.

Political analysts noted that Willkie was still sitting on the fence, and Arthur Krock reported that politicians in Washington admired Willkie's "even-handed dealing with the overtures made to him" by the two candidates. He asserted that Willkie was absolutely earnest in his plan to know what kind of foreign policy would be pursued by the candidate he supported, and that he was not satisfied by either the President or Dewey. Meanwhile, he had no intention of being used for political build-ups, public misconceptions, or designs to improve electoral chances at his expense.[18] Nevertheless, Republican liberals continued to urge Willkie to clarify his party loyalty and endorse Dewey. For personal, political, and ideological reasons, however, Willkie did not highly respect Dewey as a candidate, and though he had his secretaries compile data with which to re-evaluate the Governor's record, he was uncertain whether Dewey's newly asserted internationalism was based on principle or pressure — whether his views in 1944 or those expressed in 1941 reflected his true beliefs. Unfortunately, Willkie died before he reached a conclusion which would have provided guidance for his followers. Several people have testified that Willkie asserted, during the summer of 1944, that he would never support President Roosevelt for a fourth term. The evidence is equally formidable, however, that up until a week before his death, Willkie

---

[18] *New York Times,* August 25, 1944, p. 12. Willkie wrote a letter to Krock in which he thanked him for the article and added: "I happen to think of both Mr. Roosevelt and Mr. Dewey as what I call pragmatic politicians. If one states it kindly one says they seek to articulate the opinion of the masses. If one says it unkindly, one says that they follow the polls and engage in vote-catching. I am not interested in the characterization, but I am greatly interested in creating a body of public opinion which will force either or both of them to go in the direction in which I believe they should. In other words, I believe that either one of them can be classified under either of those general terms, internationalist or isolationist. When it became politically expedient, Franklin Roosevelt repudiated the League of Nations. When it became politically expedient, Thomas Dewey attacked the Lease-Lend Bill. Likewise, both of them have made strong statements in favor of international cooperation. In the foreign field, I want to do what I can to help force them in the latter direction. . . ." Joseph Barnes, *op. cit.,* p. 382.

was still endeavoring to force both Roosevelt and Dewey into a more extensive commitment to international cooperation, and that he had not made up his mind whether or not to advocate Dewey's election openly — or even to declare publicly that he would vote for him.[19]

Among the principal reasons for Willkie's ambivalence, in addition to the fact that he was completely identified among his followers with the Republican party, was the lure of three extremely intriguing political eventualities — all of which involved President Roosevelt — which were in latent or formative stages during the last few months of his life. The first was the possibility, during the period after the Republican convention while the Democrats were maneuvering to dump Henry Wallace, that Willkie might be tapped by Roosevelt as his vice-presidential running mate. Though much has been written since about the President's insistence upon the nomination of Harry Truman,[20] the available evidence indicates

[19] Though Drew Pearson wrote that Willkie had intimated that he would support the President, Willkie indicated at various times to Governor Baldwin, Henry Luce, and Styles Bridges that he would not support Roosevelt for re-election. *New York Times,* October 22, 1944, p. 1; October 10, 1944, p. 16, and personal interview with Senator Bridges. David Lawrence, relying on letters received from Willkie in July and August and on a conversation with him on August 30, was convinced that Willkie "had an open mind and would not make his decision until later in the campaign." He wrote that Willkie was "sincerely waiting for Governor Dewey to express himself further and to come closer to the Willkie viewpoint on international affairs." *United States News,* October 20, 1944, p. 35. H. Fred Willkie, the 1940 nominee's brother, told reporters: "I think there is no question as to where he would have stood. . . . He felt that neither party was meeting the issues squarely. He kept trying to put pressure on both of them to meet this issue. I think he eventually would have come out for Dewey if Dewey should have become a bit more liberal, especially in his foreign policy. I believe the pressure being exerted by my brother was bringing Dewey around to that liberalism." *New York Times,* October 10, 1944, p. 16. Roscoe Drummond received a letter from Willkie, written seven days before his death, in which Willkie said that he had "not finally decided" which presidential candidate he would support in the 1944 campaign. On October 2, Willkie had asked one of his personal aides to prepare for his study a documented memorandum setting forth his conception of the factors of the campaign which would properly be weighed in making his ultimate decision. Drummond, *op. cit.,* p. 467. Finally, on October 21, in order to terminate the conjecture about Willkie's support, Mrs. Willkie appealed to the press: "I am sure he had not made his decision. No one could speak for him while he was living; and I ask, out of respect for his memory, that no one should attempt to speak for him now." *New York Times,* October 22, 1944, p. 1.

[20] See particularly Rosenman, *op. cit.,* pp. 444-51, Sherwood, *op. cit.,* p. 530, and Harry S. Truman, *Years of Decisions* (Garden City, N. Y., 1955-56), pp. 190-94.

that Roosevelt had "put out feelers" to Willkie and that some sort of an offer was made to the 1940 GOP candidate.[21] By whom the offer was made and the extent to which the President was willing to be bound by such a bipartisan arrangement have never been revealed. Willkie would not discuss these details even with his closest friends, though he argued with Gardner Cowles that he had a right to consider the ramifications of the offer[22] even if, out of loyalty to his Republican friends and his distrust of the President, he had no intention of accepting it. Lem Jones, Willkie's secretary, stated that he was certain that the whole scheme was nothing more than a nebulous dream among some of Roosevelt's supporters who preferred Willkie to Truman. He also asserted that because of basic personality differences, Willkie never would have accepted any nomination under Roosevelt. In his opinion, Roosevelt would not have carried out the plan "if the chips had been actually down."[23] In any event, the plan was never consummated,[24] and Harry Truman, Roosevelt's first choice all along, was nominated on the second ballot.

The second possibility for cooperation between the President and Willkie was the proposal, negotiated between his former aide, Bartley Crum, and a presidential administrative assistant, David K. Niles, that Willkie go to Europe as Roosevelt's official civilian representative as soon as the war was concluded. Though Willkie wanted to wait until after the election before he made any decision

---

[21] On July 17, in response to a telegram from Senator George Norris to the President protesting any overture to Willkie, Roosevelt wrote: "I don't think there is any possible danger of Willkie, though feelers were put out about a week ago. . . ." Joseph Barnes, *op. cit.*, p. 371. On the other hand, Harold L. Ickes wrote to the author: "There was some talk of Mr. Willkie as a vice presidential candidate on the Democratic ticket in 1944 but I do not believe he was ever 'actually being considered.' The Democratic Party was very certain that it would win in 1944 and, in those circumstances, the leaders would have been loath to hand the vice presidential nomination to a Republican who had deserted their party (I use the word 'deserted' in no invidious sense). Besides, the administration probably felt that it had done as much as was necessary [in the way of including Republicans in the Cabinet] to foster national unity. . . ."

[22] *Ibid.*

[23] Interview with Mr. Jones.

[24] The proposal, of course, might have run into difficulty in New York even if the political leaders had managed to iron out the difficulties. Both Willkie and Roosevelt were legal residents of the Empire State, and the Twelfth Amendment to the Constitution of the United States requires the electors to vote for President and Vice-President "one of whom, at least, shall not be an inhabitant of the same state with themselves."

on the offer, Crum tried to arrange a conference between Willkie and the President for the Labor Day weekend. Willkie, however, had already planned to spend the holiday in Indiana, which he did, though he scheduled a dinner to discuss the matter with Crum on the Wednesday following his return.[25] This engagement was never kept, for it was on this Wednesday that Willkie entered the Lenox Hill Hospital. By the time the war ended and a civilian administrator was sent to Germany, all of the principals of the drama were changed.

The final, and potentially most significant, relation between Roosevelt and Willkie involved correspondence dealing with an important and fundamental change in the American party system — a realignment of parties along ideological lines. According to Rosenman, the idea of uniting the liberal wings of the two great parties belonged to Willkie, who had discussed it with Governor Pinchot, who subsequently mentioned the conversation to Roosevelt.[26] The President was delighted about the possibility and during the final week in June, 1944, he asked Rosenman to arrange to see Willkie and to tell him of his enthusiasm. "I think the time has come," he declared, "for the Democratic party to get rid of its reactionary elements in the South, and to attract to it the liberals in the Republican party. Willkie is the leader of those liberals. He talked to Pinchot about a coalition of the liberals in both parties, leaving the conservatives in each party to join together as they see fit. I agree with him one hundred per cent and the time is now — right after election. We ought to have two real parties — one liberal and the other conservative. As it is now, each party is split by dissenters. Of course, I'm talking about long-range politics, something that we can't accomplish this year. But we can do it in 1948, and we can start building it up right after the election this fall. From the liberals of both parties Willkie and I together can form a new, really liberal party in America."

Rosenman called Willkie and, after stressing that he wanted to discuss something of interest that had nothing to do with the election, arranged to have lunch with him at the St. Regis Hotel in New York on July 5. The meeting was held in complete secrecy. Rosenman told Willkie that the President had been thinking about party realignment ever since the abortive purge of 1938, and that

---

[25] Joseph Barnes, *op. cit.*, p. 378.
[26] This material is from Rosenman, *op. cit.*, pp. 463-70.

since he knew that he could not beat the Southern conservatives in
their home districts, he was ready to form a new party leaving them
out. Rosenman added: "He wants to team up with you, for he is
sure that the two of you can do it together; and he thinks the right
time to start is immediately after the election. If it is impossible for
you to start talking with him about it before election, then you can
wait until later; but he wants to do it — whether he wins or loses in
November."

Willkie agreed that he and Roosevelt were thinking along the
same lines, and observed that the 1944 Republican convention and
his own preconvention campaign had convinced him that the Republican party was completely in the control of reactionary leaders.
He talked of the bright future international cooperation could have
when sponsored by a liberal group and expressed enthusiasm that
the postwar political conflict would be waged with clear-cut issues
on both national and international affairs. "You tell the President,"
he declared, "that I'm ready to devote almost full time to this. A
sound, liberal government in the United States is absolutely essential to continued co-operation with the other nations of the world.
I know some of these reactionaries — especially those in my own
party. They'll run out on the other nations when the going gets
tough — just as soon as they can."

For more than two hours, Rosenman and Willkie analyzed men
and groups that would fall into the respective coalitions. Willkie
then expressed a willingness to discuss the plan more fully with the
President, but insisted that such a meeting be held after the election
lest it appear that he was maneuvering or being maneuvered into
an endorsement of the Democratic ticket. Rosenman reported to
the President both Willkie's enthusiasm for the plan and his reluctance to do anything about it before the election. Though Roosevelt
seemed to understand this situation, he was unable to wait, and on
July 13, a week before the conclusion of the Democratic National
Convention and only eight days after the meeting between Willkie
and Rosenman, the President wrote the following letter to Willkie
indicating that he was already making plans for the revision of the
political parties:

Dear Wendell:

I will not be able to sign this because I am dictating it just as I leave
on a trip to the westward.

What I want to tell you is that I want to see you when I come back,
but not on anything in relationship to the present campaign. I want to

talk with you about the future, even the somewhat distant future, and in regard to the foreign relations problems of the immediate future.

When you see in the papers that I am back, will you get in touch with General Watson? We can arrange a meeting either here in Washington or, if you prefer, at Hyde Park — wholly off the record or otherwise, just as you think best.

Always sincerely yours,

FRANKLIN D. ROOSEVELT

This letter, so encouraging and so innocuous on the surface, prompted Willkie to write a serious reply which, however, he neither signed nor mailed because the first note to him was leaked to the press. In the unmailed letter, Willkie stated:

My dear Mr. President:

I have your gracious note of the thirteenth. The subjects concerning which you suggest we have a talk on your return from the West are, as you know, subjects in which I am intensely interested. I am fearful, however, that any talk between us before the campaign is over might well be the subject of misinterpretation and misunderstanding. And I do not believe, however much you and I might wish or plan otherwise, that we could possibly have such a talk without the fact becoming known.

Therefore, if it is agreeable with you, I would prefer postponement of any such talk until after the November election.

I hope you will understand that I make this suggestion solely because you in a great way, and I in a small one, have the trust and confidence of people who might see in the most innocent meeting between us at this time some betrayal of the principles which each of us respectively hold so deeply.

Believe me, with great respect,

Sincerely yours,

Willkie realized that if he was to have any leverage at all on Dewey and if he was to maintain the allegiance of his liberal followers, he could not allow his motives and his position to become suspect or distorted by political columnists. Therefore, instead of sending the letter, he attempted to clarify his situation with the President personally through the good offices of former Governor James Cox of Ohio.[27] Unfortunately, this negotiation was handled so secretly and with such discretion by Cox that Roosevelt did not understand whom Cox was representing and in the end, as a result of additional leaks of information and subsequent denials by the President that he was in communication with Willkie, the 1940 Republican candidate simply issued a statement that he preferred to have no conference with the President until after the election.

---

[27] Joseph Barnes, *op. cit.*, pp. 375-76.

The President did write another letter to Willkie on August 21 explaining that when he had told reporters that he had not invited Willkie to Washington, he really had forgotten that he had dictated the previous letter before his trip to California and Hawaii. Roosevelt denied any knowledge of the source of the leak to the press and apologized for it and reiterated his invitation to Willkie to visit him either in Washington or at Hyde Park. This was the final letter from the President to the one man in the Republican party's history who had both the desire and the characteristics necessary to cooperate in the reorientation of America's political parties.[28] By 1948, both men were gone from the political scene, though the revolt of the Dixiecrats against President Truman made the situation ideal for realignment. The subject was not seriously discussed that year, however, for as Sam Rosenman wrote at the time the southern revolt was developing: "Even if Truman were willing, where is there another Willkie?"

While all of these related facets of personal bipartisanship were taking place in 1944, Willkie continued to write, criticize, argue, and advocate. On September 8, the first of his last two public articles, entitled "Cowardice at Chicago," was released in *Collier's* magazine. In it Willkie accused the Democrats and Republicans alike of "double talk, weasel words and evasion in their platforms." He criticized both parties for borrowing from the past the timidities, outworn doctrines, and mistakes long rejected by history. He wrote that the two platforms paralleled each other in that both tried to "conciliate and win all elements of the population without offending others within or without the parties." On two particular issues, "international policy" and "our Negro citizens," Willkie made his final claims on the parties in the hope that they would "arouse and make articulate a body of public opinion that would demand clear statements of purpose, not only from the presidential candidates but from the vice-presidential and congressional candidates as well."

Willkie accurately asserted that the foreign policy of the United States "is now and will be for generations the paramount, the absorbing question before us. *And upon its wise solution will depend*

---

[28] Chronologically, the negotiations between Willkie, Crum, and Niles took place after the correspondence about party realignment. Because of the apparent imminence of victory in Europe in the autumn of 1944, President Roosevelt was quite serious in his endeavor to have Willkie act for him in Europe. I have treated these events inversely in relation to what I consider to be their importance as party issues in recent history.

the domestic welfare of the American people." While stressing a permanent peace, he again criticized both party platforms for over-emphasizing "sovereignty." Willkie wanted to exchange a "small measure" of the traditional sovereignty for the greater good of pre-venting wars among men. He wanted to *"limit the sovereign right of all nations to make war at will. . . ."*

The second major point of foreign policy with which Willkie took issue was the Republican statement that both treaties and agree-ments should be subject to the consent of the Senate. He cited the history of America's major efforts to participate in international cooperation with other countries and concluded that "for fifty years the two-thirds rule in the Senate has operated to frustrate every major effort at international collaboration by this country." He did not want this history repeated. Willkie called for the United States to take the initiative in new reciprocal agreements of a multilateral nature so that an increase in world trade would result. He was certain that if the United States would eliminate the causes of international anxiety, "both in principle and in practice," hope of avoiding World War III in the foreseeable future would be in-creased. Willkie's final words on foreign policy were directed to his party: "As a Republican, I naturally hope that my party will by its forthright statement of wise and farseeing purposes . . . make the party's position clear and unmistakable. For if the Republican Party should come into power, what its authorized leaders now say will have an immense effect upon its course of action when in power. And if it should be destined to lose, its very preservation as a party will depend on whether, in our country's present critical moment, it had the courage and wisdom to be a party not of expediency but of principle."[29]

A month later, *Collier's* carried Willkie's final article, entitled "Citizens of Negro Blood." It was a summary of Willkie's often expressed ideas concerning injustice to the colored people in the United States. He charged: "the Negro lives in our midst under discriminations which differ from the racial discrimination practiced by our enemies, the Nazis, only in that ours are illegal and that we are free — if we wish — to fight against them." He called the 1944 platforms of both parties "tragically inadequate" in dealing with the Negro's problems. Though he asserted that the Republican plat-form was distinctly better than the Democratic, he scored the GOP

[29] Wendell L. Willkie, "Cowardice at Chicago," pp. 11 ff.

for demanding a constitutional amendment to abolish poll taxes, arguing that a federal anti-poll tax statute had an excellent chance of being accepted as constitutional by the Supreme Court. Willkie thought the Republican plank favoring anti-lynch legislation was equally unrealistic in that it failed to specify whether state or federal legislation was meant.[30] He also called for an immediate end to discrimination in the armed forces, again asserting that "once more the Republican remedy is inadequate."[31] On the over-all treatment by the Republican delegates to the national convention of the problems involving the Negro, Willkie concluded:

They had a magnificent chance to state in modern terms a code of practice that would make real the very principle of freedom upon which the party was founded. However, apparently over-anxious to obtain the support of the Southern delegates for the nomination of their favorite candidate, and fearing the loss in the election of racially smug Northern conservatives, they failed to measure up: they failed to gain the confidence of millions of the Negroes of America. . . .

I write this article with the deliberate intent of helping to arouse a public opinion that will require these candidates to put aside generalities, evasions and pious platitudes and deal in concise, concrete terms with this human, this national, this world problem.[32]

These articles, released in September, had been written shortly after the conventions ended in July. Late in August, Willkie went to Rushville to rest and to inspect his corn crop. On the train, he suffered the first pains of what was eventually to be a series of severe heart attacks, but he was determined to keep his condition a secret. In Indiana, when his condition became serious, he spurned the advice of an Indianapolis physician that he go into the hospital immediately, and took a train back to New York. The following day, September 7, he entered the Lenox Hill Hospital for what reporters were told was a "check-up and rest" after a "little stomach

---

[30] With reference to the Democratic civil rights plank, Willkie quoted a comment from a leader of the National Association for the Advancement of Colored People: "To call the section on the Negro a plank is a misnomer. It is best characterized as a splinter. Badgered by professional bigots from the South and dictated to by Northern political machines more interested in votes than in principle, the Democratic mountain labored and brought forth a mouse of evasion by merely asserting that rights guaranteed by the Constitution exist and that Congress 'should exert its full constitutional powers to protect those rights. . . .' "

[31] The Republican platform called for a congressional inquiry into discrimination in the armed forces. Willkie considered this both unnecessary and too time-consuming.

[32] Wendell L. Willkie, "Citizens of Negro Blood," *Collier's*, 114 (October 7, 1944), 11 ff.

upset." Later, it was revealed that the stomach disorder was complicated by a heart condition that required medical observation, but the public was never informed of the seriousness of the fourteen separate heart attacks Willkie endured in the hospital. Actually, near the end of September, his condition had improved sufficiently so that he was scheduled to be discharged from his book-strewn hospital room, and friends were preparing a place in which he could recuperate in Florida. During this period, Willkie wrote letters, edited the final draft of *An American Program,* and even granted a few interviews. Moreover, accounts of these sessions indicate that to the final days of his life, he was still extremely concerned about a liberal Republican party and a strongly international cooperative postwar policy.

On October 4, Willkie was stricken with a streptococcic throat infection. A lung congestion developed, and both afflictions affected his weakened heart muscles, producing an acute cardiac condition. With the administration of penicillin, Willkie showed steady improvement until he suffered a relapse on October 6. On October 7, Willkie ran a high temperature, but at midnight he was sleeping well. At 1 A.M., he awoke and joked with his nurses and doctors. At 2 A.M., however, he suffered another attack and had to be returned to his oxygen tent. At 2:20 in the morning of October 8, 1944, Wendell L. Willkie died of coronary thrombosis.

People across the nation were stunned by the news of Willkie's death. Thousands of telegrams, from national and international leaders, from enthusiasts and foes, from Roosevelt and from Dewey, and from many who signed their wires, "a friend," or "a follower," poured into the Willkie apartment on Fifth Avenue.[33] On a half-hour memorial radio program, Russell Davenport eulogized Willkie as a "citizen of the world . . . who rose above party to espouse principles that had to do not with immediate political victories but

---

[33] Roosevelt praised Willkie's courage which, he said, prompted him more than once to stand alone and to challenge the wisdom of counsels taken by powerful interests within his own party. Dewey called Willkie "one of the great men of our time," and Taft declared that Willkie had been an ardent, aggressive fighter for the ideals in which he believed. Bernard Baruch saw in Willkie's thinking a likeness to that of Woodrow Wilson, and the Redcaps of Pennsylvania terminal in New York sent a wire to Mrs. Willkie saying that her husband "was the most courageous champion in recent time of all minority groups. . . ." Scores of other prominent Americans spoke their tributes, and Willkie was reportedly mourned in London, Moscow, and Chungking. *New York Times,* October 9, 1944, pp. 1-15.

with the future of America and the cause of freedom." Similarly, the *New York Times* declared, in a lengthy editorial salute that was typical of newspaper comment throughout the nation: "Party, country and One World owe this man a debt which the years will not discharge. More than any other single man he fought to lead his party from isolation to cooperation on the stage of world affairs. As much as any other man he helped to shape for debate and action the great issues of the most critical years in the lifetime of the American people. . . ."

A New York funeral for Willkie was held from the Fifth Avenue Presbyterian Church on October 9. Eight days later, Wendell L. Willkie was buried in East Hill Cemetery in Rushville, Indiana. The Reverend Dr. George A. Frantz, pastor of the First Presbyterian Church at Indianapolis, speaking at this final service, stated: "If men ask, 'Where is his monument?' let them but look around at a world one in integrity like his own; one in courage like his; one in a fiery faith in democracy such as burned in him; one in a passionate dedication to freedom like that which consumed him."[34] And one year later, before 2,000 persons who attended the ceremonies for the dedication of a memorial building to Willkie in New York, Sumner Welles, the former Under Secretary of State, recounted that Willkie had spent only a few years in public life and that "within that short space of time, he became an outstanding force for human betterment, and a symbol of popular hope, not only in his own nation but throughout the world of free and democratic peoples."[35]

The world "one in integrity" was short-lived after World War II, and the world of free and democratic peoples diminished gradually as the forces of nationalism against which Willkie strove were resurrected over the earth. But Willkie's words still contain the symbol of popular hope if the world leaders would read them. Perhaps, therefore, Willkie was ahead of his time; or perhaps he envisioned a world that was too full of idealism to become a reality. Because he died when he did, Wendell Willkie, the planner, the prophet, the idea-man, never became the architect of the world organization he dreamed. That was left to other men, with different talents and different temperaments, more skilled, perhaps, in the ways of American politics, who were able to capture the prize that eluded the vigorous, courageous, and amateur democrat.

---

[34] *Ibid.,* October 18, 1944, p. 16.
[35] *Ibid.,* October 9, 1945, p. 38.

10 WENDELL WILLKIE AND THE NEW REPUBLICANISM

Roscoe Drummond once wrote that "the time will come when it can be seen that Wendell Willkie . . . made a greater contribution to the security, the welfare, the progress and the vision of his Nation than most elected Presidents."[1] Today, fifteen years after Willkie's death, any endeavor to evaluate the accuracy of this prediction must take into consideration both the development of world politics and the evolution of the Republican party.

In retrospect, it can be seen that Willkie's contribution to his party and thus to his nation was essentially in three areas: he stimulated the adoption by the Republican party of international cooperation as an accepted foreign policy; he plotted a course for a more liberal domestic policy and thus established a foundation — but only a foundation — for what eventually was called Modern Republicanism; and he gave his party a blueprint for a program of civil rights which, if followed, might well insure moral and electoral success for a long time to come.

Most clearly, Willkie did indeed contribute to the security of the nation. Before President Roosevelt died, he is reported to have said: "We might not have had Lend Lease or Selective Service or a lot of other things if it hadn't been for Wendell Willkie. He was a godsend to this country when we needed him most."[2] Later, the

---

[1] *Christian Science Monitor* (Boston), October 10, 1944, p. 14.

[2] Sherwood, *op. cit.*, II, 230.

Mackinac Island declaration in favor of participation by the United States in a postwar organization was a victory for the former Hoosier. His frequent, fiery speeches and his best-selling book predicting an interdependent world and its need for international cooperation presaged the acceptance by both parties of a more realistic foreign policy. To implement this cooperation, Willkie endorsed and demanded lower tariffs and increased international trade. On the assumption that the day of economic imperialism had come to an end, he argued for the stabilization of international currency exchange and long-term private investments — objectives that are slowly becoming realities. In Willkie's view, foreign policy and domestic policy were inseparable, and he accurately saw that what American representatives did abroad was both dependent upon and a part of the policy at home. This, in 1944, he called the great new political fact. He realized, as no contemporary of his party at the time realized, that the United States could not survive militarily, economically, or politically without close and continuing cooperation with the other nations of the world. And he recognized, as not all Republicans have since recognized, that political leadership of the world can be lost through ineptness and delay.

To be sure, Willkie's contribution cannot be evaluated apart from the era in which he lived, and that era cannot be transferred to the present. After the war, Willkie's cause was continued by Senators Vandenberg, Austin, Ball, and many others who eventually concluded he had been right; and subsequently, of course, technological developments in nuclear energy, travel, and space brought about a wide acceptance of a global concept of America's responsibilities. The by-products of these scientific advances made Willkie's "one world" a political problem and an inevitable necessity, if no longer a utopian ideal. Willkie's achievement was that he provided a base from which his successors could work; he persuaded enough members of his party to reconsider America's role in international politics so that it was impossible for the GOP to retrace its path to pre-1940 ideologies. An acknowledgment of this contribution was made on February 18, 1957, by Republican Senator Jacob Javits, who told a group in New York City: "I feel it may truly be said that Wendell Willkie was the political father of that concept of international responsibility which is so fundamental to modern republicanism."[3]

[3] *Congressional Record,* vol. 103, p. 2095 (85th Cong., 1st Sess., Feb. 21, 1957).

On the domestic scene, Willkie provided a fresh philosophy for the Republican party in business, labor relations, and civil rights. As a businessman, Willkie wanted a government under which the rules by which business operated would be consistent and stable, a government that would be willing to help the small businessman, a government which would simplify the regulations governing business, an atmosphere that would allow investment capital to be raised more easily, a revised tax structure reducing the tax load carried by small business, and government research laboratories in which particularly effectuated projects designed to aid business would be fostered. These objectives certainly have been espoused by officers within the Eisenhower administration.[4]

Simultaneously, however, Willkie opposed as a collectivist technique the artificial control of prices by business as well as by government. He realized that monopolies produced a restriction of the economy, that they were a perversion of the democratic order which eventually would destroy the right to risk and profit and would diminish civil liberties. Because business in the past had denied the principles of competition and free enterprise and had not grasped the social implications of profit-making, Willkie thought that some governmental intervention was essential. John Chamberlain wrote that even when Willkie was the utility industry's spokesman for free enterprise against government monopoly, "in the privacy of a 'well stocked' club," he used to "twit" his fellow industrialists. " 'You've got no kick,' he told a group of them on one occasion, 'the government's only doing to you fellows what Rockefeller did to the little oil men back in the Eighties.' "[5] Though Willkie's concern for business kept him a Republican to his death, he was cognizant of the fact that capitalism also must distribute its benefits to the masses by paying sufficient wages and reducing prices when possible. If

[4] D. W. Brogan wrote in 1956: "Insofar as the business community has been (a) soothed, (b) educated by 'l'experience Eisenhower,' this is a national gain, no doubt highly paid for, but not too highly paid for *if* it has really occurred. The businessman has learned that there is not an ideal 'business' way of doing things that applies equally well to all human activities from religion to sport. He has learned that the idea of an economy running itself, with no political guidance, is a utopian dream. Of course, not all businessmen have learned this. There are, as they say in the Midwest, 'exceptional children' who are very hard to teach, but the brighter members of the Eisenhower Administration have learned a lot. No administration will enter office again with *simpliciste* ideas of January, 1953." "The Eggheads and Ike," *New Republic,* 135 (September 10, 1956), 9-10.

[5] John Chamberlain, "Candidates and Speeches," p. 52.

business failed to do this, its private matters became public because they affected the public welfare, and the government was obligated to intervene in the establishment of prices, production, and profits. Willkie's frequently stated idealistic hope was that an economic climate could be created in which governmental supervision would be minimized, and he always preferred stimulation to regulation. Nevertheless, he also thought that if private enterprise abused its freedom, the government was the authority that could compel a basis for competition.

The paradox of such a position for those who must act and assume the responsibilities for action, in contrast to those who, like Willkie, only make recommendations, is the essence of the difficulty faced by any modern Republican administration. The regulation of business within any economic milieu by administrators devoted to liberating business makes for an ambivalent policy at best and no policy at all unless abuses are widely publicized. The GOP is supported by, and gives access to, the business community, and if a balance is established between business and its economic regulation, the administration's position is likely to be on the private side of the scales. The entire history of the Republican party affirms this posture, and Eisenhower has had his dilemmas in this respect. Moreover, the dilemma was also Willkie's; for it is probable that had he been elected, his liberalism within his party would have been, by association and of necessity, similar to the "dynamic conservatism" assertedly practiced by the President. But Willkie's many speeches and suggestions all indicate that he was much more of an activist than Eisenhower. Whereas Eisenhower has emphasized moderation and much of his Presidency has been marked by what he did *not* do,[6] Willkie's demands on the Roosevelt administration reveal that the "dynamic" would have been emphasized more clearly than the "conservatism." This is obviously conjecture, but it is conjecture based upon the fascinating, aggravating proposals that made Willkie such an intriguing figure on the political scene. For as Roscoe Drummond wrote: "Here was a political leader who did

---

[6] Sidney Hyman has documented several broad areas in which Eisenhower's moderate way has turned out to be a neutral way — a way of not acting when, Hyman believed, action was needed — and a way of avoiding decisions when resolute decisions would have been desirable. See "The Eisenhower Glow Is Fading Away," *The Reporter,* 17 (September 19, 1957), 12.

not know how to play safe. . . . He had utterly no ability to express cautious, discreet, expedient opinions on great issues. . . ."[7]

On the topic of labor and, more specifically, the Republican party and labor relations, Willkie's views were partially at odds with the position of most GOP representatives in Congress and in the state legislatures. Believing that America's wheels could be kept turning only if workers kept spending, Willkie *supported* a responsible, accountable, well-organized labor movement.[8] He wanted labor and management to settle their affairs among themselves, as partners in a common cause, with as little government intervention as possible. This latter position also has been adopted by the present Republican administration. But Willkie also believed that most Republicans had failed to appreciate sufficiently that for labor the essential content of freedom had changed in the twentieth century. He urged his party to acknowledge the necessary requirements for the protection of labor. Furthermore, he believed that industry had a real obligation to accept the principles of collective bargaining and unions per se; he even asserted, ten years before it became even a partial reality, that the guaranteed annual wage was both fair and necessary. Though many Republicans from northern industrial states have to a limited degree accepted this position, for economic reasons which strike at the very basis of national interest groups within the GOP, Willkie's over-all impact in this area was slight. Willkie was thinking in utopian terms rather than in partisan realities. Nevertheless, if Republicans today were willing to alter their views toward organized labor in accord with Willkie's attitudes — if they were willing to concede labor's contribution to an enlightened twentieth-century economy and stand for a recognized union movement instead of "right-to-work" laws designed to destroy labor's organizational base — they would undoubtedly be stronger at the ballot box and more powerful as a constructive force for mature capitalism.

In still another area Willkie was at variance with his adopted party in the forties and in line with developments in the fifties. Although

---

[7] *Christian Science Monitor* (Boston), October 10, 1944, p. 14.

[8] These were Willkie's views shortly before his death. They represent fairly consistently his position after 1940, but do not square completely with his record as head of Commonwealth and Southern. See the *Congressional Record*, vol. 86, pp. 19853 ff. (76th Cong., 3rd Sess., Oct. 4, 1940), for Senator Robert Wagner's assertions about Willkie's labor policies.

he won his laurels for his nomination fighting against the national government and his incessant charge against the New Deal was that it arbitrarily abused its vast authority, Willkie was no states-righter. The states, he believed, had their role to play; but most problems were nationwide in scope and had to be dealt with on a national basis. It was the central government that had to preserve the social and economic structure from the many conflicting interests. Willkie intimately understood the power that large interest groups exercised on state governments, and he realized that industrial growth and expansion could not be tied to a variety of state policies. Parenthetically, he also feared that the provincialism of the states would interfere with his view of America's objectives in international relations, and thus, he urged the Republican party to look to its heritage as a strong national-policy party and reverse the trend it had recently adopted toward "the Doctrine of States' Rights." Willkie's words went unheeded at the time, and even when national responsibility was thrust upon the party, they made no significant impact. Thus, progress in the reversal which Willkie urged has been slow and evident only in certain areas. Because of close associations with groups most powerful in state legislatures, the GOP is still, to a large extent, a states' rights organization. Eisenhower Republicans have paid substantial lip service to state competence and with projects such as school construction, conservation, social insurance and highways, they have encouraged a partnership program with the states. Eisenhower himself seems to be much less nationally oriented than was Willkie. Nevertheless, when the Bricker amendment threatened his authority in foreign affairs and when industrial expansion became an important concern, the President treated these problems in a way that emphasized Willkie's foresight.

On the topic of social security in its broadest sense, Willkie was far ahead of his party. Society, he believed, had changed in his lifetime and minimum requirements had changed too. He frequently declared his conviction that need knows no rules of eligibility or coverage, and he stood for a literal guarantee that the government provide decent education, food, clothing, and medical care. He exhorted Republicans to support, rather than oppose as they had in the past, the entire range of social benefits nationalized to reduce duplication and inefficiency and divorced from earnings. His "complete medical care for all," through a form of insurance to make it more feasible, became a part of Eisenhower's program, but it was defeated by the very forces of which Willkie warned. His federal unemployment insurance — at least in the form of grants and loans — became an available, but not an administrative, reality. Moreover, other objectives in some of these areas — increased disability insurance, old-age benefit increases, maternity benefits, and an enlarged social security system — have been realized, but their acceptance in general has not been notable among many members of the congressional wing of the Republican party.

If there was an issue in American politics that Willkie championed most completely, it was freedom; and this meant freedom for all regardless of color or creed. In the twenties, Willkie fought the Ku Klux Klan; in the forties, he fought for Negro rights against the resistance in both political parties. He was, without doubt, the outstanding advocate in the GOP for equal voting, educational, and economic rights for all Negroes. Willkie despised the reluctance of Republicans to accept a broad interpretation of federal power in the civil rights field. He saw and criticized the debilitating split in the Democratic party over the issue, and he felt that the Republican party's heritage demanded that there be no compromise with the Southern congressmen on legislation involving such basic rights. Thus, he repeatedly urged the Republican party to state unequivocally its position in favor of minority rights. Though his advocacy in this area was politically so inexpedient that no taint of self-interest or lack of sincerity can be attached to Willkie's actions, he also saw the political implications of thirteen million Negroes as "a determined, purposeful unit" at the polls[9] and more important, as part of the world-wide struggle for freedom.

It is difficult to trace Willkie's influence in this area to the Modern Republicanism of 1959. During the Truman administration, conservative Republicans often allied with Southern Democrats to block civil rights proposals in exchange for Southern assistance in maintaining the status quo on labor legislation. Though for eco-

---

[9] In seventeen states which possess well over a majority of the electoral votes, there are enough Negro voters to swing a close election. The states are: New York, Illinois, Pennsylvania, Ohio, New Jersey, Indiana, Missouri, Michigan, California, Kansas, Massachusetts, Connecticut, Maryland, Delaware, West Virginia, Kentucky, and Oklahoma.

Herbert Brownell, Jr., made a post-election analysis after the 1944 election and discovered that a shift of 303,414 votes in fifteen states outside of the South would have elected Dewey. In eight of the fifteen states, the Negro vote exceeded the number needed to shift the victory to the Republican column. See *The Nation*, September 27, 1952, pp. 248-49.

nomic reasons such a legislative position found acceptability among many of the strongest groups within the Republican ranks, it also made it impossible for the Republicans in general to operate in the civil rights struggle from a position of aggressive strength. The Old Guard-Southern coalition has had undermining effects on presidential or liberal Republicans who have had to obtain support in densely populated northern areas, and it has been one source of the intraparty conflict that has traditionally strengthened the legislative wing of the party while it has enervated the executive faction. Because of Eisenhower's personal predisposition, the pressure of events, and the activity of the National Association for the Advancement of Colored People, however, the President's record on civil rights has been such that party organizers have been encouraged by its direction. Wholly consistent with other aspects of his administration, this treatment has been moderate under most circumstances, progressive when forced, but not particularly initiatory in character. In contrast to Willkie, Eisenhower has developed politics as the art of the possible. Believing that tolerance cannot be legislated, the President has acted in spheres in which he could be influential, and has, for other situations, tried to establish a " 'moral climate' in which an equality of rights will be voluntarily accepted."[10] Thus, he was instrumental in ending discrimination in business establishments, restaurants, hotels, and municipal agencies in Washington, D.C., and in veterans' institutions and military installations. He completed, for all practical purposes, the desegregation of the armed forces begun under President Truman. Although he has never specifically endorsed the Supreme Court's repeated stand in school segregation cases and, by Willkie's standards, his action would have to be considered tardy, Eisenhower acted with vigor in Little Rock — apparently against his own feelings. And in spite of the fact that he opposes statutes such as fair employment practices measures, he nevertheless is committed to the principle that federal funds should not be provided to further segregation in any way. Whereas Willkie was intolerant of any lack of tolerance in the whole field of civil rights and civil liberties, Eisenhower has been temperate. Nonetheless, his record has been sufficiently liberal to prompt Adam Clayton Powell to assert: "No one has done more than the present Chief Executive

---

[10] Merlo J. Pusey, *Eisenhower, The President* (New York, 1956), p. 291.

in the field of civil rights!"[11] This statement, regardless of its accuracy or the source of its inspiration, is politically significant and represents a gain for Modern Republicanism in the broad area of inter-race relations. Whether or not this gain can be cemented to the Republican party as a whole, however, remains to be seen. Neither at the national conventions nor in Congress have Republicans acted in such a way as to prove to Negroes that they are truly willing to act boldly and consistently in their behalf. Too many congressional Republicans have failed to realize that the area of civil rights is the crucial key to the party's future. Studies of voter behavior indicate that the Republican party, at least at the grass roots, has a Protestant, rural, religious electorate who might be expected to give strong support to an appeal for genuine civil rights for minorities. But leadership on this point has not materialized because of a contradiction between business concepts and ethical views. The strain within the party is primarily economic in character. Negroes who have been slowly gaining social, educational, and legal equality in the North must also have the opportunity to move upward economically. What economic mobility Negroes did achieve during the last quarter-century, and particularly during the Willkie era, was acquired more or less through the organized labor movement. But because unions have been more closely aligned with the Democrats than with the GOP, most economic achievement by Negroes has been identified with the New and Fair Deal liberals who have evinced a concern for the labor rights, unemployment, housing, and recognition of minority groups.

Willkie realized that the Republican party had paid insufficient attention to these groups who make up much of the unskilled labor

---

[11] Robert J. Donovan, *Eisenhower: The Inside Story* (New York, 1956), p. 161. President Eisenhower's intentions have occasionally been better than his attention. Donovan records incidents in which the President simply wasn't aware that certain discriminatory practices were going on in the government. *Ibid.*, p. 155. Moreover, Eisenhower did not exert strong leadership when the school construction bill was up for consideration by Congress in 1956. Congressman Powell attached a civil rights amendment to the bill which provided that federal funds could not be allotted to institutions that would be segregated. It is widely believed that Republicans who supported the Powell amendment, which made the bill anathema to the Southern Democrats, and who then reversed their votes to defeat the bill in its entirety could have been brought into line by Presidential influence. For an excellent brief discussion of the Republican party and current civil rights problems, see Austin Ranney's "Politics, Parties, and Civil War" in the *American Government Annual, 1958-1959*, Ivan Hinderaker (ed.) (New York, 1958), pp. 58-60.

force. He also personally discounted the fact that any claims that these groups would make on the shared fruits of the economy would detract, in the short run, from the gains of the strongest economic elements among the Republicans. Moreover, he was not impressed by the fact that a substantial improvement in the economic status of these minorities would mean a more expensive wage pattern throughout the nation, coupled with a reduction in the supply of competitive labor. Instead, he recognized that because of the low consumption base from which these groups would begin, the economy eventually would receive a substantial lift. All of these facets of the problem were implicit in Willkie's assertions, and many Republicans would do well to review his statements today.

In any event, it can be seen that many of Willkie's ideas on policy have come partially to fruition while others have not. But his impact also has been evident without attribution in other areas of the Eisenhower administration. In personnel, such men as Douglas McKay, Arthur Summerfield, and many others became interested and active in politics as the result of Willkie's candidacy. In the economic arena his friend Sinclair Weeks, when he was Secretary of Commerce, tried to maintain a precarious balance between increasing economic freedom and the demands on the economy by centripetal forces. And in tariffs, developmental loans overseas, and revisionist thinking on the concept of sovereignty, Willkie's ideas are observable. But this is not cause and effect; it is merely that Willkie thought thoughts that fifteen years later have become political realities. Willkie's influence was by association and reconsideration of ideas. And as he would have had it, it was in this realm that he left his mark. Senator Aiken of Vermont told the author: "The effects of Willkie's speeches and his attitudes were as a trigger that got us to realizing that we no longer could live unto ourselves alone. He accepted the New Deal social philosophy and had sense enough not to buck it. He just might have been the trigger that set off Modern Republicanism." In a similar vein, Albert Leman, once editor-in-chief of the McClure newspaper syndicate and assistant to former Secretary of Commerce Weeks, declared: "Willkie was the pioneer of Eisenhower Republicanism. He prepared the way for a wider acceptance of a newer Republican doctrine, and he put back into the Republican picture a concern for progressivism. He was never really a radical; he was a moderate, middle-of-the-road Republican borrowing from the New Deal and keeping the best of traditional Republicanism. His supporters were among the first Eisenhower supporters."

The case must not be overstated, however. When Republicans meet in national convention, Willkie's name is never mentioned among the heroes of the past; he was too much of a maverick; he was too heretical and too critical. As a temporary character on the political scene, he could, at best, only forewarn, argue, exhort, and debate — and all of this within the context of only one political party in competition with his opposition in both parties. Though he performed fearlessly, and sometimes rashly, his influence was constantly discounted because he was forced to operate as only the titular head of his party while actually representing only one faction of the organization. His philosophy nevertheless ultimately became the dominant sentiment with the executive wing of the GOP, and he provided a progressive program that even today remains to be fulfilled.

Thus, what Willkie influenced was a vague consensus concerning a brand of Republicanism rather than the entire party itself. This, of course, was important. But the GOP is a complex coalition of interrelated state groups and power blocs held together by basic beliefs, economic objectives, party traditions, and regional loyalties. Though it has made an observable adjustment in favor of positive government and concern for social welfare, and many liberal Republicans have realized the political wisdom of Willkie's ideas in contrast to his occasionally impulsive actions, a substantial segment of the party has remained relatively immune to major shifts in policies, issues, and men. Hence, the party suffers from an ideological schizophrenia that Willkie frequently criticized. Dewey, Eisenhower, and Nixon have all noted this split, but because of its intricate nature, none of these men has been able to alter the situation significantly. The dilemma is a conflict within the party between the objectives of conservatives and the demands of the people for governmental services, between the western conservationists and the eastern devotees of free enterprise; between the farmers and the consumers; between business and labor; between neo-isolationists and internationalists, and among all of the other groups that try to reconcile capitalism with the welfare state. To the extent that Eisenhower has exerted the presidential power to keep the New Deal reforms while administering a conservative policy for America's economic system, he has arrived at a temporary consensus among the people that has produced electoral victories for the presidency. But he has been unable to lead his entire party to similar victories and he has been unable to heal the breach in the GOP. And to a lesser extent, it was because of this schism that Willkie did not significantly alter the character of the Republican party. More obviously than Eisenhower, he did not have the power, the personality, or the willingness to compromise that would have enabled him to be effective. In short, he was inept as a party leader. He viewed the party as a vehicle for ideas and he did not fully recognize the provincial nature of the GOP. He refused to devote his energies to partisan work divorced from philosophical considerations and by 1944, it was obvious that most orthodox Republicans who made up the backbone of the formal organization thought that Willkie had returned ideationally to the Democratic party. They believed that Willkie had come up too fast with too many new and recusant ideas. He had assisted Roosevelt too frequently. His liberalism was too outspoken, and his party loyalty too irregular. Fundamentally, a majority of the Republican leaders neither appreciated nor recognized his contribution to the future of the GOP.

Party leaders who opposed Willkie have their present-day counterparts within the orthodox wing of the Republicans who believe that Modern Republicanism is a meaningless platitude. They describe Eisenhower loyalists as political latecomers who subscribe to a federal welfare philosophy which is nothing more or less than the New Deal under another name, and who are free-wheeling freespenders who have surrendered their constructive conservatism.[12] They believe that the GOP has made serious mistakes in nominating such men as Willkie, Dewey, and Eisenhower — "me too" politicians trying to outpromise the Democrats in terms of economic reforms and welfare services — in that such men do not ideologically repre-

---

[12] This description of Modern Republicanism is a paraphrase of quotations from Republican Senator Barry Goldwater of Arizona, whom *Time* has called the leader of the Old Guard in the Senate (May 20, 1957, p. 26) and Representative A. L. Miller of Nebraska (*U. S. News and World Report,* May 3, 1957, pp. 126-38). For articles describing Modern Republicanism in various ways, see: "Just What Is Modern Republicanism," by Stewart Alsop in the *Saturday Evening Post,* 229 (July 27, 1957), 18 ff.; "The Way Ike Is Remaking His Party," in *U. S. News and World Report,* 39 (September 16, 1955), 26-27; "An Attempt to Define Our Party Lines," by William S. White, *New York Times Magazine* (May 5, 1957), p. 19; "Will Eisenhower Remake Republican Image?" *Congressional Quarterly,* 15 (January 4, 1957), 20-21; and the *Time* column noted above.

sent a majority of the Republican constituents. This is a moot point, but it is true, of course, that any present-day Republican administration will have its difficulties representing the multifarious interest groups that make up the party. There is, nevertheless, some question as to what proportion of the Republican party is represented by this right-wing philosophy. GOP Senator Clifford Case summarized its position and evaluated its strength as follows:

. . . some prominent members of our party . . . are opposed, in whole or in part, to the idea of foreign economic aid, which is a cornerstone of our current foreign policy. And in the domestic field, there are those who object on principle to the Federal Government's taking a leading role in relieving local shortages of schools, health services and similar welfare needs. Still others feel that almost every Government undertaking should be held subservient to the goal of achieving a balanced budget. Indeed, there are some who take a skeptical view of all that is embraced in what is loosely and imprecisely defined as "Eisenhower Republicanism." My belief is, however, that this represents a decidedly minority view within our party — and a diminishing one. . . .[13]

On the other hand, Senator Case notwithstanding, any examination of the Republican hierarchy in either house of Congress or of most state legislatures will reveal that except for the eastern seaboard and a few states such as Minnesota, where liberalism has been forced upon the GOP by its opposition, the conservatives are in firm control of their organizations. Loyal supporters of the late Senator Taft and of Senator Knowland controlled the Republican delegations in the Senate for nearly two decades and the senior GOP members of the House have not been strong adherents of Modern Republicanism. In 1957, the new Eisenhower supporters who were elected to the Senate were relegated to unimportant committee assignments while orthodox newcomers were given more favorable treatment. Moreover, Republican congressional support for the President in recent years, percentage-wise, has not been much higher than his support by the Democrats, and it has been constantly declining since the beginning of the 83rd Congress in 1952.[14] Finally, in the battles for control of the state political organ-

---

[13] "A Republican Prescribes for His Party," *New York Times Magazine,* February 17, 1957, p. 17.

[14] Ivan Hinderaker wrote: "While Democratic support for Mr. Eisenhower has remained fairly steady since the 83rd Congress, Republican support has dropped from 72 percent in the 83rd Congress to 67 percent in the 84th Congress to the 56 percent figure for the first session of the 85th Congress. Of 117 Eisenhower-issue roll calls in 1957, Democratic and Republican majorities were in agreement on 67, and 57 of these the Presi-

izations, Eisenhower Republicans have not fared notably well since 1954.[15] The logical conclusion is that though, as Senator Case wrote, the conservative anti-Eisenhower view may be diminishing on broad policies, the legislative statistics do not necessarily support this assumption. There are still a large number of critics of liberal Republicanism within the entire party.[16] What these critics of liberal Republicanism often fail to realize is that, given the present party and electoral systems in America, mass appeal in the large centers of population is essential; no ultraconservative Republican could win a presidential election because Americans today want the additional services from government that the Old Guard has consistently repudiated.[17] To be sure, when economic conditions are very favorable and people are secure and optimistic, voters will support a conservative who will help cement their gains. Such a conservative in America, however, must champion relatively free capitalism with its fluctuating business cycles as opposed to public planning. Inevitably, when conditions deteriorate and the voters feel insecure, the masses are the first to feel the impact and they turn to the government for redress. Presidents today are expected to insure economic stability and security when private enterprise slumps, and majorities will support candidates who are sympathetic to such expectations. The only phenomenon that saves the Republican party from being a permanent and declining minority

dent won; on 31 a Republican majority supported the President while a Democratic majority opposed, and 13 of these the President won; on 19 a Democratic majority supported the President while a Republican majority opposed, and 10 of these the President won." "Problems in Presidential Leadership," *American Government Annual, 1958-1959* (New York, 1958), p. 86.

[15] These conflicts are summarized by John R. Schmidhauser in "Where Are the Eisenhower Republicans?" *The Reporter*, 15 (September 20, 1956), 26-27.

[16] During the congressional campaign of 1958, after Eisenhower made several hard-hitting campaign speeches, William S. White commented: ". . . President Eisenhower has adopted the line of his junior, Nixon. Thus the whole Republican national leadership has been turned over to the faction made up of the orthodox Republicans, like the vice-president, and of the out-and-out old guard. . . . [This] is the faction that tried to reject General Eisenhower himself at the 1952 convention. And, for a final irony, the president is now going all-out to assist this faction to return the Republican party to the public image it had before he came along to change it." *Des Moines Register*, October 25, 1958, p. 10.

[17] For a conservative argument against this position, see Richard Lloyd-Jones' article, "The New Republican Party," in the *American Mercury*, 81 (July, 1955), 110 ff.

party is that it does contain a balancing faction that recognizes global responsibilities, that takes a more liberal view of social and welfare obligations of the government, and that this faction has been able to control the national nominating conventions. Governmental policy and the presidency today are what they are because constituents have demanded that they be such, and a negativistic approach to government — designed to deal with economic and social problems outside the arena of elective responsibility — will not consistently achieve popular majorities.

All of the recent leaders of the Republican party — and particularly Willkie — have realized this fact and thus have designed their campaigns and their programs with this current consensus in view.[18] As a result, the differences between the two parties, assuming that both are devoted to the preservation of the capitalistic system, have steadily become less marked. For example, Modern Republicanism, as described in Arthur Larson's volume, *A Republican Looks at His Party,* is closer to the Democratic position on many issues than it is to the principles of the Old Guard. And Donovan wrote that at one time Eisenhower was so frustrated by the opposition within his own party that he thought seriously about the formation of a new party.[19] The problem here presented for the Republicans is that the program necessary to win national elections is not a program that presents a clear-cut conservative opposition to the liberal Republican *or* Democratic positions. And it might be added that, theoretically, a substantial case can be made for the necessity of a strong party that really opposes. But a sterile negativism solely for opposition's sake is rarely popular. Parties exist to capture control of the government, and a party that fails

---

[18] J. D. Hicks, writing in *The Saturday Review,* stated: "In order to survive at all the Republicans eventually discovered that they must take over the very principles they had denounced most in reformers and Democrats; further, the more forward-looking among them had to force on the Old Guard a five-star General for President, a man whose record at the time of his nomination commended him almost equally to the liberals of both parties. Without him, and certainly without the liberalism he was supposed to represent, the Republicans might well have headed for another long tour of duty in the wilderness. To him they are therefore committed, for better or for worse, in sickness and in health, until such a time as they can convert a majority of the American people to the belief that the Republican Party as a whole has really changed its spots and is more to be trusted than the Democrats." "GOP: A Case History," *Saturday Review,* 39 (August 4, 1956), 19.

[19] Donovan, *op. cit.,* pp. 151-52.

to do this periodically becomes enfeebled and will sooner or later go out of existence. Thus, Willkie frequently warned that if the Republicans refused to recognize international and domestic responsibilities, it too would die. Fortunately, after 1944 there were enough leaders within the GOP who had accepted a more positive philosophy to enable the party to halt the negativistic drive toward ineffectiveness. For this, no little credit must be given to Willkie and his supporters. In 1957 on the sixty-fifth anniversary of Wendell Willkie's birth, Chief Justice Earl Warren acknowledged this debt when he declared: "In the four brief years of his political ministry he [Willkie] did as much to remove the blinders from the eyes of Americans and to change the course of the party whose standard he carried as any American without governmental portfolio in our national history."[20]

The irony of this tribute lies in the fact that in order to remove the blinders, Willkie had to sacrifice his own hold on his party. By adhering to the course in which he believed, he consistently flouted the Republican organization, thereby virtually insuring that he would never have governmental portfolio. Willkie's political errors, and they were many, can be charged to his lack of experience, his ineptness in handling men, his lack of official information, his bullheadedness, or his refusal to play a game in which he could not make the rules, but they cannot be charged to lack of principles. He sacrificed the nomination in 1944 by an adherence to those beliefs. Strangely enough, where Republicans have adopted those principles, they have succeeded; if they would adopt those they have rejected, they might well insure future success. Elmo Roper characterized Willkie's principles in describing the groups that supported Willkie most loyally:

These Willkie supporters credited their hero with being in favor of social progress for the best of all possible reasons: first, because it was good; second, because it was inevitable.

They saw in Wendell Willkie a man who believed in labor unions, not because such a belief was a political asset but because, with all their faults, unions did more good for more people than they did harm. They saw in Willkie a man who was against anti-Semitism, not because it sounded broadminded, or because it picked up a few votes or because he had some personal friends who were Jews, but because he knew that the existence of anti-Semitism or anti-any other group — was a blow at the very cornerstone of democracy. They saw in Willkie a man who was

---

[20] *Congressional Record*, vol. 103, p. 2094 (85th Cong., 1st Sess., Feb. 21, 1957).

truly a friend of the Negro — not just every fourth year and because of the Negro's political importance in New York, Chicago, and Philadelphia, but because there were ten million Negroes in this country, and since democracy has within it no room for second-class citizenships, the presence of these Negroes created a problem to be dealt with fairly and promptly and rationally.

. . . these were the qualities they were looking for: world-wide vision, complete integrity, true tolerance, a social conscience, a flaming courage, and the ability to get things done. They were looking for these things because they are the things they credited to Wendell Willkie.[21]

The beliefs here ascribed to Willkie are those he advocated before his death. Several writers have maintained that the Wendell Willkie of 1944 represented a "grown" or "changed" Willkie in comparison with the man who was president of Commonwealth and Southern. This assertion is only partially correct. With reference to individual liberty, minority rights, and international cooperation, there is a clear line of consistency from the Akron Willkie to the Willkie of 1944. On the matter of government intervention, the line is more fugitive, for there is little similarity between the writing of Willkie, the utility chief, and his "liberal platform" of 1943. Moreover, in the campaign of 1940, when he was making six to ten speeches a day, Willkie revealed inconsistent attitudes on certain issues.

After the election, however, there was no additional shift in Willkie's political philosophy. On broad humanitarian problems, considered over a period of four years, he was exceedingly consistent. Actually, after 1940 the political Willkie refused to shift with public opinion; he was even unwilling to recognize the will of Republicans when it contravened his own. He was certainly not inclined to respond to the ideas of other leaders in his party although the prospect of political defeat was evident when he rebuked them. He was a man who believed in individual freedom, "necessary" governmental guarantees for a minimum standard of living, and a system of organization for the protection of America's and the world's populace. In addition, his faith in human rights, civil liberties, racial tolerance, economic opportunity for all without discrimination, equality of education, and his emphasis on the importance of the individual over the state were principles on which he stood from his early days until his death.

These beliefs, expanded to the world, prompted Willkie to

---

[21] Elmo Roper, *You and Your Leaders, Their Actions and Your Reactions* (New York, 1957), pp. 93-94.

declare repeatedly and vigorously that international organization and cooperation were absolutely essential to the preservation of civilization. He was convinced that if many of the existing economic and political barriers were eventually destroyed, "men and women the world around" could "live and grow invigorated by independence and freedom."[22] Wendell Willkie did not have an extensive knowledge of world diplomacy, of what he called international "power politics," or even of the intricacies of world cultures or of nationalistic economic systems. What he had was a strong conviction that to have world peace, the people must be free, that the world could not survive if intense nationalism prevailed, and that the exploitation of peoples for the benefit of other nations was morally wrong. He dedicated his last years to this conviction. A few observers have written that this struggle cost Willkie his life. His battle to convert the Republican party and the peoples of America to his thinking undoubtedly placed a heavy toll on his energies. Perhaps he would have lived longer if he had retired from public life after 1940. This, however, was not in the constitution of Wendell Willkie. He was an ambitious man who wanted to be the President of the United States in order to give reality to his ideas. His devotion to the evolution of international cooperation and civil liberties would not allow him to withdraw from public life. He lived abundantly during a period of crisis, and he died in a period of idealism — still looking forward to a more fruitful and peaceful civilization.

Wendell L. Willkie's leadership was, as several people have now noted, a decisive force in the second World War and in the establishment of the United Nations.[23] In the final analysis, however, the names of Franklin D. Roosevelt, Harry S. Truman, and Dwight D. Eisenhower will loom larger on the pages of history because these men did obtain power, did play the game according to the rules, and did have the opportunity to put their policies into effect. Wendell Willkie, nonetheless, gave to American politics some of its most exciting pages and he gave the Republican party, despite his rejection, a set of policies many of which it accepted after his death. Willkie is too frequently remembered as a dynamic per-

---

[22] Wendell Willkie, *One World* (New York, 1943), p. 176.

[23] For example, see Drummond, *op. cit.,* p. 454; Davenport, *op. cit.,* p. 67; and Wayne Morse, "Wendell Willkie," *Congressional Record,* vol. 90, p. A635 (80th Cong., 1st Sess., Feb. 19, 1947).

sonality — a man of presidential timber[24] — who captured a political party but who was unable to lead what he had captured. He should be remembered for the eventual position taken by his party, at least temporarily, after the war, and for the more permanent impact of his ideas on the liberal faction within the GOP. He should also be remembered, as he wanted to be remembered, as an individual who contributed to the saving of democracy at a critical moment.

---

[24] Rexford Tugwell wrote of President Roosevelt's fascination with qualities that constituted the mysterious "presidential talent": "Franklin used to size up his rival candidates with it in view. Of all of them, only one, to the end, would seem to have the gift — that would be Willkie, some way yet in the future." *The Democratic Roosevelt* (Garden City, N.Y., 1957), p. 296.

BIBLIOGRAPHY

A. BOOKS AND PAMPHLETS

Alsop, Joseph, and Catledge, Turner. *The 168 Days.* Garden City, N.Y.: Doubleday, Doran and Company, 1938.

Barnes, Harry Elmer. *Was Roosevelt Pushed Into War By Popular Demand in 1941?* Discussion of paper read by Professor Dexter Perkins before the American Historical Association, Stevens Hotel, Chicago, December 29, 1950. (Personal copy from Mr. Barnes)

Barnes, Joseph. *Willkie.* New York: Simon and Schuster, 1952.

Bender, George H. *The Challenge of 1940.* New York: G. P. Putnam's Sons, 1940.

Bone, Hugh Alvin. *"Smear" Politics, An Analysis of 1940 Campaign Literature.* Washington, D.C.: American Council on Public Affairs, 1941.

Bryce, James. *The American Commonwealth.* New York: The Macmillan Company, 1914.

Burns, James MacGregor. *Roosevelt: The Lion and The Fox.* New York: Harcourt, Brace and Company, 1956.

Childs, Marquis. *I Write From Washington.* New York: Harper and Brothers, 1942.

Committee on Political Parties, American Political Science Association. *Toward a More Responsible Two-Party System, American Political Science Review,* vol. 44, no. 3, part 2 (September, 1950); also separately published by Rinehart and Company, 1951.

Dillon, Mary Earhart. *Wendell Willkie, 1892-1944.* New York: J. B. Lippincott Company, 1952.

Donovan, Robert J. *Eisenhower: The Inside Story.* New York: Harper and Brothers, 1956.

Fainsod, Merle, and Gordon, Lincoln. *Government and the American Economy.* New York: W. W. Norton and Company, Inc., 1948.

Field, Rudolph. *Mister American: Dwight David Eisenhower*. New York: R. Field Company, 1952.

Gosnell, Harold F. *Grass Roots Politics*. Washington, D.C.: American Council on Public Affairs, 1942.

Gunther, John. *Eisenhower, The Man and The Symbol*. New York: Harper and Brothers, 1952.

Harris, Louis. *Is There A Republican Majority?* New York: Harper and Brothers, 1956.

Hatch, Alden. *Young Willkie*. New York: Harcourt, Brace and Company, 1944.

Hinderaker, Ivan (ed). *American Government Annual, 1958-1959*. New York: Henry Holt and Company, 1958.

Howard, L. Vaughan, and Bone, Hugh A. *Current American Government*. New York: D. Appleton-Century, 1943.

Johnson, Claudius O. *American Government*. New York: Thomas Y. Crowell Company, 1951.

Kent, Frank R. *The Great Game of Politics*. Garden City, N. Y.: Doubleday, Doran and Company, 1930.

Larson, Arthur. *A Republican Looks At His Party*. New York: Harper and Brothers, 1956.

Laski, Harold J. *The American Presidency, An Interpretation*. New York: Harper and Brothers, 1940.

Lazarsfeld, P. F., Berelson, B., and Gaudet, H. *The People's Choice: How the Voter Makes Up His Mind in a Presidential Campaign*. New York: Columbia University Press, 1948.

Leighton, Isabel (ed.). *The Aspirin Age*. New York: Simon and Schuster, 1949.

Lubell, Samuel. *Revolt of the Moderates*. New York: Harper and Brothers, 1956.

Makey, Herman O. *Wendell Willkie of Elwood*. Elwood, Ind.: National Book Company, Inc., 1940.

Merriam, Charles E., and Gosnell, Harold F. *The American Party System*. New York: The Macmillan Company, 1949.

Moley, Raymond. *27 Masters of Politics*. New York: Funk and Wagnalls Company, 1949.

Moos, Malcolm. *The Republicans*. New York: Random House, 1956.

Morison, Samuel E., and Commager, Henry Steele. *The Growth of the American Republic*. New York: Oxford University Press, 1942.

Northrup, F. S. C. *The Meeting of East and West*. New York: The Macmillan Company, 1946.

Odegard, Peter H. *Prologue to November, 1940*. New York: Harper and Brothers, 1940.

Official Report of the Proceedings of the Twenty-Second Republican National Convention. Washington, D.C.: Judd and Detweiler, Inc., 1940.

Ostrogorski, M. *Democracy and the Organization of Political Parties*. New York: The Macmillan Company, 1902.

Peel, Roy V., and Donnelly, Thomas C. *The 1932 Campaign, An Analysis.* New York: Farrar and Rinehart, Inc., 1935.

Perkins, Frances. *The Roosevelt I Knew.* New York: The Viking Press, 1947.

Porter, Kirk H., and Johnson, Donald B. *National Party Platforms.* Urbana: University of Illinois Press, 1956.

Pusey, Merlo J. *Eisenhower, The President.* New York: The Macmillan Company, 1956.

Roper, Elmo. *You and Your Leaders, Their Actions and Your Reactions.* New York: Morrow, 1957.

Rosenman, Samuel I. *Working With Roosevelt.* New York: Harper and Brothers, 1952.

Rovere, Richard. *The Eisenhower Years.* New York: Farrar, Straus and Cudahy, 1956.

Schattschneider, E. E. *Party Government.* New York: Rinehart and Company, Inc., 1942.

Schlesinger, Arthur M., Jr. *Crisis of the Old Order.* Boston: Houghton Mifflin Company, 1957.

Sherwood, Robert E. *Roosevelt and Hopkins.* New York: Harper and Brothers, 1950.

Sparks, C. Nelson. *One Man — Wendell Willkie.* New York: Rayner Publishing Company, 1943.

Stimson, Henry L., and Bundy, McGeorge. *On Active Service in Peace and War.* New York: Harper and Brothers, 1947.

Stone, Irving. *They Also Ran.* New York: Doubleday, Doran and Company, Inc., 1944.

Taylor, Allan. *What Eisenhower Thinks.* New York: Thomas Y. Crowell Company, 1952.

Truman, Harry S. *Years of Decisions.* Garden City, N. Y.: Doubleday, Doran and Company, Inc., 1955-56.

Tugwell, Rexford G. *The Democratic Roosevelt.* Garden City, N. Y.: Doubleday, Doran and Company, Inc., 1957.

Vandenberg, Arthur H., Jr. *The Private Papers of Senator Vandenberg.* Boston: Houghton Mifflin Company, 1952.

Wick, James L. *How Not to Run for President.* New York: Vantage Press, Inc.

Willkie, Wendell. *Government and the Public Utilities.* Address given at a joint meeting of the Economic Club of New York and the Harvard Business School Club, New York City, January 21, 1935. (Pamphlet copy in the University of Illinois Library.)

———. *The New Fear.* Address delivered in Washington, D.C., May 1, 1935. (Pamphlet copy in the University of Illinois Library.)

———. *This is Wendell Willkie.* New York: Dodd, Mead and Company, 1940.

———. *One World.* New York: Simon and Schuster, 1943.

———. *An American Program.* New York: Simon and Schuster, 1944.

B. ARTICLES

Alexander, Jack. "The World's Greatest Newspaper," *Saturday Evening Post*, 214 (July 26, 1941), 27 ff.

Allott, Gordon. "The Role Young Republicans Played in the 1940 Campaign," *The Republican*, 6 (February, 1941), 23-24.

Alsop, Stewart. "Just What is Modern Republicanism," *Saturday Evening Post*, 229 (July 27, 1957), 18 ff.

Beichman, A. "Willkie's Choice," *The Nation*, 159 (July 15, 1944), 70-71.

Bendiner, Robert. "Pennsylvania Avenue Gets Longer and Longer," *The Reporter*, 18 (February 20, 1958), 25-27.

Berdahl, Clarence A. "Political Parties and Elections," *American Political Science Review*, 37 (February, 1943), 68-81.

———. "Presidential Selection and Democratic Government," *Journal of Politics*, 11 (February, 1949), 35-40.

Bernstein, Irving. "John L. Lewis and the Voting Behavior of the C.I.O.," *Public Opinion Quarterly*, 5 (June, 1941), 233-249.

Bridges, Ronald. "The Republican Program Committee," *Public Opinion Quarterly*, 3 (April, 1939), 299-313.

Briggs, Herbert W. "Neglected Aspects of the Destroyer Deal," *American Journal of International Law*, 34 (October, 1940), 569-587.

Brisbane, R. H. "The Negroes' Growing Political Power," *The Nation*, 175 (September 27, 1952), 248-249.

Brogan, D. W. "The American Election," *Political Quarterly*, 11 (October-December, 1940), 322-35.

———. "The Eggheads and Ike," *New Republic*, 135 (September 10, 1956), 9-10.

Bromley, Dorothy Dunbar. "The Education of Wendell Willkie," *Harper's*, 181 (October, 1940), 477-485.

Brown, Francis. "National Unity, A Willkie Formula," *New York Times Magazine*, December 14, 1941, p. 11.

"Bully for *Time*," *The Nation*, 186 (March 8, 1958), 197-98.

Burns, James MacGregor. "America's 'Four-Party' System," *New York Times Magazine*, August 5, 1956, 10 ff.

Case, Clifford. "A Republican Prescribes for His Party," *New York Times Magazine*, February 17, 1957, pp. 17-20.

Casey, Ralph. "The Republican Rural Press Campaign," *Public Opinion Quarterly*, 5 (March, 1941), 130-33.

Chamberlain, John. "Candidates and Speeches," *Yale Review*, 30 (ns) (September, 1940), 45-61.

———. "Next President Must Be Roosevelt," *Fortune*, 22 (October, 1940), 72 ff.

Coleman, M. "Wendell Willkie is Ruined," *The Nation*, 149 (July 15, 1939), 69-70.

Commager, Henry Steele. "Party Strife: Sign of Health," *New York Times Magazine*, October 6, 1940, p. 3.

Cross, Wilbur L. "Underlying Issues of the Campaign," *Yale Review*, 30 (ns) (September, 1940), 1-6.

Crossley, Archibald M. "Methods Tested During the 1940 Campaign," *Public Opinion Quarterly,* 5 (March, 1941), 83-87.

Cutler, Robert. "I Shall Vote for Eisenhower," *Atlantic Monthly,* 198 (October, 1956), 46-50.

Daniels, J. "Native at Large: Wendell Willkie and David Lilienthal," *The Nation,* 151 (August 24, 1940), 155.

Davenport, Russell W. "Whom Should the G.O.P. Nominate and Why?" *Current History,* 51 (June, 1940), 42.

———. "The Next President Must Be Willkie," *Fortune,* 22 (October, 1940), 68 ff.

———. "Wendell Willkie's Legacy to America," *New York Times Magazine,* November 19, 1944, p. 8.

———. "The Ordeal of Wendell Willkie," *Atlantic Monthly,* 176 (November, 1945), 67-73.

Davenport, W. "Willkie Way," *Collier's,* 106 (October 5, 1940), 13 ff.

Dilliard, Irving. "Can the Republicans Win?" *New Republic,* 107 (September 7, 1942), 276-77.

Evjen, Henry O. "The Willkie Campaign; An Unfortunate Chapter in Republican Leadership," *The Journal of Politics,* 14 (May, 1952), 241-56.

Feld, M. D. "Eisenhower: Constitutional Monarch?" *New Republic,* 134 (March 26, 1956), 8-9.

Fetridge, W. H. "The Case of the Republican Party," *The Republican,* 7 (July, 1942), 6-7.

Fischer, Louis. "Last Talk With Wendell Willkie," *Common Sense,* 13 (December, 1944), 417-18.

Flanner, Janet. "Rushville's Renowned Son-In-Law," *New Yorker,* 16 (October 12, 1940), 27-32.

Flynn, J. T. "Mr. Willkie and the S.E.C.," *New Republic,* 102 (May 13, 1940), 640.

Fuller, H. "Has Wendell Willkie Lost?" *New Republic,* 109 (November 29, 1943), 741-42.

Furnas, J. C. "Who Wants Willkie?" *Saturday Evening Post,* 213 (November 2, 1940), 12 ff.

Gilroy, V. "And Willkie Threw It Away," *Scribner's Commentator,* 9 (February, 1941), 46-51.

Graebner, Norman A. "The Changing Nature of the Democratic Party," *Current History,* 30-31 (August, 1956), 70-76.

Grahn, G. "My Boss Wendell Willkie," *American Magazine,* 130 (October, 1940), 14 ff.

Handlin, Oscar. "The Changing Nature of the Republican Party," *Current History,* 30-31 (August, 1956), 65-69.

———. "Do The Voters Want Moderation?" *Commentary,* 22 (September, 1956), 193-98.

Hanes, J. "I Vote For Willkie," *Atlantic Monthly,* 166 (November, 1940), 540-42.

Harrison, Selig S. "A Talk With Arthur Larson," *New Republic,* 135 (September 3, 1956), 5-6.

Hicks, J. D. "GOP: A Case History," *The Saturday Review*, 39 (August 4, 1956), 19-20.

Howe, Irving. "Poor Richard Nixon," *New Republic*, 134 (May 7, 1956), 7-9.

Hutchison, K. "Mr. Willkie's Challenge," *The Nation*, 158 (June 24, 1944), 726-27.

Hyman, Sidney. "Ike's New Republicanism," *Atlantic Monthly*, 198 (November, 1956), 6.

———. "The Eisenhower Glow is Fading Away," *The Reporter*, 17 (September 19, 1957), 11-15.

———. "Inner Circles of the White House," *New York Times Magazine*, January 5, 1958, pp. 10 f.

Johnson, Gerald W. "Horse Without Rider," *New Republic*, 138 (January 20, 1958), 8.

Johnson, Hugh. "I Am Not Nominating Him," *Saturday Evening Post*, 212 (June 22, 1940), 9 ff.

Katz, D. "The Public Opinion Polls and the 1940 Election," *Public Opinion Quarterly*, 5 (March, 1941), 52-79.

Key, V. O. "Two Political Parties in 1960?" *New Republic*, 135 (December 3, 1956), 15.

Kirchwey, Freda. "Pre-Mortem on Willkie," *The Nation*, 151 (October 12, 1940), 317-18.

———. "Roosevelt and Willkie," *The Nation*, 155 (December 19, 1942), 670.

Lerner, Max. "The Education of Wendell Willkie," *New Republic*, 107 (October 26, 1942), 536-38.

Lloyd-Jones, Richard. "The New Republican Party," *American Mercury*, 81 (July, 1955), 110 ff.

Lubell, Samuel. "Post Mortem: Who Elected Roosevelt?" *Saturday Evening Post*, 213 (January 25, 1941), 9 ff.

———. "Can The GOP Win Again in '60?" *Saturday Evening Post*, 229 (January 26, 1957), 30 ff.

Lyons, Eugene. "Notes on Wendell Willkie," *American Mercury*, 58 (May, 1944), 519-25.

"Mad At Ike? No, But . . . ," *Newsweek*, 51 (March 10, 1958), 27-31.

McCormick, Anne O'Hare. "Man of the Middle West," *New York Times Magazine*, August 8, 1940, p. 3.

"Misleading the President," *New Republic*, 138 (March 17, 1958), 5.

Mitchell, J. "How They Won With Willkie," *New Republic*, 103 (July 8, 1940), 48-49.

Moley, Raymond. "Champion and Challenger," *Saturday Evening Post*, 213 (August 24, 1940), 12 ff.

———. "Mr. Willkie's Acceptance Speech," *Newsweek*, 16 (August 26, 1940), 58.

———. "Is Willkie Slipping," *Newsweek*, 16 (September 16, 1940), 68.

———. "No Time for Gloating," *Newsweek*, 23 (April 17, 1944), 108.

———. "Harvest of Folly," *Newsweek*, 50 (November 18, 1957), 140.

Murphey, Charles J. V. "The Eisenhower Shift," *Fortune*, 53 (April, 1956), 113.

"New Republicanism At A New Low," *Business Week* (September 7, 1957), 23-25.

Oehler, C. M. "How G.O.P. 'Grass Roots' Leaders Feel About U. S. Foreign Policy," *The Republican*, 8 (January, 1944), 2-4.

Overacker, Louise. "Campaign Finance in the Presidential Election of 1940," *American Political Science Review*, 35 (August, 1941), 701-27.

Parsons, Wilfred. "The President and the Congress," *America*, 99 (April 26, 1958), 130.

Patrick, Ted. "Electing a Republican President," *Scribner's Magazine*, 104 (November, 1938), 17-21 ff.

Pear, R. H. "The American Presidency Under Eisenhower," *The Political Quarterly*, 28 (January-March, 1957), 5-12.

Peel, Roy V., with Snowden, George. "From Four Years of Politics the Candidates Emerge," *Public Opinion Quarterly*, 4 (September, 1940), 450-64.

"Plus and Minus," *The Nation*, 185 (November 16, 1957), 333.

Pringle, Henry F. "What's Happened to Willkie," *American Mercury*, 54 (January, 1942), 43-49.

Reed, Thomas H., and Reed, Doris D. "The Republican Opposition," *Survey Graphic*, 29 (May, 1940), 286-88.

"Responsible Rule and the President," *New Republic*, 137 (December 16, 1957), 5.

Reynolds, J. L. "G.O.P.'s Problem Child," *The Nation*, 151 (September 21, 1940), 235-36.

Root, Oren. "This is Wendell Willkie," *Current History*, 51 (September, 1940), 7 ff.

———. "Willkie Phenomenon; Defeated for the Presidency, He Remains a Figure of World Importance," *Current History*, 52 (March, 1941), 7-9.

Roper, Elmo. "Not Who, But Why?" *The Saturday Review*, 39 (November 3, 1956), 14-15.

———. "Public Opinion and the GOP," *The Saturday Review*, 38 (May 21, 1955), 20-22.

Rovere, Richard. "Letter From Washington," *New Yorker*, 33 (December 7, 1957), 141-44.

Rowell, Chester. "Resources of the Republican Party," *Yale Review*, 27 (ns) (March, 1938), 433-49.

Salter, J. T. "How Mr. Roosevelt Won," *Dalhousie Review*, 20 (January, 1941), 459-70.

Schlesinger, Arthur, Jr. "Can Willkie Save His Party," *The Nation*, 152 (December 6, 1941), 561-62.

Schmidhauser, John R. "Where Are The Eisenhower Republicans?" *The Reporter*, 15 (September 20, 1956), 26-27.

Sokolsky, G. E. "A Republican Examines His Party," *American Mercury*, 55 (September, 1942), 323-31.

Spangler, Harrison. "GOP's New Stand," *American Magazine*, 135 (February, 1943), 24 ff.

Stassen, Harold. "Wanted: a Forthright Republican Party," *Saturday Evening Post*, 215 (May 15, 1943), 12-13.

Taft, Robert A. "A 1944 Program for the Republicans," *Saturday Evening Post*, 215 (December 11, 1943), 17 ff.

"Taft's Reply," *The Nation*, 152 (December 13, 1941), 612.

Thompson, Dorothy. "To the Next President," *Ladies' Home Journal*, 57 (October, 1940), 4 ff.

"Toward A More Responsible Two Party System," *American Political Science Review*, 44 (Supplement) (September, 1950).

Valentine, Elizabeth R. "A Defeated Candidate Remains a Leader," *New York Times Magazine*, June 1, 1941, pp. 5 ff.

Villard, O. G. "Education of Mr. Willkie," *Christian Century*, 59 (December 16, 1942), 1559-61.

"The Way Ike is Remaking His Party," *U. S. News and World Report*, 39 (September 16, 1955), 26-27.

Wertheim, B. "Words by Willkie," *The Nation*, 151 (October 5, 1940), 292-95.

White, William Allen. "Thoughts After the Election," *Yale Review*, 30 (ns) (December, 1940), 217-27.

White, William S. "What Bill Knowland Stands For," *New Republic*, 134 (February 27, 1956), 7-10.

————. "Has Eisenhower Changed the G.O.P.?" *New York Times Magazine*, March 10, 1956, pp. 11 ff.

————. "How to Tell a Democrat from a Republican," *New York Times Magazine*, August 19, 1956, pp. 10 ff.

————. "An Attempt to Define Our Party Lines," *New York Times Magazine*, May 5, 1957, pp. 19 ff.

"Will Eisenhower Remake Republican Image?" *Congressional Quarterly*, 15 (January 4, 1957), 20-21.

"Willkie as Candidate" (editorial), *New Republic*, 109 (October 4, 1943), 442-43.

Willkie, Wendell. "New Deal Power," *New York Times Magazine*, October 31, 1937, p. 6.

————. "Brace Up, America!" *Atlantic Monthly*, 163 (June, 1939), 549-61.

————. "Idle Money — Idle Men," *Saturday Evening Post*, 211 (June 17, 1939), 7 ff.

————. "The Faith That is America," *Reader's Digest*, 36 (December, 1939), 1-4.

————. "With Malice Toward None," *Saturday Evening Post*, 212 (December 30, 1939), 23 ff.

————. "Set Enterprise Free!" *Christian Science Monitor Magazine*, March 2, 1940, pp. 1-2.

————. "We, the People," *Fortune*, 21 (April, 1940), 64-65.

————. "Five Minutes to Midnight," *Saturday Evening Post*, 212 (June 22, 1940), 10 ff.

————. "I Challenge Roosevelt," *Look*, 4 (September 10, 1940), 10-12.

————. "Patriotism or Politics," *American Magazine*, 132 (November, 1941), 14-15.

————. "The Future of the Republican Party," *The Nation,* 153 (December 13, 1941), 609-10.

————. "Let's Look Ahead," *New York Times Magazine,* February 15, 1942, p. 5.

————. "The Case for the Minorities," *Saturday Evening Post,* 214 (June 27, 1942), 14 ff.

————. "Our Sovereignty: Shall We Use It?" *Foreign Affairs,* 22 (April, 1944), 347-61.

————. "Cowardice at Chicago," *Collier's,* 114 (September 7, 1944), 11 ff.

————. "Citizens of Negro Blood," *Collier's,* 114 (October 7, 1944), 11 ff.

C. ADDITIONAL PERIODICALS CONSULTED

Editorial Research Reports (August 22, 1940).
Fortune, vols. 15-24 (1937-41).
Life, vol. 15 (1943).
Look, vols. 5-8 (1940-44).
The Nation, vols. 149-59 (1939-44).
New Republic, vols. 101-11 (1939-44).
Newsweek, vols. 13-26 (1939-45).
New Yorker, vols. 16-20 (1940-44).
Propaganda Analysis, vol. 3 (1940).
Public Opinion Quarterly, vols. 1-8 (1937-44).
Saturday Evening Post, vol. 214 (1942).
Tennessee Republican Age (February and March, 1944).
The Republican (1944).
Tide, vol. 14 (1940).
Time, vols. 35-44 (1940-44); vols. 69-70 (1957).
United States News and World Report, vols. 14-17 (1943-44); vols. 42-43 (1957).
Vital Speeches, vols. 3-4 (1937-38).

D. GOVERNMENT PUBLICATIONS

Congressional Record, vols. 81-95 (75th-81st Congresses, 1937-49).
Historical Statistics of the United States, 1789-1945. Washington, D.C.: United States Government Printing Office, 1949.
Report of the United States Senate Special Committee to Investigate Presidential, Vice-Presidential, and Senatorial Campaign Expenditures, 1940 (Senate Report No. 47, 77th Congress, 1st Session, February 15, 1941).
Supreme Court Reports
　　Ashwander et al. v. Tennessee Valley Authority et al., 297 U.S. 288 (1935).
　　Alabama Power Company v. Ickes, Federal Emergency Administrator of Public Works, et al., 302 U.S. 464 (1937).
　　Tennessee Electric Power Company et al. v. Tennessee Valley

Authority et al., 306 U.S. 118 (1938).
Schneiderman v. *United States*, 320 U.S. 118 (1942).

E. NEWSPAPERS

Chicago Daily News
Chicago Sun
Chicago Tribune
Christian Science Monitor
Daily Illini (University of Illinois)
New York Herald Tribune
New York Daily News
New York Times
PM (New York)
Philadelphia Record
Washington Post
Washington Star
Washington Times-Herald

INDEX